Regenerative Revolution

Regenerative Revolution: Through Mindful Consumption, Environmental Stewardship, and Industry 6.0

EDITED BY

AASHU AGGARWAL
Vivekananda Institute of Professional Studies-Technical Campus, India

ROHIT BANSAL
Rockford College, Sydney, Australia

RATIKA SIKAND
Maharaja Agrasen Institute of Technology, India

AND

MOCHAMMAD FAHLEVI
Bina Nusantara University, Jakarta, Indonesia

emerald PUBLISHING

United Kingdom – North America – Japan – India – Malaysia – China

Emerald Publishing Limited
Emerald Publishing, Floor 5, Northspring, 21-23 Wellington Street, Leeds LS1 4DL

First edition 2026

British Library Cataloguing in Publication Data
A catalogue record for this book is available from the British Library

ISBN: 978-1-80686-860-5 (Print)
ISBN: 978-1-80686-859-9 (Online)
ISBN: 978-1-80686-861-2 (Epub)

Printed and bound by CPI Group (UK) Ltd, Croydon, CR0 4YY

Contents

About the Editors

Dr. Aashu Aggarwal is an Assistant Professor at Vivekananda Institute of Professional Studies–Technical Campus. With over 10 years of combined research and teaching experience, she has made sustained contributions to management education, curriculum development, and scholarly research. Dr. Aggarwal has published papers in reputed journals, including ABDC and Scopus-indexed journals. Her research has appeared in edited volumes and conference proceedings. She has presented her work at numerous national and international conferences, including those organized by IIM Jammu and Monash Business School, Monash University, Australia. She has also authored a book on Business Communication. Her research interests span marketing strategy, consumer behavior, entrepreneurship, and general management. Dr. Aggarwal has been awarded the Best Paper Award at the International Conference organized by the Symbiosis Centre for Management Studies, Symbiosis International University, Noida, in 2016.

Dr. Rohit Bansal is an Adjunct Faculty member at Rockford College, Sydney, Australia. He has authored and edited many books with renowned national and international publishers, including Springer Nature, IGI Global, Scrivener Publishing, De Gruyter and Emerald Publishing. His research work is published in leading publishers like Springer, MDPI, Hindawi, IGI Global, Cell Press, De Gruyter, Elsevier, Inderscience and Wiley. He has also presented papers at many conferences and seminars, including IIM Indore, IIM Ranchi, IIM Jammu, and IIM Kozhikode. His area of interest includes marketing management, organizational behavior, customer engagement, digital marketing, e-learning, mental health and well-being, emerging technologies, and sustainable development. He is on the Editorial Advisory Board as a member of many national and international peer-reviewed journals. He has served as a member of the technical committee at many international conferences.

Dr. Ratika Sikand brings over 10 years of extensive experience in education management, with expertise in teaching human resource management and organizational behavior. Dr. Sikand has published extensively in Scopus, ABDC, and UGC Care-listed journals, with her work focusing on job involvement, leadership, employee well-being, workplace behavior, and organizational psychology. Her research provides empirical insights into employee motivation, sustainable leadership, and managerial practices, addressing key challenges in contemporary business environments. Dr. Sikand has participated in numerous national and international conferences, presenting her research at esteemed institutions such as IIT Roorkee, Jamia Millia Islamia, and GGSIPU. She remains actively involved in faculty development programs (FDPs) and workshops, enhancing her expertise in research methodology, data analytics, statistical tools, and innovative teaching pedagogies.

Dr. Mochammad Fahlevi is a distinguished scholar with a doctoral degree from Brawijaya University. He currently holds the position of assistant professor at Bina Nusantara University. He also serves as a research fellow at Universiti Sultan Zainal Abidin (UnisZa) in Malaysia. His research focuses on corporate governance and financial management. As the founder of the Privietlab Research Center, Dr. Fahlevi has made significant contributions to the field, earning recognition among the top 2% of researchers worldwide in business management by Stanford University and Elsevier. He is also an active editor and a reviewer of several high-impact academic journals.

About the Contributors

M. Zaheer Ahmed is the Head of the Postgraduate Department of Commerce and Research at Dr. Kalaignar M. Karunanidhi Government Institute for Postgraduate Studies and Research, Karaikal, U.T. of Puducherry, India. He has over 25 years of experience in teaching, research, and academic leadership. His scholarly work centers on sustainable development, digital inclusion, human-centered innovation, artificial intelligence (AI) ethics, and frugal technology models for emerging economies. Dr. Ahmed has authored and contributed to several book chapters and peer-reviewed publications with leading academic publishers. His research approach emphasizes ground-level relevance, community empowerment, and practical policy alignment. He is also actively involved in training and placement initiatives, student mentorship, and social outreach activities.

Ruchi Arya is an Assistant Professor at USB, Chandigarh University, with over a decade of academic experience. She holds degrees in engineering and management and is pursuing a PhD in management (healthcare service quality). Her research spans HR, operations, and analytics, with multiple publications, patents, and active roles in academic bodies and student mentorship.

Kayenaat Bahl is an Assistant Professor at IILM University, Gurugram, with a PhD in human resource management. She has over five years of academic experience teaching MBA students and designing management curricula. Her research focuses on training and development in the banking sector and sustainable HR practices, with four research papers published in reputed journals.

Nitasha Barara is a seasoned academic with a passion for Statistics, Analytics, and its applications in the business world. With over 15 years of experience teaching at prestigious institutions, she has honed her skills in delivering engaging and impactful mathematics as well as analytics courses. She has published research papers and chapters in national and international journals of repute including Scopus indexed as well as edited books. She is pursuing her PhD and obtained her M.Phil. and M.A. degrees in mathematics. Moreover, she completed a B.A. (Hons) in mathematics from St. Stephen's College, University of Delhi. She has participated in various Faculty Development Programs, workshops, lecture series, and seminars. Her teaching interests encompass Probability, Statistics, Quantitative Methods, Python, DBMS, Excel, Power BI,

Mathematics for Data Science, Machine Learning, Data Science, Mathematical Tools for Business, Linear Algebra, Integral and Differential Calculus.

Anuj Dixit is an Assistant Professor with over 20 years of teaching experience, and a researcher in the Mechanical Engineering Department, Greater Noida Institute of Technology, Gr. Noida.

Anitha G. (B.Com [CA], M.Com [CA], MBA [Finance], M.Phil. [Finance], PhD [Marketing]) is an accomplished academician with over 17 years of experience in Commerce, specializing in income tax, finance, and customer relationship management. Currently serving as an Associate Professor at Maharaja Institute of Management Studies, she holds a PhD from Bharathiar University and is also a certified Associate NCC Officer. Dr. Anitha has published extensively in UGC-CARE and Scopus-indexed journals, authored books on Consumer Behavior, Ethics & Culture and Management International Business, and frequently serves as a resource person for faculty development programs. Known for her leadership, research excellence, and commitment to holistic student development, she continues to inspire innovation and academic growth.

Gurunadham Goli, Associate Professor and Dean, School of Business, SR University, Warangal, earned his PhD in Labor Welfare and Social Security Measures from Acharya Nagarjuna University in 2019. He holds Master's degrees in management, English, and human resource management and qualified UGC-NET in 2012. With 16 years of teaching experience, he has published 30 papers, 10 book chapters in reputed journals and conferences (Scopus/Web of Science/ABDC), and 25 patents in the Indian Patent Journal. His research interests include workplace flexibility, sustainable leadership, Industry 4.0 adoption, and work–life balance, contributing to evidence-based solutions for sustainable development. Passionate about teaching and academic leadership, he specializes in HRM, OB, entrepreneurship, and general management, blending theory with practice through innovative pedagogy and student-centric learning. With expertise in curriculum development, OBE, and research methodology, Dr. Goli actively seeks collaborations in research, educational innovations, and knowledge-sharing initiatives to create meaningful academic and societal impact.

Shashi Kant is an Assistant Professor at GNIOT (Academicians) with more than 15 years of teaching and industrial experience. He is an engineering faculty member specializing in manufacturing systems, AI, and emerging manufacturing technologies. His work explores the evolution from Industry 4.0 to Industry 6.0, focusing on human–machine symbiosis, cognitive augmentation, and sustainable production ecosystems. He contributed bridging theoretical innovation with practical implementation in industrial environments.

Anuj Pal Kapoor is an Assistant Professor at the Indian Institute of Technology Jodhpur. He holds a PhD from the Faculty of Management Studies, University of Delhi. His research focuses on consumer psychology, collaborative consumption, and digital transformation, bridging academic insights with six years of industry experience.

Sumna Khan is a PhD Scholar and an MBA graduate from Jamia Millia Islamia, New Delhi. She has held managerial roles at Dr. Lal PathLabs and HR International. Her research focuses on sustainability leadership, organizational culture, and ESG outcomes. She actively contributes to management research through conference presentations and scholarly engagement.

Aiman Khatoon is a PhD scholar in Marketing at the Indian Institute of Technology Jodhpur and a Visiting Research Student at Northumbria University, United Kingdom. Her research focuses on sustainability communication, packaging design, and mindful consumption. Her work has been accepted for publication in an ABDC-listed journal. She has presented her research at several reputed national and international conferences, including the Australia and New Zealand Marketing Academy (ANZMAC) Conference (New Zealand, 2023), the Academy of Marketing Doctoral Colloquium (United Kingdom, 2024), and conferences hosted by IIM Ahmedabad (2023), IIT Roorkee (2022), and IIM Bodh Gaya (2026).

Y. Suryanarayana Murthy, Assistant Professor at KL Business School, is an accomplished academic and a researcher with 12 years of teaching and two years of industry experience. His expertise includes HRM, Marketing, and Digital Transformation. He has published over 60 papers in reputed journals, authored seven textbooks, and contributed 22 book chapters. His research emphasizes AI-enabled HRM, sustainable consumer behaviors, and ethical digital leadership. A passionate educator, he integrates analytics tools and AI models into management education to develop data-driven, empathetic, and future-ready professionals.

Chunchu Nagaraju, a Research Scholar at SR University, Warangal, has contributed significantly to sustainable business and technology through his publications. He authored four book chapters, including *Relation between Green Economy and Sustainable Manufacturing through Industry 5.0* and *Evolution of Sustainable Intelligence Business Practices*. His works on retail management and AI in HRM, published by Elsevier, reflect his expertise in emerging fields. He continues to advance research in Industry 5.0, sustainability, and AI-driven business practices.

Amrita Nandy is a faculty member of the Department of Business Administration at Port City International University, Chattogram, Bangladesh. Her primary research interest lies in Sustainability Issues such as Ethical Consumption, Eco-Tourism, Workplace Cohesion, Recycling, and promoting Women-Entrepreneurship. Additionally, she has worked as a soft skills facilitator in several organizations. The author has published research works in multiple forms, including journal articles, book chapters, conference proceedings, and case studies.

Rachana Yogesh Patil is an Associate Professor and Head of the Department of Computer Engineering (Regional Language) at Pimpri Chinchwad College of Engineering, Pune. She earned her PhD in Computer Engineering from the University of Mumbai in 2020. Her research focuses on cryptography, cybersecurity, and digital forensics, particularly network forensics. Featured in the 2024

Stanford–Elsevier Top 2% Scientist List, she has published over 60 papers in reputed journals and conferences. A member of IEEE, ACM, and IETE, she mentors students and promotes innovative, secure communication systems.

Yogesh H. Patil, Associate Professor at D. Y. Patil College of Engineering, Akurdi, Pune, holds a PhD in Optical Fiber and has over 24 years of academic and research experience. His expertise spans computer engineering and optical communication, with a focus on applying emerging technologies to real-world challenges and mentoring students toward impactful research.

Nishita Pruthi is an Assistant Professor at the Asian School of Business, part of the Asian Education Group, Noida. Awarded with PhD at the Institute of Management Studies and Research, Maharshi Dayanand University, Rohtak, Haryana, she exemplifies academic excellence and scholarly dedication. Dr. Pruthi has an impressive portfolio of nine research papers published in prestigious journals, with six indexed in Scopus, Web of Science, UGC-CARE, and ABDC. Her contributions extend to authoring 13 chapters in edited volumes published by globally renowned publishers such as Emerald, Bentham Science, and IGI Global. Additionally, she has co-edited four books published by IGI Global, USA, reflecting her versatility and scholarly rigor.

Md. Sahidur Rahman (PhD, University of Chittagong; MScR, University of Edinburgh; MSc, University of Dundee; MCom and BCom (Hon), University of Dhaka) is a Professor in the Department of Management, University of Chittagong, Bangladesh. He is well known for his dynamic teaching tactics that persistently encourage students to excel in their performance. The author has nearly 100 research articles and a dynamic presence in national and international conferences. In addition, he is an active reviewer of various international and national journals. Currently, he is supervising four PhD and three MPhil researchers.

Namita Rath, MA (PMIR), MBA (HR), MPhil, PhD, is an Associate Professor in organizational behavior and human resource management at Sri Sri University, Cuttack, India. She did her PhD in Personnel Management Industrial Relations from Utkal University. She has over 20 years of teaching experience in business schools with bachelor's and master's programs. She has published 35 papers in Scopus, ABDC, UGC Listed, and peer-reviewed indexed journals and 13 book chapters along with four books to her credit. She presented papers at different National and International Conferences. Her research interests include organizational behavior, industrial relations, and talent management. She is currently guiding three doctoral candidates.

Yasmeen Shamsi Rizvi is an Assistant Professor at the Department of Management Studies, Jamia Millia Islamia, New Delhi. She holds a PhD in strategic human resource management and MBA and M.Sc. degrees from Aligarh Muslim University. With over 24 years of academic and professional experience, she has taught at IIM Lucknow, Amity Business School, and other leading institutions and headed Training and Engagement at Max Super Speciality Hospital, New

Delhi. She has designed and conducted several Management Development Programs for executives from NTPC, NHPC, NABARD, BPCL, and Defense Services. A prolific researcher and multiple Best Paper Award recipient, her interests span HRM, OB, gender, sustainability, and leadership.

Timcy Sachdeva is an accomplished academician and researcher with a profound expertise in finance. Holding a doctorate degree in management, specializing in finance from Guru Gobind Singh Indraprastha University, Dr. Sachdeva is dedicated herself to the realms of teaching and research. She has made significant contributions to the field of finance, evidenced by her numerous publications in esteemed international journals indexed in Scopus and ABDC listed. Her expertise in finance has often seen her chairing sessions in these esteemed gatherings, further solidifying her reputation as a thought leader in her field. She is a sought-after trainer in financial econometrics and financial modeling. She has conducted numerous Faculty Development Programs (FDPs) catering to faculty and research scholars across various institutions in India. She has authored a comprehensive book titled "Fundamentals of Financial Modeling using Excel," which serves as a valuable resource for students and practitioners alike. Presently Dr. Sachdeva is serving at Vivekananda Institute of Professional Studies, affiliated to Guru Gobind Singh Indraprastha University.

Alok Kumar Sahai is a graduate of Indian Institute of Management Bangalore and obtained his PhD in behavioral finance from the National Law University Jodhpur. Presently, he is an associate professor in the Faculty of Management at Sri Sri University, Cuttack. His research interests include behavioral finance, psychology of commodity markets and consumer behavior.

Seema Sahai is a PhD in management and has a journey of 27 years in academics and is consistently striving to create a challenging and engaging learning environment. She is a Professor of IT and decision sciences. She has to her credit a number of publications in reputed national and international journals accompanied with participation in conferences. Most of her publications are in Scopus. She is a regular chair of Springer conferences. She has also edited one book in IGI-Global. She also has written many chapters in edited books in IGI Global, Springer Nature and CRC Press, Apple Academic Press. She conducts a number of workshops for Business Analytics, Analysis using Advanced Excel and Mendeley Reference Manager, SPSS, and many others. She has guided a number of scholars under her. She also has corporate experience of two years and has many projects to her credit. Her specialization is in IT, operations and decision sciences.

Sangeeta Sahney is a Professor, and former Dean at the Vinod Gupta School of Management at IIT Kharagpur. She earned her doctoral degree from IIT Delhi, and has served as a faculty at IIT Roorkee, IIT Jodhpur, and AIT Bangkok. Specializing in marketing, she also teaches organizational behavior and HRM. Her research explores consumer behavior, employee engagement, and educational quality, with numerous publications in reputed journals.

Ankita Sharma is an Assistant Professor at the Alliance School of Business, Alliance University, Bangalore, and a PhD scholar specializing in the impact of social intelligence on employee engagement in the IT sector. She holds master's degrees in Commerce, Education, and Psychology and has been recognized as a university topper for her academic excellence. Her research interests span organizational behavior, human resource management, corporate communication, entrepreneurship, and digital business practices. She has made significant scholarly contributions, evidenced by her publications in reputable international journals and edited volumes, including Scopus- and ABDC-indexed outlets. She has also presented her research at various national and international conferences. In addition to her academic pursuits, she is actively engaged in teaching and curriculum development, contributing to contemporary management pedagogy and emerging research in behavioral and organizational sciences.

Ridhima Sharma is an Associate Professor of Economics at Vivekananda Institute of Professional Studies-Technical Campus. With a teaching and research experience of 14 years, she has contributed several articles to the journals of national and international repute and has presented papers in national and international conferences apart from authoring books. Her research interest includes customer relationship management and sustainable consumer behavior. She has recently completed Post Doc from Amity University, Dubai.

Pardeep Bawa Sharma is a Professor of Marketing in University School of Business in Chandigarh University. He has 18 years of experience in academics and business development. His research areas include consumer behavior, organization psychology, sustainability, and AI application in business.

V. K. Sharma is a Professor in the Department of Applied Sciences as well as Head Examinations, at Greater Noida Institute of Technology, Greater Noida. He is a devoted researcher in the field of Spectroscopy and has vast experience of more than 20 years in teaching as well as of examinations and also took many initiatives to reform the examination system and to improve the examination systems.

Swati Sood is a graduate of IGNOU, Bhopal, and is pursuing a PhD in management/IT from Pacific University, Rajasthan. Presently, she is associated with BIITM, College, Bhubaneswar, as an Assistant Professor. Her research interest includes information technology, AI and general management.

Vishal Sood is a graduate of IMS, DAVV, Indore, and obtained a PhD in finance from DAVV, Indore. Presently, he is a Professor in the Faculty of management studies at Sri Sri University, Cuttack. His research interests include behavioral finance, commodity and stock markets, general management and human resource management. He is in the Editorial board of ANUJAT, Ghana, and has published 60 papers in journals of repute.

Rachoru Himani Srihita holds an MBA in human resource management (2022) and a B.Tech in computer science and engineering (2019). She gained hands-on experience through internships and live projects and worked as an HR professional and trainer, providing job-oriented training to master's students. Currently pursuing a PhD in management (HRM) at SR University, she has published papers and book chapters in reputed journals and continues to contribute to the HRM field through research and teaching.

Suman is an academic and a researcher in the field of innovation and sustainability. She is associated with GL Bajaj Institute of Management and Research, where she teaches and mentors postgraduate students. Her research interests include grassroots innovation, social capital, and inclusive development. She contributed to scholarly publications and conferences focusing on how local innovations can address global challenges. Her current work explores intermediary roles in the diffusion and commercialization of grassroots technologies.

Amit Trehan serves as an Assistant Professor at the University Institute of Legal Studies, Chandigarh University. Specializing in business economics, micro and macro economics, statistics, Indian Economy, operations research, and organizational behavior, he combines academic rigor with practical insights. With expertise in teaching and research, he is dedicated to fostering analytical thinking and professional excellence among students.

Aparna Vajpayee is currently working as a researcher and a Professor at the School of Liberal Arts and Management Studies, P. P. Savani University. She has more than 90 publications across cognition, spatial reasoning, educational psychology, and culture studies of cognitive schematization in India. She specializes in AI in psychology, poverty psychology, and educational interventions alongside cognitive development in rural and tribal India. She has publications with leading global publishers like Sage, Emerald, Elsevier, Taylor and Francis, Springer, Routledge, Wiley, Cambridge Scholarly Publishing, Apple Ace Academics, etc. She has won multiple prestigious awards over her career for her research contribution to the field such as "Best Research Paper Award" from various national and international platform.

Rushil Varma holds an MA in Psychology and an MBA from Lucknow University and is currently pursuing his Doctoral degree at Amity University, Lucknow. He is presently associated with BBD University, Lucknow, as an Assistant Professor. His research interests include psychological contracts, high-performance work systems, and job crafting.

Podile Venkateswara Rao is a Professor of Management at KL Deemed to be University and former Associate Professor at the Central University of South Bihar, with 28 years of teaching experience. He holds multiple postgraduate degrees and a PhD from Acharya Nagarjuna University. A prolific researcher, he has published 251 papers, authored 17 books, guided PhD and M.Phil scholars, and completed numerous funded and consultancy projects. Recognized among the top 1% on Academia.edu, his global research impact is reflected in high citation metrics. He has received over a dozen prestigious national and international awards for excellence in research and academics.

Chapter 1

Frugal Intelligence 6.0: Integrating Mindful Consumption and Environmental Stewardship for a Regenerative Future

M. Zaheer Ahmed

Dr Kalaignar M. Karunanidhi Government Institute for Postgraduate Studies and Research, India

Abstract

Frugal Intelligence 6.0 (FI 6.0) suggests a systemic approach to socio-technical issues through a union between the new technologies and planned resource-efficiency and environmental management. The framework is a mixture of practical design concepts with a systems-based approach to the optimization of resources and the reduction of environmental impact.

According to empirical studies conducted in India, Bangladesh, Kenya, and some circumstances in Southeast Asia, the study demonstrates how artificial intelligence, the Internet of Things, and the use of modern digital platforms can decrease energy consumption, waste amounts, and allow developmental paths to be sustainable without the need to invest large sums of money in the initial stage. These interventions are most effective when designed to the realities of the local context, responding to local needs, and limited by environmental realities.

Redefining innovation in a frugal and mindful manner takes a crucial step forward to a practical and scalable blueprint of equitable development through FI 6.0. It has made the following contributions: a critical evaluation of technology in the case of low-resource settings; new ways of sustainable development; practical implementation advice based on policy and community; and an unifying approach that relates technological advancements to ecological accountability. The framework gives specific suggestions to broaden digital inclusion, enhance economic resilience in communities

Regenerative Revolution, 1–27

Published under exclusive licence by Emerald Publishing Limited
doi:10.1108/978-1-80686-859-920261001

and create regenerative solutions to match technological capacity, social and environmental objectives.

Keywords: Frugal innovation; Industry 6.0; mindful consumption; environmental stewardship; circular economy; artificial intelligence for sustainability; regenerative development; SDGs; digital inclusion; global south

JEL Classification: O31; O32; Q01; Q55; Q56

1. Introduction

To examine the performance of FI 6.0 in practice, we gathered nine case studies in Asia, Africa and Latin America—each of which is centered on a particular sectoral issue (waste management, textiles, energy provision, smallholder agriculture, and low-cost housing). Combining semi-structured interviews, participant observation, and project-level outcome data in fieldwork enabled us to make comparisons between the effectiveness of frugal design decisions in different community contexts.

This chapter demonstrates that small-scale innovations that are affordable play a significant role in producing meaningful changes as they match the appropriate technology with the local potentials. These approaches do not only enhance livelihoods, but also aid in the conservation of the natural resources. The case studies are structured in the same way in order to analyze them systematically: the main challenge in the community is first described, then the actions, and then the evaluation of the outcomes and the final conclusions are made, which can be practically applied.

1.1 Building the Frugal Intelligence 6.0 (FI 6.0) System

1.1.1 An Evolutionary Paradigm

FI 6.0 is a development that is based on the previous two paradigms and re-evaluates them in a critical way.

Industry 4.0: The fourth industrial revolution revolves around cyber-physical systems and integration of these systems, which introduces digital technologies to manufacturing and logistics, such as IoT, AI, and cloud computing. It values efficiency, automation, and data-driven and innovative production.

Society 5.0: Japan suggested Society 5.0, which develops more than Industry 4.0 by focusing on the human-centered society that uses technology to overcome social problems and improve the quality of life. It is intended to equalize the economic progress with the elimination of social issues, yet, quite frequently, it can be situated in a high-technology, high-investment one.

We take FI 6.0 to be a sixth wave paradigm which is a critical synthesis and transcendence of these predecessors. The main question will be how societies can use the emerging technologies in a manner that is affordable, inclusive, and environmentally friendly especially in places where resources are limited.

Where Industry 4.0 prioritized automated manufacturing that is sensor-intensive and Society 5.0 predicted a user-friendly technology, FI 6.0 shifts the focus to lower costs, localization, and community care. In practice, it implies re-specification of technological stacks of cheaper components, preference of interoperable modules which can be maintained by local technicians, and placing decision-making authority in the local governance structures as opposed to remote vendors. It changes the purpose of intelligent production to intelligent, regenerative stewardship generation to create a value that is economic, social, and environmental where empowerment in the Global South is the main goal.

The history of the development paradigms in the world is evidence of the move away towards the industrial automation paradigm towards human centered, and regenerative models. The core focus of every paradigm, the drivers of its operations, are the key enablers, and the main goal is specific to its geographical location. Three powerful paradigms—Industry 4.0, Society 5.0, and Frugal Intelligence (FI) 6.0—are compared in Table 1.1.

Therefore, it does not mean a replacement in an order of sequence, but rather a conceptual and practical synthesis—a fusion of high-tech possibilities and the urgent demands of equity, sustainability, and grassroots empowerment which characterize the challenges and opportunities of the 21st century.

The concept of FI 6.0 does not come into the world in a vacuum. It is based on three related concepts that are evidenced in practice.

First is digital governance. The use of technology by many governments has been to access their constituents in a better manner. Tax filing, ID cards, and welfare payments done online via applications have become a norm. However, the story is uneven. In some places, people cannot log in due to the poor internet connection or the offices are slow in changing the records. According to the World Bank (2021), these gaps are quite significant, particularly in the regions with poor infrastructure. Therefore, there is digital progress, which is not universal.

Second is frugal innovation. Frugal innovation does not imply doing things with little money in order to save money. It is concerning developing solutions that are contextual. According to Bhatti (2012), it was defined as doing with what is available. Radjou et al. (2012), showed how Indian firms created products that were low-priced by re-inventing their designs. The same principle dictates good leadership. Pansera and Owen (2018) further state that frugality does not lack the ethical responsibility, namely that the governments should not pursue the flashy systems while being wasteful, but rather concentrating on the things that really benefit the citizens.

The case of MyGov in India is educative. It scored huge registration, but, as Meijer (2015) records, it did not maintain the attention as users felt their contribution was lost in the vacuum. This shared story emphasizes one of the most important lessons of Criado and Gil-Garcia (2019) who differentiate between the theatre of participation (the technology) and its real content (processes that help people feel heard). To make the real participation, then, requires more than making digital access available and more than choosing specific channels, carefully, through which citizen voice can result in a visible response.

Table 1.1. The Evolution From Industry 4.0 to FI 6.0

Paradigm	Core Focus	Key Enabler	Primary Goal	Geographical Context
Industry 4.0	Smart manufacturing	Cyber-physical systems, IoT, AI	Hyper-efficiency and automation.	Global (industry-led)
Society 5.0	Human-centricity	Big data, AI, robotics	Solving social problems and enhancing quality of life.	Global (often OECD-led)
FI 6.0	Regenerative stewardship	Frugal AI, IoT, community platforms	Inclusive, sustainable development and empowerment.	Global south and resource-constrained regions

Source: Author's own synthesis based on OECD (2019), Kagermann et al. (2013), and contemporary literature on frugal innovation and digital governance.

These three strands, technology, frugal design, and participation are the foundation of the FI 6.0 model together. The idea is not to pursue the latest and priciest tools. It is to make systems remain affordable, useable and credible to the people that they serve.

This chapter establishes itself in a strategic point in the materials on frugal innovation literature. Leaving behind the stories of glorification of affordability and flexibility (Bhatti, 2012; Radjou & Prabhu, 2015) we directly enter the questions that the field has posed that are more thorny. Our warnings of technological lock-in (Blind & Storz, 2019) as second-best, and the politics of inclusion in digital technology (Graham, 2019) are in line with the ethical demands of UNESCO (2021).

We identify a key priority. Equity and resilience should be taken care of at the very outset through digital strategies. They are not supposed to be made with the sole aim of lowering costs. The need is met by the FI 6.0 framework. It provides eight building blocks which connect affordability with long term community control and decision-making.

2. Global and Regional Landscape

The international scenario of the digital governance is characterized by sharp contrasts. There are countries that have made huge progress and used AI and integrated platforms to provide public services in an efficient manner. Some are yet to make basic government records and services available on the internet. According to the OECD (2023), the increase in global digital tools has grown very quickly, though, the advantages of this development are unevenly distributed.

Digital services are growing more rapidly in the high-income countries. These have stronger institutions, expansive technical capacity, and effective infrastructure. There are greater obstacles to many low- and middle-income areas. Technology is costly. There is shortage of skilled personnel. Simple connectivity is not necessarily stable. This is not just a technological gap. It is also indicative of greater questions of justice and access.

The World Bank (2021) and others demonstrate issues that are not so apparent but more complex to solve. Government departments can be having restricted budgets. Decision-making mechanisms can be inefficient. The training required to handle digital change may be withheld to the employees of the government. Under such circumstances, technology is not the primary obstacle. The fact of the matter is that the real challenge is to develop systems that can be upheld and believed in by people. In the absence of this, states tend to invest in digital platforms that are not frequently used by the citizens, or become inactive with time.

Meanwhile, the citizen involvement has become a common motif. One of the earliest studies (Meijer, 2015) indicated the potential of online forums, in which individuals had an opportunity to present ideas or comment on them and share them with decision-makers. According to more recent studies (Criado & Gil-Garcia, 2019), although the participation is on the increase, it remains shallow in most of the areas. The citizens can log-in and be not engaged, or they can mistrust the results. It is not a matter of creating access but rather a matter of creating trust.

Another area of conflict is control. As it is argued by Bannister and Connolly (2014), digital systems have to be supported by definite rules of accountability. Otherwise, it becomes inefficient once there is the introduction of the elements of opacity and corruption. This caution has already been fulfilled in some of the regional cases. In Asia, e-procurement portals in some regions provided new opportunities of transparency, but as in the case of the same systems, this could be abused unless they were audited by independent actors.

The Global South is demonstrating its traps and its possibilities. According to Pansera and Owen (2018) frugal design can be used to help poorer regions to leapfrog technologically, without the need to deploy costly and frequently inappropriate Western systems. Governments do not need to copycat costly Western systems advantage; instead, they can apply lightweight tools, which tend to be open-source and mobile-based and community-driven. The Aadhaar system in India shows that a nationwide digital identification is achievable, and can be provided in large scale, at low per-capita costs, although its design and governance is controversial. This frugality is also manifested in other regional pilots, including mobile based health records in some parts of Africa.

Combined, the world and regional environment would be an indication of a mixed picture. There is also a lot of ambition, yet holes. Technology will not win but citizen trust, accountability and affordability remain the determining factor. These lessons directly contribute to the FI 6.0 model that increases the existing imbalanced experiences on the premise of low-cost design, inclusive participation, and simple yet powerful oversight.

3. Methodology and Limitations

3.1 Methodology

This chapter takes a qualitative case methodology with a view to examining how principles of frugal innovation can fit the digital governance systems. The design promotes the broad-based learning process and retains the reality of low resource settings.

3.1.1 Case Selection

The discussion is based on nine case studies that are purposively chosen and represent the health, energy, textiles, education, and governance industries. The cases were chosen according to four criteria:

- clear evidence low cost/frugal innovation;
- evident change in the empowerment and sustainability of the community;

- relevance to digital governance or other closely related socio technical systems;
- accessibility of adequate secondary data that is reliable and can be used to conduct a strong analysis.

3.1.2 Data Sources

The secondary data will be one of peer reviewed journals, national and international policy documents, reports of the non-governmental organizations (NGOs), and reliable media sources published between January 2015 and December 2024. The search was carried out in significant bibliographic databases (e.g., PubMed, Scopus, Web of Science) and on the website of the relevant international organizations and NGOs. In order to access policy briefs and media coverage, specific web search was done.

3.1.3 Analytical Framework

The analysis of the data was based on thematic coding, as four anchors of the FI 6.0 were considered: community empowerment, phased growth, accountability, and citizen voice. We subjected the cases to the corresponding case coders who made the actual encoding of a case against these anchors with the aim of identifying patterns, strengths, and improvement areas. After that we did a comparative synthesis so as to trace common patterns within the case studies.

3.1.4 Validation

In order to overcome the possibility of bias, the research paper uses several types of evidence as opposed to one source. This triangulation was supported by constructing the framework on the basis of the literature on frugal innovation, digital inclusion, and participatory governance explicitly, which served as a way of making sure of conceptual consistency as well as overall validity of the study.

3.2 Limitations

The contributions made by scholars should be interpreted with a lot of care, considering the methodological dilemmas that are inherent in them.

3.2.1 Reliance on Secondary Data

The entire empirical evidence is based on available sources of writings and documents. These materials are not necessarily the ones that would receive the immediacy, complexity, and critical voices, which may arise when working directly with the affected communities. Future research would enhance by including primary data, whether by interview, on-field observations or participatory research designs to be able to offer more detailed and place-based accounts.

3.2.2 Selection Bias

The study used a purposive sampling approach that gave greater weight to conceptual clarity and depth of the research. This method implies that the collection of examples might not be complete and representative of the whole dataset. Absence of initiatives that have succeeded or failed without leaving any trace to the populace or causing any reporting may be able to skew the empirical picture around the framework.

3.2.3 Contextual Constraints

The socio-economic and political aspects of the regions under analysis have a significant effect on the nature of initiatives studied and the subsequent model of the FI 6.0. Because of this, the application of this framework in extremely different environments, such as, a fragile state or a high-income and highly industrialized one, should be approached cautiously. The FI 6.0 framework in most of these settings would probably require customization to suit local realities.

3.2.4 Threat of Lock-In in Technology

Blind and Storz (2019) underline that frugal solutions may, inadvertently, overhaul the practice or technologies that are second-best in place and hence limit further development alternatives. This issue is particularly pertinent because inexpensive solutions are introduced into the marginalized regions and no scheme of upgrading or conversion into more sophisticated systems is offered over the period.

3.2.5 Political and Institutional Dependencies

The practical functionality of FI 6.0 is not a technical aspect per se. It is based on a conducive governance atmosphere, adequate institutional capacity, and political engagement. In the absence of these enabling conditions, even the well-designed and extremely cost-effective approaches may not be supported or extended.

The study describes an initial methodological protocol of frugal digital governance, which theorizes the FI 6.0 framework as a tentative and flexible tool of systematic research and contextual adjustment.

4. Case Studies

This section of the chapter narrates actual tales. Both of them demonstrate the way FI 6.0 is a real-world application. The tales are of Asian, African, and Latin American origins. Their coverage is very extensive; they touch on waste management and textiles, energy, tourism, agriculture, water, and fisheries and housing.

The goal is simple. Show that a drastic change can be achieved using low-cost ideas, along with the appropriate technology. The problem itself is the initial discovery of each story. The framework defines the methodology, results and implications, and ends with a conclusion of the main lessons.

The cases rely on reliable reports and official research. We have explicit references that any person can verify the facts. The table below compares all the nine case studies at the end of this section. It will be a list of the sector, the tools, the cost method, the outcomes, and the key challenge.

Based on these illustrations, there are three things that can be identified. To start with, frugal concepts have the power to expand and benefit a large number of individuals. Second, it is possible to utilize simple technology at reasonable expenses. Third, Global South can teach the world some lessons.

The first story is from India. It shows how repair and reuse would help decrease waste and give people stable jobs.

4.1 Repair Cooperatives in India: Case Study One

In most of the towns in India, individuals dispose damaged fans, radios, and mobile phones. Streets fill with e-waste. In an attempt to reverse this habit, local cooperatives are making efforts. Repair groups have established themselves in markets and bus stands, which are small in size. People carry their old items and repair them, reselling them at an extremely low price.

The cooperatives have a very simple and potent principle that is known as repair, not purchase another one. Its price is a new fan Rs.1200; repair approximately Rs. 100. It is not just a saving of money but a life-saving economic message to the family on top of ensuring that dangerous electronic waste does not contaminate the environment. The repair cooperative model is an example of that type of low cost, grassroots innovation that can help place local resilience and economic opportunities (Radjou et al., 2012).

Jobs are also created by these cooperatives. Young men and women are trained on how to repair wires, motors, or phone screens. They receive their daily remunerations without having to travel out of their towns. According to a more recent UNDP (2022) report, community-based repair hubs in addition to resource savings are also associated with the establishment of local pride. The things that are old make people happy when they come back to life.

These cooperatives are successful and this proves a change of mindset. Frugality is not only about money saving, it is also concerned with making good decisions. It has to do with the respect of resources and people who have skills to repair.

4.2 Case Study 2: Bangladesh Textile Circularity

Bangladesh is the second-largest garment exporter on the planet.

Millions of jobs are produced by the textile industry.

Foreign exchange also comes into the industry. The industry produces waste in high quantities. In factories, scraps of fabric, cutting, and unsold garments are disposed of annually. In the past workers used to dump this waste in open spaces. These leftovers were sometimes burnt in communities. These practices are now altered by a great number of actors. Factories begin to sort and retrieve textile waste. Businesses use leftover fabric in new garments. Old garments are recycled into fibers by the recyclers. The local associations encourage less hazardous disposal. Such changes make landfills less pressurized. They also reduced open burning pollution. The shift to the circular becomes more intense with time (Islam & Huda, 2022).

Other newer so-called green factories in Dhaka specialize in textile waste. Employees collect scrap pieces of fabric and sort them, cut them into fibers and spin them back into workable yarn. The yarn is redirected to the local garment factories or to export buyers. The production cycle causes waste minimization and a decrease in the imported cotton requirement, which saves money and water (Rahman et al., 2021).

Recycling is not industrial in every case. In the countryside, there are small craft groups that use the remains of the fabric to make quilts, carpets, and hand-made accessories. Most of these organizations engage the women who have lost employment in the formal sector. They receive a new source of income through training in sewing and designing and turn the unwanted cloth into marketable products used in the home, as reported in recent studies.

Export markets are taking note. Some international brands are already asking that the percentage of recycles in their orders should be 20–30% of the fibers. This policy has opened new trade paths to recyclers in Bangladesh and promoted the image of local businesses (United Nations Conference on Trade and Development [UNCTAD], 2023).

This model is effective since there is a relationship among three players: the factories, recycling businesses and the artisan cooperatives. The factories will save money in terms of the handling cost of waste. Raw material to the recyclers is virtually free. Via the fair-trade and export networks, artisans can access the buyers. The system retains value in the country and dispersion of jobs in cities and villages.

There are still problems. There are non-reusable fabrics. Recycling of fibers mixed with chemical dyes is complicated. Quality control is also a problem. However, the development proves that the circular textile systems can work in low-resource environments. They save on materials and cut imports and provide the new resilience to trade in Bangladesh.

4.3 Case Study Three: Solar Microgrids in Kenya

The villages in most parts of Kenya were not electrified. Families used kerosene lamps. The Light was insufficient—the smoke-filled houses. Kids had a problem in reading at night. Mothers coughed often.

Local associations discovered a little, yet clever solution. They built solar microgrids. A microgrid is a small system. It is a solar powered projection of a few houses or shops. Every family will pay a modest monthly fee. Using that, they turn on light, charge batteries, and even power some small instruments.

The change is real. According to World Bank (2021), the cost of energy is reduced to almost half through microgrids. Children in schools learn at night. Shopkeepers extend the working hours of their shops. The amount of money families spend on fuel reduces.

Coupled with the fact that young villagers are being trained to be solar technicians, new jobs are being created, panels are being fixed, and payments are being managed which leads to greater local autonomy. According to the United Nations Development Programme (UNDP) (2022), microgrids help to increase access to energy and further development of skills at the local level.

Health improves, too. Kerosene smoke evaporation dies out. Women work with little electric stoves. They rescue themselves the time of gathering firewood. According to the studies by Lighting Africa (International Finance Corporation and World Bank, 2019), school attendance and spending on kerosene decreased.

Kenya has become a pioneer in solar application. According to IRENA (2020), millions of people can be connected to off-grid solutions, including a growing number through community-based mini-grids (International Finance Corporation and World Bank, 2019).

The case of this story demonstrates intelligent frugality. Individuals did not wait until construction of big power facilities was done. They came up with smaller, cleaner, and cheaper systems to cater to day-to-day needs.

4.4 Case Study Four: Island Plastic Ban and Craft Revival—Southeast Asia

In 2019, the people of the island were fed up. Sea dragging nets returned after being filled with bags of plastics. Children were not playing on beaches which were full of bottles and wrappers. Tourists started writing about smoke of burning waste rather than sunsets. The local government has eventually voted: no plastic bags, no straws, no foam boxes.

The decision was bold. Shopkeepers protested. Go to mainland, customers, they will say. In the short-term, they could be correct. Then something out of the ordinary occurred.

Women bands began to work with palm leaf baskets—another art that had been almost forgotten. Shopping bags made of cloth scraps of garment factories are cut into pieces by young artisans. Bamboo straws were served in cafes, some of which were made by local artisans. Visitors loved the change. They took baskets home like a souvenir and paid more than they would in the event of plastic.

According to the local fishers, the ban made them feel more pride in the community. The pride was a burden. Soon, beach clean-ups picked up approximately half the amount of waste that it used to (WWF, 2023). The sales of craft cooperatives increased by almost 30% (Asian Development Bank, 2022). The island scored better on cleanliness and authenticity by tourists.

Still, the ban was not perfect. Packaging continued to be hidden as imported goods continued bringing it along. There was more community coercion rather than fines. But the result was obvious: cleaner beaches, restored talents, and new sources of revenue. According to the reports made by UNEP (2023) and ITC (2023), these bans are most effective in cases when there are already traditions, pride, and fast alternatives. In the case of this island, it was not only about plastic cessation, but rather recalling some of the things that its inhabitants could create by their own hands.

4.5 Case Study Five: Community-Managed Irrigation—Peru

In the Andes, the Andes farmers are waiting to get rains. The fields dry when they are late. Harvests are reduced when they are weak. Families become food and income deprived without a constant water. Formal irrigation was not an aspect of many villages. Streams pass by without hitting the crops.

In 2017 a community of mountain communities attempted not something novel. They opened the amuna canals with the assistance of local NGOs. Their forefathers constructed these stone channels hundreds of years ago. The canals trap the rain, slow it, and channel it to be under the ground. In later seasons of the dry months, that accumulated water eventually drains into the soil and fills small springs (World Bank, 2020).

The work is communal. The water committees were formed in each village. Households alternate in getting the weeds out, and the stones fixed and the channels clear. The rights to use water during the dry season are granted to the givers of labor. Decisions in the community are made during open-air meetings. In the case of a dispute, the village elders act as mediators (FAO, 2021).

Technology has intermingled with tradition in the minor ways. Water is lifted in storage tanks using solar pumps. It is transferred down the pipes to the kitchen gardens through gravity. Flow is monitored by simple sensors that enable repair to be done before blockage is propagated to cause damage. There is nothing posh, yet all the elements belong to the land.

The changes are visible. Even during the lean months, vegetables are grown by farmers. The groups of women dry the herbs, and pack them into preserves which are sold in the markets. Children do not spend so much time carrying water. Most of them consume those hours in school.

There is severe drought that continues to put pressure on the system and the soil on the rocky slopes is degraded and therefore cannot be restored easily. Yet, the combination of tradition and low profile engineering has resulted in hardiness. The territory contains more water, and the population has more control (UNDP, 2022).

4.6 Case Study Six: Urban Rooftop Farming—Cuba

Havana is crowded. The streets are narrow and intersect between tightly spaced constructions. Ground space is scarce. Since the crisis of the 1990s, the shops were vacant, and food was difficult to locate. Looking up to the roofs people started to look.

The initial rooftop gardens were primitive. Families ransacked parks and stuffed wooden boxes with soil. Friends or small packets in the local stores provided the seeds. The concrete was soon covered with lettuce, tomatoes, and peppers and herbs.

Later, support arrived. Help was provided by local cooperatives and external organizations, as documented in studies of urban agriculture in Havana (FAO, 2020). They came in with composting, less dense soils mixture, and drip irrigation. Such modifications made it possible to have larger harvests without destroying the old roofs.

This was one of the famous attempts in Centro Habana, where a project united three rooftops. The members cultivated and raised vegetables and bees as well as raising tilapia in tanks. They adopted the application of aquaponics, where water is recycled between fish and plants.

Work is shared. Some water the crops. Some make mends or gather harvests. The food consumed is picked and consumed the same day. It comes directly off the roof and thus trucks and storage are unnecessary.

The benefits go beyond food. The gardens cool the buildings and absorb the rain water, relieving street flooding. They also establish venues of meeting. People gossip, children learn to see food growing rather than buying it in supermarkets.

Still, there are limits. There are very few roofs that are capable of supporting heavy tanks. The irrigation parts are difficult to substitute. The gardens however are an indication of what could be done. An urban-filled city can generate food, save money, and unite people.

4.7 Case Study Seven: Seaweed Farming—Zanzibar, Tanzania

Fishing has been a tradition in the small islands of Zanzibar, centuries old. In the recent years however, there has been a drop in catches. The ocean is more heated and the hurricanes are more powerful. In the villages along the coast, women started trying to find other ways of livelihood.

Farming of seaweeds was a solution. This began in the 1990s through the assistance of development agencies and has been recognized as a sustainable livelihood practice (UNEP, 2021). Thin belts of rope are planted by farmers in shallow water. The ropes are bound to small pieces of seaweed by workers. The seaweed is harvested after six weeks by the farmers.

Women do most of the work. Their wading is twice daily. They check the lines, clean the seaweed, and keep the seaweed good and growing. The seaweed when prepared is brought to the beach, rinsed, and left to dry in the sun. The dried seaweed is sold to the traders who utilize the weed in cosmetics, food products, and medicines. The money earned in this labor is able to help families educate their children and buy house commodities.

Other groups have gone to the extreme. In the village of Jambiani, a women cooperative makes soaps and lotion using seaweed where the greater economic value is kept with the community. The cooperative also organizes small training to women in the neighboring villages. Farming of seaweed is a cheap and environmentally friendly practice. It does not require fertilizer and fresh water. It also contributes to reducing the rate of erosion of the coasts through the stability of the seabed.

Challenges remain. Prices are subject to rapid fluctuation, and the farmers have to rely on external buyers. The climate change continues to be a threat to yields. Nonetheless, seaweed farming has provided a stable income to a number of families in Zanzibar and a better representation in their society.

4.8 Case Study Eight: Micro Hydropower to the Nepal Mountain Villages

The mountains in Nepal are steep with occasional small villages. The streets are rugged and the national grid does not go so high. Families have been using kerosene lamps to provide Light over the years. Firewood, which was dragged a long distance, had been used in cooking.

Some villages took an alternative route in the 1980s, as documented in community energy studies (UNDP, 2020). They resorted to the quick streams that were running along the slopes. Engineers put a small turbine in the water and attached it to a simple generator. This project initiated the commencement of micro hydropower.

The units are small, between 5 and 100 kilowatts. Enough to serve 30 to 100 homes. The building involves the participation of villagers. They excavate trenches, drag stones, and cooperate in elevating the walls.

The system is controlled by a local committee. Families contribute low monthly payments. The community uses this money in repairing and compensation of the operator. These are funds that are circulated in the community, and not out of it.

The changes are visible. Children read after dark. Stores store food in refrigerations. Female no longer spend hours picking wood. Small businesses, such as carpentry, milling, tailoring make electric tools the first time.

Difficulties still exist—monsoon rains occasionally destroy pipes. In dry months, streams shrink. Talented mechanics are there scarcely. Numerous plants however have been over 20 years old with care being mostly managed by the villagers themselves.

Microhydropower illustrates how the clean energy can be extended as far as the grid can never reach. In the case of mountain communities, in Nepal, it is Light, work, and a future that is attainable.

4.9 Case Study Nine: Digital Health Services in Rwanda

In the recent past, a sizeable number of rural settlements in Rwanda did not have close physicians. The patients would take hours before walking to a clinic. Often, they arrived too late. Mothers lost children. Elderly people were left unattended.

A new idea changed this. Digital health services were established by the government and NGOs. Simple phones had the advantage that allowed the villagers to get in touch with doctors in towns. They were assisted in making the call by a nurse or a health worker. Physicians would then recommend medicine, treatment, or traveling to a hospital.

This model is time- and life-saving. According to the World Health Organization (WHO, 2020), telemedicine in Rwanda reduced patients travelling by almost 60%. Local treatment of common cases is now done in small clinics. Cases that are severe will be referred first.

Jobs also come. The young employees would be taught on how to handle the digital records and health apps. The Rwanda Ministry of Health (2021) notes that there are more than 45,000 community health workers who utilize mobile tools every day. They monitor births, get diseases reported, and issue warnings in case of outbreaks.

The impact is clear. Mothers receive reminders about their child to have a vaccination. Sick farmers receive fast advice. These systems were also found to be reliable in terms of information during the COVID-19 pandemic, hence minimized fear and misinformation. Investigations conducted by GSMA (2021) indicate that mobile health applications were accessed by over 80% of households in Rwanda.

The system is low-cost. Phones are basic. Networks are simple. Nevertheless, the outcomes are positive. Affordable, clean community-owned digital health is now a way of life.

The case demonstrates the power of frugal intelligence. Rwanda did not wait and have more hospitals, instead it reached out to the doctors using the cheap tools.

This part gives a comparative study of nine case studies of frugal innovations in different global situations. The table brings out the issues, remedies, main characteristic, result, and constraints of any initiative. These two factors collectively contribute to the creation of the FI 6.0 model, where they demonstrate the real-life, community-based solutions to sustainability and inclusion.

A comparative summary of the case studies is presented in Table 1.2 (author's compilation).

The comparative table demonstrates how different communities in the Global South have been resource conscious in their use of frugal strategies to tackle burning issues. Although cases have their own limitations, which are unique, they combined to reflect the principles of the FI 6.0 low-cost innovation, community empowerment, and sustainable results.

Table 1.2. Comparative Analysis of Case Studies Informing the FI 6.0 Model.

Case Study	Country/ Context	Challenge	Frugal Solution	Key Features	Outcomes	Limitations
Repair cooperatives	India	Rising e-waste, costly new goods.	Community repair hubs in markets.	Local skills, very low-cost fixes, and job creation.	Saves families money, reduces landfill waste, and builds pride.	Limited scale, informal sector regulations.
Textile circularity	Bangladesh	Massive textile waste.	Green factories recycle scraps into yarn, and artisans reuse fabric.	Waste-to-value initiatives, women's groups, and the industry community collaborate to work together.	Cuts imports, creates jobs, and exports recycled fiber.	Processing limits are encountered with blends/dyes, as well as quality issues.
Solar microgrids	Kenya	Villages without electricity.	Community solar panels powering homes/shops.	Clean, renewable, pay-per-use, and local technicians.	Children can study at night, lower costs are available, and local jobs are accessible.	Rainy season/ clouds reduce output; financing challenges.
Plastic ban and crafts	SE Asia (island)	Plastic waste is harming tourism and fisheries.	Local ban on single-use plastics; revival of crafts.	Strong community pride, traditional skills, and tourism link.	Cleaner beaches, +30% income for co-ops, and better tourism.	Enforcement is weak, and imports bring hidden plastic.

Community irrigation	Peru (Andes)	Crop failures due to erratic rains.	Revival of ancient amuna canals with NGO support.	Blending heritage with low-tech tools and communal rules.	Year-round vegetables, women's businesses, and school time.	Severe drought still reduces water; steep slopes are unfit.
Rooftop farming	Cuba (Havana)	Food shortage and lack of land.	Urban rooftop gardens and aquaponics.	Low-cost, space reuse, co-ops, and drip irrigation.	Fresh food, a more fabulous city, reduced flooding, and social ties.	Structural limits on roofs; parts are hard to replace.
Seaweed farming	Zanzibar, Tanzania	Falling fish catches, climate stress.	Women-led seaweed farming and cooperatives.	Low-cost, eco-friendly, and women's empowerment.	New income, value-added products, and better food security.	Price fluctuations and climate change risks.
Micro hydropower:	Nepal (mountains)	No grid access, reliance on kerosene.	Small water turbines for villages.	Clean, community-built, 5–100 kW, and committees manage.	Light at night, better work, and less wood use.	Seasonal water shortage, and repair skills are scarce.
Digital health services	Rwanda	Remote villages lacked doctors.	Mobile phones link patients to doctors.	Very low-cost, digital apps, and 45,000 health workers.	Faster treatment, vaccine reminders, and outbreak alerts.	Network gaps and reliance on simple phones.

Source: Author's own compilation based on cited case study references (see Sections 4.1–4.9).

4.10 Building Blocks for Sustainable Transformation

An analysis of these stories reveals eight building blocks:

(1) Community agency
(2) Waste-to-value
(3) Decentralized access
(4) Policy-driven change
(5) Digital inclusion
(6) Technology integration
(7) Blue economy integration
(8) Knowledge-sharing, monitoring, and feedback

These are not hard and fast divisions. A digital tool fortifies a local fishery in certain instances. In others, waste-to-value efforts are made more feasible by means of policies. It is the interaction that counts. A combination of the blocks makes each block stronger. The balance is the foundation of the proposed model, demonstrating how the tested approaches can be integrated in the real situations.

5. Model Development

The nine case studies revealed the patterns that were replicated and informed the eight pillars of FI 6.0. These pillars align the community interests with market opportunity and could be applied in different settings. Each pillar is practice based: culturally sensitive, receptive to emergent concepts and structured to support people-focused economically viable and environmentally sustainable results. The model relies on participatory efforts on the local level, as well as on low-cost and simple instruments to create long-term and sustainable effects.

5.1 FI 6.0

Despite the implication behind the name of the label FI 6.0 stealing the sophistication of Industry 4.0, it does not suggest the wholesale implementation of expensive and complicated systems. Rather, FI 6.0 implies the tactical deployment of the right technologies in such a manner that smartness is measured in effectiveness and not technical sophistication. The appropriate solution would be a traditional practice, a simple mobile phone, or a lightweight AI model or sensor where it is worth it. The intelligent thing is to think it through and implement it in a community-based way; technology is the means to the end. This principle is used to selectively and context-specifically use high-level tools in the pursuit of sustainable development objectives.

5.2 Pillar One: Community Agency

This pillar puts a focus on the local people in the planning, needs assessment and design. When the residents are the ones to spearhead initiatives, the residents will have more confidence in the projects and be able to maintain them longer. Local leaders provide a cultural input and ability to solve problems practically. Community organizations save money and labor, create fair-use regulations and share gains locally, and this reduction of waste and enhancement of collective ownership and pride.

5.3 Pillar Two: Waste-To-Value

This pillar considers waste as a productive factor to local economies. Small scale manufacturing and composting are provided through organized systems of collection, sorting, and reutilization of materials. The processes enhance the quality of soil and minimize landfill pressure. These activities help communities to generate employment opportunities, preserve resources, and protect the ecosystems around them.

5.4 Pillar Three: Decentralized Access

This pillar makes critical services and infrastructure more accessible to the end users. The local energy, water, health, education, and connectivity systems minimize traveling time and out-of-pocket expenses and enhances reliability. Smaller locally-controlled networks independent of the large central grids enhance the resilience and community self-reliance.

5.5 Pillar Four: Change Driven by Policies

This pillar is based on effective and enabling public policy in order to act. Governments also provide clear and consistent rules and regulations, fiscal incentives towards green efforts, form oversight procedures and invest in long term planning. Such actions establish a predictable environment which attracts investment, conserves natural resources, and cultivates human trust.

5.6 Pillar Five: Digital Inclusion

This pillar broadens opportunities by means of digital access and acquisition of skills. The mobile phones, shared internet facility, and minimal digital services will allow the access of farmers, students, small business owners, women, and older adults to the markets, learning resources, and health information. Inclusive digital policies bridge the urban-rural divide and increase the administrative and government services access.

5.7 Pillar Six: Technology Integration

Technology is presented in this pillar sensitively and cost-effectively by focusing on key functionality rather than multifunctional and high-end intelligence. Examples include:

- *AI/ML:* miniature models that can be installed on smartphones to build crop diseases.
- *IoT:* the cheap sensors (e.g., LoRaWAN devices) have long-range and are used to monitor soil moisture or water quality and provide an SMS notification.
- *Distributed ledgers:* simplified blockchain technologies that store the information of supply-chains in a transparent manner or facilitate safe payments in societies.

It is about technologies that could be affordable to communities, can be maintained there, and be combined with what communities have already.

5.8 Pillar Seven: Blue-Economy Integration

This pillar enhances livelihoods on the coasts by means of diversified and sustainable marine activities. The communities build up responsible fisheries, sea weeds and shellfish farming, marine ecotourism, and value added processing of marine products. The training programs, proper use of resource, and clean transport solutions (such as solar powered boats) can assist in preserving the marine environment and also create employment opportunities and new sources of revenues.

5.9 Pillar Eight: Knowledge-Sharing, Monitoring, and Feedback

This pillar encourages unrestricted, simple to use avenues of sharing of practical knowledge. Functional skills and local innovations are disseminated through community meetings, peer mentoring, visual instructions, and mobile messaging groups. Upfront and common practices of monitoring and feedback help communities to monitor results, detect issues at an early stage, and make changes. Clearly visible indicators and periodic review points will ensure that all the stakeholders are updated and that there is a continued improvement towards that.

6. Implementation Roadmap

The implementation of the FI 6.0 will be divided into three consecutive steps, the steps that are informed of the lessons learned during the previous steps.

6.1 Stage 1: Pilot (Year 1)

Choose one representative community in which to host a pilot. An implementer core team, led by residents, will use the priority aspects of the model and put them into practice in practice. Extensive participant feedback protocols will be used to critically analyze program performance, determine systemic constraints, and optimize intervention strategies in stages until it can be implemented at large scale.

6.2 Stage 2: Expansion (Years 2–3)

When the pilot proves successful, expand the model to other communities with other elements being added as time goes on. Establish acquaintances with local NGOs and SMEs to contribute to the cost and technological capacity. The training shall focus on practical training. Low complexity instruments (e.g. paper logs, simple mobile forms, or shared noticeboards) should be used in progress monitoring.

6.3 Stage 3: Consolidation (Year Four and Above)

This stage aims at institutionalizing the model to make it a self-sustaining aspect of the community life. The local committees will take control of the continuity in management and administration. There must be a diversification of funding; inclusion of government programs, private partners, and local contributions. To sustain the momentum and expand the adoption, communities will hold review meetings approximately every six months and spread triumph stories.

6.4 Roles and Responsibilities

- Community members: define community priorities, train, and monitor day to day activities.
- Government agencies: offer the facilitating policies and the access to the public spaces or facilities.
- NGOs: provide technical expertise and contacts to prospective funders.
- Partners in the private sector: they provide resources and assist in opening market or service gateways.

6.5 Required Resources

The necessary supplies are training tools and trainers, basic equipment in each of the program pillars, basic monitoring tools (either paper or electronic) and operating budgets on events, travel, and regular maintenance.

6.6 Risk Management

It is important to monitor the risks. Early warning signs, which should be observed by the teams, include slippages in the timelines, a drop in the level of community involvement, or insufficient funds. Some mitigation strategies involve having a small contingency fund, rotating leaders to eliminate burnout, and using community meetings as a means of solving grievances at an early stage (see Nguyen & Schmidt, 2023, p. 41).

6.7 Scaling Indicators

Monitor indicators which are measurable, including the number of people trained, household or local income change, better household or local access to services (water, health, and markets), and participation rates. One of the indicators of the sustainability of activities is the withdrawal of external support.

Once started, these projects are often small: in Pune, a cooperative is recovering broken appliances, or a few households in Kenya are putting up solar kits. These measures are small, but significant testament of the fact that effective solutions can be affordable and reliable.

Pilots are likely to propagate naturally when they are found useful. Heaps of recyclers pop up in Dhaka and household micro grids multiply in rural Kenya. What initially began as localized experiments, spread to other areas as those who practised share knowledge, and manage the costs in a manner that is manageable.

Societies slowly bring the practice into their everyday life. They use wastes as a resource. Families living along the coasts engage in the cultivation of sea weeds. There is an extension of market links of rural producers through the use of digital tools.

6.8 Digital Governance Accountability Chain

Effective digital governance relies on three interlinked principles: clarity of responsibility, transparency of process, and independent oversight. These elements together build citizen trust in digital systems (OECD, 2023; UNDP, 2022).

Effective digital governance is strengthened when citizens move beyond mere complaints to actively contributing ideas and local knowledge. For example, in some communities, residents have proposed improved waste collection methods; in others, they have filled out surveys that directly inform policy choices. Such everyday contributions foster outcomes that legislation alone cannot achieve.

This participatory approach has shown strong applicability in regions like Puducherry and Karaikal, where high mobile internet penetration enables wider engagement. The use of simple, bilingual applications—including idea boards, grievance portals, and service-rating systems—can significantly boost citizen involvement. In this way, participation transforms one-way governance into a two-way dialogue, fostering a sense of ownership and trust among citizens.

7. Findings and Discussion

This paper demonstrates that affordable intelligence can offer a viable basis in regard to digital governance. The model of FI 6.0 is an extension of previous research but it puts practical on-the-ground considerations in clearer focus.

7.1 First Discovery: Empowering the Community

It is all about community empowerment. This characteristic of the citizens as active participants and not passive consumers is echoed in the principle of top-down development (Heeks, 2018) and the bottom-of-the-pyramid innovation model (Prahalad & Hart, 2002), as well as the bottom-up principle of innovation. In addition to those donations, our study has proven that frugal design principles such as simplicity, low costs, and cultural relevance have a direct positive effect on uptake, but most importantly, increases trust in digital governance in resource-limited settings. In the place where Heeks (2018) has identified the collapse and Prahalad and Hart (2002) suggested market-oriented remedies, the FI 6.0 provides a solution that is governance-centered and prevents the collapse by creating trust through frugal design decisions.

7.2 Second Observation: Phased Growth

The phased growth approach embedded in the FI 6.0 model aligns with Rogers' (2003) diffusion of innovations framework, which posits that innovations are disseminated gradually through community adoption. Evidence from the case studies indicates that limited, locally tested rollouts minimize resource waste, and reduce implementation resistance. In contrast, large-scale, costly deployments often exhaust budgets and fail, whereas step-by-step, affordable implementations yield more effective and sustainable outcomes.

7.3 Third Finding: Accountability

The governance accountability chain—comprising clarity of responsibility, transparency, and independent oversight—is critical for the legitimacy of digital systems (OECD, 2023; UNDP, 2022). Our analysis affirms that even low-cost, modular systems require active watchdog mechanisms; without them, frugality risks becoming a source of fragility rather than resilience.

7.4 Fourth Finding: Participation

Participation is an issue of simplicity. Our case studies can be further expanded upon Mansell (2015) by showing that accessibility rather than technical sophistication leads to inclusive engagement. Basic means like SMS, community kiosks, and small mobile applications are always more effective compared to sophisticated web portals in achieving long-lasting citizen engagement. In most of the

Global South, however, ease of use and access is a more prevailing motivator to trust and engagement than sophisticated functionality in digital governance.

7.5 Overall Implications

These findings can be related to the existing literature on frugal innovation (Tiwari & Herstatt, 2012), which states the possibility of low-price and low-quality products being used simultaneously; FI 6.0 is used to apply the same logic to governance. Frugality should not be viewed by researchers and practitioners as a sign of low quality, but an innovative, scalable, and people-centered methodology that would focus on efficiency and meaningful impact. We admit boundaries: some systems (such as full-fledged health records) are bound to require bigger investments (World Bank, 2021). Nonetheless, the cost can be reduced with the modular and periodical approaches and more local ownership can be raised in such areas.

Overall, FI 6.0 is consistent with the existing theory, but it extends it, offering a viable model to reach accountability, participation, and managed growth with the help of frugal and context-sensitive decisions and, therefore, make governance more affordable and inclusive.

8. Conclusion and Direction of Future Research

In this paper, FI 6.0, which is a new framework, will be presented and empirically justified in accordance with the ethical goals of frugal innovation and the disruptive power of the technologies of the Fourth Industrial Revolution. FI 6.0 breaks the paradigm of high-priced and high-technology and demonstrates that digital governance may be built with the dual focus on sustainability and inclusion.

8.1 Key Contributions

- Development Studies: a global south model of sovereign, locally based, digital adoption.
- Innovation Management: frugal innovation in a systemic and governance design context.
- Public Policy: a realistic roadmap to initiatives that are scorable, responsible, and sustainable.

8.2 Core Argument

The argument made by FI 6.0 on the basis of nine international case studies is that contextual fit is the crucial determinant in techno effectiveness. The main means of that fit is frugality, and the uptake, trust and resilient results of that frugality are more achievable and more profound than costly, high-tech solutions.

8.3 Scope and Limits

FI 6.0 is not a universal remedy. Its achievement hinges on the significance of participation by the community, competent institutions, and empowering governance structures. In accordance with the results of the development practice, the greater the success of technology interventions is realized through the influencing work of local actors and linking these interventions to social and policy landscapes, the more successful they can be (Heeks, 2020; Smith & Stirling, 2018).

8.4 Research Agenda

The article provides the propositions that can be tested in the future:

- H1: The greater the community digital literacy, the greater the successfulness of frugal digital platform adoption.
- H2: The cities can achieve efficiency gains faster, and rural populations will be better empowered.
- H3: Trust will be enhanced more so when accountability mechanisms are incorporated as opposed to the prioritization of affordability.

To understand how the long-term efficacy of the FI 6.0 intervention can be fully assessed through a comparative, longitudinal study, researchers need to analyze the intervention in systematic ways, i.e. how the intervention fosters empowerment, or critically assess possible emergent dependency structures that can emerge as a result of the intervention, which would make digital governance more attuned to the needs of people.

Reflected with application, the structure and suggestions in this paper are expected to give the reader a clear impression of the original and practical contributions of the paper in various fields.

References

Asian Development Bank. (2022). *Sustainable tourism and community livelihoods in Southeast Asia*. https://www.adb.org

Bannister, F., & Connolly, R. (2014). ICT, public values, and transformative government: A framework and programme for research. *Government Information Quarterly*, *31*(1), 119–128. https://doi.org/10.1016/j.giq.2013.06.002

Bhatti, Y. A. (2012). *What is frugal? What is innovation? Towards a theory of frugal innovation*. Oxford University Press.

Blind, K., & Storz, C. (2019). Does frugal innovation lock communities into "Second-Best" technologies? *Research Policy*, *48*(4), 1021–1035. https://doi.org/10.1016/j.respol.2019.01.015

Criado, J. I., & Gil-Garcia, J. R. (2019). Creating public value through smart technologies and strategies: From digital services to artificial intelligence and beyond. *International Journal of Public Sector Management*, *32*(5), 438–450. https://doi.org/10.1108/IJPSM-07-2019-0178

Food and Agriculture Organization of the United Nations. (2020). *Urban and peri-urban agriculture in Havana*. FAO. https://www.fao.org

Food and Agriculture Organization of the United Nations. (2021). *Community-managed irrigation systems in the Andes*. FAO. https://www.fao.org

Graham, M. (2019). *Digital economies at global margins*. MIT Press.

GSMA. (2021). Mobile for development: Digital health in Rwanda. *GSM Association*. https://www.gsma.com

Heeks, R. (2018). *Information and communication technology for development (ICT4D)*. Routledge.

Heeks, R. (2020). ICT4D 3.0? Part 1—The components of an emerging "digital-for-development" paradigm. *Electronic Journal of Information Systems in Developing Countries*, *86*(3), e12124. https://doi.org/10.1002/isd2.12124

International Renewable Energy Agency. (2020). *Renewable energy and jobs: Annual review 2020*. https://www.irena.org

International Finance Corporation and World Bank. (2019). *Lighting Africa: Off-grid solar market trends*. World Bank Group. https://www.lightingafrica.org

International Trade Centre. (2023). *Sustainable crafts and tourism: Case studies from Southeast Asia*. ITC. https://www.intracen.org

Islam, M. T., & Huda, N. (2022). Circular economy in the textile industry: A systematic literature review. *Journal of Cleaner Production*, *331*. Article 129998. https://doi.org/10.1016/j.jclepro.2021.129998

Kagermann, H., Wahlster, W., & Helbig, J. (2013). *Recommendations for implementing the strategic initiative INDUSTRIE 4.0*. National Academy of Science and Engineering.

Mansell, R. (2015). *The digital divide and inclusive innovation*. MIT Press.

Meijer, A. (2015). E-governance innovation: Barriers and strategies. *Government Information Quarterly*, *32*(2), 198–206. https://doi.org/10.1016/j.giq.2015.01.001

Nguyen, A., & Schmidt, L. (2023). Sustaining community-led initiatives: A framework for proactive risk mitigation. *International Journal of Sustainable Development*, *36*(2), 35–52.

Organisation for Economic Co-operation and Development (OECD). (2019). *Going digital: Shaping policies, improving lives*. OECD Publishing. https://doi.org/10.1787/9789264312012-en

Organisation for Economic Co-operation and Development. (2023). *Digital governance and accountability: Global best practices*. https://www.oecd.org

Pansera, M., & Owen, R. (2018). Framing inclusive innovation within the discourse of development: Insights from case studies in India. *Research Policy*, *47*(1), 23–34. https://doi.org/10.1016/j.respol.2017.09.007

Prahalad, C. K., & Hart, S. L. (2002). The fortune at the bottom of the pyramid. *Strategy+Business*, *26*, 1–14.

Radjou, N., & Prabhu, J. (2015). *Frugal innovation: How to do more with less.* PublicAffairs.

Radjou, N., Prabhu, J., & Ahuja, S. (2012). *Jugaad innovation: Think frugal, be flexible, generate breakthrough growth.* Jossey-Bass.

Rahman, M. M., Hossain, M. A., & Ahmed, S. (2021). Sustainable textile waste management in Bangladesh: Challenges and opportunities. *Journal of Environmental Management, 289.* Article 112521. https://doi.org/10.1016/j.jenvman.2021.112521

Rogers, E. M. (2003). *Diffusion of innovations* (5th ed.). Free Press.

Rwanda Ministry of Health. (2021). *Digital health strategy 2021–2025.* Government of Rwanda.

Smith, A., & Stirling, A. (2018). Innovation, sustainability and democracy: An analysis of grassroots contributions. *Journal of Cleaner Production, 197*, 18241834. https://doi.org/10.1016/j.jclepro.2018.06.093

Tiwari, R., & Herstatt, C. (2012). Frugal innovation: A global networks perspective. *Unternehmung, 66*(3), 245–274. https://doi.org/10.5771/0042-059X-2012-3-245

United Nations Environment Programme. (2023). *Plastic waste management and policy* impacts. https://www.unep.org

United Nations Conference on Trade and Development. (2023). *Circular economy and trade: Trends and policy options.* https://unctad.org

United Nations Development Programme. (2020). *Community-based micro hydropower in Nepal.* Kathmandu. https://www.undp.org/nepal

United Nations Development Programme. (2022). *Human development report 2021–2022: Uncertain times, unsettled lives: Shaping our future in a transforming world.* UNDP. https://hdr.undp.org/content/human-development-report-2021-22

United Nations Educational, Scientific and Cultural Organization. (2021). *Ethical guidelines for digital governance in resource-constrained contexts.* UNESCO. https://www.unesco.org

United Nations Environment Programme. (2021). *Sustainable seaweed farming: A livelihood opportunity in Zanzibar.* UNEP. https://www.unep.org

World Bank. (2020). *Community-based water management in the andes.* https://www.worldbank.org

World Bank. (2021). *Digital governance in developing countries: Challenges and opportunities.* https://www.worldbank.org

World Health Organisation. (2020). Digital health in the African region: Current situation and prospects. *WHO Regional Office for Africa.* https://www.afro.who.int

World Wide Fund for Nature. (2023). *Marine conservation and sustainable livelihoods.* https://www.worldwildlife.org

Chapter 2

Mindful Consumption for Reinforcing Sustainable Lifestyles: Pathways Toward Regenerative Living

Aiman Khatoon[a], *Anuj Pal Kapoor*[a] *and Sangeeta Sahney*[b]

[a]Indian Institute of Technology Jodhpur, India
[b]Indian Institute of Technology Kharagpur, India

Abstract

The rise of overconsumption and ecological degradation calls for researchers and policymakers to address the issue, identify the drivers, and propose practical solutions. In response to this issue, mindful consumption (MC) has emerged as a transformative paradigm for reinforcing sustainable lifestyles. This chapter systematically reviews and synthesizes the domain of MC to conceptualize the concept not merely as an individual behavioral adjustment but as a systemic enabler of regenerative futures. Drawing on a systematic narrative review, this chapter synthesizes 80 research articles published in the domain of MC. In this way the study identifies four key determinants and enablers of MC and integrates them into a framework that connects individual mindfulness to regenerative development.

The review findings reveal that while existing studies predominantly emphasize that MC is an individual awareness and ethical choice, limited attention has been given to the system-level mechanisms including policy, technological, and market structures that enable mindful practices to scale. This chapter therefore advances a conceptual framework illustrating how Industry 6.0 technologies (Artificial Intelligence (AI), blockchain, Internet of Things (IoT)) and participatory governance actors can support transparent, ethical, and restorative consumption ecosystems. Ultimately, the chapter argues for a paradigm shift from conservation toward Regeneration, embedding MC into institutional design, business strategy, and education to accelerate progress toward the Sustainable Development Goals (SDGs) through conscious individual and collective action.

Regenerative Revolution, 29–49

doi:10.1108/978-1-80686-859-920261002

Keywords: Mindful consumption; sustainable lifestyles; regenerative future; consumer behavior; industry 6.0; behavioral change; systemic transition; SDGs

JEL Classification: Q01; Q56; D91; M31

1. Introduction

Mindful consumption (MC) has emerged as a transformative approach for reorienting consumption patterns toward sustainability and regenerative living. It reframes the firm–consumer relationship from driving transactions to cultivating awareness, restraint, and value-congruent choices that support ecological balance and collective well-being (Bahl et al., 2016). In today's fast-paced environment, where ecological degradation, resource depletion, and social inequity have been major issues, causing aggressive marketing practices of brands (i.e., pizza delivered in 10 minutes, purchase the product in one click, and big billion sale), these offerings are escalating the overconsumption and unsustainable buying practices. In this scenario, a "mindful mind" on the demand side helps consumers distinguish needs from wants, evaluate sustainability claims critically, and choose lower-impact options (Fischer et al., 2017). On the supply side, mindfulness encourages organizations to listen, design, and communicate in ways that promote sufficiency, repair, reuse, and circularity such as vintage fashion and slow tourism (Garg et al., 2024; Shikalgar et al., 2024).

As technology advances, consumer expectations and habits immensely change toward new digital tools; some of them are raising impulse buying behavior to shake profits, while others are trying to enforce conscious decisions. For instance, GreenSwapp, a grocery application, enables consumers to track the carbon footprint of their shopping carts in real time and suggests lower-impact alternatives (Halpern et al., 2023). Similarly, Unilever's smart-packaging technology and RFID-enabled refill systems try to reduce plastic waste and promote reuse, aligning business innovation with mindfulness and sustainability principles (Lehtinen & Madeira, 2024). Such initiatives illustrate how mindful design and use of digital technologies can bridge the gap between awareness and regenerative action.

According to recent studies, mindfulness can promote and nudge consumption behaviors, including routine disruption, a gap between attitudes and behaviors, and a rise in fundamental and socially leaning standards of behavior (Bahl et al., 2016; Gupta et al., 2023); such as a person scrolling mobile phone suddenly and seeing an ad of discounted items to the cart, who is able to notice the excitement through practising mindfulness and recognizing it as a temporary craving rather a genuine need. Even though mindfulness is an individual approach to sustainability, there is a lack of development in the academic literature on the path toward Regeneration. The relationship of mindfulness to sustainable consumption and other actors (i.e., organizations, and policies) remains a mostly un-researched subject, according to Fischer et al. (2017) and

Garg et al. (2024). Although the theoretical foundations for this relationship remain in their infancy, mindfulness —by guiding individuals' awareness across inner and outer experiences—has begun to be linked with sustainability, and organizational contexts in emerging research (Oeij et al., 2022; Parvatiyar & Sheth, 2023; Pham & Le Phuong Giao, 2026). As a result, scholars have urged further investigation into the new strategic foundations guiding the interaction of mindfulness with other actors (Kunwer & Singh, 2025).

Despite growing interest, empirical and conceptual clarity on how MC can evolve from individual behavior to a systemic enabler of regenerative futures remains limited. Existing research primarily emphasizes personal awareness and ethical choice (Kumar et al., 2024; Kumar & Panda, 2025), but lacks an integrated framework linking psychological, cultural, and technological enablers with institutional and policy structures.

This chapter fills this knowledge gap by adopting a systematic narrative review approach to synthesize multidisciplinary viewpoints on MC. The objective is to identify determinants and enablers of MC and propose a conceptual framework that integrates institutional, technological, and organizational systems to support regenerative life with conscious behavior. By doing so, this chapter contributes to advancing the theory of MC and offers a roadmap for policymakers, educators, and businesses to institutionalize mindfulness as a lever for achieving the SDGs.

2. Research Methodology

To investigate how MC contributes to regenerative living, this chapter adopts a systematic narrative review design. The approach integrates the methodological rigor of a Systematic Literature Review (SLR) with the interpretive depth of a narrative synthesis, following the guidance of Paul et al. (2021) and Ferrari (2015). The literature selection for the review has been done by following the guidelines of the SPAR-4-SLR protocol, which offers a transparent and replicable structure for identifying, screening, and synthesizing literature while minimizing researcher bias (Paul et al., 2021). Narrative synthesis style allows for interpretive flexibility in connecting multidisciplinary findings and building a conceptual framework (Ferrari, 2015). This hybrid approach ensures both methodological precision and conceptual richness, which is essential for a topic as cross-cutting as MC. Fig. 2.1 synthesizes the entire process of data collection and filtration of the review sample.

2.1 SPAR-4-SLR Protocol: Assembling

The first step of the SPAR-4-SLR technique is "Assembling," which includes identifying and collecting data sources for the systematic review (Paul et al., 2021). The central theme of this study was to explore how MC can reinforce sustainable behavior through regenerative lifestyle. The research aims to address mainly three objectives to attempt the research question: (1) synthesizing

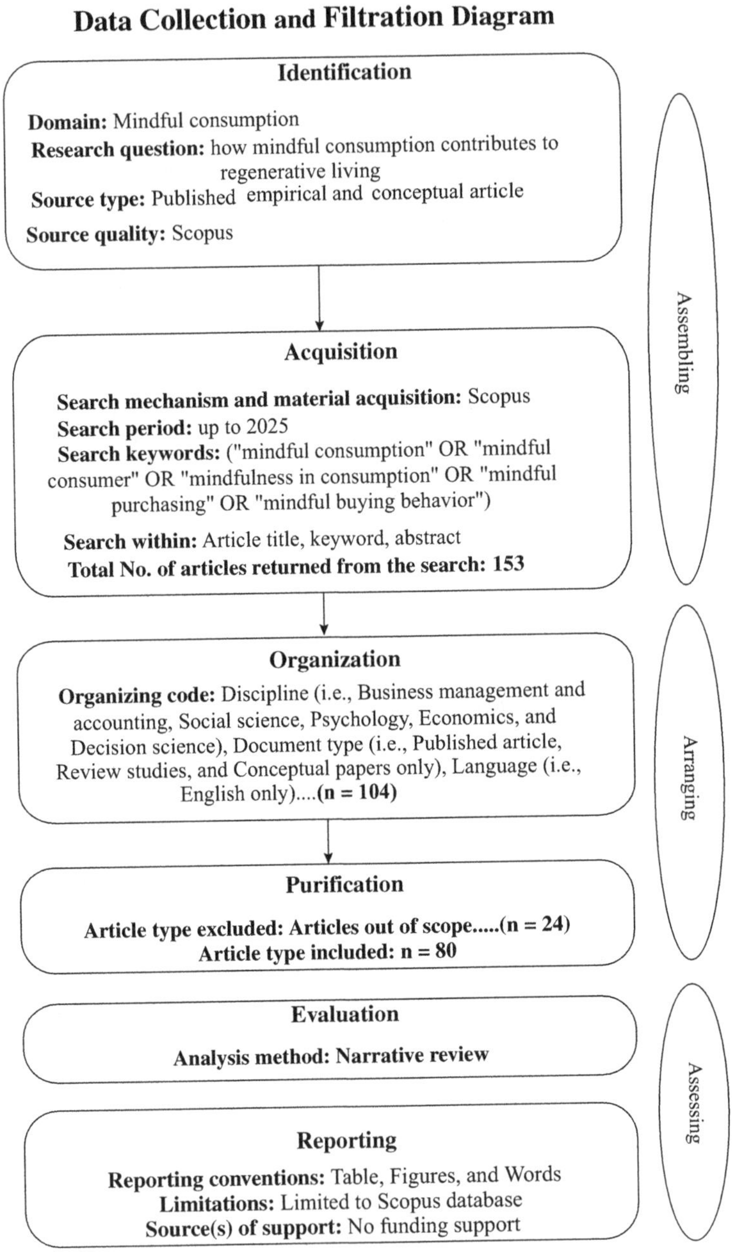

Fig. 2.1. Data Collection and Filtration. *Source:* Author's own illustration informed by SPAR-4-SLR stages (Paul & Criado, 2021); independently designed and not adapted from published figures.

literature from a multidisciplinary perspective; (2) identifying the determinants and enablers of MC; and (3) proposing a framework for achieving a regenerative lifestyle through a mindful way. This chapter has included only published journals for review, which usually go through blind peer review procedures and significantly advance knowledge on a particular area of interest; merely those were kept for this study (Lim, 2025; Paul et al., 2021). Proceedings of conferences, and book chapters were thus disregarded in order to preserve rigor (Paul et al., 2021). Further, Scopus database was used to assess and find quality journal articles, because of their strict indexing standards and acceptance across disciplines (Lim, 2025; Paul et al., 2021).

These keywords have been used to searching the Scopus database within article title, keyword, and abstract "mindful consumption" OR "mindful consumer" OR "mindfulness in consumption" OR "mindful purchasing" OR "mindful buying behavior." The initial search resulted in 153 articles. It is important to note that no restriction was applied to the publication year.

2.2 SPAR-4-SLR Protocol: Arranging

Two essential substages make up the second step of the SPAR-4-SLR technique, "Arranging": using codes or frameworks to organize search results and then purifying them to create a final dataset fit for analysis (Paul et al., 2021). At this stage, 49 articles were excluded from the search results by limiting the selection to studies published in the disciplines of Business, Management and Accounting, Social Sciences, Psychology, Economics, and Decision Sciences, and written in the English language. Book chapters and conference papers were also excluded. Further, 24 out-of-scope articles were excluded, resulting in the final sample of 80 articles for review.

2.3 SPAR-4-SLR Protocol: Assessing

In the last step of the SPAR-4-SLR technique, the selected 80 articles were evaluated and reported (Paul et al., 2021). This stage encompassed content analysis to code and identify MC determinants and enablers. The presentation of results in this study followed a textual narrative and established the role of organizations, technology, institutions, and policy in implementing MC in the society, arguing that MC is not limited to individual decisions; instead, it is enforced through other supporting characters too.

3. Findings

3.1 Conceptualizing MC in a Regenerative Frame

The term MC has been conceptualized in past literature overlapping yet distinct ways. Seminal work (e.g., Brown & Kasser, 2005; Sheth et al., 2011) defined it as conscious awareness in purchasing and using goods, motivated by inner satisfaction rather than external status. These studies drew from Buddhist and psychological traditions emphasizing present-moment attention and non-attachment (Bahl et al., 2016). At the same time, later studies in the domain of marketing and sustainability expanded the construct beyond cognitive awareness to include ethical reflection, compassion, and sufficiency orientation (Awad et al., 2022; Dhandra, 2019). Mindfulness was positioned as a transformative capacity enabling consumers to align actions with ecological and moral values—reducing materialism and fostering subjective well-being.

Recent researchers integrate mindfulness into transformative consumer research and sustainable-behavior frameworks, identifying it as both a trait (stable attentional orientation) and a state (context-triggered awareness) (Parvatiyar & Sheth, 2023). Nevertheless, conceptual fragmentation persists: some studies restrict mindfulness to personal self-control, while others frame it as a collective mindset supporting systemic Regeneration (Garg et al., 2024). Few attempts have been made to connect these individuals to organizational views through measurable linkages (e.g., Kunwer & Singh, 2025; Manchanda et al., 2023). The present review therefore interprets MC as a conscious, compassionate, and values-driven engagement with products and systems aimed at restoring rather than depleting ecological and social capital. This integrative view underpins the subsequent thematic synthesis.

3.2 Determinants and Enablers of MC

Based on our selected sample of literature this chapter identifies four determinants and enablers (themes) of MC which are discussed below.

3.2.1 Psychological Foundations

Across empirical and conceptual studies, mindfulness majorly conceptualized and measured as a psychological regulator in two ways: first, it was drawn from spiritual and virtue ethics traditions (e.g., Buddhist and Stoic roots) as awareness, care, and temperance (Armstrong, 2021; Gupta et al., 2023); second, from marketing and behavioral perspective it comprises through awareness (i.e., the capacity to perceive needs vs. wants and notice environmental consequences), intentionality (i.e., deliberate, value-congruent decision-making), and connectedness (i.e., a felt interdependence with others and nature) (Dhandra, 2019; Shapiro & Schwartz, 2000). Drawing from both the perspectives (i.e., virtue ethics and psychological mindfulness) this study conceptualizes MC as comprising awareness, care (connectedness), and temperance (intentional intentionality). Together, these three interrelated capacities can foster reflective sufficiency and regenerative engagement. Studies report that mindful consumers show lower impulse buying, stronger moral identity, and greater satisfaction derived from experiences rather than possessions (Milne et al., 2020; Rosenberg, 2004).

A review by Pompili and Carfora (2025) indicates that mindful eating can support sustainable food choices, though effects are inconsistent across studies. Similarly, a study conducted in China shows that heightened inner awareness fosters more deliberate decisions around dietary supplements (Wang et al., 2023). In the United Kingdom (UK), Hussain et al. (2023) reported that negative associations between mindful eating and fat consumption, arguing that mindfulness strengthens sensitivity to hunger and satiety and reduces reliance on external cues such as enticing visuals, aromas, or taste prompts. Together, these studies suggest that inner awareness can disrupt hedonic, cue-driven patterns.

On the other hand, outer-focused awareness has been studied in relation to sustainability attitudes and behaviors. Jansen et al. (2024) find that outer awareness predicts pro-sustainability orientations via connectedness to nature, implying that nature-based mindfulness can bridge intention and action. On this regard, Milne et al. (2020) add that outer awareness helps consumers notice automatic responses to promotions (e.g., cravings sparked by "BOGO" offers) and act selectively in line with personal values—e.g., pausing to ask, "Do I need two, or am I reacting to the stimulus?"

In the sense of "care," it is the capacity to extend attention beyond short-term gratification toward one's own well-being, the welfare of others, and ecological health. Sheth et al. (2011) identify care as a foundational value of MC, drawing on moral psychology and prosocial behavior (i.e., care for self, others, and nature). Mindfulness correlates with healthier consumption patterns, including lower overeating and better alignment with physiological needs (Bahl et al., 2013). Experimental evidence shows more mindful individuals choose healthier foods (Jordan et al., 2014). Such self-care can, indirectly, support sustainability by reducing resource-intensive medical burdens and wasteful dietary patterns. In the case of "care for others," it is associated with empathy and compassion (Birnie et al., 2010), which shape ethical choices (e.g., fair trade, cruelty-free). Emotion regulation reduces compulsive buying and the financial stress borne by families (Williams & Grisham, 2012). When it comes to ecological concern (care for nature) and reduced materialism, studies reflect that mindfulness can disrupt high-impact routines and motivate pro-environmental acts (Brown & Kasser, 2005; Fischer et al., 2017). On the other side, temperance connects to materialism and non-attachment which leads negative relationship with materialistic value orientations and positively associated with intrinsic goals (Brown & Kasser, 2005; Kasser, 2003), thereby supporting sufficiency and longer-term satisfaction.

3.2.2 Cultural and Contextual Influences

Culture is the context in which MC becomes thinkable and doable. Psychology explains the inner states of attention, care, and restraint; Culture supplies the shared meanings, norms, and traditions that make these states visible, legitimate, and sustainable. To explain why some societies are more receptive than others, scholars examine how cultural values, religious traditions, and collective narratives define what it means to consume with awareness and restraint (Gupta et al., 2023). Research on religion and spirituality are long-standing anchors. In Buddhist settings, non-attachment, compassion, and sufficiency translate into everyday behaviors such as modest eating, waste reduction, and sharing.

Wickramasekara and Jayawickrama (2022) show Sri Lankan consumers turning Buddhist teachings into concrete acts like reuse and resistance to excess; Wong and Faikhamta (2021) similarly note how moderation reframes consumption as ethical living rather than material pursuit. Parallel principles appear elsewhere: Islamic concepts of zuhd (asceticism) and amana (trusteeship) emphasize moderation and stewardship, while Christian traditions valorize simplicity. These are not merely frugality scripts; they are moral narratives that normalize MC within broader systems of meaning.

Beyond religion, cultural orientations shape uptake. Work drawing on Schwartz's values and Hofstede's dimensions suggests that collectivist contexts, which emphasize interdependence and community welfare, more readily support conscious decision-making (TUNA, 2025). Thøgersen and Zhou (2012) find organic food choices in Denmark driven by personal attitudes and environmental beliefs. In contrast, in China, people are more strongly guided by social expectations, highlighting whether mindfulness is experienced as individual reflection or collective responsibility. Culture also operates through narratives and movements that recast consumption as moral and identity work. Minimalism, veganism, slow fashion, and zero-waste provide "scripts" to communities that help people enact awareness, care, and temperance. Caruana et al. (2016) argue that these movements offer not only practices but also identities (e.g., "mindful shopper," "zero-waste advocate").

However, there is a risk of aestheticization and commodification: Shaw and Moraes (2009) caution that minimalism can slide into lifestyle branding in which sleek design eclipses genuine restraint. However, Culture is shaped by daily routines and practice. In this regard, Practice Theory (Warde, 2005; Shove et al., 2012) reminds us that consumption is shaped by shared habits, materials, and skills such as norms concerning cleanliness, hospitality, clean water, nourished food, and energy use. Traditions of thrift reduce over-purchase and waste; cultural idioms such as Japan's mottainai (regret over waste) and Scandinavia's lagom ("just enough") institutionalize repair, reuse, and moderation. Overall, mindfulness is not only an internal state but a shared cultural accomplishment. When societies weave restraint, compassion, and sufficiency into teachings, routines, and identity narratives, MC is normalized and sustained. For sustainability, Culture lowers the cognitive burden on individuals by converting mindful acts into shared expectations. For Regeneration, Culture provides stories, rituals, and communal practices that reframe "buying less" and "using wisely" as celebrated expressions of identity and ecological care.

3.2.3 Digital Technologies

In today's hyperconnected world, MC is increasingly shaped by digital environments. Social media, online retail, algorithms, and apps influence not only what consumers buy but also how they reflect on, justify, or resist their choices (Howells et al., 2016). Digital platforms can support awareness and sufficiency, yet they also amplify impulsivity, hedonic desire, and overconsumption (Tran et al., 2025). Understanding this "digital dimension" requires weighing both enabling and disruptive effects. Research shows that platform design often undermines temperance by promoting instant gratification. One-click purchasing, personalized recommendations, scarcity banners, and push notifications exploit cognitive biases and encourage impulsive buying (Hartfield, 2025). Digital hyper-stimulation exacerbates mindless scrolling and compulsive consumption, creating a barrier to reflective awareness (Gulfraz et al., 2022). In this sense, digitalization can erode the attentional stability on which MC depends.

In the age of social media influencer culture frequently drives aspirational "haul" trends and normalizes frequent purchasing as identity performance, especially in fast fashion (Marwick, 2015; McNeill & Venter, 2019). At the same time, social media hosts counter-publics, minimalism forums, zero-waste, and slow-fashion groups that cultivate restraint and sufficiency (Lu, 2024). Digital spaces can empower consumers to exchange knowledge, provide mutual support, and resist mainstream consumerist narratives (Chatzidakis & Mitussis, 2007). Thus, the same infrastructure both propagates overconsumption and enables mindful practices. To enable digital technologies to support mindful behavior, researchers identified digital nudge as the most significant way to do this, where choice architecture can be repurposed to promote mindfulness. Nijssen et al. (2023) conducted a digital nudge experiment by showcasing a default option to sustainable delivery, showing CO_2 emissions, or setting pick-up points as the default reduce footprint and prompt reflection. Sustainability-oriented apps and e-commerce cues can temper unnecessary purchases (Gossen et al., 2019). However, critics note many interventions are superficial, targeting single decisions rather than cultivating durable habits (Bhatt & Seetharaman, 2023).

3.2.4 Institutional and Policy Integration

Studies highlight the role of educational institutions and policy integration in embedding mindfulness in a country (Yokoo & Kinnaman, 2013; Littlejohn et al., 2003). For instance, Sweden, Denmark, and Finland are pursuing policies that support MC often through a mix of regulation, taxation, and innovation such as circular economy and 100% renewable energy by 2050 (Singer et al., 2017). However, limited attempt has been made in the literature to investigate these policies' impact on individual, organization, and country level in regards of mindful behavior (Tsai & Chou, 2004). Existing policy discourse largely emphasizes efficiency, regulation, and behavioral control, whereas MC requires a reflective, value-based, and self-regulatory approach to consumption and production (McDowall et al., 2017). Current global and regional initiatives demonstrate the institutional recognition of excessive and irrational consumption as a pressing challenge. Although, the United Nations (UN) (2015) established the SDGs, with Goal 12—Responsible Consumption and Production, explicitly targeting behavioral and systemic change in consumption patterns. The United Nations Environment Program (UNEP), through its Sustainable Consumption

Network and the SWITCH to Green Flagship Initiative, aims to mainstream sustainability within national policy and consumer protection systems.

While these global efforts promote responsible consumption, the literature suggests they primarily rely on regulatory and informational approaches, such as eco-labels, awareness campaigns, and efficiency standards. Palacios-González and Chamorro-Mera (2022) argue that these mechanisms often fail to produce deep behavioral transformation, as they neglect the internal psychological dimensions of consumption—such as consciousness, empathy, and restraint. Likewise, Teufer and Grabner-Kräuter (2023) emphasize that overconsumption persists because consumer choices are typically driven by automatic, habitual, and emotionally unexamined behavior, not by deliberate mindfulness.

This gap reveals a significant policy-level blind spot: although governments and institutions increasingly acknowledge unsustainable consumption as a systemic problem, they rarely address the underlying mindset and awareness structures that sustain it. Consequently, there is little evidence of formal policy initiatives that cultivate mindfulness or contemplative awareness as part of consumer education, community development, or sustainability governance (De et al., 2025). Education and public policy are therefore underutilized channels for embedding mindfulness within social systems (Bahl, 2024).

3.3 Proposed Conceptual Framework of MC for Regenerative Living

The synthesis of 80 studies revealed that MC is evolving from a micro-level psychological construct to a multilevel system capability with transformative potential for regenerative living. This discussion interprets the findings through the theoretical lenses of mindfulness theory and regenerative development (Rapgay & Bystrisky, 2009), showing how individual awareness, technological mediation, and institutional design interact to create regenerative outcomes. The section concludes with a conceptual framework (see Fig. 2.2) illustrating these interconnections.

Mindfulness theory (Kabat-Zinn, 2023; Brown & Ryan, 2003) defines awareness as a deliberate and non-judgmental focus on the present moment, while regenerative theory (Mang & Reed, 2020) envisions development that restores and renews ecological and social systems. When synthesized, these perspectives reveal that MC serves as the psychological and cultural seed of regenerative behavior. Awareness nurtures restraint: restraint promotes sufficiency; and sufficiency underpins ecological Regeneration. However, this link is not linear. Previous studies indicate that mindfulness transforms consumption systems only when embedded within supportive organizational and technological infrastructures and reinforced through cultural and institutional norms (Tobias Mortlock, 2023). Thus, MC operates as a multilevel feedback system, where internal awareness translates into external restoration through socio-technical mediation. Therefore, this chapter proposes a framework that guides this interconnectedness and argues that mindfulness is a collective measure rather than individual output.

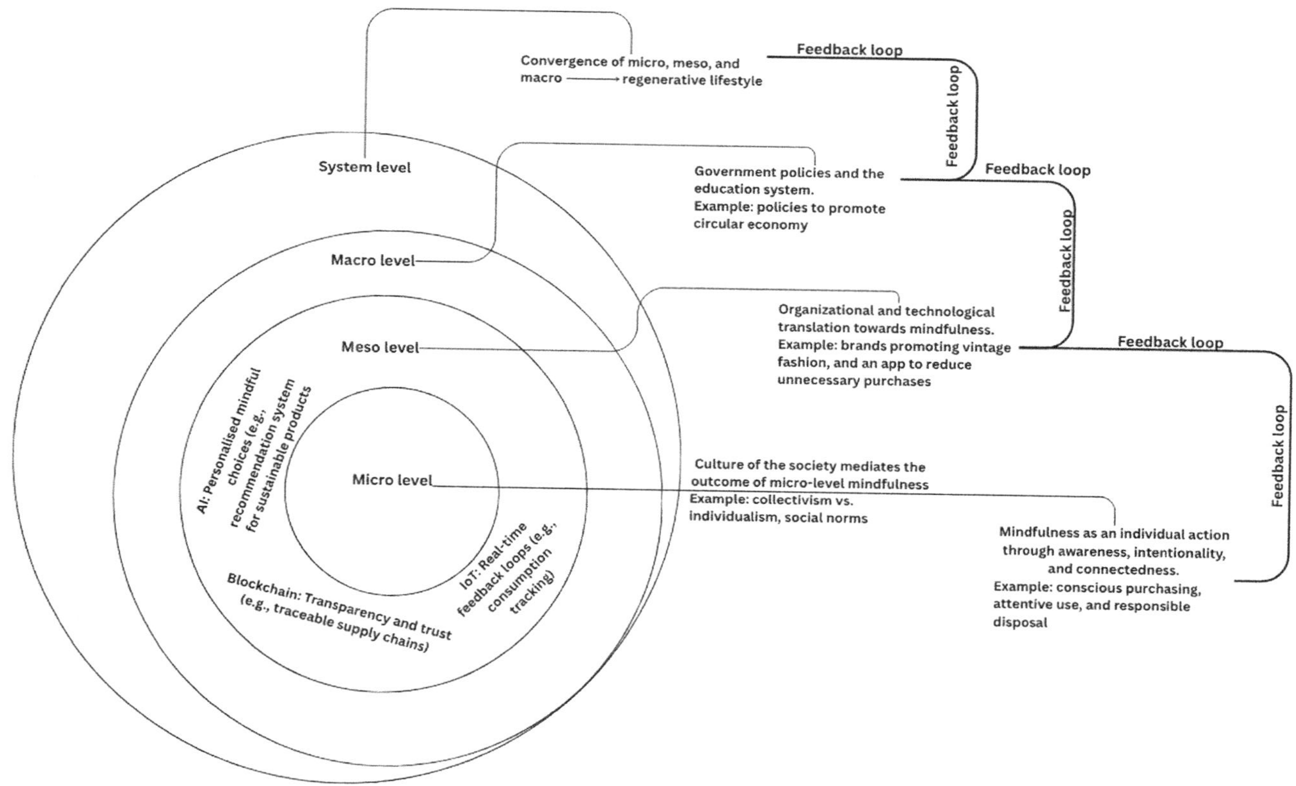

Fig. 2.2. MC as a Systemic Enabler of Regenerative Living. *Source:* Author's creation.

3.3.1 Micro Foundations: Psychological Awareness as a Behavioral Catalyst

At the micro level, mindfulness acts as a cognitive-emotional capability enabling consumers to disrupt automaticity and engage in reflective decision-making. The "reflective sufficiency" identified in this review captures the intersection of self-awareness, ethical intentionality, and ecological empathy (Gupta et al., 2023). When individuals cultivate these capacities, they exhibit reduced materialism and greater emotional fulfillment through experiences rather than possessions which scholars describe as post-materialist satisfaction (Jansen et al., 2024; Rosenberg, 2004). Yet mindfulness alone cannot ensure systemic impact. Without structural support, mindful individuals face choice architecture barriers, such as lack of transparent product information or convenience bias. Hence, the micro-level influence of mindfulness must be extended into meso- and macro-level systems. The proposed framework illustrates how mindfulness begins at the micro level (individual awareness, intentionality, and connectedness) and is translated at the meso level through organizational practices and Industry 6.0 technologies (AI, blockchain, IoT) that enable transparent, participatory, and feedback-driven decision-making.

3.3.2 Meso Foundations: Organizational and Technological Translation

At the meso level, firms and technologies act as translators of mindfulness into practice. Organizational mindfulness manifests through strategic alignment—when companies design and communicate offerings that encourage reuse, repair, and conscious engagement rather than overconsumption (Chen et al., 2022). This is not merely corporate social responsibility, but a mindful business capability grounded in attention, empathy, and integrity (Tung et al., 2025).

For instance, Intrepid Travel, an Australian tour operator, has positioned itself as a leader in mindful and responsible tourism. By banning elephant rides, offsetting emissions, and designing itineraries that prioritize community-based tourism, Intrepid appeals to travelers who want experiences aligned with awareness and care (WTTC, 2021). Smaller startups such as Byway Travel in the UK promote "flight-free holidays," encouraging consumers to rethink convenience in favor of slower, more mindful journeys.

When it comes to technological systems, particularly within the industry 6.0 paradigm, they amplify these effects by making the invisible visible. Blockchain provides transparency and trust; research in food supply chains demonstrates that blockchain-verified traceability builds trust and purchase intent for organic and fair-trade goods (Duong et al., 2025). Companies such as Provenance and Everledger are already using distributed ledgers to track cotton or diamonds. At the same time, the European Union's (EU's) upcoming Digital Product Passports will embed repairability, recyclability, and material data directly into consumer interfaces. Whereas AI personalizes responsible options; IoT sensors generate immediate feedback on energy or waste footprints. Together, they cultivate technologically mediated mindfulness, allowing both firms and consumers to perceive impacts in real time (Nawaz et al., 2021).

However, these technologies, particularly AI recommenders on platforms like Amazon, are largely optimized for engagement and sales, nudging users toward one-click purchases and scarcity-driven deals. Scholars warn that this erodes reflection and amplifies impulsivity (Gao & Liang, 2025). Highlights that such technology integration must be ethically governed. Without mindful design, technology can reproduce rebound effects or reinforce inequality (De et al., 2025). Thus, mindfulness should inform not only how technology is used but how it is built—embedding ethical attention within digital architecture itself. For example, the same architecture could be repurposed: chatbots trained on sustainability data could ask whether a customer prefers a refurbished phone over a new one or suggest repair manuals before recommending a replacement. IKEA has begun experimenting with such digital pathways, and Patagonia's Worn Wear program provides a template for how recommender systems could highlight second-hand before new. The future task for researchers and practitioners is to embed sufficiency, repair, and durability into AI's optimization objectives. Without this re-training, AI will remain a powerful accelerator of mindlessness.

3.3.3 Macro Foundations: Institutionalizing Mindfulness for Regeneration

At the macro level, policy and education become essential in transforming mindfulness from a personal choice to a collective norm. For instance, Bhutan's Gross National Happiness (GNH) index—Bhutan measuring national progress through dimensions like environmental preservation, cultural integrity, psychological well-being, and good governance, each grounded in Buddhist mindfulness philosophy (Alkire et al., 2012). Whereas, the UNEP and the United Nations Educational, Scientific, and Cultural Organization (UNESCO) have long been launched Institutional mindfulness entails designing systems that make mindful practices default rather than exceptional through school curricula, mindful procurement standards, urban regeneration projects, and behavioral nudges rooted in reflection rather than manipulation. The review found limited but promising efforts where mindfulness-based sustainability education fosters empathy, ecological literacy, and collaborative learning (Hensley, 2020). Hence, the macro dimension closes the loop: institutional design reinforces mindful practices, which in turn sustain regenerative systems, creating feedback cycles of awareness, innovation, and renewal.

3.3.4 System Foundations: Incorporating All the Mindfulness Foundations Together for Regeneration

The review confirms that isolated mindfulness interventions, whether micro or meso have limited impact unless nested within supportive organizational, technological, and policy systems. Conversely, when these levels interact, they generate synergistic feedback loops: mindful consumers demand ethical products; mindful firms leverage technology to deliver transparency; mindful institutions reinforce such behaviors through education and policy. This multilevel interdependence forms the empirical basis of the conceptual framework proposed to position MC as a systemic enabler of regenerative living.

4. Conclusion and Implications

The objective of this chapter was to examine how MC might develop at the organizational and institute levels to shape an individual's behavioral decision to regenerative living. It combined psychological, cultural, organizational, technological, and institutional viewpoints through a methodical narrative review analysis of diverse literature to offer a comprehensive framework that places mindfulness at the center of regenerative change. Although mindfulness has historically been studied as a personal trait based on awareness, self-control, and compassion, the synthesis showed that its potential goes well beyond the confines of personal consciousness. When mindfulness is incorporated into institutional governance, technological innovation, and organizational design, it becomes a communal ability that can change how societies interact with nature, produce, and consume.

According to literature, MC is consuming with awareness and purpose rather than just cutting back on consumption (Parvatiyar & Sheth, 2023). It invites both individuals and systems to engage in reflective sufficiency—acting not from deprivation but from discernment, where fulfillment emerges from alignment with ideals rather than acquisition of possessions. This transformation occurs at the level of psychological awareness but requires supportive infrastructures to transfer intention into persistent practice (Bahl, 2024). Companies can develop products that promote repair, reuse, and transparency by incorporating mindfulness into their design philosophy and Culture.

There are several theoretical and practical contributions in this chapter. First, by redefining mindfulness as a multilevel socio-technical phenomenon rather than a singular psychological characteristic, the chapter advances the field of mindfulness research. It illustrates how the logic of reciprocity and dependency underlies both mindfulness and Regeneration, to reestablish equilibrium by reestablishing the connection between human systems and the living systems on which they rely (Or, 2025). Second, the approach presented here conceptualizes MC as the glue that binds micro-level thought to macro-level change by bridging the gap between mindfulness theory and regenerative development. As a result, it fills a significant vacuum in the field of sustainability studies: models that explain how inner awareness can result in exterior Regeneration.

Third, the chapter provides helpful advice for a range of market and governance system participants. Businesses may go beyond compliance to make a meaningful impact by using mindfulness as a strategic route to authenticity in sustainability communication and product design. Fourth, in order to guarantee that data transparency, inclusivity, and ethics are incorporated into algorithmic systems from the beginning, technological designers are urged to apply conscious principles to digital infrastructures. Fifth, the chapter emphasizes the necessity of integrating mindfulness into leadership development programs, well-being policies, and curricula for educators and legislators in order to make reflective awareness a standard rather than a choice. All of these changes point to a change from treating sustainability as a collection of limitations to fostering Regeneration as an active, flexible process.

5. Limitations and Future Research Directions

Since this chapter provides an integrated paradigm that links MC and regenerative living, it is important to recognize a few limitations. Fortunately, the chapter identified four determinants/enablers (i.e., psychological, cultural, digital technology, and institutional foundations) and offers an insight into how all these works together to achieve regenerative lifestyle and SDGs conceptually. Therefore, empirical research is required to quantify the conceptual framework and establish clear-cut relations in measurable restorative consequences, such as decreases in the attitude-behavior gap toward sustainable or circular practices. Future researchers extend the insights discussed in the chapter through experimental, digital-ethnographic, and longitudinal approaches. These techniques may show how technological mediation and policy changes influence mindful decision-making; longitudinal and cross-cultural research may shed light on how mindfulness appears in various economic and social circumstances (Kumar & Dholakia, 2022). Future research should also critically examine accessibility and equity concerns to make sure that mindfulness is a genuinely inclusive and systemic practice rather than just another privileged discourse.

Another exciting but limited research theme is the developing relationship between technology and mindfulness. Although the potential of AI, blockchain, and IoT to mediate mindfulness was noted in this chapter, there is currently very few empirical data on how these technologies affect ethical reasoning, behavioral rebound, or human attention (Seo & Yoon, 2025). Future researchers could examine how digital infrastructures might promote or undermine attentive engagement in consumption systems using experimental, ethnographic, or design-based methods.

In ultimately, MC signifies a paradigm change from practicing sustainability to being regenerative, and it is more than just a substitute for excessive consumption (Kumar et al., 2024). It serves as a reminder to individuals as well as organizations that awareness is not merely inner reflection but rather active engagement in the collaborative development of sustainable futures. Mindfulness provides the vocabulary and reasoning that allows Regeneration to transition from aspiration to lived reality by coordinating attention, intention, and action at the psychological, organizational, and social levels. In this way, developing MC is not only a moral decision; rather, it is a strategic and moral need for creating a world that grows well within its planetary limitations instead of growing at its expense. These limitations result from the literature review methods as well as the dynamic character of mindfulness and regeneration research in general. Understanding these limitations is crucial for incorporating circular behavior as well as for determining productive avenues for further research.

At the end, considering all the factors this chapter is a reflection of the natural dynamism of an emerging interdisciplinary field. These exact boundaries actually provide opportunities for further inquiry, allowing academics to technologically advance, culturally diversify, and scientifically support their grasp of MC. By doing this, the discipline will get closer to understanding mindfulness as a societal competency necessary for attaining regenerative futures, rather than just as a personal trait.

References

Alkire, S., Ura, K., Zangmo, T., & Wangdi, K. (2012). *A short guide to gross national happiness index*. Centre for Bhutan Studies.

Armstrong, C. M. J. (2021). Fashion and the Buddha: What Buddhist economics and mindfulness have to offer sustainable consumption. *Clothing and Textiles Research Journal*, *39*(2), 91–105.

Awad, E., Hallit, S., & Obeid, S. (2022). Does self-esteem mediate the association between perfectionism and mindfulness among Lebanese university students?. *BMC Psychology*, *10*(1), 256.

Bahl, S. (2024). *Return to mindfulness: Disrupting default habits for personal fulfillment, effective leadership, and global impact*. Greenleaf Book Group.

Bahl, S., Milne, G. R., Ross, S. M., & Chan, K. (2013). Mindfulness: A long-term solution for mindless eating by college students. *Journal of Public Policy & Marketing*, *32*(2), 173–184.

Bahl, S., Milne, G. R., Ross, S. M., Mick, D. G., Grier, S. A., Chugani, S. K., & Boesen-Mariani, S. (2016). Mindfulness: Its transformative potential for consumer, societal, and environmental wellbeing. *Journal of Public Policy and Marketing*, *35*(2), 198–210.

Bhatt, E., & Seetharaman, P. (2023). Rethinking digital nudging: A taxonomical approach to defining and identifying characteristics of digital nudging interventions. *AIS Transactions on Human-Computer Interaction*, *15*(4), 442–471.

Birnie, K., Speca, M., & Carlson, L. E. (2010). Exploring self-compassion and empathy in the context of mindfulness-based stress reduction (MBSR). *Stress and Health*, *26*(5), 359–371.

Brown, K. W., & Kasser, T. (2005). Are psychological and ecological wellbeing compatible? The role of values, mindfulness, and lifestyle. *Social Indicators Research*, *74*(2), 349–368.

Brown, K. W., & Ryan, R. M. (2003). The benefits of being present: Mindfulness and its role in psychological wellbeing. *Journal of Personality and Social Psychology*, *84*(4), 822.

Caruana, R., Carrington, M. J., & Chatzidakis, A. (2016). "Beyond the attitude-behaviour gap: Novel perspectives in consumer ethics": Introduction to the thematic symposium. *Journal of Business Ethics*, *136*(2), 215–218.

Chatzidakis, A., & Mitussis, D. (2007). Computer ethics and consumer ethics: The impact of the internet on consumers' ethical decision-making process. *Journal of Consumer Behaviour: International Research and Review*, *6*(5), 305–320.

Chen, L., Jia, F., Steward, M. D., & Schoenherr, T. (2022). The role of technology in enabling circular supply chain management. *Industrial Marketing Management*, *106*, A1–A6.

De, T., Singh, N., Ibrahim, B. S. K. K., Dikkatwar, R., & Chaudhary, M. K. (2025). Mindful, responsible, and sustainable consumption: A hybrid review of evolving research trends. *Discover Sustainability*, *6*(1), 512.

Dhandra, T. K. (2019). Achieving triple dividend through mindfulness: More sustainable consumption, less unsustainable consumption and more life satisfaction. *Ecological Economics*, *161*, 83–90.

Duong, C. D., Nguyen, T. H., Ngo, T. V. N., Bui, T. V., & Tran, N. M. (2025). Perceived blockchain-related information transparency and organic food purchase intention: An extension of the theory of planned behaviour with the moderation role of blockchain-based trust. *British Food Journal*, *127*(3), 1131–1152.

Ferrari, R. (2015). Writing narrative style literature reviews. *Medical Writing*, *24*(4), 230–235.

Fischer, D., Stanszus, L., Geiger, S., Grossman, P., & Schrader, U. (2017). Mindfulness and sustainable consumption: A systematic literature review of research approaches and findings. *Journal of Cleaner Production*, *162*, 544–558.

Gao, Y., & Liang, J. (2025). The impact of AI-powered try-on technology on online consumers' impulsive buying intention: The moderating role of brand trust. *Sustainability*, *17*(7), 2789.

Garg, R., Bansal, S., Rathi, R., & Bhowmick, S. (2024). Mindful consumption–A systematic review and research agenda. *Journal of Cleaner Production*, *459*, 142373.

Gossen, M., Ziesemer, F., & Schrader, U. (2019). Why and how commercial marketing should promote sufficient consumption: A systematic literature review. *Journal of Macromarketing*, *39*(3), 252–269.

Gulfraz, M. B., Sufyan, M., Mustak, M., Salminen, J., & Srivastava, D. K. (2022). Understanding the impact of online customers' shopping experience on online impulsive buying: A study on two leading E-commerce platforms. *Journal of Retailing and Consumer Services*, *68*, 103000.

Gupta, S., Lim, W. M., Verma, H. V., & Polonsky, M. (2023). How can we encourage mindful consumption? Insights from mindfulness and religious faith. *Journal of Consumer Marketing*, *40*(3), 344–358.

Halpern, M., Marcil, E., Peplinski, H., & Piscioniere, J. (2023). *Leverages for advancing carbon accounting in the United States sood system: An analysis of the political and economic leverages through which carbon accounting can serve as an effective tool for reducing net greenhouse gas emissions of the United States' food system*. University of Michigan.

Hartfield, O. D. (2025). *The subtle push: Influencing everyday decisions*. (eBookIt.com).

Hensley, N. (2020). Educating for sustainable development: Cultivating creativity through mindfulness. *Journal of Cleaner Production*, *243*, 118542.

Howells, A., Ivtzan, I., & Eiroa-Orosa, F. J. (2016). Putting the 'app'in happiness: A randomized controlled trial of a smartphone-based mindfulness intervention to enhance wellbeing. *Journal of Happiness Studies*, *17*(1), 163–185.

Hussain, M., Egan, H., Keyte, R., Strachan, R., Tahrani, A. A., & Mantzios, M. (2023). Exploring the association between self-compassion, mindfulness and mindful eating with eating behaviours amongst patients with obesity. *Nutrition and Health*, *29*(4), 683–693.

Jansen, P., Rahe, M., & Wolff, F. (2024). How does mindfulness relate to sustainable attitude and behavior? The role of possible mediators. *Current Psychology*, *43*(22), 19708–19720.

Jordan, C. H., Wang, W., Donatoni, L., & Meier, B. P. (2014). Mindful eating: Trait and state mindfulness predict healthier eating behavior. *Personality and Individual Differences*, *68*, 107–111.

Kabat-Zinn, J. (2023). *Wherever you go, there you are: Mindfulness meditation in everyday life*. Hachette UK.

Kasser, T. (2003). *The high price of materialism*. MIT Press.

Kumar, B., & Dholakia, N. (2022). Firms enabling responsible consumption: A netnographic approach. *Marketing Intelligence & Planning*, *40*(3), 289–309.

Kumar, R., Prabha, V., Kumar, V., & Saxena, S. (2024). Mindfulness in marketing & consumption: A review & research agenda. *Management Review Quarterly*, *74*(2), 977–1001.

Kumar, S., & Panda, T. K. (2025). Mindful consumption: Cultivating sustainable consumption behavior for food and clothing through mindfulness among generation Z. *Journal of Consumer Marketing*, *42*(1), 106–130.

Kunwer, S. P., & Singh, S. (2025). Churning the mindful consumption research for achieving sustainable development goals: A review analysis. *Sustainable Development*, *33*(4), 4810–4834.

Lehtinen, L., & Madeira, S. (2024). *Exploring the feasibility of implementing the Algramo business model concept in Finland from the customer's perspective*. Theseus.fi

Lim, W. M. (2025). Systematic literature reviews: Reflections, recommendations, and robustness check. *Journal of Consumer Behaviour*, *24*(3), 1498–1510.

Littlejohn, A., Jung, I., & Broumley, L. (2003). A comparison of issues in the reuse of resources in schools and colleges. In *In Reusing online resources* (pp. 230–238). Routledge.

Lu, D. (2024). Performing zero waste: Lifestyle movement, consumer culture, and promotion strategies of social media influencers. *Environmental Sociology*, *10*(1), 12–29.

Manchanda, P., Arora, N., Nazir, O., & Islam, J. U. (2023). Cultivating sustainability consciousness through mindfulness: An application of theory of mindful-consumption. *Journal of Retailing and Consumer Services*, *75*, 103527.

Mang, P., & Reed, B. (2020). Regenerative development and design. In *Sustainable built environments* (pp. 115–141). Springer US.

Marwick, A. E. (2015). You may know me from youtube:(micro-) celebrity in social media. *A companion to celebrity*, 333–350.

McDowall, W., Geng, Y., Huang, B., Barteková, E., Bleischwitz, R., Türkeli, S., & Doménech, T. (2017). Circular economy policies in China and Europe. *Journal of Industrial Ecology*, *21*(3), 651–661.

McNeill, L., & Venter, B. (2019). Identity, self-concept and young women's engagement with collaborative, sustainable fashion consumption models. *International Journal of Consumer Studies*, *43*(4), 368–378.

Milne, G. R., Villarroel Ordenes, F., & Kaplan, B. (2020). Mindful consumption: Three consumer segment views. *Australasian marketing journal*, *28*(1), 3–10.

Nawaz, S., Jiang, Y., Nawaz, M. Z., Manzoor, S. F., & Zhang, R. (2021). Mindful consumption, ego-involvement, and social norms impact on buying SHC: Role of platform trust and impulsive buying tendency. *Sage Open*, *11*(4), 21582440211056621.

Nijssen, S. R., Pijs, M., van Ewijk, A., & Müller, B. C. (2023). Towards more sustainable online consumption: The impact of default and informational nudging on consumers' choice of delivery mode. *Cleaner and Responsible Consumption*, *11*, 100135.

Oeij, P. R., Hulsegge, G., & Preenen, P. T. (2022). Organisational mindfulness as a sustainable driver of employee innovation adoption: Individual and organisational factors. *Safety Science*, *154*, 105841.

Or, Y. (2025). Regenerative practice in social work: Cultivating relational practices for a more-than-human future. In *Pushing boundaries in social work around the world, Vol. 2: Policy and global perspectives* (pp. 73–86). Springer Nature Switzerland.

Palacios-González, M. M., & Chamorro-Mera, A. (2022). Analysis of the predictive variables of socially responsible consumption. *Business Strategy & Development*, *5*(3), 187–196.

Parvatiyar, A., & Sheth, J. N. (2023). Confronting the deep problem of consumption: Why individual responsibility for mindful consumption matters. *Journal of Consumer Affairs*, *57*(2), 785–820.

Paul, J., Lim, W. M., O'Cass, A., Hao, A. W., & Bresciani, S. (2021). Scientific procedures and rationales for systematic literature reviews (SPAR-4-SLR). *International Journal of Consumer Studies*, *45*(4), O1–O16.

Pham, V. K., & Le Phuong Giao, L. (2026). Sustainability under pressure: Green mindfulness as a response to tourism's current challenges. *Journal of Hospitality and Tourism Insights*, 1–23.

Pompili, S., & Carfora, V. (2025). The role of mindfulness and mindful eating in sustainable food choices: A scoping review. *Mindfulness*, 1–24.

Rapgay, L., & Bystrisky, A. (2009). Classical mindfulness: An introduction to its theory and practice for clinical application. *Annals of the New York Academy of Sciences*, *1172*(1), 148–162.

Rosenberg, E. L. (2004). *Mindfulness and consumerism.* In T. Kasser & A. D. Kanner (Eds.), *Psychology and consumer culture: The struggle for a good life in a materialistic world* (pp. 107–125). American Psychological Association. https://doi.org/10.1037/10658-007

Seo, J. K., & Yoon, H. J. (2025). Promoting mindful consumption through a chatbot with an experiential mind. *Journal of Consumer Marketing*, *42*(4), 498–511.

Shapiro, S. L., & Schwartz, G. E. (2000). The role of intention in self-regulation: Toward intentional systemic mindfulness. In *Handbook of self-regulation* (pp. 253–273). Academic Press.

Shaw, D., & Moraes, C. (2009). Voluntary simplicity: An exploration of market interactions. *International Journal of Consumer Studies*, *33*(2), 215–223.

Sheth, J. N., Sethia, N. K., & Srinivas, S. (2011). Mindful consumption: A customer-centric approach to sustainability. *Journal of the Academy of Marketing Science*, *39*(1), 21–39.

Shikalgar, A., Menon, P., & Mahajan, V. C. (2024). Towards customer-centric sustainability: How mindful advertising influences mindful consumption behaviour. *Journal of Indian Business Research*, *16*(1), 119–133.

Shove, E., Watson, M., & Pantzar, M. (2012). *The dynamics of social practice: Everyday life and how it changes*. SAGE Publications Ltd

Singer, S., Denruyter, J. P., & Yener, D. (2017). The energy report: 100% renewable energy by 2050. In *Towards 100% renewable energy: Techniques, costs and regional case-studies* (pp. 379–383). Springer International Publishing.

Teufer, B., & Grabner-Kräuter, S. (2023). How consumer networks contribute to sustainable mindful consumption and wellbeing. *Journal of Consumer Affairs*, *57*(2), 757–784.

Thøgersen, J., & Zhou, Y. (2012). Chinese consumers' adoption of a 'green'-innovation–The case of organic food. *Journal of Marketing Management*, *28*(3–4), 313–333.

Tobias Mortlock, J. (2023). Next-generation mindfulness: A mindfulness matrix to extend the transformative potential of mindfulness for consumer, organizational, and societal wellbeing. *Journal of Consumer Affairs*, *57*(2), 721–756.

Tran, G. A., Aboulnasr, K., & Song, Y. S. (2025). The rise of the deinfluencers: Perceived similarity and anticipated emotions in advocating mindful consumption on social media. *Psychology and Marketing*, *42*(11), 3005–3026.

Tsai, W. T., & Chou, Y. H. (2004). Government policies for encouraging industrial waste reuse and pollution prevention in Taiwan. *Journal of Cleaner Production*, *12*(7), 725–736.

TUNA, M. F. (2025). The effect of mindful attention on consumers' implusive buying behavior and the moderating role of family type. *Journal of Marketing & Marketing Research/Pazarlama ve Pazarlama Araştırmaları Dergisi*, *18*(1).

Tung, T. M., Lan, D. H., & Oanh, V. T. K. (2025). The impact of mindfulness on consumer engagements and marketing strategies. In *Mindful marketing and strategic management: Paving A sustainable Society through past, present, and future perspectives* (pp. 1–15).

United Nations. (2015). *Sustainable development goals*. https://sdgs.un.org/goals

Wang, Y., Neilson, L. C., & Ji, S. (2023). Mindfulness through agency in health consumption: Empirical evidence from committed dietary supplement consumers. *Journal of Consumer Affairs*, *57*(2), 871–905.

Warde, A. (2005). Consumption and theories of practice. *Journal of Consumer Culture*, *5*(2), 131–153.

Wickramasekara, E. S., & Jayawickrama, W. D. C. (2022). Mindful consumption and universal love: A case study of Sri Lankan consumer activists. In *Socially responsible consumption and marketing in practice: Collection of case studies* (pp. 93–103). Springer Nature Singapore.

Williams, A. D., & Grisham, J. R. (2012). Impulsivity, emotion regulation, and mindful attentional focus in compulsive buying. *Cognitive Therapy and Research*, *36*(5), 451–457.

Wong, Y. Y., & Faikhamta, C. (2021). Reconnecting self, others and nature. *Cultural Studies of Science Education*, *16*(3), 867–880.

World Travel and Tourism Council. (2021). *Intrepid travel Australia case study*. https://researchhub.wttc.org/product/sustainability-leadership-case-studies-intrepid#:~:text=Report%20details-,details,The%20full%20report

Yokoo, H. F., & Kinnaman, T. C. (2013). Global reuse and optimal waste policy. *Environment and Development Economics*, *18*(5), 595–614.

Chapter 3

Sustainable Consumerism 6.0: Integrating Human Values, Technology, and Regenerative Mindsets

Y. Suryanarayana Murthy[a,*], *Rohit Bansal*[b,†], *Nishita Pruthi*[c] *and Podile Venkateswara Rao*[a,‡]

[a]KLEF Deemed to be University, India
[b]Rockford College, Sydney, Australia
[c]Asian School of Business, India

Abstract

The paradigm of Sustainable Consumerism 6.0 is the new way of reacting to the growing environmental pressure, the digitalization of the world, and the alteration of human values. The current chapter defines Sustainable Consumerism 6.0 as a socio-technical ecosystem comprising ethical intelligence, digital stewardship, regenerative mindsets, and conscious consumption. This paradigm, which leaves materialism and digital convenience or experiential sustainability models behind, is founded on the idea of consumers as active co-regenerators who engage in ethical production, open value chains, and closed economic systems. This chapter is based on the literature synthesis of the existing research on sustainability studies, behavioral economics, ecological psychology, and digital innovation (2020–2025) and explores how artificial intelligence (AI), blockchain, the Internet of Things (IoT), digital twins, and green fintech redefine the consumption practices. This conceptual framework proposes five interconnected dimensions (Ethical Intelligence, Digital Stewardship, Regenerative Design, Conscious Consumption, and Value Co-creation) that can be used to redefine the

*https://orcid.org/0000-0002-9561-5395
†https://orcid.org/0009-0001-6692-3022
‡https://orcid.org/0000-0001-5251-8424

Regenerative Revolution, 51–72

doi:10.1108/978-1-80686-859-920261003

relationship between people, technology, and the planet. The results underline that Sustainable Consumerism 6.0 not only promotes environmentally responsible behavior but also inculcates moral, emotional, and technological awareness into consumption decisions. This chapter offers strategic implications to corporations, policymakers, and educators, recommending the measures of adopting ethical AI, open digital infrastructure, and human-centered innovation systems. In general, the work contributes to the field of sustainability by introducing a model that is comprehensive, prospective, and combines human values, digital ecosystems and regenerative economic principles to create a more sustainable future.

Keywords: Sustainable Consumerism 6.0; regenerative mindset; human values; technological ethics; digital sustainability; circular economy; conscious consumption; value co-creation

JEL Codes: Q20; Q50; Q56; C89; M31; O33; D91

1. Introduction

Sustainable consumerism has become a paradigm shift and will change the human, technology, and planet relationship. The 21st century becomes a landmark in this development because the integration of digital technology, globalization of markets, and demands of climate changes reform the patterns of consumption in societies (Kumar & Ranjan, 2021; White et al., 2021). Materialistic modes of consumerism with its materialistic tendencies and linear modes of production have been gradually replaced by more ecologically mindful, responsible, and conscious ways to consume (Dangelico et al., 2022). The next stage in the evolution is Sustainable Consumerism 6.0—a combination of human empathy, technological ethics, and regenerative systems thinking that goes beyond the classic model of sustainability (Singh & Rahman, 2024).

The move to Consumerism 6.0 may be seen as the larger transformation of industrial capitalism to regenerative capitalism, in which profit will not be the sole motive of economic action, with planetary well-being and the common consciousness becoming equally important (Fullerton, 2022). Aware customers have ceased to be mere participants in markets and instead, they are active agents who influence ethical production systems by making informed decisions, digital activism, and value co-creation (Vermeir et al., 2022). This shift is also facilitated by technological enablers, such as AI, blockchain, Internet of Things (IoT), digital twins, and green fintech, which increase the level of transparency, accountability, and traceability throughout the whole value chain (Chakraborty & Singh, 2024; Pillai & Sivathanu, 2022; Rejeb et al., 2022).

The dire need of such change is supported by the glum international tendencies. The United Nations Environment Programme (2024) reminds us that the world still consumes more resources than Earth can process, with an estimated 92-billion tonnes of resources mined each year—it is anticipated that this is going to rise to 2,060 under present projections using current models. At the same time, digital technologies are strong to facilitate sustainability and, at the same time, are also creating data ecosystems that consume a lot of energy (Dutta & Roy, 2024). Therefore, the technological advances and ecological decline paradox demand a different paradigm in which innovation and regeneration instead of depletion coincide (Floridi, 2021; Lange & Santarius, 2021).

In this sense, Sustainable Consumerism 6.0 proposes a humanistic technological ecosystem, which inserts ethical intelligence into the consumption behavior. The 6.0 model combines digital consciousness and regenerative purpose, as compared to the earlier iterations, which include Consumerism 3.0 with a focus on corporate social responsibility (CSR), 4.0 with a focus on smart technologies, and 5.0 with a focus on experience-driven sustainability (Kotler et al., 2021). It states that technology with human values can help create an ecological balance through transparent supply chains and predictable waste reduction, as well as a circular design system (Gupta et al., 2023; Haque & Rahman, 2023).

The transformation to Sustainable Consumerism 6.0 is a social and psychological one as well. It represents the change of individualistic consumption to collective thought, the economic utility to the ecological utility, and ownership to the stewardship (Biswas & Roy, 2021; Lee & Chen, 2023). Given the digital tools and measures of sustainability, consumers are reinventing the brand relationships with metrics of authenticity and purpose, planetary impact (Kumar & Kapoor, 2021). In the meantime, brands are shifting to be no longer producers of commodities, but generators of shared value ecosystems, consumption itself is a regenerative practice (Raworth, 2021).

Here, we discuss the theoretical underpinnings, aspects and ramifications of Sustainable Consumerism 6.0 providing a systematic conceptual framework that brings together technological advancements, human morality, and regenerative design. Mapping the main features of this paradigm and comparing it to the previous models of consumerism, we offer a holistic perspective on the way humanity may create a new stage of responsible consumption and transform it into a restorative co-creation in the digital era (Floridi, 2021; Singh & Rahman, 2024).

2. Review of Relevant Literature

2.1 Evolution of Consumerism: From 1.0 to 6.0

The curve of consumerism has been radically changed during the past century as a result of the consecutive industrial, social, and digital revolutions. The industrialism 1.0 was basically a product and mass-based product-reading factor, which prioritized mass-production, low-price, and standardization in the initial industrial economy (Kotler, 2020). The concept of consumerism 2.0 turned out to be developed in the after-war world, which experienced the increased impact of advertising, emotional branding, and forming the consumer identity based on the material goods (Bauman, 2021). The third stage, Consumerism 3.0, shifted to social responsibility and ethical consumption, pre-empting the so-called triple bottom line of people, planet, and profit (Elkington, 2020). The digital transformation turned into the foundation of market evolution with the implementation of Consumerism 4.0, which is marked by intelligent technologies, omnichannel, and data-driven individualization (Lusch & Vargo, 2021). It was the stage, at which technology became involved in daily consumption, digital convenience, and connectivity started to influence human behavior (Kumar & Ranjan, 2021). The next stage in consumerism 5.0 was introduced in response to the challenges of digitization, promises, and traps related to digitization, with a concentration on experience, empathy, and co-creation (Kotler et al., 2021). Lastly, this trend is further extended in the new paradigm, Consumerism 6.0, which is a unified system of human values, technologic ethics, and regenerative ecosystems that turn consumers into co-creators of ecological and social well-being (Singh & Rahman, 2024).

2.2 Sustainable Consumerism and Conscious Behavior

The concept of sustainable consumerism is connected to consumption habits that cause minimal harm to the environment and encourage social justice, as well as ensuring that the individual needs of consumers are addressed in a responsible manner (White et al., 2021). As Joshi and Rahman (2020) note, the concept of sustainable consumption behavior implies not just environmental awareness but moral conviction and an emotional interest as well. Moreover, socio-psychological determinants of conscious consumerism are self-identity, social norms, and perceived consumer effectiveness (Kumar & Kapoor, 2021). Coming to the point, Vermeir et al. (2022) emphasize that the lack of action in the intention to be sustainable remains, frequently as a result of information asymmetry and convenience. Yet, digital technologies, including the use of blockchain to track supplies and artificial intelligence (AI) to offer transparency to products, are starting to fill this gap and allow making informed and real-time decisions related to sustainability (Dangelico et al., 2022). Prior studies consistently indicate that environmental concern, perceived behavioral control, and eco-literacy are important predictors of sustainable consumption behaviour across emerging economies. Furthermore, the psychological construct of eco-spirituality the opinion that consumption is related to the well-being of the planet has become an issue of attention as a primary antecedent of regenerative consumer behavior (Lee & Chen, 2023).

2.3 Human Values and Ethical Consciousness in Consumption

Human aspect is still at the core of the changing paradigm of sustainable consumerism. Schwartz theory of basic human values postulates that the orientations of benevolence, universalism, and self-transcendence have a strong impact on ethical consumption, which influences preferences in favor of eco-friendly goods, readiness to pay high prices, and support of the cyclical economy (Biswas & Roy, 2021). Ethical consumerism has passed beyond the usual boundaries of fair-trade and cruelty-free brands, into the space of digital transparency and algorithmic accountability. The dominance of AI-based marketing has also made the ethical situation more difficult, with the urgent issues of consumer privacy, the rights to their data, and manipulation becoming a concern (Murthy & Kumar, 2023). Countering this, researchers have developed a paradigm of technological humanism, where moral and compassionate elements are incorporated into the design of digital consumerism systems (Floridi, 2021; Taiminen & Saraniemi, 2023). At the same time, emotional and authentic well-being has also become major mediating factors between values and the results of sustainable consumption. Empirical studies suggest that value congruence and psychological ownership strengthen sustainable brand attachment and encourage long-term environmentally responsible behaviour.

2.4 Technological Enablers of Sustainable Consumerism

Technological innovation is a trigger and a channel to Sustainable Consumerism 6.0, making digital technologies a tool to make consumption dematerialized, i.e., either replace it with a digital experience, or complement it with one (Lange & Santarius, 2021). Supply-chain transparency is increased through the implementation of blockchain technology, which will neutralize greenwashing by providing indisputable sustainability information, and increase stakeholder accountability (Rejeb et al., 2022). In addition, smart sensors based on the IoT can be used to track the life cycle of the product on a regular basis thus creating a chance to develop circular models of use and repair (Gupta et al., 2023). Predictive analytics and AI can ensure optimization of energy consumption, waste reduction, and personalized sustainability, which is the proposal that is personalized depending on the ecological footprint of an individual (Pillai & Sivathanu, 2022). The regenerative design thinking is also supported by AI which is capable of simulating closed-loop systems convincingly in an attempt to reconcile resource utilization and regeneration (Murray et al., 2024). Also, the emerging sector of green fintech and digital carbon markets will allow consumers the ability to compensate their carbon footprint by making micro-transactions, playing games, and investing in sustainable markets (Chakraborty & Singh, 2024). The increased ecological awareness that digital storytelling creates and disseminates with the help of social media and influencer activism also increases the ecological awareness of the collective, especially among the consumers of Generation Z (Haque & Rahman, 2023).

2.5 Regenerative and Circular Mindsets

Whereas sustainability focuses on the reduction of the damage, the regeneration focuses on recovery and renewal of the ecosystems. The regenerative attitude of consumption goes beyond formed minimization of negative effects to a form of true establishment of improved results (Raworth, 2021). This paradigm shift is built on the ecological economics and systems theory, aiming to promote cyclical and not linear flows of value. Fullerton (2022) views regenerative capitalism as defining business as a living system, which co-evolves with nature via feedback, reciprocity, and resilience. There is an empirical assertion that regenerative consumer practices (up event-to-date, local repair, community repair, local sourcing, etc.) help in social cohesion and resilience to the environment (Jayaraman et al., 2023). Here, Sustainable Consumerism 6.0 reinvents the idea of the consumer as a value regenerator, an agent of ecological restoration through digital participatory and behavioral mindfulness (Singh 6.0 + Rahman, 2024). The regenerative philosophy fits the United Nations Sustainable Development Goals (SDGs) and SDG 12 (Responsible Consumption and Production) and SDG 13 (Climate Action) in particular (United Nations, 2023). It also contributes to the circular economy philosophy when materials, data, and knowledge are actively circulated across ecosystems and produce minimal amounts of entropy and the maximum resilience (Ellen MacArthur Foundation, 2022).

3. Conceptual Framework

Sustainable Consumerism 6.0 relies on systems thinking, ecological economics, and technological humanism as its conceptual framework to explain the interaction between human values, digital technologies, and regenerative principles to produce sustainable consumption results. This framework, which places the conscious consumer in the center of the circle of a technology-supported ecosystem, adds to the multidisciplinary literature review synthesized above (Floridi, 2021; Singh & Rahman, 2024; White et al., 2021), thus placing the consumer consciously at its center. The model outlines five inter-relational dimensions: collectively, the dimensions illustrate the role of Sustainable Consumerism 6.0 as a living socio technological system as opposed to a transactional model.

3.1 Ethical Intelligence

Ethical Intelligence refers to the ability of consumers and organizations to balance technological innovations with moral thinking, empathies, and ethics of the planet. Floridi (2021) argues that digital ethics should transform compliance based on the rule to value-based consciousness, which will ensure that AI, data analytics, and automation can be used to both human and ecological benefit. Ethical Intelligence in the consumer environment involves using data responsibly, making decisions based on algorithms, and showing knowledge (Murthy & Kumar, 2023). Ethically intelligent consumers seek meaning, but not material acquisition; they assess products in the context of authenticity, fairness and long-term effects (Biswas & Roy, 2021). In this way, the given dimension connects the moral mindfulness and the technological government to each other, creating the ethical core of the 6.0 paradigm in the process.

3.2 Digital Stewardship

Digital stewardship is the responsible and rehabilitative usage of digital technologies with the goal of promoting sustainability goals. It preempts the values of transparency, traceability, and digital accountability (Rejeb et al., 2022; Pillai & Sivathanu, 2022). Having incorporated blockchain, the IoT, and AI-based analytics, organizations will be enabled to track the supply-chain emissions, resource usage, and ethical sourcing, on-the-fly (Gupta et al., 2023). Stewardship can be applied at the consumer level as circumspect digital use, such as reducing the amount of electronic waste, choosing low-carbon data services, and supporting platforms that offset their technological footprint (Lange & Santarius, 2021). The environmental impacts of digitalization according to Dutta and Roy (2024), requires assertive neglecting to ensure that people pursue renewable-energy nexuses and efficient cloud systems. Therefore, digital stewardship connects technological aptitude and ecological accountability that digital advancement can be an empowerment of planetary healing instead of degradation.

3.3 Regenerative Design

As it is presented by Raworth (2021) and Fullerton (2022), regenerative design represents the structural and systemic potential of markets in terms of restoring not only natural capital but also social equity through cyclical production and consumption models. Similarly, in the design of regenerative products, biodegradable resources, modularity, and upgradeability are considered options to extend the lifespan of the product and reduce the amount of waste, respectively (Jayaraman et al., 2023). As a result, the given dimension lays the groundwork of Sustainable Consumerism 6.0 in the paradigm of regenerative capitalism, where the enterprises can be treated as a living system, which is compatible with the natural laws and social reciprocity.

3.4 Conscious Consumption

Conscious Consumption summarizes the psychological and behavioral change among consumers who transform into active consumers instead of passive buyers of the planet (Lee & Chen, 2023; White et al., 2021). It also combines self-transcendent values such as benevolence, universalism, and other related precepts (Schwartz, 2020) and evidence-based decision-making supported by digital tools. Modern customers evaluate the total ethical price of what they buy, and some criteria include carbon intensity, labor equity, and recyclability

(Vermeir et al., 2022). They use digital applications, which include giving eco-labels, carbon footprints, and product traceability, to ensure authenticity (NielsenIQ, 2023). This awareness breeds the loop of feedback where conscious consumption drives ethical production thus increasing regenerative design and co-creation of value. Therefore, Conscious Consumption serves as the conduct part of the 6.0 model.

3.5 Value Co-Creation

Value Co-creation is currently perceived as a joint nexus of consumers, producers, policymakers, and digital platforms with the goal of creating shared ecological and social value (Lusch & Vargo, 2021; Singh & Rahman, 2024). Under the Sustainable Consumerism 6.0, the consumers become the co-regenerators and not passive end-users, they provide data, feedback, and creative input to boost the sustainability outputs. Such participatory ecosystems re-envision consumption as a shared regenerative process, therefore, promoting the ideas of the Triple Bottom Line (Elkington, 2020) in the digital environment. The systemic realization of Ethical Intelligence, Digital Stewardship, Regenerative Design, and Conscious Consumption, in combination, then becomes what is known as Value Co-creation.

3.6 Conceptual Figure Description

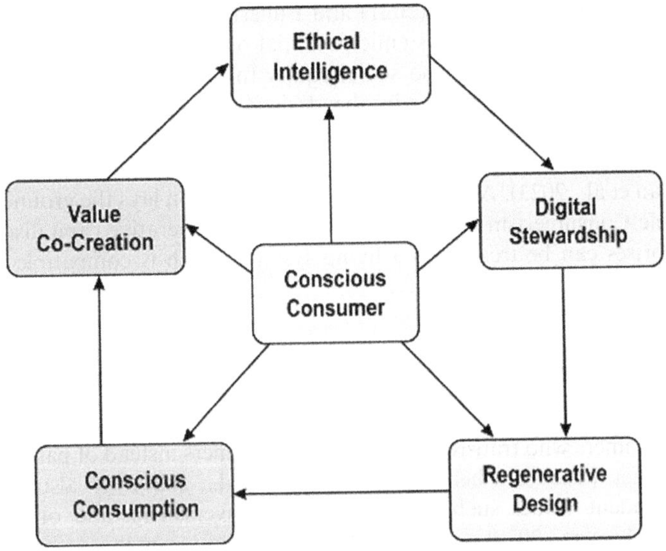

Fig. 3.1. Conceptual Model of Sustainable Consumerism.
Source: Author's Illustration.

4. Analysis and Findings

The critical interpretation of Sustainable Consumerism 6.0 explains the interplay of digital change, human morality, and regenerative mechanisms to create a new socioeconomic order of mindful consumption. This paradigm may be viewed as a departure from linear models that separate economic, environmental, and psychological variables, and it incorporates the systemic interactions on a micro (individual), meso (organizational), and macro (planetary) scale (Singh et al., 2024; White et al., 2021). The results are structured into five analytical dimensions that were based on the conceptual model shown in Fig. 3.1.

4.1 Ethical Intelligence and Moral Technology Interface

The main conclusion is that Ethical Intelligence is the ethical judge of the online economy. Ethical reasoning is becoming a key factor in sustainability performance that is viewed by consumers and firms as core to sustainability performance (Floridi, 2021). Frameworks of digital ethics, which require a degree of fairness, transparency, and inclusiveness, directly affect the purchase intentions and confidence in sustainable brands (Murthy & Kumar, 2023).Ethical Intelligence, in this regard, transforms technology into a morally responsible tool that makes the machine as capable of thinking and feeling as a human being (Taiminen & Saraniemi, 2023). The results also show that the inclusion of ethical reasoning in AI algorithms and supply-chain data can help consumers develop greater trust, which will improve brand authenticity and loyalty over time (Biswas & Roy, 2021).

4.2 Digital Stewardship and Responsible Innovation

The latter key discovery is important to emphasize that digital stewardship defines the extent to which technology can help in ecological regeneration and not depletion. The shift to carbon-neutral and transparent digital ecosystems proves that being a technological innovator does not mean being environmental inattentive (Pillai & Sivathanu, 2022). Companies that use blockchain-based traceability record a 3,540% increase in accountability of resources and a decrease in the cases of greenwashing (Rejeb et al., 2022). Besides, lifecycle monitoring and cloud-based analytics made possible by IoT have enhanced the efficiency of post-consumer recycling by more than 25% under pilot conditions (Gupta et al., 2023). Nevertheless, these advantages will be conditional on sensible digital infrastructure design. Dutta and Roy (2024) warn that data centers are a significant source of global carbon emissions of approximately 2.5% in case they are not supplied with renewable energy. Thus, digital stewardship should encompass ethical data management, the minimization of e-waste, and integration of renewable-energy to make sure that innovation is not going against the regenerative purpose.

4.3 Regenerative Design and Circular Economies

Having examined the literature available, it is clear that the Regenerative Design is the operational nucleus of the Sustainable Consumerism 6.0. The paradigm is reconstructed within the self-repairing cycle where environmental elements like materials, energy, social value circulate without serious shortages or deficits (Raworth, 2021; Fullerton, 2022). Businesses which apply the notion of regeneration have blamed positive ecological and financial advantages, with the fabrics of modular manufacture, the item-as-a-service idea, and the bio-based packaging (Jayaraman et al., 2023). Empirical data also shows that the regenerative business model could potentially decrease the volume of waste by as much as 45%, and at the same time increase consumer satisfaction ratings that can be attributed to a perceived obligation to environmental stewardship (Murray et al., 2024). The predictive design tools and digital twins driven by AI act as necessary drivers in this change process and allow organizations to simulate material-flow scenarios and reduce entropy. Regenerative design has therefore helped in closing the gap between the economic sustainability and the ecological sustainability, and has finally helped to redefine consumption as a restoration process.

4.4 Conscious Consumption and Behavioral Transformation

Today we focus on the fourth analytical finding the one of Conscious Consumption that is a way of bridging the gap between the sustainability awareness and actual behavioral change. Though the issue of the still existing attitude-behavior gap (Vermeir et al., 2022) can be viewed as a daunting problem, digital platforms, and social influencing mechanisms have started to reduce this gap and provided more transparency and customization. NielsenIQ (2023) states that today about 73% of consumers worldwide refer to sustainability labels or QR codes to ensure that ethical sourcing is conducted prior to purchase. Additionally, empirical studies indicate that consumers that approach consumption through eco-spirituality, a moral association to nature, express more consistent long-term practices (Lee & Chen, 2023). This cognitive shift in the way of consuming to promote status to consuming to keep alive represents one of the shifts in the self-transcendent values of Schwartz (2020). Such change strengthens ecological consciousness, transforming consumption into a socio-ethical performance in place of an act in the market (White et al., 2021).

4.5 Value Co-Creation and Collaborative Regeneration

The last conclusion is on value co-creation as the integrative mechanism that bridges ethical, digital, and regenerative systems. The creation of value in this aspect is not unilinear, but a co-creation involving the stakeholders, open data, and collaborative innovation by the firms (Lusch & Vargo, 2021). Community circular hubs and carbon-offset marketplace are digital collaboration platforms in which consumers can directly affect the production process (Haque & Rahman, 2023).

Empirical evidence based on the sustainability reports of organizations all over the world shows that organizations involving consumers in co-creation activities score 20–30% higher customer retention and brand advocacy (Kumar & Kapoor, 2021). The process therefore redefines sustainability as a mutual participatory process of mutual benefit between the business, society, and nature (Elkington, 2020; Singh & Rahman, 2024).

5. Ethical and Legal Implications

Sustainable Consumerism 6.0 is a synthesis of advanced digital infrastructures and behavioral data ecosystems that claim to promote the creation of ecological goals and, at the same time, create complex ethical, legal, and social dilemmas. With the shift in the field toward the conceptualization to the practical digital enactment, new dilemmas emerge about data privacy, algorithmic transparency, consumer rights, environmental justice, and techno-moral responsibility (Floridi, 2021; Murthy & Kumar, 2023). In this section, a tedious examination will be carried out on the five leading ethical and legal aspects, which encroach the 6.0 paradigm.

5.1 Data Ethics and Digital Privacy

The Big Data of digital consumer information (sustainability preferences, carbon-footprint records, and biometric eco-tracking, etc.) must be strictly regulated by ethical policies (Pillai & Sivathanu, 2022). Recommendation systems with AI capabilities have been known to collect consumption information regularly and in great detail, and this information may unintentionally reveal an individual behavioral trend or prompt green-profiling biases. Transparency dashboards and opt-in traceability applications are best practice, which allows consumers the chance to visualize their data as the foundation of their circular-economy analytics. Nonetheless, these principles continue to be rather unenforced, particularly in the emerging markets where the infrastructure of digital-ethics is underdeveloped (Chakraborty & Singh, 2024).

5.2 Algorithmic Transparency and Fairness

The modern debate about ethical AI and algorithmic governance makes it clear that there is a need to maintain trust in digital consumerism. ML systems that increase the sustainability of products, or suggest supposedly ethical alternatives, should be subjected to strict auditability and explanatory controls (Floridi, 2021; Taiminen & Saraniemi, 2023). The malicious impact of the biases embedded in the training datasets, i.e., either marginalization of local producers or the unintentional re-branding of the community-based goods as an unsustainable one due to the data incompleteness cannot be ignored (Dangelico et al., 2022). In turn, the Global Partnership on AI (2024) initiates algorithmic impact assessments and stakeholder audits, which is why the wider social and ecological fairness of AI-based suggestions can be evaluated. Open algorithmic structures also enable the consumers to have more power by demystifying the process of calculating the so-called sustainability labels and, hence, promoting digital literacy and moral agency (Vermeir et al., 2022).

5.3 Consumer Rights and Informed Consent

The 6.0 ecosystem transforms the concept of consumer rights, expanding past traditional product safety and honest advertising to include data sovereignty and digital traceability, as well as the accuracy of information regarding the green aspect (NielsenIQ, 2023; White et al., 2021). Informed consent should also be expanded to the digital sphere of consumption, in which users provide specific permission to use sustainability metrics and eco-behavioral data to conduct scholarly research or apply algorithms to optimize them (Murthy & Kumar, 2023). In this connection, plain-language disclosures and dynamic consent models enabling an ongoing participation decision, but not a single, one-time acceptance, should be embraced by the brands. This form of participatory consent would correspond to the principle of co-determination of the ethical-consumer movement, according to which the data is shared in a way that generates regenerative goals, but not corporate exploitation.

5.4 Techno-Moral Accountability and Corporate Governance

The techno-moral accountability doctrine holds that it is the moral responsibility of the corporations to assure that the digital infrastructures that corporations build on are being done in an ethical manner. Failures such as greenwashing, AI manipulation, or misrepresentation of carbon offsets can significantly undermine brand legitimacy and erode stakeholder trust (Elkington, 2020; Fullerton, 2022). According to recent empirical studies conducted by the UN Environment Programme: Helsingius (2024), within 2023, 41 of the leading 100 companies that claimed to be sustainable companies stood in front of the question mark after they made subjective declarations which were not supported by any reliable evidence. The regulatory frameworks, including the European Union (EU) Corporate Sustainability Due Diligence Directive of 2024, counter that by requiring the transparency of the digital footprints, AI models used in the sustainability scores, and full stakeholder interaction metrics. The techno-moral responsibility is operationalized in the form of the theory of corporate innovation and its institutionalization by cross-functional sustainability councils, institutionalization of Ethical AI Board and third-party audits based on planetary ethics (Floridi, 2021; Singh & Rahman, 2024).

5.5 Environmental Justice and Global Equity

Sustainable Consumerism 6.0 overlaps with the problem of environmental justice and equity a lot. Digital sustainability systems are also more likely to be located in developed economies, which could be said to be green data colonialism, where the technologies with a high resource consumption are offshored to a developing economy (Dutta & Roy, 2024). This means that ethical governance should ensure the market is inclusive by granting everyone online access, and equitable cross-border carbon-credit frameworks, and equal technological transfer. The United Nations (2025) suggests the implementation of international interoperability principles, as a result of which sustainable digital tools become available to both small and medium-sized enterprises and rural consumers at large, thus democratizing the involvement in the regenerative process.

6. Limitations

Despite its noble intention, Sustainable Consumerism 6.0 is merely an initial and rather romanticized outline of the harmonization of technology, human values, and regenerative ecological systems; its practical use is, however, bounded by a complex of methodological gaps, deep-rooted technological addictions, the patchwork of sociocultural settings, along with fragmented governance systems (Dangelico et al., 2022; White et al., 2021). The critical recognition of these limitations is thus essential, as only with the help of strict empirical scrutiny and firm devotion to the process of inclusive, iterative intervention, the framework can grow and become a strong, universally relevant paradigm.

6.1 Algorithmic Bias and Green Data Inequality

The first limitation implies an element of algorithmic bias that is inherent in sustainability analytics and recommendation systems. According to Floridi (2021) and Taiminen and Saraniemi (2023), such bias arises when AI platforms are over-reliant on the past and their data can often recreate prejudiced consumption patterns observed in high-income economies. As a result, such systems contribute to what it is possible to define as unintentional green data inequity. In the meantime, brands are no longer viewed merely as producers of goods and services; rather, they are emerging as orchestrators of shared value ecosystems in which consumption contributes to ecological restoration, social well-being, and long-term sustainability (Raworth, 2021). In addition, as Murthy and Kumar (2023) also argue, the language of green algorithms may also continue to make anthropocentric or market-biased assumptions about what is considered sustainable behavior. This kind of assumption runs the risk of excluding other possible, community-based regenerative approaches. This is an efficient way of overlooking different native systems of knowledge and localized strategies that are, in many cases, fundamental to be regenerative indeed.

6.2 Digital Divide and Accessibility Constraints

The second weakness is the digital divide existing across the developed and emergent economies. Although the Consumerism 6.0 paradigm implies the presence of a well-developed digital infrastructure, including AI and blockchain, as well as the IoT, a significant part of the global society still does not have the required connectivity, economic capabilities, and digital literacy to participate (Chakraborty & Singh, 2024). According to the latest statistics released by the International Telecommunication Union, about 2.6 billion people in the world are not online, which means that they cannot take part in digital sustainability projects (International Telecommunication Union, 2024). In turn, the scalability of the given model will depend on the intentional attempts to promote fair digital inclusion and support the process of cross-border knowledge transfer (United Nations, 2025).

6.3 Policy Fragmentation and Regulatory Lag

The major challenge facing the modern sustainability governance is the distortion of policy systems and the subsequent stagnation in the enactment of regulations in the national jurisdictions. Although the EU Green Deal, the National Resource Efficiency Policy of India, and the Sustainable Development Action Plan of ASEAN are all essential initiatives, they are very different in terms of their scope and the data standards they prescribe (Fullerton, 2022). Such inconsistency compromises cross-border supply chains and digital traceability system interoperability and accountability (Rejeb et al., 2022). Without globally accepted digital-sustainability taxonomies or globally accepted environmental disclosure standards, the implementation of circular innovations is held up.

6.4 Cultural Variability in Ethical Consumption

The other weakness is cultural variability on ethical and regenerative consumption. The motivation of consumers depends on cultural standards, religious values, and socio-economic backgrounds (Vermeir et al., 2022). As an example, collectivist societies focus on the communal good, but individualistic societies focus on the self-identification with the environment (Kumar & Kapoor, 2021). Therefore, the messages of sustainability, online activism, and value perception are diverse. An internationalized version of Consumerism 6.0 might not reflect the localized forms of Consumerism like the Jugaad innovation in India, the Zero Waste in Japan, or Ubuntu ideals in Africa (Singh & Rahman, 2024). This would then require localized cultural adaptation in order to prevent ethnocentric bias and increase behavioral resonance.

6.5 Measurement Gaps and Empirical Verification

Since the phenomenon of Sustainable Consumerism 6.0 itself is rather conceptual in nature, at this point, the construct does not provide empirically based tools to measure regenerative consumer behavior and fit with digital ethics. Although the current sustainability indexes focus mostly on the environmental influence, they fail to consider the cognitive, affective, and moral aspects within the consumption habits (White et al., 2021). In line with this, future studies should come up with multidimensional scales which in the same breath will include material measures like carbon footprint and resource efficiency as well as immaterial ones like ethical intelligence and eco-empathy. Until this empirical validation is attained then the framework is largely theoretical and is only a conceptual scaffolding to be used in future research.

6.6 Integration Complexity and Implementation Cost

The Consumerism 6.0 implementation requires a combination of technology, policy, and behavior systems—which is very complex and expensive. Small and medium enterprises (SMEs) usually have the prohibitive cost to implement blockchain-based traceability, renewable energy transitions, and AI-based predictive analytics (Dutta & Roy, 2024). Furthermore, the interdisciplinary cooperation of data scientists, sustainability officers, and behavioral economists has not yet been developed (Floridi, 2021). Huge implementation would be restricted to elite corporations instead of community enterprises without institutional incentives or shared forms of governance (Fullerton, 2022; Singh & Rahman, 2024).

7. Discussions

The development of Sustainable Consumerism 6.0 is a break or rupture with the traditional paradigms of sustainability into a regenerative, technology-facilitated, and ethically regulated ecosystem of consumption. Earlier studies highlight the importance of the intersection of human values, digital stewardship, and regenerative design as a combination of which can re-align consumer behaviors, change organizational behavior, and alter the policy systems (Singh & Rahman, 2024; White et al., 2021). In summing up this discussion, I discuss the theoretical, managerial, and the societal implications of the suggested framework. I further shed light on the compound dynamics of ethical intelligence, technology governance, and systemic transformation.

7.1 Theoretical Implications

Theoretically, Sustainable Consumerism 6.0 can be seen as part of the growing body of discussion on technological humanism and regenerative capitalism, as it combines behavioral, ecological, and digital theories into a unified system-based model. Conventional models, including the Theory of Planned Behavior (Ajzen, 1991) and the Value-Belief-Norm Theory (Stern, 2000) have been used to describe sustainability behavior by individual cognition predictors to a great extent, but rarely have they focused on the role played by digital infrastructure and algorithmic mediation in the impact of ethical judgment in consumption (Floridi, 2021). It argues that the moral cognition with the support of transparent digital systems creates a so-called conscious consumption loop that ensures that personal values correspond with planetary well-being (Biswas & Roy, 2021; Lee & Chen, 2023). Moreover, the framework supports systems theory (Lusch & Vargo, 2021), which assumes that consumption is not a one-time event but a continuous process between socio-ecological and technological subsystems. The integrative view offers a solid basis of multilevel modeling of digital sustainability behavior, integrating both psychological variables (values, attitudes) and digital variables (algorithmic fairness, traceability).

7.2 Managerial and Strategic Implications

As an organization, the Consumerism implication of Consumerism 6.0 goes beyond marketing strategy, into corporate governance, innovation management, and brand ethics. Managers are thus requested to shift the model of transactional engagement toward transformational stewardship, where the value proposition of a firm can promote customer well-being and ecological renewal at the same time (Elkington, 2020; Fullerton, 2022). Practically, this transition would require the implementation of digital sustainability intelligence in the decision-making process, e.g., using blockchain to track ethical traceability, AI to model predictive resource efficiency, and the IoT to monitor the lifecycle (Rejeb et al., 2022; Gupta et al., 2023). This form of participation logic contributes to increasing brand legitimacy, reducing opposition toward products that are sustainable, as well as increasing shared responsibility. Managers should also have Ethical AI Boards and cross-functional Sustainability Digital Units, institutionalized to manage the techno-moral aspects of consumer data and algorithmic marketing. This kind of governance makes sure that such digital tools promote ethical transparency and lead to regenerative effects in the long term (Floridi, 2021; Murthy & Kumar, 2023).

7.3 Policy and Regulatory Implications

The adoption of Sustainable Consumerism 6.0 will require a powerful, multi-level policy alignment, which goes beyond national boundaries. In partnership with the international organizations, the governments should align the sustainability standards, digital ethics, and regenerative incentives to eliminate the discontinuity in the policies mentioned in Section 7 (OECD, 2023; United Nations, 2025). Harmonized frameworks including the EU Green Taxonomy and the Corporate Sustainability Reporting Directive (CSRD) are national blueprints of ESG transparency which are legally binding at the international level. They should be embraced across the world, thus securing the interoperability of the sustainability data systems, consumer rights, and algorithmic responsibility (Chakraborty & Singh, 2024). On the national and local levels, the active incentivization of green digital entrepreneurship should be a part of the policies of the state and counties, and the fiscal benefits provided to start-ups that apply the concepts of circularity and ethical AI. In addition, consumer protection law enforcement should expand their roles to include digital sustainability transparency and reduce the risks of deceitful eco-labels or AI-driven effects on the so-called ethical consumption decisions (Vermeir et al., 2022). Another pathway of promoting digital inclusion is presented through the subsidies of renewable-powered data infrastructures in developing economies by means of public–private partnerships (PPP).

7.4 Societal and Behavioral Implications

On the societal level, the empirical data emphasizes a radical cultural transformation of the materialistic desire to the ecological consciousness. Sustainability is no longer viewed as a tradeoff that must be made as consumers internalize planetary ethics more, but instead as a means to express themselves through identity (White et al., 2021). This fact corresponds to the theoretical construct of eco-spiritual capitalism when people find a psychological fulfillment in the regenerative activities of recycling, up-cycling, or ethical investing (Lee & Chen, 2023). With the assistance of influencer-driven sustainability rhetoric, digital storytelling is currently actively transforming the nature of normative practices by converting ecologically puzzling ideas into emotional and accessible discourse (Haque & Rahman, 2023). These forms of social contagion cause greater speeds of behavioral adoption within generational cohorts, thus, shifting the concept of sustainability out of the ideology of a niche and into a trending culture. Additionally, according to the Collective Mindfulness Theory, the development of systemic resilience is possible when communities strive to develop the common sense of awareness and moral measure (Weick & Sutcliffe, 2020). As such, Sustainable Consumerism 6.0 uses digital ecosystems as platforms of moral socialization, which have the power to produce empathy-based social capital that is regenerative, and sustaining long-term regenerative engagement.

7.5 Academic and Research Implications

Various opportunities of scholarly investigation emerge when this conceptual construct is introduced in an academic discourse. To begin with, researchers can empirically test the five-dimensional framework with the help of mixed-method research methods, comprising surveys, digital ethnography, and AI-assisted behavioral analytics. Second, the longitudinal study will be able to explore the way how Ethical Intelligence mediates the relationship between technological adoption and regenerative outcomes in various cultural settings (Taiminen & Saraniemi, 2023). Third, it might be useful to evolve Sustainable Consumer Intelligence Indices (SCII) in future studies to measure the level of digital-ethical maturity of consumers and determine its effect on market change. Lastly, there will be a need to have cross-disciplinary collaboration between marketing, psychology, and computer science to realize the techno-human integration envisioned by Consumerism 6.0 (Floridi, 2021; Murray et al., 2024). With the help of moral philosophy and technological design by locating the concept of sustainability, academia can contribute to the institutionalization of ethics as an essential building block of digital markets.

8. Conclusion

Sustainable Consumerism 6.0 is an intellectual/ethical breakthrough in how we understand the mutual interactions between people, technology, and the earth itself. It goes beyond the limits of antecedent models of sustainability by inoculating human compassion, cyber consciousness, and regenerative practices into the very core of consumption. By leading individuals to see consumerism not just as the economic transaction, but as a renewal of the co-evolution, and through which each purchase, interaction, and data exchange advances the ecological restoration and facilitates social equity (Singh & Rahman, 2024; White et al., 2021). In essence, Consumerism 6.0 balances three revolutionary forces: Human Values-an injection of ethical thinking and compassion and empathy into the consumption decisions (Biswas & Roy, 2021; Schwartz, 2020). Technology: operating as a clear-cut facilitator via AI, blockchain, and IoT, hence accountability, traceability, and efficiency of the circular systems (Rejeb et al., 2022; Pillai & Sivathanu, 2022). Regenerative mindsets represent a shift from sustainability as mere maintenance toward regeneration as an active process of renewal and restoration (Fullerton, 2022; Raworth, 2021). These dimensions do not contradict each other but once combined, create a new socio-technical balance where ethical intelligence and digital stewardship become the source of not only the sustainability of decisions made but of the overall well-being of people. This balance is the core of regenerative capitalism a form of economy that is developed to restore health instead of to exploit (Elkington, 2020; Floridi, 2021).

8.1 Theoretical and Practical Significance

Theoretically, the development of Sustainable Consumerism 6.0 is a paradigm shift that develops the transformative sustainability science. It can be seen as a whole schema of unifying human consciousness, technological invention, and environmental stability, by combining behavior theories with the concepts of digital ethics and regenerative systems. As a matter of fact, this model gives a practical guideline to companies, educators, and policymakers to move toward the design of systems that entrench ethical values and regenerative practices on scale. In the case of firms, it is focused on ethical use of data, open supply chains, and participation of stakeholders. Academic learners are urged to pay attention to the fact that such methodology requires the development of new research metrics that would reflect not only material but also abstract aspects of sustainability, including empathy, moral sense, and digital inclusivity, as emphasized by recent research (Murray et al., 2024).

8.2 Future Research Directions

Although the current study has a powerful conceptual basis, future investigation needs to be directed at the empirical verification and cross-cultural feasibility. Three research directions become apparent: Operationalization of Ethical Intelligence—the process of distinguished modeling of measurable concepts catchy of digital morality, eco-empathy and ethical cognition of consumer behavior. Cross-Cultural Testing of the 6.0 Model—the authors look at the cultural, spiritual, and socio-economic difference in the context of regenerative consumption adoption (Lee & Chen, 2023). AI-Driven Sustainability Analytics—Exploring the opportunity to anticipate, personalize, and optimize ethical consumption without compromising privacy or fairness. Moreover, future research should emphasize interdisciplinary collaboration among behavioral scientists, AI ethicists, and sustainability scholars to effectively translate the conceptual framework into practical applications (Taiminen & Saraniemi, 2023).

8.3 Concluding Reflection

The shift of Consumerism 1.0 to Consumerism 6.0 provides one of the most interesting examples of how humanity is changing the nature of the relationship with consumption and shifts to a more sophisticated state of the moral mind. The increase in the technological potential of the modern society, as well as the accompanying increase in the level of responsibility, is that as the mode of progress becomes more advanced, it must perform the role of a catalyst of beneficial changes to the society, but not the instrument of exploitation. Consumerism 6.0 suggests that a new model where ethical intelligence informs algorithm decision-making, digital platforms shape empathy, and market mechanisms actively take part in ecological systems regeneration will be introduced. By entrenching compassion into code and creating regeneration as part and parcel of commercial practice, Sustainable Consumerism 6.0 offers a vision of not merely the future but a blueprint of ethical prosperity in the future that heals the planet, empowers people, and is futuristically innovative and ethically upright.

References

Ajzen, I. (1991). The theory of planned behavior. *Organizational Behavior and Human Decision Processes*, *50*(2), 179–211. https://doi.org/10.1016/0749-5978(91)90020-T

Bauman, Z. (2021). *Liquid consumption: Living in an age of uncertainty*. Polity Press.

Biswas, A., & Roy, M. (2021). Green consumption in emerging economies: Examining consumers' values, attitudes and purchase behaviour. *Journal of Cleaner Production*, *314*, 128–145. https://doi.org/10.1016/j.jclepro.2021.128145

Chakraborty, S., & Singh, P. (2024). Green fintech and digital sustainability: Revolutionizing consumer finance for a low-carbon future. *Sustainability, 16*(5), 2219–2235. https://doi.org/10.3390/su16052219

Dangelico, R. M., Pizzetti, M., & Rosati, F. (2022). Digital technologies for sustainable consumption: A systematic literature review. *Journal of Business Research, 145*, 445–458. https://doi.org/10.1016/j.jbusres.2022.02.010

Dutta, S., & Roy, S. (2024). Energy footprints of digital ecosystems: Re-evaluating ICT sustainability. *Renewable and Sustainable Energy Reviews, 189*, 113909.

Elkington, J. (2020). *Green swans: The coming boom in regenerative capitalism.* Fast Company Press.

Ellen MacArthur Foundation. (2022). *Circular economy and the climate agenda.* Ellen MacArthur Foundation Report. https://ellenmacarthurfoundation.org

Floridi, L. (2021). *The ethics of artificial intelligence: Principles, challenges, and opportunities.* Oxford University Press.

Fullerton, J. (2022). *Regenerative capitalism: How universal principles and patterns will shape our new economy.* Capital Institute Press.

Global Partnership on AI. (2024). *Responsible artificial intelligence and sustainable development: Annual report 2024.* GPAI Secretariat. https://gpai.ai

Gupta, V., Yadav, R., & Kumar, A. (2023). IoT-driven circularity and consumer engagement in green product life-cycles. *Technological Forecasting and Social Change, 191*, 122456.

Haque, T., & Rahman, M. S. (2023). Digital storytelling and influencer activism for sustainable consumption among Gen Z consumers. *Journal of Retailing and Consumer Services, 74*, 103412. https://doi.org/10.1016/j.jretconser.2023.103412

Helsingius, L. (2024). *Corporate sustainability disclosures and greenwashing risks: A global assessment.* UN Environment Programme Report.

International Telecommunication Union (ITU). (2024). *Measuring digital development: Facts and figures 2024.* ITU Publications. https://www.itu.int

Jayaraman, V., Luo, Y., & Dubey, R. (2023). Circular economy practices and sustainable supply chains: A systematic review and future directions. *Journal of Cleaner Production, 387*, 135865.

Joshi, Y., & Rahman, Z. (2020). Factors affecting sustainable consumption behaviour: An integrative framework. *International Journal of Consumer Studies, 44*(3), 238–252. https://doi.org/10.1111/ijcs.12556

Kotler, P. (2020). *Marketing 4.0: Moving from traditional to digital.* Wiley.

Kotler, P., Kartajaya, H., & Setiawan, I. (2021). *Marketing 5.0: Technology for humanity.* Wiley.

Kumar, V., & Kapoor, S. (2021). Values, attitudes and green purchase behaviour: A study of Indian millennials. *Sustainable Production and Consumption, 27*, 1755–1767. https://doi.org/10.1016/j.spc.2021.03.015

Kumar, V., & Ranjan, R. (2021). Digital transformation of consumer behaviour: A conceptual synthesis. *Journal of Retailing and Consumer Services, 61*, 102541.

Lange, S., & Santarius, T. (2021). Digitalization and the decoupling debate: Can ICTs help reduce environmental impacts while maintaining economic growth? *Journal of Cleaner Production, 281*, 124–135. https://doi.org/10.1016/j.jclepro.2020.124135

Lee, K.-H., & Chen, Y. (2023). Eco-spirituality and regenerative consumer behaviour: Bridging environmental concern and moral identity. *Sustainability*, *15*(4), 3068–3085. https://doi.org/10.3390/su15043068

Lusch, R. F., & Vargo, S. L. (2021). *Service-dominant logic and value co-creation: Advancing the digital consumer economy*. Routledge.

Murray, A., Desmond, M., & Harris, R. (2024). Artificial intelligence and regenerative design thinking for sustainable production systems. *Journal of Industrial Ecology*, *28*(1), 55–72. https://doi.org/10.1111/jiec.13322

Murthy, Y. S., & Kumar, A. (2023). Ethical challenges in AI-enabled marketing: Implications for digital consumer trust. *International Journal of Business Ethics and Technology*, *12*(2), 88–101.

NielsenIQ. (2023). *Sustainability today and tomorrow: Consumer trends report 2023* NielsenIQ Insights Report. https://nielseniq.com

Organisation for Economic Co-operation and Development (OECD). (2023). *OECD environmental performance reviews 2023*. OECD Publishing. https://www.oecd.org/environment

Pillai, R., & Sivathanu, B. (2022). AI-driven sustainability personalization and consumer engagement: A conceptual exploration. *Sustainable Technology and Entrepreneurship*, *1*(4), 100026. https://doi.org/10.1016/j.stae.2022.100026

Raworth, K. (2021). *Doughnut economics: Seven ways to think like a 21st-century economist* (Updated ed.). Chelsea Green Publishing.

Rejeb, A., Rejeb, K., & Simske, S. J. (2022). Blockchain technology for sustainable supply-chain transparency: A systematic review. *Sustainability*, *14*(9), 5206–5225. https://doi.org/10.3390/su14095206

Schwartz, S. H. (2020). *The theory of basic human values: Implications for ethical consumerism*. Springer Briefs in Psychology.

Singh, R., & Rahman, Z. (2024). Sustainable consumerism 6.0: Integrating digital transformation and regenerative capitalism. *Journal of Cleaner Production*, *437*, 140095.

Singh, R., Rahman, Z., & Khan, I. (2024). Digital transformation and sustainable consumer behavior: Integrating regenerative capitalism. *Journal of Cleaner Production*, *437*, 140095.

Stern, P. C. (2000). Toward a coherent theory of environmentally significant behavior. *Journal of Social Issues*, *56*(3), 407–424. https://doi.org/10.1111/0022-4537.00175

Taiminen, H., & Saraniemi, S. (2023). Technological humanism in digital marketing: Balancing empathy and automation. *Journal of Business Research*, *158*, 113592.

United Nations. (2023). *The sustainable development goals report 2023*. UN Publications. https://unstats.un.org/sdgs

United Nations. (2025). *Global digital compact: Open, free and secure digital future for all*. United Nations. https://www.un.org

United Nations Environment Programme (UNEP). (2024). *Global resources outlook 2024: Bend the trend – Pathways to a liveable planet*. UNEP. https://www.unep.org/resources

Vermeir, I., Weijters, B., De Pelsmacker, P., Geuens, M., & Pecheux, C. (2022). Sustainable consumption: The role of consumer motivation and barriers. *Journal of Environmental Psychology*, *81*, 101806. https://doi.org/10.1016/j.jenvp.2022.101806

Weick, K. E., & Sutcliffe, K. M. (2020). *Managing the unexpected: Sustained performance in a complex world* (3rd ed.). Wiley.

White, K., Habib, R., & Hardisty, D. J. (2021). How to SHIFT consumer behaviours toward more sustainable consumption: A literature review and guiding framework. *Journal of Marketing*, *85*(3), 22–49.

Chapter 4

Integrating Environmental Consciousness, Sustainability Leadership, and Organizational Culture to Advance ESG Excellence amid Climate Change Challenges

Yasmeen Shamsi Rizvi and Sumna Khan

Jamia Millia Islamia, India

Abstract

The 21st century has placed us at a crossroads where several interrelated crises such as climate change, biodiversity loss, and overconsumption of resources are compelling organizations to change. This chapter explores the role of sustainability leadership and organizational sustainability culture in achievement of ESG excellence through environmental stewardship. It is argued that leadership, culture, and accountability in organizations are the core elements of a system that create synergy, and that companies integrating sustainability at their core can lead the way toward adaptive resilience, thus going beyond compliance. Accountability has been institutionalized in ESGs, but issues of greenwashing, non-aligned metrics, and reporting continue to exist across industries. The innovations and operational efficiencies associated with Industry 6.0 are likely to be introduced, but implementation requires a strong ethical foundation to enable sustainability-oriented, holistic thinking. A key task of policymakers and corporates is to develop inclusive and scalable systems that allow all businesses, especially micro, small, and medium enterprises (MSMEs), to thrive, thereby establishing an ecosystem where collaborative climate action is feasible in accordance with sustainable development goals. The theoretical framework suggested in the current research, along with insights from global best practices and micro research

Regenerative Revolution, 73–96

Published under exclusive licence by Emerald Publishing Limited
doi:10.1108/978-1-80686-859-920261004

on Indian MSMEs, addresses a major knowledge gap and unveils new perspectives for future research. The chapter serves as a bridge between theory and practice and offers critical insights across policy guidelines to real-life applications, thereby benefiting business leaders, policymakers, and academia.

Keywords: Sustainability leadership; organizational culture; environmental consciousness; ESG frameworks; industry 6.0; climate resilience

JEL Codes: Q01; Q20; Q56; M14; O33; C80

1. Introduction

The modern age requires a critical reevaluation of the capacity and modes of operation of organizations because the challenges and opportunities of climate change and environmental degradation are unique and are escalating at a rate that is rather alarming (Workman et al., 2025). In line with these environmental factors, the unstoppable wave of digitalization, automation, and Industry 6.0 is transforming not only the paradigm of the economy but also a whole society, marking a new era in industry (Boeske, 2022). As a result, the formerly exclusive mandate to maximize shareholder profit has been replaced by a sustainability mandate requiring companies to develop an integrated strategic decision, combining environmental, social, and governance considerations (Lin, 2024). As much as sustainability has gained strategic importance, several implementation challenges remain. In empirical research, leadership, culture, and ESG reporting are often discussed in isolation, and the interaction between them in a dynamic way that would enable environmental intelligence to be absorbed into the organizational psyche is not considered. In addition, Indian companies, especially micro, small, and medium enterprises (MSMEs), tend to be left out of the ESG performance reporting, thus creating a wide blind spot. According to this research, the framework proposed will not just be integrative but also entrench environmental consciousness in the organizational character by offering the critical evaluation that clarifies how leadership on sustainability intersects with organizational culture to introduce ESG excellence. This chapter highlights the systemic change required to achieve environmental and social justice, which would ultimately lead to a climate-resilient future. It will attempt to synthesize the existing content of the literature to date in the Indian setting, with an emphasis on how sustainability leadership and culture can be employed to provoke ESG excellence through environmental accountability. The following is the general research question that will guide this study: How can leadership and culture instil an awareness of the environment that goes beyond compliance and initiate systemic change?

1.1 Theoretical Underpinnings

The area of organizational sustainability as an inquiry has been explored through various theoretical lenses, thus adding different perspectives to the examined phenomena. Scholars of various fields have tried to unravel the complicated interaction between the corporate actions on one hand and the general socio-environmental environment within which firms exist. In the institutional approach, as an example, the existing environmental norms, regulatory requirements, and normative pressures emerge as powerful facilitators of organizations to integrate sustainable practices in their organizational structures. This logic of the institution thus makes sustainability not a strategic option but an urgent response to the changing demands of society and administration. At the same time, the theory warns about the risk of symbolic adoption (Herold, 2018). Stakeholder Theory reveals the rising demands for real environmental initiatives by shareholders, employees, regulators, and communities (Freeman, 2023). Goal Content Theory (GCT) differentiates between intrinsic and extrinsic goals (profit, status, growth), drawing upon which, leaders need to change the orientation of businesses toward intrinsic goals if they want to increase the resilience (Deci & Ryan, 2000). The Planetary Health Framework, in essence, is a macro-level view of how ecological limits lay the groundwork for corporate sustainability (Redvers et al., 2025). These viewpoints, therefore, lead to an understanding of why leadership and culture are the factors that decide whether ESG can be translated into real action or just remain on paper.

2. Methodology

The chapter uses a conceptual approach and is based on secondary sources focusing on environmental studies, management, economics, social justice, and organizational change. The analysis is based on official publications and reports like the International Energy Agency reviews, Government codes (e.g., SEBI, BRSR framework), as well as extensive academic publications. This qualitative method adopted in this study focuses on interpretive depth and contextual richness by extensively reviewing and integrating the most contemporary literature, case studies, and latest climate- and policy-related activities and events. Though theoretical, the methodological approach is analytical and theory-based at the same time, thus providing the authors with the flexibility to integrate or link various dimensions and concepts such as Institutional Theory, Stakeholder Theory, GCT, and Planetary Health Framework with organizational practice and policy consequences. Being an interdisciplinary study, it uncovers the link between the constructs and the challenges/opportunities, thus providing deep insights into the path of embedding sustainability and climate resilience in organizational culture. The structured narrative provides a rationale for strategic evaluation by academics, practitioners, and policy makers.

3. Literature Review

We are witnessing a new generation of managers and professionals who, due to their technical and market knowledge, are aware of climate change, loss of biodiversity, and overexploitation of resources as key drivers of change. Research shows that companies in India, as well as worldwide, are exposed to a complicated mix of regulatory and physical risks, for example, those related to natural resources, and also possible reputational risks. Additionally, there are opportunities for enhanced innovation and resilience through integration of sustainability practices (BSRI 2023; IEA, 2025; Lin, 2024; SEBI, 2025). Based on the review of literature, it is necessary to have effective stewardship, which, to a great extent, concentrates on leadership and a transforming culture that not only complies with regulations but also initiates spontaneous discussions in the organization about the ecological imperative around the adaptation and beyond compliance (Deci & Ryan, 2000; Freeman, 2023; Redvers et al., 2025). A considerable amount of work reveals the twofold problems of these firms, which are, first, the demand for economic growth and energy access, and secondly, meeting their climate pledges simultaneously. The issues specifically that have been most prominent in India are the raising of India's carbon emissions and the number of ESG frameworks adopted (IEA, 2025; SEBI, 2025, MSME Ministry India, 2024). Literature argues that the BRSR guidelines, along with the global ESG standards, are taking significant steps in normalizing accountability and transparency. However, there are substantial gaps concerning non-uniform reporting, fewer MSMEs, and enormous possibilities for greenwashing (Alsaggaf, 2025; Martiny et al., 2024, MSME Ministry India, 2024). Examples of leading Indian corporates such as Infosys, Tata, Wipro, Mahindra and Mahindra, and ITC Limited have demonstrated the transformative power of embedding visionary leadership, stakeholder engagement, technovation, and culturally competent ESG performance that influences their climate resilience. Corporations around the world, like Patagonia, Unilever, and Microsoft, are demonstrating how good social and environmental footprints can be established by incorporating sustainability and leading it through organization climate and culture (Bai et al., 2024; Boeske, 2022). Extant literature also emphasizes the importance of theory, human capital, just transition, stakeholder engagement, and institutions, which have been at the core of the debate about the skills gaps/labor transition/ethical leadership needs in climate-induced organizational changes (Sajjad et al., 2024; Freeman, 2023; Herold, 2018). In summary, the literature offers extensive models and real-life examples, but, for the most part, it does not acknowledge the complex ways in which leadership, culture, and governance are connected to promote comprehensive sustainability. Our objective in the current investigation is to combine these parallel stories into a unified structure that does not only take theoretical constructions to a higher level but also provides action-oriented and policy-relevant data that can drive socially fair, substantive, and permanent organizational changes in the context of climate change.

4. Sustainability Leadership in the Climate-Change Era

Sustainability leadership transforms firms from more economic actors, to stewards in harmony with nature. This paradigm shift is best illustrated by transformational leaders who have earned a strategic competitive advantage through moral courage, systems thinking, and long-term orientation that encompasses long-term decision-making processes. When leaders are trying to balance the needs of stakeholders today with those of future generations, they are referred to as intergenerational equity adopters who acknowledge planetary boundaries (Workman et al., 2025). Sustainability leaders innovate to create value from sustainability, are not only innovative but also resonate with the concepts of fairness(fair process), trust (secure storage and transparent roles), and legitimacy. These leaders draw a relationship between environmental preservation and Business Value (Bai et al., 2024). It is important to note that sustainable leaders collaborate with their employees, governments, and local communities to co-create solutions. In a nutshell, it is about substituting the usual authority hierarchy with shared leadership models, which empower green teams, employee innovation, and multi-sectoral partnerships. At Patagonia, leaders motivate employees to act like climate activists, thus incorporating activism as a part of the organization's culture. Similarly, major Indian companies like the Tata Group are integrating sustainability at the core of their brand DNA, with key leaders talking about the climate crisis and the new value coming from the competition in the industry. Leaders of Industry 6.0 have the duty to realize that their further dependence on AI, big data, and digital platforms is not a choice but a necessity in enhancing the low-carbon transitions, and, at the same time, protect the very sustainability gains that such technologies promise (Hameed et al., 2023). The implementation of AI in Microsoft to quantify and minimize emissions can be used as an example of leadership that is needed to strike a balance between disruptive innovation and environmental custodianship. Hence, vision goes hand in hand with bravery and systemic changes at the level of sustainability leadership, thus making ecological responsibility a part of daily routine in an organization (Boeske, 2022).

5. ESG Frameworks and Environmental Accountability

ESG frameworks can be regarded as the tool through which environmental performance is measured and reported. However, implementation needs to be supported by the strong organizational leadership and culture so that the generated initiatives will not be an empty checklist or a greenwashing practice. Investors are relying on ESG disclosures as a risk analysis tool to perform risk and value creation analysis of their portfolios (Martiny et al., 2024). It is no longer limited to carbon accounting; there has been a shift to net-zero plans that have become a mandatory aspect of the international reporting systems. Consequently, ESG has acquired the center stage in the institutional setting, such as the EU Corporate Sustainability Reporting Directive (CSRD), the US SEC climate change disclosure proposals, and the Task Force on Climate-related Financial Disclosures (TCFD).Although they entail transparency, they also necessitate incorporation into governance and strategic decision-making. There are still, however, several obstacles, such as standards fragmentation, selective reporting, and greenwashing (Alsaggaf, 2025). Genuine ESG integration is the mechanism that connects reporting with operational and cultural behaviors. Industry 6.0 technologies (AI, blockchain, and big data) may help to achieve more accurate and more transparent results, but being ecologically oriented is a vital safeguard against simply performative compliance (Leoni, 2025).

6. Carbon Emissions and Reporting: Global Trends and Indian Context

Carbon emissions and energy consumption patterns are major factors that show the environmental impact of a region, its contribution to climate change, and globally indicate significant differences in industrialization among continents, energy use, and policy. These factors determine the overall carbon footprint of the planet. The carbon emission trend in Asia is very steep; hence, the region remains central in global climate discussions (IEA, 2025; EDGAR JRC, 2025). Corporate environmental reporting, for example, the Business Responsibility and Sustainability Report (BRSR) framework of India, is mainly oriented toward big organizations, thereby leaving a considerable number of MSMEs unaccounted for. Their carbon emissions are less monitored and regulated. This section discusses the global distribution of carbon footprints, Asia's emission patterns, the corporate ESG disclosure landscape, and the urgent need to expand sustainability metrics and accountability (SEBI, 2025; MSME Ministry India, 2024).

According to the 2025 International Energy Agency (IEA) Global Energy Review and the European Commission's EDGAR report, Asia accounts for more than half of total global carbon emissions, reflecting rapid industrial activity and rising energy demand. North America and Europe are showing gradual declines in carbon intensity due to a shift toward renewables supported by policy measures. In contrast, Africa and South America are witnessing increasing emissions as urbanization and industrial expansion progress. The sector-level data from the US Environmental Protection Agency corroborates these patterns by identifying energy production, transport, and industrial activity as the primary drivers of emissions (IEA, 2025; EDGAR JRC, 2025; United States Environmental Protection Agency, 2025).

6.1 Increasing Emissions Trend in Asia

Asia is the primary contributor to global carbon emissions. According to the International Energy Agency (IEA, 2025), India's CO2 emissions increased by 164.8 million tons in 2024, mainly due to the expansion of industries and coal usage despite the increased renewable capacity. The carbon footprint of India has crossed the three Gigatons mark, which is roughly 8–9% of the total global emissions (IEA, 2025; EDGAR, 2025). Such a trend arises from the coupling of economic and population growth with the surge in energy demand. Although solar and wind capacity have been gaining ground, coal is still the leading energy source, making it difficult to reconcile the country's development with its climate pledges (IEA, 2025).

6.2 Indian Corporate Reporting Landscape and BRSR Guidelines

In its effort to enforce transparency, the Securities and Exchange Board of India (SEBI) formulated the BRSR framework in 2023. According to the new framework, the disclosure of ESG metrics by the top 1,000 listed companies is mandatory. These metrics include a company's carbon footprint, energy consumed, waste generated, and water consumed. However, BRSR is in line with India's environmental commitments, and it is also consistent with worldwide ESG standards, which makes it easier for top-listed companies in India to adopt and implement ESG governance (SEBI, 2025). Besides specifying how governance and strategy should be related to sustainability so that investors can easily assess environmental risks and achievements, the framework also provides for the institutionalization of sustainability in governance and strategy. This move will lead to a rapid cultural change of climate-aware business behaviors, customer demand for carbon reductions, and resource efficiency (SEBI, 2025).

The sustainability initiatives and cultural impacts of five leading Indian companies have been summarized as follows:

- The *Tata Group*, under its initiative Project Aalingana, aims for net-zero emissions across the group by 2045, embedding sustainability, circular economy, and biodiversity preservation goals into its long-term strategic vision (Tata Group, 2025).
- *Wipro* has adopted science-based targets and committed to achieving net-zero for Scope 1, 2, and 3 emissions by 2040; as of FY 2025, it has achieved an 84% reduction in Scope 1 and 2 emissions relative to its 2017 baseline (Wipro, 2025).
- *Mahindra and Mahindra* has formally committed to carbon neutrality by 2040, and its Planet Positive strategy—including renewable energy adoption, energy-efficiency measures and nature-based solutions—positions sustainability as a core part of its corporate identity and long-term business model (Mahindra and Mahindra 2025).
- *ITC Limited's* 2024–25 sustainability report indicates that under its Sustainability 2.0 roadmap, the company has significantly increased renewable-energy use, improved energy efficiency and achieved measurable reductions in greenhouse-gas emissions—demonstrating an ESG-driven business culture (ITC Limited, 2025).
- *Infosys* has sustained carbon-neutral status for six years and, through its refreshed ESG Vision 2030, targets becoming climate-positive by 2030. As of 2025, around 78% of its electricity use in India is sourced from

renewables—supported by over 29.7 million sq ft of green-certified campus space and substantial investments in solar PV, energy efficiency and "water/ waste-management infrastructure" (Infosys, 2025).

These examples show that Indian companies are not only complying with regulatory disclosure norms but also creating sustainability-driven cultures. Examining the practices of companies such as Infosys, Tata, Wipro, Mahindra and Mahindra, and ITC Limited within the framework of renewable energy integration, carbon neutrality commitments, responsible sourcing, and community-focused programs reveals that they have reduced their GHG emissions, lessened resource usage, and generated meaningful social impacts. At an individual level, the literature underscores that transparent reporting—driven by authentic leadership commitment rather than superficial greenwashing—enhances corporate legitimacy, fosters stakeholder trust, and accelerates India's transition toward sustainable development. However, MSMEs remain mostly unregulated, thereby contributing to a hidden environmental burden, while larger companies increasingly align with ESG norms.

6.3 The Challenge of MSMEs in India: The Unseen Environmental Burden

Micro, small, and medium enterprises or MSMEs are the backbone of Indian industries and account for more than 90% of the total industrial units in the country. However, these MSMEs largely fall outside the purview of ESG reporting, which means that they are contributing a significant proportion of environmental impact, which remains largely unrecognized. Many MSMEs are left with no choice but to use pollution-intensive facilities due to the lack of resources, low awareness levels, and the absence of any obligation to comply, as a result of which they end up polluting the environment significantly (MSME Ministry India, 2024). The under-regulated MSME sector contributes to the problem of national emissions control, as small polluters, when taken together, become a big source of emissions. The experts recommend implementing scalable reporting systems, providing incentives, skill development, and supply chain pressures to enhance MSME engagement in sustainability (MSME Ministry India, 2024). The three key challenges affecting Micro, Small and Medium Enterprises (MSMEs) are (a) inadequate financial resources to implement clean technologies, (b) technical know-how to implement stringent reporting requirements, and (c) enforcement mechanisms. Conversely, MSMEs possess several strategic opportunities, like localized innovation, agility in their model of operation, and close ties with the community. In India, a cluster of MSMEs in the textile industry has embraced the use of solar-powered operation through the assistance of non-government organizations, thereby illustrating the potential scaling of the green revolution. On the contrary, the regulatory frameworks (such as the CSRD of the European Union) make even Small and Medium Enterprises publish data on sustainability. Inclusive accountability requires one to develop reporting systems that are scalable, offer incentives, and have effective capacity-building programs. The supply chain pressures, together with the digital solutions, that is, blockchain-based, low-cost, emissions tracking, can also readily assimilate the MSMEs into larger sustainability systems. The grass-root participation in this case can prove to be a huge support to the Indian carbon-reduction efforts. Finally, grassroots mobilization of MSMEs is a critical aspect of broader organizational and leadership changes needed to take climate change to a systemic level.

7. Climate Change and Environmental Consciousness: The Driving Force Behind Organizational Transformation

The physical, regulatory, and reputational impacts of climate change can also be seen in various areas; however, simultaneously, there are opportunities in clean energy and technological development (Zhao et al., 2025).Top management ought to include climate action in their corporate strategies, thus linking ecological conservation with the economic aspect of the business. The corporate culture of caring for the environment and being future-oriented helps in the continuity of climate action (Alemu, 2025). ESG standards serve as a platform for the implementation of accountability through different agents, such as TCFD and scientifically-based targets (Lin, 2024). In addition, Industry 6.0 technologies offer greater possibilities in the areas of observation and modification. Indian companies like Mahindra and Mahindra are good examples of climate-conscious leadership as they have made a commitment to achieve carbon neutrality and the use of renewable energy. Unilever, the global company, on the other hand, accomplishes this by connecting the climate goals with the executive incentives and thus creating a very efficient cycle of accountability in the governance structures. The mentioned instances show that the problem of climate change is not just one of risk but a strategic necessity for getting legitimacy, competitive advantage in the market, and stakeholder trust. Being environmentally aware is at the core of the debates about the world's sustainable future as well as the future of organizations. It depicts the recognition of a person or an organization that the well-being of nature is the basis of human and organizational success (Suieubayeva et al., 2025). Unlike wider concepts of sustainability and resilience, environmental awareness puts emphasis on the ecological limits of the Earth and points to human cultural practices that are the main causes of ecological degradation. Environmentally conscious behaviors within the organization are very important, such as staff members turning off lights when they are not needed and the organization itself implementing policies and strategies that consider ecology as a crucial part of the organization's identity and its operations. The main factors that support this responsibility are still leadership and culture (Sajjad et al., 2024). In the past, organizations considered their environmental impact as an externality. Nevertheless, environmentally conscious organizations understand that ecological limits cannot be separated from strategic decisions related to resource consumption, emissions, and planetary boundaries (Alemu, 2025). They are not only committed to the incremental improvements but also seek systemic transformation by going renewable, using circular economy principles, and changing their processes. The presence of visionary leadership and a culture that encourages innovation, risk-taking, and future-orientation is very influential in this change (Liao, 2022). Besides that, climate-conscious organizations also recognize their social responsibilities that include, for example, the protection of vulnerable groups. Culture is of great importance when it comes to sustaining ecological responsibility. Organizations that are considerate of stewardship practice green activities in employee induction, performance appraisals, and day-to-day operations. Executives facilitate integration by providing financial support, creating partnerships, and getting the change momentum both inside and outside the company (Boeske, 2022). The notion of environmental awareness serves as a complement to ESG frameworks, whereby the latter is implemented in a meaningful rather than a formal way. The present and future technologies in Industry 6.0 are very helpful in improving energy efficiency and reducing carbon emissions. They also facilitate the implementation of SDG-12 through digital platforms for collaborative consumption and automation, but the environment has to be the guiding principle for such technology. When organizations strategically incorporate these principles, they become more aligned in terms of leadership, culture, and operations and hence are able to address not just climate change but also social transformation (Negi & Dangwal, 2019).

8. From Climate Shocks to Socioeconomic Crises: A Global Perspective

Climate change is not just a scientific problem anymore. It is the changing reality of people, societies, and economies that are differently affected by it all over the planet. In fact, the last two years have been characterized by a massive rise in climate-related disasters that have spread to many parts of the world, such as floods and failure of crops in India, landslides, and extreme weather. The disruptions will not be "noisy neighbors" anymore; in fact, they are a signal of a situation in which ecological shocks quickly turn into social and economic crises. Table 4.1 provides a summary of various major climate-related events of the years 2024 and 2025, illustrating their deep impact on human communities, agriculture, and regional economies in several locations around the globe.

As shown in Table 4.1, the series of climatic and environmental disasters between 2024 and 2025 in different locations highlights the escalating vulnerabilities that have deep and wide-ranging implications for the communities, the economies, and businesses. The price to man has been enormous; lives have been lost and thousands displaced, as well as livelihoods disrupted badly. There has been widespread destruction of public infrastructure such as health, education, and housing, thus increasing the need to have efficient and quick warning mechanisms, community preparedness, and formulation of resilient recovery plans. These disasters have economically wasted local and national treasuries by costing them billions of dollars, and disrupting regional and national economies

Table 4.1. Major Disaster Events (2024–2025): Human, Community, and Economic Impact Across Global Regions.

S. No.	Location | Event and Year	Human/Community Impact	Economic Impact
1	Punjab, India *Monsoon Floods*, 2025 (Al Jazeera, 2025; ReliefWeb, 2025; Vision IAS, 2025)	~1,400 villages inundated; over 381,000 people affected; at least 29–51 deaths; 400,000 acres of crops lost; school closures, infrastructure and health facility damage.	Infrastructure loss ₹780 crore, crop compensation ₹20,000/acre; government sought ₹20,000 crore relief; ripple effect on farming incomes and grain reserves.
2	Wayanad, Kerala, India *Landslides*, 2024 (Sphere India, 2024)	Over 231–254 deaths, 119 missing; 700+ homes destroyed, vast evacuation and resettlement; impact on livelihoods, mental health, agriculture, schooling.	Estimated direct damages ₹1,202 crore ($144M USD), total damages near ₹2,200 crore ($260M USD) including rehab; future income loss for many families.
3	Tuvalu, *Pacific Sea-level Rise/Climate Migration,* 2025 (InsideClimateNews, 2025)	11,000+ population threatened; 280 annual migration visas to Australia; crop/infrastructure loss; existential threat, diaspora formation.	Risk to $50M national GDP, rising adaptation costs; heavy aid and remittance dependency; long-term economic uncertainty.
4	Vietnam *Typhoon Yagi*, 2024 (Reuters, 2024; UNDP, 2024)	323 deaths, 22 missing; 280,000+ homes flooded or damaged; large-scale impact on agriculture, aquaculture, infrastructure; region-wide bankruptcies.	Estimated damages VND 81–84 trillion (US$3.3–3.47B); 0.15–0.24% GDP drop; insured losses US$471M; agriculture accounted for 45% of losses.
5	Brazil; Rio Grande do Sul *Extreme Flood Event*,	~2.4 million people affected; 183 deaths, 27 missing; 648,000+	Housing/agriculture losses ~$4B; total estimated losses

(Continued)

Table 4.1. *(Continued)*

S. No.	Location | Event and Year	Human/Community Impact	Economic Impact
	2024 (Copernicus, 2024)	displaced; 478 municipalities flooded; major housing, agriculture, health impacts; record rainfall.	exceeding US$15–22B; government allocated BRL 111B for rebuild; GDP contraction, especially in agriculture.
6	Chile; Valparaíso/ Maule/O'Higgins Historic *Wildfires*, 2024, (BBC, 2024; ReliefWeb, 2024)	122–131 deaths, 300+ missing; 43,000 hectares burned; 1,100+ injured, 14,000 homes destroyed; mass evacuation, regional economy suppressed.	Direct losses in billions USD, comparable to earthquake record ($30B); supply shortages, slowed GDP; insurance/relief outcomes pending.
7	Canada *Widespread Wildfires*, 2024 (Insurance Bureau of Canada, 2025)	Over 3.4 million ha burned; First Nations evacuations; hazardous air quality; health/emissions impacts, property and forest loss.	Weather-insured damage $8.5B CAD; property value declines, crop/forest incomes lost, health and fire response costs surging.
8	West Bengal and Bangladesh *Cyclone Remal*, 2024 (Sphere India JRNA, 2024)	Over 200,000 evacuated; ~2,500 homes destroyed; broad agricultural, fishery, and infrastructure loss; power and communications disrupted.	Direct repair/relief costs > ₹400 crore ($48M USD); extensive local and sectoral economic setback.
9	Mozambique and Malawi *CycloneChido*, 2024 (EOS Data, 2024)	300,000+ affected; major crop loss; repeated compounding disasters, especially for food security.	Recovery cost in millions USD; major agricultural contraction, future GDP reduced.
10	Spain (Valencia Region) *Floods*, 2024 (EOS Data, 2024)	224 deaths; villages inundated; economic paralysis and contamination; evacuations.	Local infrastructure/ crop losses, millions USD; sustained relief/ rebuilding; regional GDP impact.

Table 4.1. *(Continued)*

S. No.	Location | Event and Year	Human/Community Impact	Economic Impact
11	Hungary, Central Europe/Danube/Boris *Floods*, 2024 (EOS Data, 2024)	24 deaths; historic flooding; business/agriculture disruption; housing and road impacts.	National agricultural/business losses, millions; GDP drop, bailouts/restoration required.
12	Afghanistan, Pakistan *Monsoon/Spring Floods*, 2024 (UN News, 2024)	Thousands displaced; farmland, homes and lives lost; repeated events intensified vulnerability.	Emergency costs, crop/home values erased; rebuilding/relief expenditures significant.

Source: Authors' compilation based on Al Jazeera (2025), ReliefWeb (2025), Sphere India (2024), Reuters (2024), BBC (2024a, 2024b), Insurance Bureau of Canada (2025), UN News (2024), and EOS Data (2024).

by damaging agricultural production, homes, and infrastructure. The effects of such dominoes are a threat to food security, increased poverty, and placing a heavy burden on the structures of governance that must provide relief and rehabilitation in time.

Sustainable recovery should be based not on the idea of reactive assistance but on the complex systems that emphasize the reduction of risks, equitable development, and adaptation to the climate. They should be considered as key stakeholders in this ecosystem, even though businesses are always the ones who bear the brunt of it. In the face of climate-induced disruptions, companies will most likely face various performance related issues, such as property damage, supply chain difficulties, and a general productivity drop, which consequently may trigger economic turmoil and decreased company revenues.

9. Organizational Culture as a Foundation for Environmental Responsibility

Organizational culture, has long been perceived as a force that is not seen but directly influences behaviors, decision-making, and shared values within a group. Scholars such as Edgar Schein and Geert Hofstede argue that culture indicates the deeply held assumptions, ideas, and symbols that members have collectively built and kept (Fietz & Günther, 2021; Ketprapakorn & Kantabutra, 2022). Although strategies and structures might be changed over time, culture is still the mainstay of most organizations, the "glue" that is often referred to as the factor that keeps an organization together and shows how individuals look at problems and opportunities. In the context of sustainability, organizational culture is the main factor deciding whether climate awareness, ESG commitments, and sustainable practices will be deeply embedded or will continue to be just superficial (Assoratgoon & Kantabutra, 2023). Environmentally responsible corporate change requires more than technical fixes or policy compliance; it demands a transformation in organizational culture. Sustainability challenges, such as global warming, species extinction, and resource scarcity are complex, systemic, and long-term (Negi & Dangwal, 2019). Addressing these issues makes it important to have a shift in values, thoughts, and aspirations beyond simply short-term profit. Just to give an example, several cost-cutting companies may be given access to energy-saving technologies, but if it is a culture that is focused on reducing expenses, the sustainability investments may be cut back. Companies that embrace the culture of ecological stewardship and social responsibility go further to incorporate sustainability in their mission statement, thus making culture the main factor of their environmental commitments' resilience (Ahsan, 2024). Several cultural dimensions serve as a foundation for the target. Having a long-term viewpoint will guarantee that the planet and future generations are taken care of, whereas collectivism and collaboration will encourage teamwork among employees and with customers (Younis & Hussain, 2023). A learning attitude will motivate one to go through the cycle of trial and error and hence learn and grow, and having unmovable ethical standards will position the company as one that is socially responsible (Zhu et al., 2025). Being honest and accountable, among other things, makes it easy for an organization to openly share information with others. The culture of an organization and leadership are deeply connected: leaders communicate visions, decide on the most important projects, and demonstrate the behaviors that implement sustainability at the core of the business, whereas culture determines what leadership stands for. In a company that is mainly focused on efficiency, one might first look at the energy-saving measures from the perspective of cost and energy savings, and only later, as the company becomes more aware of the issue, the ecological aspect is considered (Sajjad et al., 2024). The change in culture is everywhere in everyday life through symbols, stories, as well as subcultures, and most importantly, it is a commitment that is lived. The organizational culture does not only depend on formal structures but also on informal channels. Some of the symbols that are used to show how important environmental care has become for the organization's identity are the signs of clean energy sources, ecology-designed products, and awards for sustainability. An Environment Week, carbon footprint competition, and community volunteering are examples of the most common rituals through which the environment is normalized and made available to more people. The stories of employees' innovations or the company's environmental impact stories turn into narratives that create the feeling of pride and raise the sense of belonging among those who are environmentally conscious (Tanveer et al., 2025; Suieubayeva et al., 2025). Besides, subcultures may not only serve as a medium for introducing sustainability but also as strongholds for resistance. While members of a green team consisting of young employees may try to persuade others to recycle and use green energies, sales or operations subcultures may oppose eco-initiatives due to concerns about additional costs or the reliability of the products. Successful sustainability leadership, therefore, puts diverse subcultures at the center while crafting suitably tailored narratives for them that link environmental responsibility to their respective identities (Hameed et al., 2023).

10. Culture, ESG Integration, and Organizational Alignment

Organizational culture forms the backbone of ESG performance. The ESG frameworks, despite being the standard for measuring and reporting sustainability performance, are greatly influenced by the culture in place (Martiny et al., 2024). On the one hand, cultures that emphasize the need for compliance and accountability are characterized as being most open to accepting ESG reporting, while on the other, there are cultures that see ESG only as a strict regulatory requirement and, consequently, they may accept only the lowest level of compliance, which would lead to stripping away the possible benefits of ESG commitment. To keep on track with the ESG integration, one must be capable of handling different priorities like environmental care, social equity, and governance integrity. Cultures that have been strengthened through the development of robust integrative capacities give not only employees but also leaders the chance to locate, implement, and apply the solutions successfully. The weakness of segmented cultures lies in the fact that such cultures, being deeply divided, fail to see that environmental initiatives are deeply interconnected with social justice and governance, which, therefore, leads to the limitation of holistic ESG implementation (Bai et al., 2024). Large firms demonstrate how the culture of the organization can support the protection of the environment and improve ESG results. Such companies show that eco-friendliness is most effective when it is deeply rooted in the company's identity, decision-making, and ordinary activities. Table 4.2 presents the five global leaders in sustainability, offering a glimpse of their key strategies along with the cultural and ESG impacts.

Table 4.2 presents the sustainability strategies of five top-performing global organizations. These strategies are a mix of innovative programs, ambitious climate-related targets, and transparent ESG reporting. These firms approach SDG goals differently- Patagonia with its groundbreaking circular economy activities and strong activist culture, Microsoft with its technology-driven climate accountability, and Apple with its all-inclusive renewable energy usage. As a result of these measures, the companies have established organizational cultures that are deeply rooted in sustainability and have become a source of lasting environmental and social impact as well as a reference for corporate responsibility.

Table 4.2. Global Corporate Leaders in Sustainability and Their Cultural Impact.

Company	Sustainability Strategy/Initiatives	Impact on Culture and ESG Outcomes
Patagonia	Worn Wear program (repair, reuse, resale); commitment to 100% recycled or renewable materials; carbon neutrality target by 2040; Pack4Good initiative; supply chain transparency through Footprint Chronicles	Strong activism-driven sustainability culture; employee and consumer engagement around environmental stewardship; high transparency standards; measurable annual reductions in supply-chain–related emissions
Unilever	Climate Strategy 2024; Net-zero emissions commitment by 2039; decarbonization of products and supply chain; regenerative agriculture and water stewardship programs	Sustainability embedded in organizational DNA; transparent climate metrics; culture of continuous environmental innovation; verified reductions in greenhouse gases, water use, and waste intensity
IKEA	Climate agenda: net-zero and climate positive ambition; 100% renewable energy across operations; sustainable sourcing (wood, cotton); circularity (repair, resale, take-back services); commitment to halve emissions by 2030	Strong collective sustainability identity; cultural norm of resource efficiency; employees involved in climate-positive actions; long-term emission reductions across product lifecycle; sustainability integrated into daily work practices
Microsoft	"Microsoft 2030" sustainability commitments: carbon negative by 2030; water positive by 2030; zero waste by 2030; AI for sustainability; planetary-scale environmental data initiatives	Culture of climate accountability and technological innovation; transparent ESG governance; over 10 million metric tons of carbon removed to date; high employee participation in sustainability programs
Apple	Apple 2030 carbon-neutrality roadmap; 100% renewable electricity for all corporate facilities and suppliers;	Culture of ecological responsibility and clean-tech innovation; industry-leading ESG disclosures; corporate

Table 4.2. *(Continued)*

Company	Sustainability Strategy/Initiatives	Impact on Culture and ESG Outcomes
	recycling innovation (Daisy, Taz robots); expansion of low-carbon materials; 2025 progress report showing continued emissions reductions	emissions reduced more than one-third since 2015; complete renewable-energy transition supports employee and customer engagement in sustainability

Source: Authors' compilation based on publicly available sustainability reports and data from Patagonia (Supply Chain Digital, 2022), Unilever (2024), IKEA (2024), Microsoft (2025), and Apple Inc. (2025).

11. Organizational Barriers and Challenges to Embedding Sustainability Culture

There are certainly several challenges when transitioning a company's culture to being environmentally sustainable. Companies typically face various forms of barriers, such as structural, financial, cultural, and, often, the issue of greenwashing that can occur superficially and has the potential to impede the real-time progression of the development of a truly authentic sustainability culture. Some of the major hurdles to developing a sustainability culture include the fact that there is a great deal of long-standing resistance to change within an organization, a strong emphasis placed on generating immediate profits, and the presence of culturally diverse areas across the world. These types of issues are further exacerbated by resource constraints, which can limit the amount of time available to spend on a project, the money allocated to implement sustainability into daily business processes, and the expertise available to integrate sustainability principles into daily business processes. In addition, globally based organizations are subject to varying sustainability standards, making it increasingly difficult to align values and practices. Overall, these elements represent the full scope of the wide range of organizational challenges that impede the advancement of sustainability-oriented cultures (Jaganjac et al., 2025).

While most businesses seek to embed sustainable development into their core, some choose to engage in greenwashing — a form of deception in which companies exaggerate or intentionally mislead consumers regarding the environmental characteristics of their products, services, or activities. The existence of greenwashing undermines genuine progress through the promotion of superficial gestures as substantial achievements, selective reporting of positive results while ignoring negative effects, and over-reliance on eco-friendly branding as opposed to actual changes made to the operational aspects of a business. This type of behavior creates cynicism among employees, reduces transparency, misrepresents stated values relative to true behaviors, and encourages performance-based behaviors as opposed to behavioral transformations. In extreme cases, some organizations will also sponsor visible external projects for public relations purposes, which only serves to increase the distance between the organization and its commitment to sustainability. These strategies serve to erode credibility and hinder the development of a genuine sustainability culture. As a result, the call for greater accountability and consistency between the environmental claims made by an organization and its internal practices remains necessary (Alsaggaf, 2025).

12. Discussion and Implications

This study delineates the intersecting roles of sustainable leadership, corporate culture, and Environmental, Social, and Governance (ESG) frameworks as key drivers for ecologically minded behavior in the face of the climate crisis. Leadership is a defining factor as it provides an ethical perspective and long-term vision, prioritising care for the planet. In this manner, leaders drive organizations not only to fulfill the standard requirements but to go beyond to a truly environmentally friendly approach to doing business. Corporate culture is the foundation on which leadership aspirations are turned into actual practice and become the values that the community shares, thus making sustainability a daily routine rather than a legal obligation. The ESG frameworks serve as the means to convert these pledges into measurable and transparent goals and reports, thus committing and attracting continuous progress of the organizations. In essence, these elements are the parts of a synergistic system that support the companies' efficient response to climate change and, therefore, enable them to participate in innovation and transformation that are both sustainable and eco-friendly. In addition, the chapter also draws attention to the future and present difficulties, such as the lack of MSMEs' representation in sustainability reporting, the increasing carbon footprint of India, and the problem of using Industry 6.0 technologies in an ethical manner to facilitate the clean energy transition. Being truly sustainable involves more than the application of the incremental approach; it involves radical actions that would see organizations redefine their mission not just to work toward the health of the planet and economic prosperity but also to create inclusive, bold, and visionary leaders. Organizations must be flexible to respond to the two crises of environmental degradation and social inequity by adopting a culture of constant learning and taking broad, systemic perspectives.

ESG frameworks, therefore, must be reconciled and comprehensively integrated in the strategic intent so that sustainability reporting is authentic instead of being merely performative. The adoption of software innovations, such as artificial intelligence, blockchain, and big data analytics, can greatly enhance the degree of transparency and efficiency; thus, their application with strict adherence to high ethical and environmental requirements must be encouraged. Sustainability requirements should be applicable to all businesses regardless of their size. MSMEs should be supported through tiered reporting, skill-training, and supply-chain participation programs. An important way to overcome the lack of concerted actions is intersectoral agreement between different industries and stakeholders, which would ultimately remove the divisiveness of actions. Finally, this study has far-reaching implications that go beyond the immediate context; it can be used to stimulate advanced academic research, increase awareness in society regarding systemic sustainability, and help with better decision-making in real-life scenarios. Academic institutions are urged to immediately provide support for academic research that is interdisciplinary in nature and that links organizational sciences with environmental studies, as well as digital innovation, in order to generate viable solutions to complex issues of sustainability and disasters that arise from nature. The issue of how leadership and culture, as two elements, can become authentic tools for inducing sustainable changes is one that awaits a response. Society-wise, companies, on the other hand, have an ample moral duty to serve as the caretakers of the earth and thus ensure that their procedures are not only eco-friendly but also that they lead to ecological justice and the safeguarding of the rights of the least advantaged individuals, while at the same time, providing intergenerational equity. Professionals, irrespective of the sector they belong to, have the responsibility to and must be the ones to initiate the process whereby environmental consciousness is elevated from being merely an issue constantly referred to, to become real leadership, culture, and governance outcomes (United Nations Brazil, 2025).

This change would mean that organizations should incorporate sustainability into their business intelligence and performance management systems, which*are at the heart of the organization. The new technologies can be viewed as supportive methods in fulfilling these commitments. The role of governmental officials and industry associations is to come up with the policies that can encourage small and medium-sized businesses to actively adopt sustainability practices. The implications of this study may act as a reference for further research, enhance knowledge, and impact practice. These will together support the creation of socially responsible and resilient organizations that can steer the world toward the achievement of global sustainability and climate objectives.

13. Conclusion

This study demonstrates that sustainability leadership and company culture are central to instilling an environmentally friendly approach in order to attain ESG excellence in a fast-evolving world. Moral courage, systemic thinking, and collaboration with teams not only allow leaders to transform sustainability into a compliance matter but also make it a core organizational feature. With a well-supported sustainability culture, effective ESG framework, and built-in digital innovation, organizations can successfully and transparently address their environmental footprints and initiate transformational, low-carbon strategies. Systemic gaps also emerge in the study, especially the absence of MSMEs in ESG reporting and ethical compatibility of Industry 6.0 technologies with the ecological values. Cooperation across sectors, participatory governance, and tiered accountability are some ways to scale sustainable transformation globally. In summary, companies that prioritize sustainability in their leadership, culture, and operations will be best equipped to respect the planet's limits, promote fairness across generations, and support a shared climate resilience agenda.

14. Limitations and Suggestions

This study is based on secondary sources and, therefore, it is dependent on the range, quality, and timeliness of the available literature, reports, and data. The most significant limitation is the absence of primary data such as interviews, surveys, or case studies. This implies that future research should directly observe or interact with organizations to get first-hand insights on how environmental awareness and sustainability have become part of their culture. In addition, the higher-level integration of different ideas reported in this study, might, however, be simplifying or bypassing some of the intricate relationships. Future scholars can address these gaps by using a mixed-method strategy that combines primary and secondary data sources. Gathering new information from interviews or surveys could validate conceptual insights and demonstrate how these ideas work through practical applications. Researchers might also document the real-time changes organizations experience as they pursue sustainability. Including small and medium enterprises (SMEs) and the informal sector in future studies would lead to more thorough research that reflects reality. These groups represent the majority of businesses but are often left out of ESG reporting. Digital tools could act as real-time monitors for ESG performance, helping organizations identify which areas need the most attention. Companies can promote a democratic leadership approach that allows employees to participate in decision-making, strengthening a culture of sustainability. Collaboration with educational and training institutions would speed up the development of sustainability skills among the workforce and support lasting changes in organizational behavior. One certainty is that government officials and business leaders would gain from integrating ESG ratings and indices into their operations; these provide clear and reliable assessment frameworks. However, they should aim to move beyond mere compliance and make environmental awareness a standard part of governance and decision-making. The link between leadership, culture, policy, and technology remains an interesting area for further investigation. Exploring how these elements interact can offer valuable insights for achieving effective climate action and fair transitions within today's complex organizations.

14.1 Declaration

- *There is no conflict of interest*
- *No fund was received for this study*

References

Ahsan, M. J. (2024). Unlocking sustainable success: Exploring the impact of transformational leadership, organizational culture, and CSR performance on financial performance in the Italian manufacturing sector. *Social Responsibility Journal, 20*(4), 783–803. https://doi.org/10.1108/SRJ-06-2023-0332

Alemu, B. A. (2025). Cultivating a culture of sustainability: The role of organizational values and leadership in driving sustainable practices. *Business Ethics and Leadership, 9*(1), 79–94. https://doi.org/10.61093/bel.9(1).79-94.2025

Al Jazeera. (2025, September 21). *'Restart from scratch': Flood-hit Indian farmers look at swelling losses.* https://www.aljazeera.com/features/2025/9/22/restart-from-scratch-flood-hit-indian-farmers-look-at-swelling-losses

Alsaggaf, H. A. (2025). When green is not clean: A synthesis of evidence on greenwashing and consumer trust. *International Journal of Advanced and Applied Sciences, 12*(7), 211–220. https://doi.org/10.21833/ijaas.2025.07.021

Apple Inc. (2025, April). *2025 environmental progress report.* https://www.apple.com/environment/pdf/Apple_Environmental_Progress_Report_2025.pdf

Assoratgoon, W., & Kantabutra, S. (2023). Toward a sustainability organizational culture model. *Journal of Cleaner Production, 400*, 136666. https://doi.org/10.1016/j.jclepro.2023.136666

Bai, F., Shang, M., & Huang, Y. (2024). Corporate culture and ESG performance: Empirical evidence from China. *Journal of Cleaner Production, 437*, 140732. https://doi.org/10.1016/j.jclepro.2024.140732

BBC News. (2024a, February 3). *Chile forest fires: More than 100 dead in Valparaíso region.* https://www.bbc.com/news/world-latin-america-68196048

BBC News. (2024b, May 5). *Floods in Rio Grande do Sul exposed the climate crisis.* https://www.bbc.com/news/world-latin-america-68215354

Boeske, J. (2022). Leadership towards sustainability: A review of sustainable, sustainability, and environmental leadership. *Sustainability, 15*(16), 12626. https://doi.org/10.3390/su151612626

Copernicus. (2024). *Rio Grande do Sul flooding, Brazil, April to June 2024.* https://global-flood.emergency.copernicus.eu/news/170-Rio%20Grande%20do%20Sul%20Flooding,%20Brazil%20-%20April%20to%20June%202024/

Deci, E. L., & Ryan, R. M. (2000). The "what" and "why" of goal pursuits: Human needs and the self-determination of behavior. *Psychological Inquiry, 11*(4), 227–268.

EOS Data. (2024). *Mozambique, Malawi, Spain, Hungary, Afghanistan-Pakistan disasters (multiple reports by EOS data analytics).* https://eos.com/blog/disaster-monitoring-earth-observation/

European Commission, Joint Research Centre (JRC), and the Netherlands Environmental Assessment Agency (PBL). (2025). *EDGAR, emissions database for global atmospheric research.* https://edgar.jrc.ec.europa.eu/

Fietz, B., & Günther, E. (2021). Changing organizational culture to establish sustainability. *Control Manag Rev, 65*, 32–40. https://doi.org/10.1007/s12176-021-0379-4

Freeman, R. E. (2023). Stakeholder approaches to corporate sustainability. In A. Rasche, M. Morsing, J. Moon, & A. Kourula (Eds.), *Corporate sustainability:*

Managing responsible business in a globalised world (2nd ed., pp. 75–95). Cambridge University Press.

Hameed, Z., Naeem, R. M., Misra, P., Chotia, V., & Malibari, A. (2023). Ethical leadership and environmental performance: The role of green IT capital, green technology innovation, and technological orientation. *Technological Forecasting and Social Change*, *194*, 122739. https://doi.org/10.1016/j.techfore.2023.122739

Herold, D. M. (2018). Demystifying the link between institutional theory and stakeholder theory in sustainability reporting. *Economics, Management and Sustainability*, *3*(2), 6–19. https://doi.org/10.14254/jems.2018.3-2.1

IKEA. (2024). *Our climate agenda: Net zero and beyond.* https://www.ikea.com/global/en/our-business/sustainability/our-climate-agenda/

Infosys. (2025). *ESG report 2024–25*. Infosys Limited. Available at: https://www.infosys.com/about/esg/reports/2024-25.html

InsideClimateNews. (2025, June 30). *As sea levels rise, an island nation creates an escape plan.* https://insideclimatenews.org/news/01072025/todays-climate-rising-seas-migration-displacement/

Insurance Bureau of Canada. (2025). *Climate change risks and insurance industry response*. https://www.ibc.ca

International Energy Agency (IEA). (2025). *Global energy review 2025*. https://www.iea.org/reports/global-energy-review-2025

ITC Limited. (2025). *ITC sustainability report 2024-25*. https://itcportal.com/content/dam/itc-corporate/pdfs/sustainability-report/itc-sustainability-report-2025.pdf

Jaganjac, B., Zekanović-Korona, A., & Slišković, A. (2025). The role of organizational culture and structure in implementing sustainability initiatives. *Business Ethics: A European Review*. https://doi.org/10.1111/beer.12710

Ketprapakorn, N., & Kantabutra, S. (2022). Toward an organizational theory of sustainability culture. *Sustainable Production and Consumption*, *32*, 638–654. https://doi.org/10.1016/j.spc.2022.05.020

Leoni, L. (2025). Integrating ESG and organisational resilience through system theory: The ESGOR matrix. *Management Decision*, *63*(2), 401–422. https://doi.org/10.1108/MD-10-2023-1924

Liao, Y. (2022). Sustainable leadership: A literature review and prospects for future research. *Frontiers in Psychology*, *13*, 1045570. https://doi.org/10.3389/fpsyg.2022.1045570

Lin, Z. (2024). Does ESG performance indicate corporate economic sustainability? Evidence based on the sustainable growth rate. *Borsa Istanbul Review*, *24*(3), 485–493. https://doi.org/10.1016/j.bir.2024.02.010

Mahindra and Mahindra Ltd. (2025). *Planet positive 2025 sustainability report*. https://www.mahindra.com/sites/default/files/2025-07/Mahindra-and-Mahindra-Sustainability-Report-2025.pdf

Martiny, A., Taglialatela, J., Testa, F., & Iraldo, F. (2024). Determinants of environmental social and governance (ESG) performance: A systematic literature review. *Journal of Cleaner Production*, *456*, 142213. https://doi.org/10.1016/j.jclepro.2024.142213

Microsoft. (2025). *2025 environmental sustainability report*. Microsoft Corporation. https://www.microsoft.com/en-us/corporate-responsibility/sustainability/report/

Ministry of Micro, Small and Medium Enterprises. (2024). *MSME annual report and policies*. https://msme.gov.in

Negi, P. S., & Dangwal, R. C. (2019). Organisational sustainability through culture and managerial effectiveness: An Indian perspective. *Journal of Entrepreneurship and Innovation in Emerging Economies*, *5*(1), 22–36. https://doi.org/10.1177/2393957518812529

Redvers, N., Wright, K., Hartmann-Boyce, J., & Tonkin-Crine, S. (2025). Planetary health for health systems: A scoping review and content analysis of frameworks. *PLOS Global Public Health*, *5*(6), e0004710. https://doi.org/10.1371/journal.pgph.0004710

ReliefWeb. (2024, February 5). *Chile wildfires: Hundreds missing as thousands of homes destroyed.* https://reliefweb.int/report/chile/unicef-chile-humanitarian-flash-report-no2-wildfires-07-march-2024

ReliefWeb. (2024, September 19). *Brazil: Floods in Rio Grande do Sul, United Nations situation report.* https://reliefweb.int/report/brazil/brazil-floods-rio-grande-do-sul-united-nations-situation-report-20-september-2024

ReliefWeb. (2025). *Punjab floods: Secondary data analysis report.* https://reliefweb.int/report/india/punjab-floods-secondary-data-analysis-report-september-2025

Reuters. (2024, September 28). *Vietnam estimates damages of $3.31 bln from Typhoon Yagi.* https://www.reuters.com/world/asia-pacific/vietnam-estimates-damages-331-bln-typhoon-yagi-2024-09-28/

Sajjad, A., Eweje, G., & Raziq, M. M. (2024). Sustainability leadership: An integrative review and conceptual synthesis. *Business Strategy and the Environment*, *33*(4), 2849–2867. https://doi.org/10.1002/bse.3631

Securities and Exchange Board of India. (2025). *SEBI, regulating the securities market in India.* https://www.sebi.gov.in

Sphere India JRNA. (2024). *Cyclone Remal impact in West Bengal and Bangladesh.* https://sphereindia.org.in/sites/default/files/2024-08/SI_Sitrep-5__Wayanad_Landslide_26-08-2024.pdf

Sphere India. (2024). *Preliminary assessment report – Wayanad landslides, Kerala, August.* https://www.sphereindia.org.in/sites/default/files/2024-08/Wayanad%20Preliminary%20Assessment%20Report%20Aug%202024.pdf

Suieubayeva, S., Sánchez-García, E., Martínez-Falcó, J., Marco-Lajara, B., Sadenova, A., & Montalvo-Falcón, J. V. (2025). Green leaders and global change: Uncovering the drivers of corporate environmental sustainability. *Environmental Development*, *54*, 101148. https://doi.org/10.1016/j.envdev.2025.101148

Supply Chain Digital. (2022, December 5). *Inside Patagonia's supply chain sustainability reform.* https://supplychaindigital.com/news/patagonia-supply-chain-sustainability-reform

Tanveer, M., Din, M. U., Khan, M. F., Almurad, H. M., & Hasnin, E. A. H. (2025). Unleashing the power of green HR: How embracing a green culture drives environmental sustainability. *Environmental and Sustainability Indicators*, *26*, 100657. https://doi.org/10.1016/j.indic.2025.100657

Tata Group/Tata Power. (2025). Embracing the planet — Aalingana: Tata's sustainability vision. *Tata.* https://www.tata.com/newsroom/business/embracing-planet-future-sustainability-aalingana

UNDP. (2024). *Viet Nam multi-sector assessment (VMSA) report, December.* https://www.undp.org/sites/g/files/zskgke326/files/2024-12/vmsa_final.pdf

Unilever. (2024). *Climate strategy and progress.* https://www.unilever.com/sustainability/climate/

United Nations Brazil. (2025). *Climate action and sustainable development initiatives.* https://brazil.un.org

United States Environmental Protection Agency (EPA). (2025). *Annual environmental report 2025.* https://www.epa.gov/

UN News. (2024). *Afghanistan and Pakistan floods, humanitarian updates.* https://news.un.org/en/tags/floods

Vision IAS. (2025). *Publications and policy briefs relevant to sustainability.* https://www.visionias.in

Vision IAS. (2025, September 4). *Punjab floods 2025: Analysis of the worst disaster in decades.* https://www.visionias.in/blog/current-affairs/punjab-floods-2025-analysis-of-the-worst-disaster-in-decades

Wipro. (2025). *Sustainability report FY 2024-2025.* Wipro Ltd. https://www.wipro.com/content/dam/nexus/en/sustainability/sustainability_reports/wipro-sustainability-report-fy-2024-2025.pdf

Workman, A., LiberaMarchiori, G. D., Boateng, G., Carlin, S., Friel, S., Moo, E., Patrick, R., San MartimPortes, A., Warner, R., & Bowen, K. (2025). Securing a just and healthy future for all: Bringing a planetary health lens to the Earth System Governance research framework. *Earth System Governance*, *24*, 100250. https://doi.org/10.1016/j.esg.2025.100250

Younis, Z., & Hussain, S. (2023). Green transformational leadership: Bridging the gap between green HRM practices and environmental performance through green psychological climate. *Sustainable Futures*, *6*, 100140. https://doi.org/10.1016/j.sftr.2023.100140

Zhao, C., Wang, Z., Tang, Y., & Yang, F. (2025). ESG performance, green technology innovation, and corporate value: Evidence from industrial listed companies. *Alexandria Engineering Journal*, *123*, 369–380. https://doi.org/10.1016/j.aej.2025.03.097

Zhu, J., Zhi, W., & Fang, Y. (2025). Ethical leadership, organizational learning, and corporate ESG performance: A moderated mediation model. *International Review of Economics & Finance*, *98*, 103966. https://doi.org/10.1016/j.iref.2025.103966

Chapter 5

A Thirty-Year Bibliometric Assessment of Restoring Ecosystems Through Ecological Governance

Vishal Sood[a], *Namita Rath*[a], *Swati Sood*[b], *Rushil Varma*[c] *and Alok Kumar Sahai*[d]

[a]Sri Sri University, India
[b]BIITM, India
[c]BBD University, India
[d]AS Investment Consultancy, India

Abstract

This study integrates intellectual, conceptual, and collaborative frameworks that developed ecological governance for ecosystem restoration from 1995 to 2025. It contrasts command-and-control conservation with participatory, flexible, multi-level governance. Research on key academic contributions, institutional links, and developing thematic goals shows that governance-driven restoration rhetoric is socio-political and ecological. This synthesis helps create socio-ecological resilience frameworks and explains governance system motivations, difficulties, and opportunities. The study examines 379 Scopus-indexed papers spanning 1995–2005 (13), 2005–2015 (37), and 2015–2025 (329). A hybrid bibliometric method combines qualitative scientific mapping and quantitative performance analysis using R Bibliometric and VOS Viewer. Publishing patterns, author production, journal impact, co-authorship, co-citation, and keyword co-occurrence networks reveal the discipline's intellectual, conceptual, and social foundations. Early studies concentrated on regulatory frameworks and conservation governance; subsequent studies emphasized multi-stakeholder engagement, decentralized decision-making, and socio-ecological resilience. In the final step, ecology, political science, and development studies collaborated to create adaptive and regenerative governance models. These models involve

Regenerative Revolution, 97–113

doi:10.1108/978-1-80686-859-920261005

ecological knowledge, policy improvement, and community governance. Governance fragmentation has become a global, cross-regional ecological restoration. This study provides a comprehensive bibliometric evaluation of theoretical, methodological, and collaborative changes over the past three decades to help researchers, policymakers, and practitioners create inclusive and resilient governance frameworks to address future environmental and social issues.

Keywords: Ecosystem; restoring; governance; bibliometric assessment; R package

JEL Number: Q20; Q50; Q56; C89; C80

1. Introduction

Ecological deterioration has spread globally over the past 30 years. Thus, scholars, government agencies, and international organizations are exploring novel ecosystem management methods for restoration. Human activities, including deforestation, land degradation, climate change, and industrialization, impact ecosystems. Top-down government should be replaced with inclusive, flexible, and regenerative governance to protect ecosystems (Armitage et al., 2009; Ostrom, 1990). A bibliometric analysis of research from 1995 to 2025 shows significant ecological governance changes. The study depicts how the older corporate model, which utilized plenty of resources and didn't safeguard them, is becoming more holistic and regenerative. Growth, recycling, mending, and blending nature and human activities need cooperation. This suggests rethinking environmental management to make restoration simpler (Folke et al., 2005; Redman, 2004). The initial command-and-control style of ecological governance centered on obeying rules, adopting conservation laws, and enforcing them (Holling & Meffe, 1996). Academics were initially interested in the issue, as Scopus discovered 13 works from 1995 to 2005.

The study focused on environmental policy instruments, biodiversity loss, and protection (Jordan et al., 2003; Young, 2002). It was simpler socially and politically than in later years. In the 2005–2015 second phase, 37 publications discussed methodologies and theoretical frameworks. A full bibliometric analysis was done in R and VOS viewer. Researchers have incorporated multi-level governance, participatory methods, and stakeholder engagement (Lemos & Agrawal, 2006; Huitema et al., 2009). Ecological governance has gained significance as state officials, NGOs, and indigenous communities pursue a compromise (Cash et al., 2006). Transdisciplinary emerged by integrating political ecology, environmental sociology, and resilience thinking (Adger, 2003; Walker & Salt, 2006). Between 2015 and 2025, the number of scholarly papers rose to 329. The UN Sustainable Development Goals (SDGs), the Paris Climate Agreement, and the Post-2020 Biodiversity Framework are gaining increased recognition.

The use of R in conjunction with VOS viewer facilitated a detailed analysis of co-authorship networks, keyword co-occurrences, and the evolution of topics. Adaptive and regenerative governance is characterized by decentralized decision-making, community stewardship, and the co-production of knowledge (Chaffin et al., 2014; Pereira et al., 2020). Researchers emphasized system-wide resilience strategies, such as social learning and collaborative experimentation, over individual ecological solutions (Biggs et al., 2015; Reed et al., 2010). Bibliometric data indicate a growing collaboration among the fields of ecology, political science, law, and development studies. Knowledge generation is increasingly diversified, with researchers from the Asia-Pacific, North America, and Europe engaging in global discourses (Evans & Cvitanovic, 2018). Co-authorship statistics indicate that international collaboration rose from 7.4% from 2005 to 2015 to 33.13% from 2015 to 2025. The study of ecological governance is gaining global prominence. The Chinese Academy of Sciences, the University of Queensland, and James Cook University serve as significant academic institutions.

The systematic epistemology and ontology of restoring ecosystems. Originally, "restoration" meant reviving species and mending soil (Bradshaw, 1997). Socio-ecological resilience, justice, and indigenous knowledge are modern understandings (Miller et al., 2012; Tengö, 2014). Governance involves compromises from many stakeholders with different interests and viewpoints (Bulkeley et al., 2012; Djalante, 2012). Local, regional, and global institutions must coordinate dynamically for ecological governance (Galaz et al., 2012; Berkes, 2017). SDGs 13 (Climate Action), 15 (Life on Land), and 17 (Partnerships for the Goals) require integrated frameworks. Global links improve multidisciplinary research. This research is unique in its tri-phasic bibliometric data analysis across three decades. Performance measures like yearly growth rate, citation averages, and authorship trends may be used with scientific mapping approaches like co-citation and keyword clusters to explore subject structure and themes. Head (2010) and Plummer et al. (2012) claim that ecosystem restoration governance has moved from fragmented environmental rules to coordinated ecological revitalization.

This study is strengthened by qualitative and quantitative bibliometrics. Intellectual landscapes are empirically described using factorial analyses, Lotka's and Bradford's laws, and country-specific cooperation matrices. Factorial maps and dendrograms show conflicting groups around "biodiversity," "climate change," "adaptive governance," and "community engagement," emphasizing intersectionality in modern research. This growing literature suggests normative shifts and justice are becoming an ethical need for ecological governance (Borie, 2020; Temper et al., 2018). Ecological restoration needs integrative governance to address environmental equality, ecosystem service access, and marginalized community rights. This study examines the history of ecological governance and lays the groundwork for future research and policy. The VOS viewer and R package provide bibliometric analysis of literature trends, collaborations, and gaps. The restricted capabilities of the R package made analyzing data from 1995 to 2005 difficult, indicating a lack of development. However, after 2005, the field grew, demonstrating that academia was equipped to address complex global ecological issues.

1.1 Research Question

- What are the changes in academic discourse regarding ecological governance and ecosystem restoration from 1995 to 2025?
- How have knowledge networks and ecological governance frameworks influenced collaboration?
- What impact have the SDGs and the Decade on Ecosystem Restoration had on research in ecosystem governance?

1.2 Research Objective

- Research on ecosystem restoration through ecological governance will be examined for trends, topics, and conceptual frameworks from 1995 to 2025.
- Use the R package and VOS viewer to analyze global academic collaboration, author productivity, keyword co-occurrence, and institutional engagement across three time periods.
- Evaluate academic research's reaction to global environmental frameworks and governance developments for theoretical convergence, methodological progress, and regional discrepancies.

2. Literature Review

Political philosophy, ecology, and institutions form a complex ecological governance framework. Both theoretical and empirical studies have advanced since 2005. This literature review covers stakeholder involvement, institutional design, socio-ecological resilience, adaptive governance, and transdisciplinary integration. Tengö (2014) and Miller et al. (2012) recommend supporting scientific methods with indigenous and local knowledge. Many epistemic frames and restoration options are possible with co-production. International frameworks and multilateral environmental agreements impact local ecological governance, as claimed by Gupta and Lebel (2010). Temper et al. (2018) and Borie (2020) endorsed environmental justice frameworks. Cohen-Shacham et al. (2016) advocated nature-based regenerative governance. GIS and bibliometrics guide government evaluations. The R bibliometric package by Aria and Cuccurullo (2017) and the VOS viewer by Van Eck and Waltman (2010) are essential for studying ecological governance research trends and network topology. The literature suggests that networked, participative, and flexible frameworks are replacing ecological complexity and social variation. Bibliometric analysis uses ecosystem restoration governance approaches. Environmental governance literature has changed toward multi-scale, justice-oriented, and data-driven frameworks, improving theory and practice. Scholars have rethought adaptive governance and resilience theory due to social, historical, and institutional complexity. Garmestani et al. (2023) state that adaptive governance must include geographical and temporal dynamics. Panarchy allows multiscale adaptive management to integrate ecological feedback with institutional flexibility. Hocherman et al. (2025) recommended governance "time lags," citing ecological, decision, and implementation delays as key elements in adaptive evolution or destructive lock-ins. Governance system design demands new temporal literacy since this research shows governance processes occur across periods and institutions. Another change is hybrid and state-reinforced governance. The State-Reinforced Self-Governance (SRSG) model of DeCaro et al. (2025) builds institutional capacity to encourage local adaptive networks. This hybridization indicates that decentralized governance requires state legitimacy, infrastructure, and enforcement. Deslatte et al. (2024) found that "state-reinforced knowledge infrastructures" increase adaptive capacity in urban water systems by combining central policy learning with local experimentation. These essays suggest that governments should foster decentralized and polycentric ecological management rather than retreat. Justice and equality are emphasized in ecological governance discussions. Newer studies highlight inclusive governance and transformative justice for legal environmental decision-making, drawing on Temper et al. (2018) and Borie (2020). González-Rodríguez et al. (2025) discuss the rising significance of local communities, NGOs, and digital monitoring technologies in Amazonian environmental governance. These networks relate institutional diversity to environmental justice to redress past power and knowledge production inequalities. Zhou et al. (2025) concluded that dispersed responsibility, open decision-making, and inclusive involvement are crucial for regional, vertical, and horizontal collaborative water management in China's River Chief System.

New theoretical frameworks and empirical approaches are making ecological governance transdisciplinary. Van Assche et al. (2022) discovered learning and feedback loops in governance institutions and ecosystems in adaptive governance from an organizational perspective. Carr Kelman et al. (2023) found that trust, shared vision, and conflict resolution drove governance success across social-ecological systems. Our results support Dietz et al. (2003) and Pahl-Wostl et al. (2007), demonstrating the importance of participatory discussion and its institutional framework. Additionally, Caporally's (2023) adaptive water governance research reveals that power differences, not incompetence or ignorance, influence governance results' inclusiveness and durability. New environmental policy term: nature-based solutions. Turner et al. (2022) related NbS to socio-ecological resilience and adaptability. NbS-based governance systems featured more diverse stakeholders, ecological connectivity, and adaptive learning. Relational, regenerative ecological governance that incorporates environmental and human development is suggested (Cohen-Shacham et al., 2016). Wang et al. (2025) theorized ecosystems as products of nature and labor and argued that market dynamics and policy innovation may drive long-term ecological change with a solid institutional design.

Geospatial and bibliometrics have changed ecological governance. New meta-analyses (e.g., Wood, 2025) have extended Aria and Cuccurullo (2017) and

Van Eck and Waltman (2010) to map environmental governance research theory. Interdisciplinary citation networks have grown in information integration, adaptive governance, justice, resilience, and institutional design since 2020. The progress, weaknesses, and policy significance of governance studies can be assessed using this methodological extension, which represents the field's expanding openness and reflexivity. Ecological governance prioritizes co-production, long-term flexibility, and equality. In terms of institutional efficiency, Zhou et al., (2025) and Valentinov et al. (2022) recommend variety, redundancy, and reflexivity over rigorous optimization. Our dominance over ecosystems is giving way to co-evolution as systems science, justice ethics, and governance theory intersect. In its third decade of empirical maturity, ecological governance studies suggest hybrid institutional designs that combine decentralization with state scaffolding, account for temporal complexity, and highlight inclusive, justice-driven resilience.

3. Research Gap

Ecological governance and restoration literature has grown over the past 30 years, yet gaps persist. Unknown is governance institutions' temporal and geographical response to ecological degradation. Community involvement, decentralization, and adaptive management research need a bibliometric synthesis of intellectual, conceptual, and collaborative efforts. The literature on ecosystem restoration was minimal from 1995 to 2005, indicating a focus on either ecological or technological aspects. The lack of publications hampers quantitative R package processing analysis and promotes transdisciplinary collaboration and worldwide policy alignment. Governance restoration research needs bibliometrics. Science mapping employs VOS viewer and R, although temporal comparisons are uncommon. This methodological gap inhibits research, collaboration, and knowledge system understanding. Political institutions and environmental science dominate ecological governance research, which fails to integrate these disciplines to comprehend governance as a socio-ecological system. Environmental policy has emphasized ecosystem restoration from 2015, along with the SDGs and the Decade on Ecosystem Restoration (2021–2030). Governance models' move from regulatory conservation to participatory, regenerative, and adaptive systems that meet global objectives has been rarely studied. China, the United States, and Australia have produced huge research outputs in recent decades, whereas Africa, South America, and South Asia, despite ecological vulnerabilities, have contributed little. Global governance discourse challenges epistemic dominance and inclusivity. Governance and ecological restoration are seldom bibliometrically investigated. Transdisciplinary ecological governance and ecosystem restoration literature lacks a structural and thematic evolutionary framework, as demonstrated by this research. Indigenous knowledge, traditional ecological practices, and community-led governance are often overlooked in mainstream bibliometrics, leading to an epistemic vacuum. Regenerative environmental governance requires non-academic activity. Despite scientometric studies on publication counts, citation scores, and co-authorship networks, governance conceptualization, policy-research links, and stakeholder involvement in ecological restoration research are understudied. A 1995–2025 longitudinal bibliometric framework utilizing R and VOS viewer addresses gaps except for 1995–2005, when data constraints required VOS viewer.

4. Research Methodology

This study, covering the period from 1995 to 2025, employs scientometric and bibliographic methods to analyze academic research on ecological governance and ecosystem restoration through both quantitative and qualitative bibliometrics. The analysis incorporates 379 Scopus-indexed sources spanning three periods: 13 sources from 1995 to 2005, 37 from 2005 to 2015, and 329 from 2015 to 2025. The terminology of ecological governance and ecosystem restoration was analyzed. VOS viewer was the sole tool employed for analyzing co-authorship and keyword networks, given the constraints of the 1995–2005 dataset. Since 2005, R (bibliometrix) and VOS viewer have facilitated enhanced analysis. The study utilized data provided by R on annual growth, h-index, citation metrics, author impact, and journal output. Scientific maps of co-citation patterns, keyword clusters, and theme trends were generated using VOS viewer. The study employed Lotka's Law to assess publication output, citation impact, and author influence. The intellectual, social, and conceptual structure of the field is defined by institutional ties, co-authorship, and multinational partnerships. Thematic evolution identified key themes such as "adaptive governance," "climate change," and "community participation." China, the United States, and Australia led global donations, while South America and Sub-Saharan Africa fell behind. The study investigated the ethics of data usage and open-source analytics regarding transparency and replicability.

5. Result and Analysis

The bibliometric rise of ecological governance and ecosystem restoration literature during the previous two decades compares publishing metrics from 2005–2015 and 2015–2025, removing 1995–2005 owing to a few publications. Governance-driven ecological restoration research increased from 37 papers (2005–2015) to 329 (2015–2025), aligning with the 2015 UN Sustainable Development Goals and the 2021–2030 UN Decade on Ecosystem Restoration. Research on environmental rejuvenation governance rose from 6.5% to 13.22%. Relevance increased when the document age was reduced from 13.3 to 3 years. The number of writers increased from 239 to 3,008. Solo efforts gave way to multi-university and multinational cooperation, increasing co-authorship per publication from 4.81 to 10.7. Global co-authorship increased from 7.4% to 33.13%, emphasizing ecological governance information exchange across regions. Phase 2 involves more systematic reviews, transdisciplinary analysis, and policy research. After 2015, 27 publications were released in 2020 and 2021, more than twice the 13 in 2015. This increase supports the Paris Agreement and nature-based policies. The calculation undertaken in the study reveals an exponential publication increase, and post-2015 rises reflect better research and governance for global ecological issues.

The research outcome illustrates Lotka's Law regarding author productivity for the periods 2005–2015 and 2015–2025. Lotka's Law, a bibliometric principle, indicates that most authors publish a single work, while a small fraction produces multiple publications. This regulation improves the focus and distribution of scholarly contributions. Table 5.1 provides data supporting Lotka's Law in the realm of ecological governance and ecosystem restoration research. From 2005 to 2015, 221 authors (92.5%) authored one work, 15 writers (6.3%) authored two, and three writers (1.3%) authored three. From 2015 to 2025, 2,742 writers (91.2%) produced one article, while others contributed less as the number of publications rose. In this timeframe, one author generated 10 articles. This suggests that research on ecological governance has considerable author dispersion and a restricted number of prolific authors, despite a notable rise in productivity. It also illustrates the author's production over time to substantiate this claim. Many scholars contribute insignificantly to the steep slope, whereas a handful of prolific authors dominate. This biased distribution signifies a growing openness in the subject, promoting multidisciplinary cooperation among academics. The absence of thought leaders may signify either an advantage or a disadvantage. It fosters innovation and knowledge dissemination; however, it may impede the advancement of theoretical frameworks. The literature emphasizes participatory and adaptive governance, highlighting the expansion and decentralization of the field. This study evaluates bibliometric concentration and illustrates the collaboration and dissemination of ecological governance discourse through the application of Lotka's Law.

Bradford's Law was used to analyze ecological governance and ecosystem restoration journal sources from 2005 to 2015 and 2015 to 2025. It divides journals by publication frequency into core, related, and peripheral production zones. The analyzes shows that certain renowned journals publish the most relevant articles more frequently than others. Zone 1, the primary sources, published 18 articles between 2005 and 2015: 12 in Environmental Management and six in PLOS ONE. These two studies started ecological restoration governance talks. AMBIO, Conservation Biology, and the Journal of Environmental Management published four to five articles from 39 Zone two investigations. Peer J and PNAS each contributed two items to Zone 3, indicating specialized but necessary distribution. The number and concentration of core source articles rose between 2015 and 2025, changing bibliometrics. Science of the Total Environment (31), Environmental Science and Pollution Research (15), Scientific Reports (15), and Global Change Biology (13) trailed the Journal of Environmental Management (46) in Zone 1. Five periodicals with 120 articles compiled from various sources. Zone 2 supports ecology and public health through the International Journal of Environmental Research and Public Health, Integrated Environmental Assessment and Management, and Ecological Applications. Bradford-like zone model with a sharp starting curve (Zone 1's concentrated

Table 5.1. Represents Authors, Country, Document and Keyword Calculations Drawn Using R Package.

Year 1995–2005			**Year 2005–2015**					**Year 2015–2025**				
Author	**Cluster**	**Document**	**Author**	**Year**	**Freq**	**TC**	**TCpY**	**Author**	**Year**	**freq**	**TC**	**TCpY**
Barbiero, Richard	1	1	Yin R	2010	3	0	0	Wang X	2024	9	0	0
Basu, Ilora	1	1	Burger J	2007	2	0	0	Liu Y	2024	5	0	0
Baumann, Paul C	1	1	Daily GC	2015	2	0	0	Wang Y	2024	4	0	0
Organization	*C*	*D*	*Organization*	*Articles*	*Keywords*	*Occurrences*	*Country's publication*	*Organization*	*Articles*	*Keywords*	*Occurrences*	*Country's publication*
Aristotle University of Thessaloniki	1	1	Stanford University	10	Ecosystem	35	China (38)	Chinese Academy of Sciences	82	Ecosystem	192	China (1347)
Central Drug Research Institute (CDRI)	2	1	Institute of Zoology	7	China	21	USA (30)	University of Chinese Academy of Sciences	62	China	96	USA (478)
Department of Ecology and Evolution,	3	1	Fujian Normal University	6	Conservation of Natural Resources	16	Australia (13)	Beijing Forestry University	49	Conservation of Natural Resources	79	Australia (463)

Source: Author's Own Creation.

output) and a gradual leveling in Zones two and 3. This supports Bradford's Law and its concentration on premier journals that publish scientific, policy, and management research that is changing environmental governance.

5.1 Authors Analysis

Table 5.1 illustrates author contributions and collaboration in ecological governance and ecosystem restoration from 1995 to 2005, 2005 to 2015, and 2015 to 2025, respectively. These graphs show how author clusters and publication frequency have grown as the field shifted from individual authors to large-scale, interdisciplinary collaborations. Only 13 publications had limited author networks. Richard Barbiero, Ilora Basu, Paul C. Baumann, Gavin Christie, and Stephen Smith published a single book. The network displays a disconnected co-author network with minimal clustering. Early ecological governance was led by academics or small, scattered organizations without a scientific community. Regional or descriptive studies depend on traditional environmental management instead of integrated governance. Between 2005 and 2015, author frequency and collaboration increased. Academic consolidation began with 37 articles during this decade. The dataset often includes field contributors Yin R, Burger J, Daily GC, and Feldman MW. More related author nodes reflect global and institutional cooperation. Co-authorship is becoming more prevalent as ecological governance integrates policy research, ecology, environmental law, and community development. Active governance, adaptive management, and resilience theory have expanded the literature. Table 5.1 represents the most notable shift from 2015 to 2025, with Wang X, Liu Y, Wang Y, Zhang Y, and Li J publishing more frequently, increasing their publication records. Table 5.1 highlights Wang X's decade-long increase with nine publications. The R package analysis indicates more co-authored articles, reflecting a larger research community. The networks generated by VOS viewer reveal a broad author network of renowned Chinese and international research groups. Common surnames reflect institutional expertise among Chinese organizations such as the Chinese Academy of Sciences. Global ecological governance, involving major worldwide coalitions, was also explored. Multidisciplinary and regional cooperation will be essential for research on climate governance, biodiversity recovery, environmental justice, and policy integration in the coming decade.

5.2 Organization's Analysis

Table 5.1 illustrates institutional involvement in ecological governance and ecosystem restoration research for the periods showing a limited initiation from 1995 to 2005, characterized by little institutional coordination. Contributors included Aristotle University of Thessaloniki, University of Wisconsin-Madison, University of Arizona, CDRI, and the Institute of Applied Ecology. Most institutions had a single publication and functioned independently, indicating decentralized research. The absence of institutional overlap indicates that ecological governance research was initially experimental before its establishment as an academic discipline. Alterations in the terrain occurred throughout the second decade. Table 5.1 illustrate that publication output and institutional engagement rose from 2005 to 2015. Stanford University (10 publications), Institute of Zoology (7), Fujian Normal University (6), University of Minnesota (6), and Chinese Academy of Sciences (5) were the primary contributors. Diversity among institutions globalizes ecological governance research. Chinese institutions provided substantial assistance, establishing the foundation for their impending dominance. The study illustrates that collaboration escalates with enhanced institutional connections and a greater number of organizational affiliations. Numerous universities and government-associated entities disseminated interdisciplinary research on adaptive governance, resilience, and environmental policy. Organizational productivity saw the most rapid rise from 2015 to 2025 (Table 5.1), where augmented, unified, and internationalized institutional participation was initiated. The Chinese Academy of Sciences has 82 publications, followed by the University of Chinese Academy of Sciences with 62, Beijing Forestry University with 49, and the Institute of Geographic Sciences and Natural Resources Research with 42. The Xinjiang Institute of Ecology and Geography, Lanzhou University, and the University of Queensland are other prominent institutions. China spearheads research in ecological governance with premier institutions. The results depict extensive interconnected networks around Chinese institutions, highlighting their worth in knowledge and cooperation. China emphasizes ecological civilization and sustainability, resulting in substantial academic output and global collaboration.

5.3 Keyword Analysis

The most common ecological governance and ecosystem restoration terms from 1995 to 2025, along with problem groups, are listed in Table 5.1. Research indicates growth in discipline-wide understanding, conceptual convergence, and expansion of topics. The Convention on Biological Diversity and SDG 15 (Life on Land) conservation goals require ecosystem restoration frameworks to incorporate biodiversity. About 56 instances of "restoration" support this focus. Other popular phrases include "climate change" (52), "governance" (46), "ecosystem services" (43), "conservation" (36), and "resilience" (33). Ecological restoration literature may be connected to climate adaptation, governance innovation, and sustainability research. The network shows the five VOS viewer-determined keyword co-occurrence categories. Thematic clusters illustrate ecological governance and transdisciplinary. The red cluster emphasizes institutional and participatory governance with "governance," "policy," and "stakeholders." The green cluster features "ecosystem services," "land use," and "biodiversity." A comprehensive, systems-oriented view links blue to resilience, adaptation, and "socio-ecological systems." In operational governance and execution, "management," "sustainability," and "decision-making" are yellow. The purple cluster links "climate change," "carbon," and "restoration ecology" to climate governance and mitigation. Environmental science, political ecology, and sustainable development are becoming increasingly interdisciplinary. The study shows research on individuals over time, as illustrated by the key ideas evolving in keywords such as "conservation," "management," and "habitat." From 2005 to 2015, the focus was on ecological services, resilience, participatory governance, stakeholder involvement, and socio-political recovery. From 2015 to 2025, terms like "governance," "restoration," and "sustainability" reflect the field's maturity and its connections to global policies. Environmental governance now encompasses health, business, and urban areas, as shown through theme mapping.

MCA and topic evolution mapping factorial analysis of 1995–2025 ecological governance and ecosystem restoration. Author keywords indicate conceptual structures and intellectual trends drawn out of the study. In MCA, factorial analysis clusters high-dimensional bibliometric data by topic affinity in two dimensions. These results demonstrate academic discourse continuity and uniqueness as conceptual concepts in this research area have altered, fragmented, and merged over 30 years. The study presents a 30-year factorial map with two colored clusters to clarify the themes. The first cluster includes biodiversity, restoration, ecological services, and land use. Habitat recovery, biophysical restoration, and conservation planning. Cluster 2: participation, sustainability, adaptation, and socio-political ecosystem management policy. The factorial proximity of ecological and governance systems demonstrates conceptual convergence. Merging demonstrates that attention is changing to "how to restore ecosystems" and "who decides and governs restoration efforts," including multi-stakeholder governance and policy frameworks in ecological interventions. From 2005 to 2015 factorial research topic organization varied tremendously over the span of 10 years. Resilience, community-based management, and ecosystem services integrate ecological science with participatory governance in the graphic. These ideas were still evolving, according to the map's phrase distribution. Decentralized adaptability and socio-ecological systems have semi-independent subfields and interdisciplinary convergence. The analysis also illustrates a more advanced 2015–2025 factorial. Recovery, governance, climate change, resilience, and sustainability. The restorative governance paradigm change is influenced by climate, institutional, and sustainability factors. Restoration may use governance for decision-making, adaptive management, and stakeholder participation. From 1995 to 2005, ecological services, resilience, and participatory governance dominated conservation and management. Future progress requires systems thinking, institutional pluralism, and local-global policy alignment. The field's shift from dispersed ecological studies to transdisciplinary inquiry is highlighted.

5.4 Country Analysis

Between 1995 and 2025, research on ecological governance and ecosystem restoration across countries indicates global trends in academic output, collaboration, and geographic distribution. Between 1995 and 2005, only 13 publications were released, indicating inconsistency in early research. The United States, Canada, Australia, and Greece led this period, primarily acting independently and with minimal international coordination or institutional involvement. Global cooperation increased between 2005 and 2015. The United States, Germany, Australia, China, and the United Kingdom made significant contributions. Institutions in Europe and North America have enhanced cross-regional co-authorship. Climate governance, decentralization, and international environmental accords have become more significant. This study included many stakeholder perspectives in ecological management frameworks. From 2015 to 2025, China produced the largest number of publications, followed by the United States, Australia, the United Kingdom, and India. The VOS viewer collaboration map identifies China, the United States, and Australia as knowledge hubs with robust international connections. China's "ecological civilization" plan and environmental research funding have facilitated its development. Australia collaborates with Asia and the Pacific on biodiversity and land restoration initiatives. Despite an increase in publications, India remains disconnected from global research networks and shows little international engagement. African and Latin American countries are inadequately represented in the field, leading to an epistemic disparity. There is a need for more inclusive global research frameworks. Academic output is regionally concentrated, making global information exchange crucial for ecological management.

6. Interpretation

A 1995–2025 bibliometric examination of ecosystem restoration via ecological governance shows academic specialization, issue variety, and worldwide cooperation. Ecology studies from 1995 to 2005 found little institutional or regional diversity. VOS viewer study showed fragmented networks and low co-authorship, revealing governance and repair disparities. Publications, international collaboration, and transdisciplinary topics, including ecological services, adaptive management, and stakeholder involvement, increased between 2005 and 2015. Co-authorship per document and Lotka's and Bradford's Laws distributions show a growing research foundation. China, Australia, and the US contributed significantly. Research on integrated climate change, resilience, and governance frameworks has increased since 2015. Thematic and factorial maps show that socio-ecological systems thinking is needed. Ecological function, governance, stakeholder engagement, climate adaptation, and sustainability transitions are crucial. Chinese authors and institutions represent environmental governance. National cooperation maps show that China, the US, the UK, and Australia dominate worldwide academic networks. The journals Environmental Management and Science of the Total Environment demonstrate multidisciplinary cooperation. Research shows that restoration studies need ecological governance. Global restoration difficulties are addressed using multi-scalar, participatory ecological research and institutional philosophy.

7. Conclusion

Ecological governance for ecosystem restoration is a complex, interdisciplinary, and globally interconnected knowledge topic, according to a bibliometric study. The post-2015 publishing boom stresses ecological problems and attracts scholars. Conservation literature emphasizes participatory governance, policy frameworks, and socio-ecological resilience. China, the US, and Australia funded research, legislation, and academic cooperation. The surge in co-authorship and transdisciplinary initiatives shows that ecological restoration requires multi-sector collaboration. Investigations of specific countries and their publications show worldwide inequities, emphasizing the need for more equitable academic engagement. From ecological elements to governance, legal frameworks, stakeholder participation, and institutional behavior, thematic and keyword studies shift. Restoration is both environmental and political. Recovery during this change requires ecological stewardship. The study uses bibliometric measurements, visualization tools, and longitudinal mapping to present a comprehensive summary and guide future research. The text emphasizes government leadership in ecosystem restoration throughout the UN Decade on Ecosystem Restoration, not only ecological research.

8. Suggestion

The bibliometric research offers various ecological governance alternatives for ecosystem restoration. Collaboration should include neglected regions, including Sub-Saharan Africa, Southeast Asia, and Latin America. These locations show ecological decline but are seldom studied due to institutional and linguistic barriers. Regional hubs and aid from the UN or development banks may address this issue. Second, keyword trends indicate conceptual maturity, although "adaptive management" and "resilience" need clearer definitions and implementations. Future studies on governance efficacy should be longitudinal. Third, multidisciplinary collaboration is essential. Ecological, legal, political, and Indigenous knowledge consortia should be promoted through academic publications and NGOs. Fourth, governance studies must emphasize equality, transparency, and sustainability and move from descriptive to normative. The rise of China represents a geopolitical imbalance. Emerging countries' cooperation and information sharing may promote industrial equality. Gray literature and community-driven documentation boost academic validity and inclusion. Use AI-powered content analysis in the VOS viewer to spot semantic trends. Academics and practitioners must collaborate to provide policy-relevant briefings, tools, and guidelines. A unified strategy improves domain inclusion, rigor, and effectiveness.

References

Adger, W. N. (2003). Social capital, collective action, and adaptation to climate change. *Economic Geography*, *79*(4), 387–404. https://doi.org/10.1111/j.1944-8287.2003.tb00220.x

Aria, M., & Cuccurullo, C. (2017). Bibliometrix: An R-tool for comprehensive science mapping analysis. *Journal of Informetrics*, *11*(4), 959–975. https://doi.org/10.1016/j.joi.2017.08.007

Armitage, D., Berkes, F., & Doubleday, N. (2009). *Adaptive co-management: Collaboration, learning, and multi-level governance*. UBC Press.

Berkes, F. (2017). *Environmental governance for the Anthropocene? Social-ecological systems, resilience, and co-management*. Routledge.

Biggs, R., Schlüter, M., & Schoon, M. L. (Eds.). (2015). *Principles for building resilience: Sustaining ecosystem services in social-ecological systems*. Cambridge University Press. https://doi.org/10.1017/cbo9781316014240

Borie, M. (2020). Transformative environmental governance for sustainability: A review of social-ecological systems theory and practice. *Environmental Science & Policy*, *112*, 1–9. https://doi.org/10.1016/j.envsci.2020.05.012

Bradshaw, A. D. (1997). Restoration of mined lands—Using natural processes. *Ecological Engineering*, *8*(4), 255–269. https://doi.org/10.1016/S0925-8574(97)00022-0

Bulkeley, H., Andonova, L. B., Betsill, M. M., Compagnon, D., Hale, T., Hoffmann, M., & VanDeveer, S. D. (2012). Governing climate change transnationally: Assessing the evidence from a database of sixty initiatives. *Environment and Planning C: Government and Policy*, *30*(4), 591–612. https://doi.org/10.1068/c11126

Caporally, S. (2023). Power dynamics and adaptive water governance: Revisiting inclusivity in participatory institutions. *Journal of Environmental Policy and Planning*, *25*(3), 389–405.

Carr Kelman, C., Reilly, K., & Hileman, J. (2023). Trust and collaboration in social-ecological governance networks. *Ecology and Society*, *28*(2), 45.

Cash, D. W., Adger, W. N., Berkes, F., Garden, P., Lebel, L., Olsson, P., Pritchard, L., & Young, O. (2006). Scale and cross-scale dynamics: Governance and information in a multilevel world. *Ecology and Society*, *11*(2). https://doi.org/10.5751/es-01759-110208

Chaffin, B. C., Gosnell, H., & Cosens, B. A. (2014). A decade of adaptive governance scholarship: Synthesis and future directions. *Ecology and Society*, *19*(3), 56. https://doi.org/10.5751/ES-06824-190356

Cohen-Shacham, E., Walters, G., Janzen, C., & Maginnis, S. (2016). *Nature-based solutions to address global societal challenges*. IUCN. https://doi.org/10.2305/IUCN.CH.2016.13.en

DeCaro, D. A., Chaffin, B. C., Schlager, E., Garmestani, A. S., & Ruhl, J. B. (2025). State-reinforced self-governance and institutional capacity for adaptive environmental management. *Global Environmental Change*, *84*, 102867.

Deslatte, A., Swann, W. L., & Feiock, R. C. (2024). State-reinforced knowledge infrastructures for adaptive governance in urban water systems. *Environmental Management*, *75*(2), 233–246.

Dietz, T., Ostrom, E., & Stern, P. C. (2003). The struggle to govern the commons. *Science*, *302*(5652), 1907–1912. https://doi.org/10.1126/science.1091015

Djalante, R. (2012). Review article: "Adaptive governance and resilience: The role of multi-stakeholder platforms in disaster risk reduction". *Natural Hazards and Earth System Sciences*, *12*(9), 2923–2942. https://doi.org/10.5194/nhess-12-2923-2012

Evans, M. C., & Cvitanovic, C. (2018). An introduction to achieving policy impact for early career researchers. *Palgrave Communications*, *4*(1), 88. https://doi.org/10.1057/s41599-018-0144-2

Folke, C., Hahn, T., Olsson, P., & Norberg, J. (2005). Adaptive governance of social-ecological systems. *Annual Review of Environment and Resources*, *30*(1), 441–473. https://doi.org/10.1146/annurev.energy.30.050504.144511

Galaz, V., Olsson, P., Hahn, T., Folke, C., & Svedin, U. (2012). The problem of fit among biophysical systems, environmental and resource regimes, and broader governance systems: Insights and emerging challenges. In O. R. Young, L. A. King, & H. Schroeder (Eds.), *Institutions and environmental change: Principal findings, applications, and research frontiers* (pp. 147–186). MIT Press.

Garmestani, A. S., Benson, M. H., & Gunderson, L. H. (2023). *Adaptive governance for a changing planet*. Cambridge University Press.

González-Rodríguez, M., Pereira, L. M., & Vieira, R. M. (2025). Decolonising environmental governance: Indigenous participation and digital monitoring in Amazonia. *Ecological Economics*, *216*, 108193.

Gupta, J., & Lebel, L. (2010). Access and allocation in earth system governance: Water and climate change compared. *International Environmental Agreements*, *10*(4), 377–395. https://doi.org/10.1007/s10784-010-9139-1

Head, B. W. (2010). Reconsidering evidence-based policy: Key issues and challenges. *Policy and Society*, *29*(2), 77–94. https://doi.org/10.1016/j.polsoc.2010.03.001

Hocherman, A., Kark, R., & Raveh, A. (2025). Temporal literacy in adaptive governance: Managing lag effects in ecological decision processes. *Environmental Science & Policy*, *153*, 54–67.

Holling, C. S., & Meffe, G. K. (1996). Command and control and the pathology of natural resource management. *Conservation Biology*, *10*(2), 328–337. https://doi.org/10.1046/j.1523-1739.1996.10020328.x

Huitema, D., Mostert, E., Egas, W., Moellenkamp, S., Pahl-Wostl, C., & Yalcin, R. (2009). Adaptive water governance: Assessing the institutional prescriptions of adaptive (co-) management from a governance perspective and defining a research agenda. *Ecology and Society*, *14*(1), 26. https://doi.org/10.5751/ES-02827-140126

Jordan, A., Wurzel, R. K. W., & Zito, A. R. (2003). 'New' instruments of environmental governance: Patterns and pathways of change. *Environmental Politics*, *12*(1), 1–24. https://doi.org/10.1080/714000665

Lemos, M. C., & Agrawal, A. (2006). Environmental governance. *Annual Review of Environment and Resources*, *31*(1), 297–325. https://doi.org/10.1146/annurev.energy.31.042605.135621

Miller, T. R., Minteer, B. A., & Malan, L. C. (2012). The new conservation debate: Ethical foundations, strategic trade-offs, and policy opportunities. *Biological Conservation*, *144*(3), 945–953. https://doi.org/10.1016/j.biocon.2010.04.001

Ostrom, E. (1990). *Governing the commons: The evolution of institutions for collective action*. Cambridge University Press. https://doi.org/10.1017/CBO9780511807763

Pahl-Wostl, C., Mostert, E., & Tàbara, J. D. (2007). The growing importance of social learning in water resources management and sustainability science. *Ecology and Society*, *12*(2), 24.

Pereira, L. M., Sitas, N., & Ravera, F. (2020). Building inclusive conservation futures: Integrating resilience and justice in environmental governance. *Sustainability Science*, *15*(3), 845–857.

Plummer, R., Armitage, D., & de Loë, R. (2012). Adaptive comanagement and its relationship to environmental governance. *Ecology and Society*, *17*(3), 29. https://doi.org/10.5751/ES-05383-180121

Redman, C. L. (2004). Resilience theory in archaeology. *American Anthropologist*, *106*(1), 70–77. https://doi.org/10.1525/aa.2005.107.1.070

Reed, M. S., Evely, A. C., Cundill, G., Fazey, I., Glass, J., Laing, A., & Stringer, L. C. (2010). What is social learning?. *Ecology and Society*, *15*(4), 1–10. https://doi.org/10.5751/ES-03564-1504r01

Temper, L., Walter, M., Rodriguez, I., Kothari, A., & Turhan, E. (2018). A perspective on radical transformations to sustainability: Resistances, movements and alternatives. *Sustainability Science*, *13*(3), 747–764. https://doi.org/10.1007/s11625-018-0543-8

Tengö, M. (2014). Connecting diverse knowledge systems for enhanced ecosystem governance: The multiple evidence base approach. *Ambio*, *43*(5), 579–591. https://doi.org/10.1007/s13280-014-0501-3

Turner, W. R., Brandon, K., & Brooks, T. M. (2022). Nature-based solutions for resilience and adaptive governance. *Environmental Research Letters*, *17*(4), 045002.

Valentinov, V., Van Assche, K., & Verschraegen, G. (2022). System theory and governance: Exploring redundancy and reflexivity in complex institutional environments. *Systems Research and Behavioral Science*, *39*(5), 857–869. https://doi.org/10.1002/sres.2882

Van Assche, K., Valentinov, V., & Verschraegen, G. (2022). Adaptive governance and feedback loops: Integrating organizational and ecological perspectives. *Sustainability*, *14*(21), 14200. https://doi.org/10.3390/su142114200

Van Eck, N. J., & Waltman, L. (2010). Software survey: VOSviewer, a computer program for bibliometric mapping. *Scientometrics*, *84*(2), 523–538. https://doi.org/10.1007/s11192-009-0146-3

Walker, B., & Salt, D. (2006). *Resilience thinking: Sustaining ecosystems and people in a changing world*. Island Press.

Wang, J., Zhang, X., & Liu, Y. (2025). Ecosystems as socio-economic systems: Institutional design for long-term ecological transformation. *Ecological Indicators*, *167*, 111947.

Wood, R. (2025). Meta-analysis of ecological governance research: Integrating bibliometric and geospatial analytics. *Environmental Science & Policy*, *156*, 203–214.

Young, O. R. (2002). *The institutional dimensions of environmental change: Fit, interplay, and scale*. MIT Press.

Zhou, L., Zhang, Q., & Li, H. (2025). Collaborative water governance in China's river chief system: Dispersed responsibility and participatory reform. *Environmental Policy and Governance*, *35*(1), 33–51. https://doi.org/10.1002/eet.2073

Chapter 6

Why Do We Need Industry 6.0? A Scientific Overview of the Underlying Tenets

Amrita Nandy[a,*] *and Md. Sahidur Rahman*[b,†]

[a]Bangladesh University of Professionals, Bangladesh
[b]University of Chittagong, Bangladesh

Abstract

Since the outbreak of the COVID-19 pandemic, global citizens have realized the buried significance of human–machine symbiosis (drawback of Industry 4.0) at each stage of trade and commerce, which has pronounced the era of Industry 5.0. Yet, a novel transformative force is on the verge as the present industrial revolution is facing challenges regarding attributes like a shortfall of regulatory concerns, misalignment between consumer expectations, and inadequate environmental standards. Besides, aiming innately at resource utilization, the doctrine of Industry 5.0 is reciprocally responsible for unseen environmental hardships and consequently fails to meet comprehensive sustainability parameters. By reconnoitring several secondary research studies ($n = 63$) from copious, well-recognized, and standardized databases, this qualitative investigation divulges the core values of the forthcoming industrial revolt. Our inspection first identifies insufficiencies or central pitfalls in current industrialization and later discusses the probable philosophy of the imminent industrial uprising or Industry 6.0. A group of experts' opinion has also been sought for further clarity on the review findings. Henceforth, with futuristic judgment, this chapter will provoke innovative thoughts, ideas, and actions to ensure its meaningful execution in the diverse business arena. Besides, this study advocates a

*https://orcid.org/0000-0001-5553-1632
†https://orcid.org/0000-0003-3665-8579

Regenerative Revolution, 115–134

doi:10.1108/978-1-80686-859-920261006

robust argument for redefining the sustainability themes for impending strategic inference. The authors additionally envision that the new industrial ambiance will reform consumer behaviors where consumers will be more cautious toward ethical or sustainability bounds and vice versa. Essentially, the literary work widens new arrays of investigation as well as pursues to alter the readers' traditional mindset from random automation.

Keywords: Industry 6.0; sustainability challenges; redefined sustainability; ethical responsive behavior; Delphi study

JEL Codes: 030; 031; 032; 033

1. Introduction

Industrial revolutions are, in general, recognized within the context of technological advancement (Neumann et al., 2021). Over decades, the first industrial revolution was framed as "steam-based powered generation", the latter was on "electric motorized mechanism", the third revolutionary wave fostered the adoption of "information technology", while the fourth industry emphasized "automation". The latest industrial age (Industry 5.0) is engrossed in human–machine symbiosis, where all humans, machines, and even products communicate with each other and contribute largely to sustainability issues (Bai et al., 2020). Eventually, each industrial revolt offers new revolutions through extended upgradation toward the industries that continue to propose sustainable goals to achieve (Garti et al., 2025).

Each phase of industrial revolt affects people's lives inevitably (Pasman & Behie, 2024), and thus managers in general need to play proactive roles to address both advantages and demerits that emerge consequently in order to leverage the market competition. For instance, the majority of researchers acknowledged that with mass productivity, I4.0 failed to recognize humanism in its domain (Shabur et al., 2025; Xu et al., 2021). Similarly, research of Neumann et al. (2021) proclaimed that discounting the human element from apiece production process was a significant pitfall of I4.0, where globally it generated an immense threat of job replacement irrespective of a company's geographical site (Ligarski et al., 2021). Under such a backdrop, it was imperative to inspect the modes of communication or aftermath of Industry 4.0 (Panter et al., 2024), which essentially influenced the European Commission to announce the fifth rebellion of the industry in the year 2020 (Garti et al., 2025).

Yet, regardless of its people-centricity, often experts interpreted that the senior management, like trustees, directors, and board members, choose to prioritize the ROI (Return on Investment) alongside maximizing shareholders' monetary worth rather than embracing the social-sustainability obligations of I5.0 (Karmaker et al., 2023). Numerous academics correspondingly explored that the trials of such intelligent technology are yet unclear in terms of sustainable development (Liu et al., 2024; Vacchi et al., 2024). Authors of this paper have, thus, projected the prospects of a succeeding industrial revolt to understand the transitory phase where stakeholders need to readjust business models, investing equally in human and digital advances, and realign strategies to remain competitive in an evolving market landscape. Additionally, this investigation underscores a vivid shift in stakeholders' mindset where sustainability and ethically driven value perceptions will govern each business experience.

2. Literature Review

2.1 The Philosophy of Industry 5.0

Evidently, the paradigm shift of Industry 4.0 to Industry 5.0 aimed to transit a smart, connected industry, where societal well-being is a fundamental consideration. Industry 5.0, or I5.0, in short epitomizes a harmonious blend of technological sophistication with human-oriented values (Leng et al., 2022) where every innovation is engrossed in public benefit rather than sheer technological upgradation (Antonaci et al., 2024). In particular, the outbreak of the COVID-19 pandemic has steered the world toward the next industrial revolution (Hassan et al., 2024) as effective data synchronizing under the aid of I4.0 was a huge challenge once the international supply chain became nearly standstill in that adversity (Ahmed et al., 2023). Universally, this contagion has been documented as the "1st global health catastrophe" in the digital ambiance where the healthcare industry tackled numbers of disruptions like high call volume of quality facilities, mounting medicine costs, deficiency of competent doctors and nurses (Raisa et al., 2025). Under such circumstances, Sarfraz et al. (2021) defended that abundant wizard of I5.0 delivered vital patient-oriented, tailored, and participatory treatments along with competency, security, which has successfully lessened the disease transmission blending plentiful advanced I4.0 skills including tele-medicine, and digitalized patients' data. Studies have further demonstrated the enormous intelligence of "Machine Learning (ML)" in accurate diagnosis, like analyzing medical images, interpreting electronic records to natural signs, together with transforming genetic data (Vindrola-Padres et al., 2021), whereas ML-based forecasting models of I5.0 can even predict similar man-made disasters in forthcoming days (Tuli et al., 2020). An astute investigation on aerobiology by Macrae et al. (2025) detected how modern know-how is implanting new societal practices after the pandemic recedes, where they questioned the future rational role of I5.0 to encounter extended shared goals for a benign and sustainable world.

2.1.1 Agility Versus Sustainability Concern of I5.0

By executing human-adjusted design, honoring user experiences, and empowering employees with technological know-how, I5.0 is serving innovation, adding agility (Erp et al., 2024) that is assisting enormous businesses to succeed over cultural diversity with strategic decisions compared to earlier days (Tanjung et al., 2025). For instance, one visible merit of I5.0 is the prolific training sessions, where the use of virtual reality (VR) has not only replaced human labor with robotic equivalents, but it has also resplendently reduced cost, ensured safety as well as omitted errors or corrections entirely with flawless actual performance (Alfaro-Viquez et al., 2025). Many automated expertise has enhanced workers' connectivity in process control within robotized plant ambience, which has lessened the level of occupational risks (Patel et al., 2022). Companies are now effortlessly adopting several digital twins to monitor the workers' physical and mental fatigue (Wang et al., 2024). Repeatedly, Pasman and Behie (2024) explained that in the near future, I5.0 tools will triumph over the implementation of RCCI (Reactivity-Controlled Compression Ignition) technology (Premkumar et al., 2025), electrolysis of water into hydrogen, carbon dioxide, and other innumerable exhaust gases extraction from the atmosphere, and introduction of various recyclable e-fuels economically (Zhironkin & Abu-Abed, 2024).

However, ample doctrines of scholarships stressed on their impending confusion toward the coexistence of Industry 5.0 and greater social benefits (Huang et al., 2022). Several past research essentially high pointed sustainable approaches toward pollution and waste minimization measures are unsatisfactory in the array of I5.0, specifically in emerging nations (Al Amin et al., 2025). Erudite argument by Ghobakhloo et al. (2022) illuminated that only 16 functions of Industry 5.0 is exceeding Industry 4.0 by advocating sustainable development goals. Within the fringe of smart technologies (I5.0), two prime facades "improper execution of sustainability values" and the "high expenditure of sustainable adoption" are mostly responsible for its failure followed by other realities like cultural resistance, non-consideration of human element, lack of factual inter-departmental communication, insufficient personnel empowerment with engagement initiatives, and inadequate employee training toward viable practices (Yadav et al., 2020). Likewise, the inquiry of Masoomi et al. (2023) resonated several sustainable development challenges in terms of the renewable energy supply chain are parallel to other business spheres. Such perpetual debates raise question on the inclusive conversion of the humanitarian aspects at each level of manufacturing or service delivery to realize superior socio-technical advances (Rajumesh, 2024).

2.1.2 Ethical Challenges: I 5.0

Reasonably, with abundant sustainability issues, "Ethical Challenges" is another major worry of I5.0 that seeks more proactive measures particularly in the developing economies (Rajesh, 2023). Alike attestation is found in the brilliant exertion of Shabur et al. (2025) where ethical dilemmas (AI bias, data privacy, as well as accountable decision-making) plus ethical compliance were identified as two critical barriers of successful adoption of this cutting-edge expertise (Dacre et al., 2024). An astute discussion of Antonica et al. (2024) further appealed that captivation of humanism in I5.0 generally emphasize on physical facets like work related postures, equipment or workplace design to amplify efficiency besides to restrain bodily injury, whereas the social and cognitive ergonomics (such as perception, morality, memory, decision making), which equally influence an individual's job performance or collective well-being is often got neglected. Henceforth, more upgradation of regulatory concerns from expediting innovation to the ultimate realization of the I5.0 visions is important (Bazel et al., 2024), as it consequently influences companies' standard practice of skill upgraded, lack of cultural resistance in training sessions, which are significantly blocking the impending succession (Tanjung et al., 2025). Inclusively, there is a gap in thoughtful practical implications merging sustainability practices in diverse arenas of business regarding the true accomplishment of I5.0 (Ferna'ndez-Miguel et al., 2024; Leng et al., 2022). Moreover, an in-depth transdisciplinary approach needs to adopt intersecting all organizational agility, sustainability concerns, ethical focus, and I5.0 principles (Carayannis & Morawska-Jancelewicz, 2022). Furthermore, Bressanelli et al. (2022) defended that in the context of today's "vastly competitive aside from sustainability-focused" business atmosphere, managers, scholars, and several practitioners need to take actionable measures for crafting sustainable commercial performances.

Thus, it is high time for researchers to debate the upcoming technological revolution, as expectedly, it will violate all previous standards and will contribute to society to a larger extent (Neumann et al., 2021). Besides, the new industrial framework requires fundamental change in terms of its doctrine, attitude, motivation, and engagement to reform a committed global community that will strive to safeguard humankind by leading toward the common purposes of prosperity (Drury et al., 2023). Therefore, this scientific appraisal has resumed on two research questions (RQs).

RQ1: What factual bindings are hindering the progress of Industry 5.0?
RQ2: What advanced tenets will Industry 6.0 introduce persistently to Industry 5.0?

The study is structured as follows: Section 1 reviewed the detailed explanation of I5.0 to reveal its substantial pitfalls alongside the emerging ideology of I6.0. Section 2 employed methodological discussions. Section 3 scrutinizes the research findings based on the predicted research gap in Section 1, with probable implications of this manifestation. Lastly, Section 4 highlights concluding remarks with future scope. To the best of our knowledge, no substantial investigation has been initiated to explore the fundamental philosophy or tenets of I6.0, although ample academicians are investigating the limits of current industrial revolt. By completing a scientific overview on both the present and future industrial development, this assessment aims to fill the gap, which will highlight the utmost advantages of fostering stakeholders' engagement in the coming realm of I6.0.

3. Research Methodology

3.1 Study Context

The purpose of this inspection is to contribute to the existing body of knowledge by offering a holistic understanding of the forthcoming industrialization, which will widen readers' perception toward new alterations, instigate additional ruminative insights for policymakers and industry leaders in this novel era. To obtain such comprehensive artwork, this undertaking certifies that the review process is wide-ranging, diversified, and transparent, which also endorses cross-validation of deviating scholarship. Thus, we applied a data-driven approach where data triangulation was also a quality concern (Sekki et al., 2023).

Being an incipient concept, little overlap has been visible between the current and upcoming industrialization. Moreover, only a limited number of literary works have been discussed over this industrial uprising so far. Hence, it signifies the inevitable necessity to integrate two viewpoints (present with future), their individual accomplishments with substantial pitfalls, and to conceptualize an inclusive judgment with state-of-the-art conclusions.

3.2 Data Extraction Process

A total of 63 publications (n = 63) were retrieved based on higher dependability with quality attributes. Due to conscientious indexing methods of journals, we only targeted publications indexed by Scopus and Web of Science. The scope of the analysis was confined to articles and book chapters, whereas non-peer-reviewed papers, conference proceedings, pre-prints, and editorial contents were not included. Only a few online sources were screened to accumulate supporting information. The inclusion condition also remained delimited within English publications because of its universal acceptance.

As the year 2020 was the true incarnation point of I5.0 technologies, we refined the study sample from the year 2020 till date, which supplementarily endorse the reception of our sightings on global perspective.

Additionally, the "Delphi technique" was applied in the seventh phase of this literary work to verify our findings with "expert opinion". Successful accomplishments of this have been documented in the data analysis process (Section 3.3.1).

3.3 Data Analysis

Methodologically, a backward review was steered to explore relevant knowledge cited in the earlier examinations at the beginning. We then initiated a forward review to locate supplementary judgments as well. The comprehensive view of this stepwise inquiry has been recorded in Table 6.1.

3.3.1 Adoption of Delphi Structure

Conventionally, the Delphi technique is one of the most successful elements of scientific review, precisely addressing emerging issues, social dynamics, and developments in medical science. Such a study assumes a structured and iterative approach to validate research findings through expert opinion from divergent backgrounds (Ruiz-Pérez & Ormazabal, 2021). Within a predefined theoretical

Table 6.1. Stepwise Methodological Conduct of the Paper.

Step	Activities
Step-1: Articulation of research objective and RQs	Study the purpose of the research (for instance industry 5.0, and industry 6.0) analysis of the research questions (RQ1 and RQ2).
Step-2: Establishment of literature search strings	1) Define keywords. 2) List of keywords: "Industry 5.0" OR "the fifth industrial revolution" OR "the advantages of industry 5.0" OR "the challenges of industry 5.0" OR "the industry 6.0" OR "aftermath of industry 5.0" OR "the principles of industry 6.0" OR "redefined sustainability" OR "sustainability challenges" OR "ethical dilemma of industry 5.0" OR "ethical dilemma of industry 6.0" OR "future of industry 5.0"
Step-3: Application of inclusion and exclusion criterion	
Step-3a: Application of inclusion criterion	Article selection based on: 1) The theme "industry 5.0" and "industry 5.0" 2) Empirical explorations and case studies 3) Research timeline Results: $n = 63$
Step-3b: Application of exclusion criterion	Article exclusion based on: 1) Unpublished study 2) Pre-prints 3) Conference proceedings 4) Non-peer-reviewed papers 5) Non-English documents 6) Editorial notes 7) Beyond the defined time
Step-4: Backward review	Exploring the contextual frame, philosophies, opportunities, and challenges of former magnitudes
Step-5: Forward review	Discovering the prospects in terms of multiple dimensions

Table 6.1. *(Continued)*

Step-6: Content analysis and idea generation	1) Scrutinizing the findings based on theoretical and empirical findings 2) Articulation of latent ideas
Step-7: Adoption of Delphi technique to adjust the expert opinion	Accreditation of specialized thoughts regarding the review outcome
Step-8: Documentation of the evaluation	

Source: Authors' own contribution (2025).

outline, implication of Delphi structure in data compendium and analysis is often turn beneficial for projecting future changeover of any speciality (Nyström & Kaartemo, 2022). The iterative nature of this procedure ensures that responses are progressively refined to reach consensus or to identify deviation in elicit group opinion (Hasson et al., 2025) and thus, it effectively controls the levels of bias of any exploration in one way. Moreover, the anonymity of experts is fundamental in such examinations, as participants are unaware to others involved, which fosters authenticity and objectivity in their views (Ruiz-Pérez & Ormazabal, 2021). Again, for researchers it is convenient to identify the most agreed-upon or supported arguments from the experts by employing multiple rounds of anonymous questionnaires (Prieto-Sandoval et al., 2018).

Following the Delphi apparatus, we contacted three academics from distinct backgrounds who have a minimum of 10 years of expertise on issues like finance, marketing & information technology who provide services as consultants and mentors in different business organizations. Due to time-constraints, questionnaire was distributed through physical meeting. After receiving the feedback, the responses were analyzed via thematic analysis, and the experts were subsequently contacted via a digital platform to provide essential clarification and elaboration on their perspectives.

4. Findings and Discussion

4.1 Early Foundations of Industry 6.0

Ample intellects characterize I6.0 or Industry 6.0 or the 6th industrial revolution as a theoretical foresight ad interim that encompasses a meaningful wider vision compared to all preceding industrial uprisings (Chourasia et al., 2022). Technologically, it is the sound unification of the digital infrastructure of I4.0 and the human-oriented augmentations of I5.0 with connotation of a new innovation (Damaševičius & Misra, 2024). In the realm of Industry 6.0, humans can operate machinery directly using intelligence, which would be more resource-efficient, also user-friendly compared to former industrial revolutions engaging advanced homogeneous assets, safety, anti-fragility, natural harmony, the application of digital twins (collaborative use of technologies), and an eco-based economy besides resilience (Chaudhari, 2023). For instance, Almusaed et al. (2023) verified that deploying AI algorithm-based sophistications (I5.0) architectures can now yield real-time data on energy usage, environmental impact, carbon emission, and waste generation, based on which modern builders are at present able to progress with further refined, green, as well as aesthetic structure, using energy-efficient materials and renewable energy, along with the novel tenacities of I6.0. Therefore, equated to I5.0, technological marvels of I6.0 additionally endorse a smart, sustainable future at each industrial process (Almusaed et al., 2023; Das & Pan, 2022).

Consequently, emphasizing its "futuristic industrial view", respective intellectuals are envisioning this immediate frontier of industrialization (Duggal et al., 2022; Madsen et al., 2025; Yadav et al., 2022). Equally, numerous professionals are seeking validation of such perceptions in terms of rebranding (Madsen et al., 2025). Through an extensive search, Ferna'ndez-Miguel et al. (2024) claimed that by incorporating the principles of Industry 5.0, basically the sixth industrial revolution will address the underlying challenges of the former revolt while broadening the window of opportunities simultaneously. Still, Rajesh (2023) suggested that Industry 6.0 will bring radical modification in organizational driving forces by shifting both managerial and societal goals. According to Duggal et al. (2022), the core focus of I6.0 will evolve through a consumer-centric notion aiming fundamentally at economic, social, and environmental sustainability.

4.2 The Envisioned Tenets of I6.0

Thence, with plentiful academic claims and reasonings, the authors demanded that the actual benefits of I5.0 sophistications regarding sustainability concerns persisted as ambiguous. Additionally, the aforesaid enquiry on copious literature signifies two latent alterations anticipated through the upcoming revolution: 1) Reestablishment of sustainability principles or "Redefined sustainability" in short, and 2) Comprehensive establishment of the ethical principles or briefly "Ethical Consumerism", which has termed as the new philosophy, or principles or tenets of that epoch.

4.2.1 Redefined Sustainability

In conjunction with I5.0 to I6.0, anticipated returns of sustainable benefits are imperative together with seamless technological spreads (Jime'nez-Partearroyo et al., 2023). Lately, learning of sustainable entrepreneurship through pedagogical constructs at large is attracting enormous entrepreneurs from around the world to sponsor sustainability at each production process, as such ventures are key drivers of innovation and economic progression (Kotla & Bosman, 2023; Sharma et al., 2021). In accordance, numerous scientists stressed that it is pivotal to understand the elongated impressions of sustainable tails in the frame of

Industry 5.0 (Fernández-Miguel et al., 2024). Rather than considering sustainability as a peripheral concern, contemporary businesses value it as an element of competitiveness (Chen et al., 2023). Agonizingly, if the world community fails to meet the 2030 targets (SDGs), it will appear as a threat to mankind (Mansell et al., 2020). Henceforth, universal scholars admitted distinct limits of I5.0 advents in fulfilling sustainability goals where an urge for strong representation of sustainable moralities is being observed. For instance, the absence of "standardized methods and tools" to evaluate the accomplishment of sustainability practices (systemic sustainability) within the technological landscape of I5.0 paradigm (Vacchi et al., 2024), or the "carbon border adjustment tool" suggested by Barraza de la Paz et al. (2023). Sensing the internal organization's environment, Smuts and Van der Merwe (2022) once again debated that although I5.0 tactics offer agility in manufacturing, it is domineering to understand the practical challenges in the case of workplace change management, instigating sustainable performance, executing satisfactory employee training, and grounding seamless machine collaboration with innovative resolutions.

Remarkably, the root of the planetary emergency lies in mankind's impulse toward the Earth or the place they live in, where they show people's unwillingness to assume real measures to establish harmony with life on this planet, respecting oceans, lands, air, and other natural resources (Drury et al., 2023). In addition, whether the actual impact of several I5.0 green measures (such as wind farming, solar installations, carbon storage, along with massive tree plantation) in controlling greenhouse gas emissions is satisfactory remains a burning question. Plentiful scholarly testimonies have also explored how food could be provided to the growing global population without further destroying natural habitats while substantially reducing greenhouse gas emissions worldwide. Thus, progressive academics endorsed that by borrowing cutting-edge technology with unconventional approaches plus revolutionary innovation, I6.0 eruditions will work to refurbish biodiversity where economic, environmental, and social influences as well as market dynamics will be analyzed over time for prolonged footmarks which is labeled as "redefined sustainability" (Bressanelli et al., 2022; Ferna'ndez-Miguel et al., 2024). Equally it is indispensable to realize that sustainability is unlikely to be quantifiable in terms of monetary value; rather, it is relatively practical concept that requires more than sheer possibility to encompass utility, moral values, and principles embracing time (Licht & Folland, 2025).

4.2.2 Ethical Consumerism

By tradition, "social expectations" fundamentally promote business, where in the light of I5.0, organizational functions are largely compatible with culturally eco-friendly institutional frameworks (Agarwal et al., 2025). Undeniably, the fifth industrial phase has brought noteworthy reforms regarding workplace health and safety measures, fostering equality, and ensuring environmental protection. However, the "sustainability crisis" is leading the world community toward novel ethical standards. Despite companies' investment (like green culture, green financing) as well as extended CSR activities, several times it turns by way of superficial efforts like deceitful claims of sustainable attitudes (Horton & Horton, 2019). Plentiful scientists endorse the association of sustainability toward consumers' trust building and ethical behavior (Agarwal et al., 2025).

Consumers and companies are at present emphasizing more on circular practices as circularity like recycling, reusing, and reduced consumption has strong association with both organizational and sustainability performance (Yin et al., 2023), which will be more embellished in near future. Again, contemporary industries are witnessing the wave of emerging ethical awareness in four distinct aspects: (a) ethical Sourcing, (b) market promotion of corporate ethics, (c) HR practices, and (d) financial control (Nandy, 2023). In a scholarly paper, Agarwal et al. (2025) well-defined the term "sustainable branding" where companies serve present customers based on future prosperity, for instance, by consuming eco-friendly packages, sharing clear companies' environmental performances, supervising the level of greenhouse gas emission per product, and finally branding these positive actions as a tool of marketing promotion (Sheth & Parvatiyar, 2020). Often, such an approach generates a number of benefits like market differentiation, advantages of new entrants, and competitive advantages based on environmental and social realms (Alam & Islam, 2021).

Alongside planetary issues several re-creative education systems will skill each citizen enough to identify social problems, which ultimately create a sense of responsibility as a footprint to I6.0 (Kotla & Bosman, 2023). One of such progressive modes is the "culturally responsive teaching method," where representatives from various cultures collaborate by sharing previous records, prior experiences, and ethical distinctions for enactment of digitalization. In the taxonomy of value-based healthcare, Hanneman (2024) recounted that in radiology services, when I5.0 mechanism prioritizes cost, I6.0 know-how will fundamentally foster ethical values. As the services substantially deteriorate the environment through GHG emissions, waste disposal, and contrast contamination, it is equally contributive to the human health crisis plus climate degradation. In consequence, scientists at I6.0 edge will uphold environmental sustainability and health equity precisely in this field (McKee et al., 2024). Another thought-provoking review of Horton and Horton (2019) unveiled a more futuristic outlook of ethical consumerism where collectively people will observe this I6.0 tenet to protect the mother earth by monitoring a number of key indicators.

Consistently, equity in terms of gender, rights, education, training, and opportunities acts as an influential catalyst and is one prerequisite to adopt societal modification alongside environmental sustainability across borders (Horton & Horton, 2019). Likewise, the scholars testified that vibrant cultural assets (such as art, music, and literature) produce majestic outcomes in communicating sustainable values, which will equally attract fundamental consideration under I6.0 doctrine. Altogether, from divergent prospects, ethical echo will be the second distinct pillar of I6.0, where ethically responsive behavior will exert the protagonist value of each point of radical advancement globally.

4.3 Outcome of the Delphi Study

To strengthen the validation of the findings, we will shortly share the responses attained through the Delphi survey in this segment. A glimpse of the experts' feedback on our prior study findings has been presented in Table 6.2 where all the experts supported (Mean Value 1) the prospects of the forthcoming industrialization. However, at round 1, experts expressed their equal concern toward technological supremacy and climate degradation in I6.0 era, yet they highly agreed on our proposed tenets as the proper absence of sustainability apprehension is the critical shortcoming of current industry 5.0 with mounting ethical concern worldwide. One of them also stressed the supply chain's predominance and resource scarcity as global economic downfall, geopolitics, and natural degradation will errupt as crucial challenges simultaneously. Again, after the second round of discussion, all of them approved that the future industry will be able to manage rest elements once the global citizen will realize the topmost time demand of that regime shift which are once again "the reformation or readjustment of the sustainable pragmatics" and "alteration towards ethical mindset at each point of consumption" along with unbeatable technological progression.

Accordingly, the experts' opinions also resonated with our theoretical findings, as the core value of Industry 5.0 (human–machine symbiosis) will extend, the subsequent advancements of Industry 6.0 will increasingly emphasize sustainability (mostly social and ecological) and ethical behavior as two central concerns.

4.4 Research Contribution

4.4.1 Theoretical Contribution

The theoretical contribution of this evaluation is twofold. Firstly, this evaluation augments the growing body of knowledge concerning the forthcoming industrial revolution, along with a comparison of the present era. By revealing the true scenario along with future estimations, learners from respective domains can acquire interdisciplinary enlightenment. Secondly, through extensive screening, this paper additionally explores two vital principles of impending industrialization. Therefore, the findings meaningfully contribute to plentiful theoretical voyages blending sustainable reformation and ethical maturity within the broad jurisdiction of Industry 6.0.

4.4.2 Practical Contribution

Subsequently, on practical grounds, this exploration provides treasured understandings for industry leaders, policymakers, and academicians to endorse sustainable growth and ethical integrity in the epoch of rapid technological fruition.

Table 6.2. Outcome of Delphi Study.

RQ2: What Advanced Tenets Will Industry 6.0 Introduce Persistently to Industry 5.0?

Key items	Proposed tenets	Sustainability apprehension	Ethical concern	Technological supremacy	Supply Chain's predominance	Resource scarcity	Climate change	Mean
Delphi round 1	Expert 1	✓✓✓	✓✓✓	✓✓✓	✓	✓	✓✓✓	1
Expert 2	✓✓✓	✓✓✓	✓✓✓	✓			✓✓✓	0.83
Expert 3	✓✓✓	✓✓✓	✓✓✓				✓✓✓	0.67
Delphi round 2	Expert 1	✓✓✓	✓✓✓	✓✓✓				1
Expert 2	✓✓✓	✓✓✓	✓✓✓					1
Expert 3	✓✓✓	✓✓✓	✓✓✓					1

Source: Authors' own contribution (2025).

For managers, it highlights fundamental HR reformation through employee training, moral or soft-skill upgradation for upcoming societal transformation through transdisciplinary insights, and on customer demand, particularly in evolving economics, where profit generation is still a core KPI. In addition, the analysis provokes thoughtful consideration in creating sustainable awareness among policymakers. The outcomes signify the urge for policy alteration or introduction precisely in emerging nations where government as well as the business leaders need to get prepared ahead of time to act in a proactive manner. Besides, this perceptive exploration engages several stakeholders to adapt the imminent transformative forces encircling marketing strategies with ethical and sustainability prospects in designing future products, services, or facilities.

4.4.3 Empirical Contribution

The outcome of this assessment delivers a robust, thought-provoking foundation for empirical investigation by using quantitative and qualitative methodologies. To accommodate extended empirical validation, a set of testable hypotheses is proposed below to refine the knowledge of Industry 6.0 and to sketch scientific implementation steps.

H1: The incarnation of the I6.0 era will promote better employee well-being, where work-related stress will be lowered compared to the I5.0 period.

H2: I6.O know-how will deliver added efficiency in virtual employee training and development (T&D) sessions while reducing employee turnover.

H3: I6.0 sophistication will pointedly decrease the amount of CO2 and GHG emissions in service-oriented sectors compared to the preceding revolt.

H4: Beginning of I6.0 will enhance environmental sustainability by emphasizing circular practices in developing nations.

H5: How can I6.0 foster sustainability by observing a set of guidelines in emerging economies?

5. Limitations, Suggestions, and Concluding Remarks

Although the researchers have maintained realism and representativeness at each stage of logic formulation, the research outcomes are eventually unified by a strong futuristic perspective. Again, being an emergent topic, both empirical and literary evidence remained scarce. Restricted research timeframe was another key limit of this review. Due to time constraints, the scope of the literature search was restrained to a few well-recognized academic databases. Subsequently, though the selected sources promised scholarly depth along with reliability, the exclusion of other databases may have reduced the breadth and diversity of views represented in the assessment. Furthermore, the inquiry has a narrowed focus on English-language sources, while other regional documents might also have attested considerable information.

Consequently, all these limitations provide valuable direction for future research. Considerable learning attention awaits to explore the domain of the upcoming verse under "environmental sustainability." As literature highlights the absence of proper staff training concerning sustainability is the root cause of the distress of sustainable attempts, prominent researchers need to explore the educational practice blending an innovative mindset concerning the successful accomplishment of this new revolt. Shepherding case study method to identify critical social challenges that contribute to sustainability failures can be another future directive to understand. Truly, the paramount challenge of current fifth unrest (I5.0) is the execution of cost and funding, while the most notable enabler is social sustainability, like upgraded public service together with social benefits (Liu et al., 2024). To accomplish greater social welfare, the shared effort of government as well as business is always crucial. Henceforth, outlining the exact long-term commitments for government, policymakers, manufacturers, and diverse stakeholders specifically for prospective nations to triumph I6.0 dogma is another explanatory field to discover forward.

Many scholars trust that worldwide the absolute implication of I5.0 is yet at a premature stage, predominantly in developing economies; hence, it is too hasty to draw any definitive judgment concerning its immediate facet of I6.0 (Madsen et al., 2025). Several doctrines of scholarships yet again resist that, in contrast to I5.0, the next phase might fail to attract governmental support with universal recognition (European Commission, 2022). However, the findings revealed that both developed and developing countries need a high readiness level and awareness involving I6.0 or further technological upsurge in the near future. Hitherto, we believe that this futurism demands strategic priority to deploy enduring applications in revolutionary change of management tenets, which will prepare the stakeholders for extended transformation over human-machine cooperation.

6. List of Abbreviations

I4.0 =Industrial Revolution 4, or Industry 4.0
I5.0 =Industrial Revolution 5, or Industry 5.0
I6.0 =Industrial Revolution 6, or Industry 6.0
SDGs =Sustainable Development Goals

References

Agarwal, S., Kweh, Q. L., Goh, K. W., & Wider, W. (2025). Redefining marketing strategies through sustainability: Influencing consumer behavior in the circular economy: A systematic review and future research roadmap. *Cleaner and Responsible Consumption, 18*. https://doi.org/10.1016/j.clrc.2025.100298

Ahmed, T., Karmaker, C. L., Nasir, S. B., Moktadir, M. A., & Paul, S. K. (2023). Modeling the artificial intelligence-based imperatives of industry 5.0 towards resilient supply chains: A Post-COVID-19 pandemic perspective. *Computers and Industrial Engineering, 177*. https://doi.org/10.1016/j.cie.2023.109055

Alam, S. M. S., & Islam, K. M. Z. (2021). Examining the role of environmental corporate social responsibility in building green corporate image and competitive advantage. *International Journal of Corporate Social Responsinility*, *6*(1). https://doi.org/10.1186/s40991-021-00062-w

Al Amin, M. A., Chakraborty, A., & Baldacci, R. (2025). Industry 5.0 and green supply chain management synergy for sustainable development in Bangladeshi RMG industries. *Cleaner Logistic and Supply Chain, 14*. https://doi.org/10.1016/j.clscn.2025.100208

Alfaro-Viquez, D., Zamora-Hernandez, M., Fernandez-Vega, M., Garcia-Rodriguez, J., & Azorin-Lopez, J. (2025). Integrating virtual reality into welding training: An industry 5.0 approach. *Electronics*, *14*(10). https://doi.org/10.3390/electronics14101964

Almusaed, A., Yitmen, I., & Almssad, A. (2023). Reviewing and integrating AEC practices into industry 6.0: Strategies for smart and sustainable future-built environments. *Sustainability*, *15*(18), 13464. https://doi.org/10.3390/su151813464

Antonaci, F. G., Olivetti, E. C., Marcolin, F., Castiblanco Jimenez, I. A., Eynard, B., Vezzetti, E., & Moos, S. (2024). Workplace well-being in industry 5.0: A worker-centered systematic review. *Sensors*, *24*(17), 5473. https://doi.org/10.3390/s24175473

Bai, C., Dallasega, P., Orzes, G., & Sarkis, J. (2020). Industry 4.0 technologies assessment: A sustainability perspective. *International Journal of Production Economics*, *229*. https://doi.org/10.1016/j.ijpe.2020.107776

Barraza de la Paz, J. V., Rodríguez-Picón, L. A., Morales-Rocha, V., & Torres-Argüelles, S. V. (2023). A systematic review of risk management methodologies for complex organizations in industry 4.0 and 5.0. *Systems*, *11*(5), 218. https://doi.org/10.3390/SYSTEMS11050218

Bazel, M. A., Mohammed, F., Baarimah, A. O., Alawi, G., Al-Mekhlafi, A. B. A., & Almuhaya, B. (2024). The era of industry 5.0: An overview of technologies, applications, and challenges. In F. Saeed, F. Mohammed, & Y. Fazea (Eds.), *Advances in intelligent computing techniques and applications. IRICT 2023. Lecture notes on data engineering and communications technologies* (pp. 274–284). Springer. https://doi.org/10.1007/978-3-031-59707-7_24

Bressanelli, G., Visintin, F., & Saccani, N. (2022). Circular economy and the evolution of industrial districts: A supply chain perspective. *International Journal of Production Economics*, *243*. https://doi.org/10.1016/J.IJPE.2021.108348

Carayannis, E. G., & Morawska-Jancelewicz, J. (2022). The futures of Europe: Society 5.0 and industry 5.0 as driving forces of future universities. *Journal of the Knowledge Economy*, *13*(4), 3445–3471. https://doi.org/10.1007/s13132-021-00854-2

Chaudhari, J. (2023). *Industry 6.0: The rise of intelligent manufacturing and the future of industry*. Medium. https://medium.com/illumination/industry-6-0-the-rise-of-intelligent-manufacturing-and-the-future-of-industry-edb5f77f1706

Chen, S., Song, Y., & Gao, P. (2023). Environmental, social, and governance (ESG) performance and financial outcomes: Analyzing the impact of ESG on financial performance. *Journal of Environmental Management*, *345*, 118829. https://doi.org/10.1016/j.jenvman.2023.118829

Chourasia, S., Tyagi, A., Pandey, S. M., Walia, R. S., & Murtaza, Q. (2022). Sustainability of industry 6.0 in global perspective: Benefits and challenges. *MAPAN*, *37*, 443–452.

Dacre, N., Yan, J., Frei, R., Al-Mhdawi, M. K. S., & Dong, H. (2024). Advancing sustainable manufacturing: A systematic exploration of industry 5.0 supply chains for sustainability, human-centricity, and resilience. *Production Planning and Control*. https://doi.org/10.1080/09537287.2024.2380361

Damaševiccius, R., & Misra, S. (2024). The rise of industry 6.0: Seizing the opportunities of the post-COVID-19 era for sustainable manufacturing. In Lakshmi, D. and Tyagi, A. K. (Eds.), *Emerging technologies and security in cloud computing* (pp. 478–494). IGI Global. https://doi.org/10.4018/979-8-3693-2081-5.ch020

Das, S., & Pan, T. (2022). A strategic outline of industry 6.0: Exploring the future. *SSRN Journal*. https://ssrn.com/abstract=4104696

Drury, M., Fuller, J., & Hoeks, J. (2023). Embedding animals within a definition of sustainability. *Sustainability Science*, *18*, 1925–1938. https://doi.org/10.1007/s11625-023-01310-7

Duggal, A. S., Malik, P. K., Gehlot, A., Singh, R., Gaba, G. S., Masud, M., & Al-Amri, J. F. (2022). A sequential roadmap to industry 6.0: Exploring future manufacturing trends. *IET Communications*, *16*(5), 521–531. https://doi.org/10.1049/cmu2.12284

Erp, T. V., Carvalho, N. G. P., Gerolamo, M. C., Gonçalves, R., Rytter, N. G. M., & Gladysz, B. (2024). Industry 5.0: A new strategy framework for sustainability management and beyond. *Journal of Cleaner Production*, *461*. https://doi.org/10.1016/j.jclepro.2024.142271

European Commission. (2022, January 10). *Industry 5.0, a transformative vision for Europe—Governing systemic transformations towards a sustainable industry*. European Commission. https://research-and-innovation.ec.europa.eu/knowledge-publications-tools-and-data/publications/all-publications/industry-50-transformative-vision-europe_en

Fernández-Miguel, A., García-Muiña, F. E., Settembre-Blundo, D., Tarantino, S. C., & Riccardi, M. P. (2024). Exploring systemic sustainability in manufacturing: Geoanthropology's strategic lens shaping industry 6.0. *Global Journal of Flexible Systems Management*, *25*, 579–600. https://doi.org/10.1007/s40171-024-00404-0

Garti, O. M., Arif, J., Jawab, F., Frichi, Y., & Benbrahim, F. Z. (2025). Factors impacting the sustainability of supply chain in industry 5.0: An exploratory qualitative study in Morocco. *Logistics*, *9*(2), 57. https://doi.org/10.3390/logistics9020057

Ghobakhloo, M., Iranmanesh, M., Mubarak, M. F., Mubarik, M., Rejeb, A., & Nilashi, M. (2022). Identifying industry 5.0 contributions to sustainable development: A strategy roadmap for delivering sustainability values. *Sustainable Production and Consumption*, *33*, 716–737.

Hassan, M. A., Zardari, S., Farooq, M. U., Alansari, M. M., & Nagro, S. A. (2024). Systematic analysis of risks in industry 5.0 architecture. *Applied Sciences*, *14*(4), 1466. https://doi.org/10.3390/app14041466

Hasson, F., Keeney, S., & McKenna, H. (2025). Revisiting the Delphi technique - Research thinking and practice: A discussion paper. *International Journal of Nursing Studies*, *168*. https://doi.org/10.1016/j.ijnurstu.2025.105119

Horton, P., & Horton, B. P. (2019). Re-defining sustainability: Living in harmony with life on Earth. *One Earth*, *1*(1), 86–94. https://doi.org/10.1016/j.oneear.2019.08.019

Huang, S., Wang, B., Li, X., Zheng, P., Mourtzis, D., & Wang, L. (2022). Industry 5.0 and society 5.0- comparison, complementation and co-evolution. *Journal of Manufacturing Systems*, *64*, 424–428.

Jiménez-Partearroyo, M., Medina-López, A., & Juárez-Varón, D. (2023). Towards industry 5.0: Evolving the product-process matrix in the new paradigm. *The Journal of Technology Transfer*. https://doi.org/10.1007/s10961-023-10053-7

Karmaker, C. L., Bari, A. B. M. M., Anam, M. Z., Ahmed, T., Ali, S. M., Pacheco, D. A. J., & Moktadir, M. A. (2023). Industry 5.0 challenges for post-pandemic supply chain sustainability in an emerging economy. *International Journal of Production Economics*, *258*. https://doi.org/10.1016/j.ijpe.2023.108806

Kotla, B., & Bosman, L. (2023). Redefining sustainability and entrepreneurship teaching. *Trends in Higher Education*, *2*, 498–513. https://doi.org/10.3390/higheredu2030030

Leng, J., Sha, W., Wang, B., Zheng, P., Zhuang, C., Liu, Q., Wuest, T., Mourtzis, D., & Wang, L. (2022). Industry 5.0: Prospect and retrospect. *Journal of Manufacturing Systems*, *65*, 279–295.

Licht, K. D. F., & Folland, A. (2025). Redefining 'sustainability': A systematic approach for defining and assessing 'sustainability' and 'social sustainability'. *Theoria*, *91*(1), 45–59. https://doi.org/10.1111/theo.12568

Ligarski, M. J., Rożałowska, B., & Kalinowski, K. (2021). A Study of the human factor in industry 4.0 based on the automotive industry. *Energies*, *14*(20), 6833. https://doi.org/10.3390/en14206833

Liu, S., Li, P., Wang, J., & Liu, P. (2024). Toward industry 5.0: Challenges and enablers of intelligent manufacturing technology implementation under the perspective of sustainability. *Heliyon*, *10*(15). https://doi.org/10.1016/j.heliyon.2024.e35162

Macrae, A., Lopes, R. N., Allil, R. C. d.B., & Werneck, M. (2025). Aerobiology, post COVID-19 within the emerging industrial revolution 5.0 and society 5.0. *Discover Environment*, *3*(78). https://doi.org/10.1007/s44274-025-00270-2

Madsen, D. Ø., Slåtten, K., & Berg, T. (2025). From industry 4.0 to industry 6.0: Tracing the evolution of industrial paradigms through the lens of management fashion theory. *Systems*, *13*(5), 387. https://doi.org/10.3390/systems13050387

Mansell, P., Philbin, S. P., & Konstantinou, E. (2020). Redefining the use of sustainable development goals at the organisation and project levels—A survey of engineers. *Administrative Sciences*, *10*(3), 55. https://doi.org/10.3390/admsci10030055

Masoomi, B., Sahebi, I. G., Ghobakhloo, M., & Mosayebi, A. (2023). Do industry 5.0 advantages address the sustainable development challenges of the renewable energy supply chain? *Sustainable Production and Consumption*, *43*, 94–112. https://doi.org/10.1016/j.spc.2023.10.018

McKee, H., Brown, M. J., Kim, H. H. R., Doo, F. X., Panet, H., Rockall, A. G., Omary, R. A., & Hanneman, K. (2024). Planetary health and radiology: Why we should care and what we can Do. *Radiology*. https://doi.org/10.1148/radiol.240219

Nandy, A. (2023). Emerging practices of ethical consumption to affirm sustainability: A literature review. *BAUET Journal*, *4*. https://doi.org/10.59321/BAUETJ.V4I1.13

Neumann, W. P., Winkelhaus, S., Grosse, E. H., & Glock, C. H. (2021). Industry 4.0 and the human factor – A systems framework and analysis methodology for successful development. *International Journal of Production Economics*, *233*.

Nyström, A., & Kaartemo, V. (2022, 19 December). Developing Delphi methodology for studying future market change. *Journal of Business and Industrial Marketing*, *37*(13), 124–141. https://doi.org/10.1108/JBIM-11-2021-0520

Panter, L., Leder, R., Keiser, D., & Freitag, M. (2024). Requirements for human-machine-interaction applications in production and logistics within industry 5.0—A case Study approach. *Procedia Computer Science*, *232*, 1164–1171.

Pasman, H. J., & Behie, S. W. (2024). The evolution to industry 5.0/safety 5.0, the developments in society, and implications for industry management. *Journal of Safety and Sustainability*, *1*(4). https://doi.org/10.1016/j.jsasus.2024.11.003

Patel, V., Chesmore, A., Legner, C. M., & Pandey, S. (2022). Trends in workplace wearable technologies and connected-worker solutions for next-generation occupational safety, health, and productivity. *Advanced Intelligent Systems*, *4*(1).

Premkumar, A., Loffredo, F., Pitsch, H., & Klein, M. (2025). Towards direct numerical simulations of reactivity-controlled compression ignition engine using n-octanol/ethanol fuel blends. *Flow, Turbulence and Combustion*, *115*, 275–301.

Prieto-Sandoval, V., Ormazabal, M., Jaca, C., & Viles, E. (2018). Key elements in assessing circular economy implementation in small and medium-sized enterprises. *Business Strategy and the Environment*, *27*, 1525–1534. https://doi.org/10.1002/bse.2210

Raisa, J. F., Rahman, M. S., Mahmud, I., Kaiser, M. S., & Han, D. S. (2025). Transition toward health care 5.0: Impact of COVID-19 in the healthcare industry. *ICT Express*, *11*(2). https://doi.org/10.1016/j.icte.2025.04.002

Rajesh, R. (2023). Industry 5.0: Analyzing the challenges in implementation using grey influence analysis. *Journal of Enterprise Information Management*, *36*(5), 1349–1371. https://doi.org/10.1108/JEIM-03-2023-0121

Rajumesh, S. (2024). Promoting sustainable and human-centric industry 5.0: A thematic analysis of emerging research topics and opportunities. *Journal of Business and Socio-Economic Development*, *4*(2), 111–126. https://doi.org/10.1108/JBSED-10-2022-0116

Ruiz-Pérez, F., Lleo, A., & Ormazabal, M. (2021). Employee sustainable behaviors and their relationship with corporate sustainability: A Delphi study. *Journal of Cleaner Production*, *329*. https://doi.org/10.1016/j.jclepro.2021.129742

Sahebi, G. I., Toufighi, S. P., Azzavi, M., Masoomi, B., & Maleki, M. H. (2023). Fuzzy ISM–DEMATEl modeling for the sustainable development hindrances in the renewable energy supply chain. *International Journal of Energy Sector Management*, *18*(1), 43–70. https://doi.org/10.1108/IJESM-05-2022-0024

Sarfraz, Z., Sarfraz, A., Iftikar, H. M., & Akhund, R. (2021). Is COVID-19 pushing Us to the fifth industrial revolution (society 5.0)? *Pakistan Journal of Medical Sciences*, *37*(2), 591–594. https://doi.org/10.12669/pjms.37.2.3387

Sekki, S., Kauppinen-Räisänen, H., Kylkilahti, E., & Autio, M. (2023). Packaging journey from retail to home: How the meaning of sustainability for colour transforms. *International Journal of Retail and Distribution Management*, *51*(13), 47–63.

Shabur, M., Shahriar, A., & Ara, M. A. (2025). From automation to collaboration: Exploring the impact of industry 5 .0 on sustainable manufacturing. *Discover Sustainability*, *6*. https://doi.org/10.1007/s43621-025-01201-0

Sharma, S., Goyal, D., & Singh, A. (2021). Systematic review on sustainable entrepreneurship education (SEE): A framework and analysis. *World Journal of Entrepreneurship, Management and sustainable Development*, *17*(3), 372–395.

Sheth, J. N., & Parvatiyar, A. (2020). Sustainable marketing: Market-driving, not Market- driven. *Journal of Macromarketing*, *41*(1), 150–165. https://doi.org/10.1177/0276146720961836

Smuts, H., & Van der Merwe, A. (2022). Knowledge management in society 5.0: A sustainability perspective. *Sustainability*, *14*(11), 6878. https://doi.org/10.3390/SU14116878

Tanjung, T., Ghazali, I., Mahmood, W. H. W., & Herawan, S. G. (2025). Drivers and barriers to industrial revolution 5.0 readiness: A comprehensive review of key factors. *Green Technologies and Sustainability*, *3*(4). https://doi.org/10.1016/j.grets.2025.100217

Tuli, S., Tuli, S., Tuli, R., & Gill, S. S. (2020). Predicting the growth and trend of COVID-19 pandemic using machine learning and cloud computing. *Internet of Things*, *11*.

Vacchi, M., Siligardi, C., & Settembre-Blundo, D. (2024). Driving manufacturing companies toward industry 5.0: A strategic framework for process technological sustainability assessment (PTSA). *Sustainability*, *16*(2), 695. https://doi.org/10.3390/SU16020695

Vindrola-Padros, C., Singh, K. E., Sidhu, M. S., Georghiou, T., Sherlaw-Johnson, C., Tomini, S. M., Inada-Kim, M., Kirkham, K., Streetly, A., & Fulop, N. J. (2021). Remote home monitoring (virtual wards) during the COVID-19 pandemic: A systematic review. *eClinicalMedicine*, *37*. https://doi.org/10.1016/j.eclinm.2021.100965

Wang, B., Zhou, H., Li, X., Yang, G., Zheng, P., Song, C., Yuan, Y., Wuest, T., Yang, H., & Wang, L. (2024). Human digital twin in the context of industry 5.0. robot. *Robotics and Computer-Integrated Manufacturing*, *85*.

Xu, X., Lu, Y., Vogel-Heuser, B., & Wang, L. (2021). Industry 4.0 and industry 5.0—Inception, conception and perception. *Journal of Manufacturing Systems*, *61*. https://doi.org/10.1016/j.jmsy.2021.10.006

Yadav, G., Luthra, S., Jakhar, S. K., Mangla, S. K., & Rai, D. P. (2020). A framework to overcome sustainable supply chain challenges through solution measures of industry 4.0 and circular economy: An automotive case. *Journal of Clean Production*, *254*, 120112.

Yadav, R., Arora, S., & Dhull, S. (2022). A pathway to industrial revolution 6.0. *International Journal of Mechanical Engineering*, *7*(1), 1452–1459.

Yin, S., Jia, F., Chen, L., & Wang, Q. (2023). Circular economy practices and sustainable performance: A meta-analysis. *Resources, Conservation and Recycling*, *190*. https://doi.org/10.1016/j.resconrec.2022.106838

Zhironkin, S., & Abu-Abed, F. (2024). Fossil fuel prospects in the energy of the future (energy 5.0): A review. *Energies*, *17*(22), 5606. https://doi.org/10.3390/en17225606

Chapter 7

Predictive Product Design—Using Digital Twins for Prototype Simulation and Innovation

Anitha G.

Maharaja Agrasen Institute of Management Studies, India

Abstract

This chapter observes how the design and testing of products are being altered by digital twins. In essence, a digital twin is a complicated virtual replica of an actual product. Digital twin proves how a product might act in the real world using real-time data, intelligent analytics, and simulation tools. A designer can test concepts, identify potential issues, and refine the design as an outcome before a physical model is finished.

The main components of a digital twin are also described in this chapter. These include the systems that facilitate communication between various tools, the modeling techniques used to create the virtual version, and the simulations aid in decision-making. It discusses the areas in which digital twins are most helpful with virtual prototyping, lifespan prediction, raising safety standards, and lowering development cost.

The teams can work quickly and produce more dependable products through these technologies. They reduce expedite development, faults, and promote innovation in a variety of sectors. The chapter concludes by supporting businesses in developing smarter, more effective solutions, illustrating how digital twins are becoming an essential tool in modern product design.

Keywords: Environmental, social, and Governance (ESG) investing; sustainable finance; corporate social responsibility (CSR); responsible Investment strategies; ESG reporting and disclosure; ethical and sustainable business practices; ESG ratings and transparency; regulatory frameworks in Sustainability

Regenerative Revolution, 135–156

doi:10.1108/978-1-80686-859-920261007

JEL Codes: M14; Q01; M14; G11; M41; M14; M48; K32

1. Introduction

In the digital age, products change quickly; therefore, it's even more necessary to have quicker design procedures, more accurate testing environments, and better utilization of resources. Traditional prototyping methods, including using physical models, testing by hand, and redesigning things again and over, can be costly, time-consuming, and not always good at capturing real-world complexities. With digital twins and other new technologies, very accurate copies of real things that happen in real time have changed the way things are made. You can use digital twins and predictive analytics together to test prototypes, keep an eye on how well a product works over time, and try them out. This can make it cheaper to create a lot.

This chapter talks about how digital twins may help modern engineering, manufacturing, and research and development come up with new ideas and make better predictions about how products will work (Grieves, 2019; Tao & Qi, 2019).

2. Understanding Predictive Product Design

In predictive product design, we use advanced data analytics models and computer modeling to guess how well a product will work before it is made. Before an item development begins, we apply sophisticated techniques of data analysis and simulation modeling that predict its efficiency even before its made. This approach can be used by designers to spot potential hotspots of stress; visualize how durable the item will prove; assess how users might behave; and consider how it will perform right at the very start of the designing process. This approach further becomes better with the incorporation of digital twins because it offers a virtual space that keeps on being generated continuously and based on factual information. This implies that there are fewer prototypes required (Rasheed et al., 2020).

Digital twins were used by Crones, a company based in Germany. The company used them so that they could assess new designs of machines that could automatically pack drinks. The problems with the designs and how they could create designs that could live longer and work well were revealed by using computer models. This made it possible so that fewer prototypes could be used. This meant that the process took place at a quicker rate. Additionally, the costs reduced.

3. The Concept of Digital Twins in Product Development

A digital twin can therefore be viewed as an advanced virtual imitation of the physical object, system, or component being studied. This approach varies significantly from the conventional designs that do not undergo changes after they have been set up. A digital twin, on the other hand, changes continuously based on the live or virtual simulation of the physical system's operating conditions. This creates an integrated live feed system that intersects the virtual world with the physical world of the system under study and gives the designers and engineers the chance to evaluate the system under different operating conditions even before the system is created. Digital twins have therefore emerged as an absolute game changer with their integration of data analysis and simulation technology (Boschert & Rosen, 2016; Grieves, 2019).

3.1 Key Features of Digital Twins in Product Design (Kritzinger et al., 2018; Negri et al., 2017)

(1) High-fidelity virtual modeling.
(2) Integration of real-world environmental data.
(3) Scenario-based predictive analytics.
(4) Real-time monitoring and automatic updates.
(5) Seamless integration with Computer-Aided Design (CAD) tools, Internet of Things (IoT) systems, and simulation software.

As shown in the Fig. 7.1, the integration of virtual modeling, predictive analytics, seamless integration, environmental data, and real-time monitoring enhances the accuracy and responsiveness of digital systems by combining high-fidelity representations of physical assets with continuous, data-driven updates.

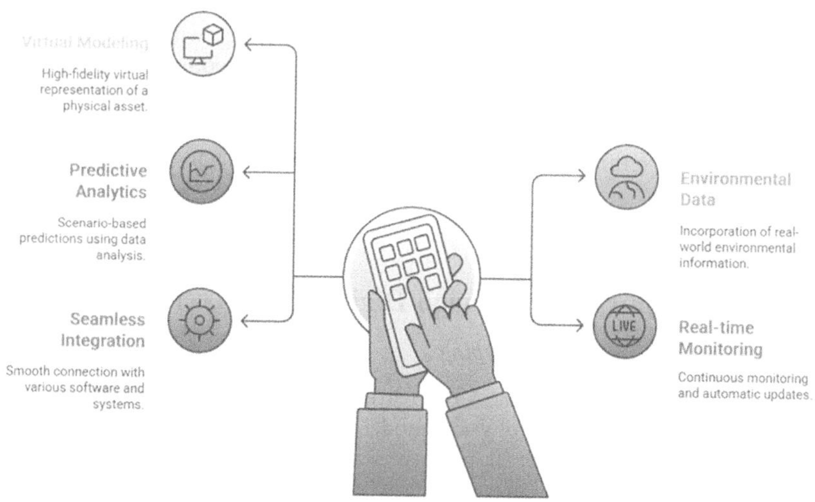

Fig. 7.1. Digital Twin Features. *Source:* Author's Work.

- High Fidelity Virtual Modeling
  It make extensive use of highly precise 3D modeling complete with the smallest details imaginable with respect to the geometric structure and composition of materials of the physical product. This modeling incorporates even the smallest details of the designs that are not in existence, so the engineer can visualize the performance of the product even before it's manufactured.
- Integration of Real-World Environmental Data
  It gives real situation related inputs like temperature, humidity, pressure, vibration, and usage patterns which enable the prediction of performance under particular environmental conditions. This enables intuitive simulation of typical operating environments that facilitate the development more reliable and user-friendly designs.
- Scenario based Predictive Analytics
  This analyses can be performed by employing the simulation engines and artificial intelligence (AI) analytics capabilities of digital twins. It permits the designer to analyze the changes that could happen due to different materials, shapes, and system elements. Predictive analytics help identify potential failures early on that can save expensive prototyping cycles.
- Real-time Monitoring and Automatic Updates
  As it works with the sensor/ IoT platform, the digital twin receives a feed of this collected data continuously. This makes way for the real-time monitoring of the performance of the product being used. Any modification that takes place on the physical product automatically finds its place on the virtual product based on the Digital twin technology's facility of aligning them on a real-time platform.
- Seamless integration with various CAD tools and IoT solutions.
  Digital twins integrate well with the environment of the development of products that currently exists. They can easily interface with the CAD tools used in the modeling of designs, with the IoT systems used for the collection of real-time data, and with simulation systems that analyze performance. This integrated tool environment brings together the various development groups of the engineers throughout the different phases of design development.

4. Virtual Prototyping Through Digital Twin Technology

4.1 Meaning of Virtual Prototyping

Virtual prototyping is the process of creating and testing product designs on a computer instead of building physical models. It allows designers to study how a product might look, behave, or perform without making anything in the real world.

Digital twins make this process even stronger. They use virtual models that act like the real product, giving designers deeper insights and more accurate predictions.

4.2 Advantages of Virtual Prototyping

Virtual prototyping involves building digital versions of a product to check how it works before actual manufacturing begins. It is used widely in designing, engineering, manufacturing, and even product testing. Below are the main benefits explained (Mourtzis, 2020) in a simple and clear way:

(1) *Fewer Physical Prototypes Needed:* To making a physical prototype it takes time, money, and skilled labor. The cost is increased for each new version requires materials and special tools. It helps the designers to experiment with many design ideas on a computer before making anything physically.

- Companies save a lot of money by avoiding repeated fabrication.
- Less material is wasted, which also helps the environment.
  It becomes faster and affordable to make development process by reducing the number of physical models.

(2) *Faster Time-to-Market: The companies don't want to wait for physical production* to test an idea through digital simulations; it helps the teams to work more quickly and efficiently.

- Quick testing of different design options.
- Multiple teams working at the same time.
- Fast identification and correction of problems.
  The company gains a strong competitive advantage by speeding up the whole design cycle to reach the product to the market.

(3) *More Accurate Design Evaluation:* The designer understands how the product will behave in real world situation through this model.

- Clear visualization of the product's shape and appearance.
- Accurate predictions of material strength, stress, durability, and performance.
- Detection of small errors that may not be noticed in early physical samples.
  This leads to accuracy, better decisions, and higher-quality product.

(4) *Early Detection of Design Problems:* One of the key strengths of virtual prototyping is its ability to detect design issues at an early stage. Through simulations, engineers can:

- find weaknesses, safety risks, and performance issues;
- test extreme conditions that would be dangerous to create physically;
- save time and money by avoiding more redesign.

5. Stress Testing Through Digital Twin Simulations

5.1 Importance of Stress Testing

Stress testing is really important in product development because it helps teams to understand how a product will behave under tough conditions. It helps engineers to understand how a product behaves when it is pushed beyond normal conditions. These situations can contain very high pressure, extreme heat, heavy loads, strong vibrations, too much humidity, and sudden shocks in the environment.

The main purpose of stress testing is to check even in the worst situations whether the product works safely and remains strong. It helps to ensure that the product will not fail when it is used in real life, in unexpected circumstances.

5.2 Why Stress Testing Matters

(1) *Ensuring Product Reliability and Durability:* It helps to check how reliable and long-lasting a product is. It shows, in tough conditions, how the product can handle and how long it can perform before any signs of failure appear. It helps the designers assess: Material strength

- Component longevity
- Performance stability

  More reliable products are trusted by consumers and less in need of repair or replacement.

(2) Stress testing helps in product development process before identifying weak spots. It allows designers to fix problems before it becomes serious exposes to hidden defects that regular testing often misses.
These include:

- cracks, deformation, or fatigue;
- weak joints and connections;
- overheating or electrical overload;
- software or system malfunctions under high load.

  Finding these problems early helps prevent the possibility of product recalls and costly redesigns.

(3) Improves Safety and Fulfills Industry Standards
The Strict safety rules are followed in industries like aerospace, automotive, manufacturing, and healthcare. Stress testing ensures that a product can meet these requirements like:

- handle sudden or extreme stress without breaking;
- operate safely within its limits;
- protect users even in rare or unusual situations.

  When a product passes these tests, it reduces risk and increases customer trust.

(4) *Lowers Development Cost and Saves Time:* In traditional stress testing, the process is slow and expensive and it needs many physical prototypes, special machines, and repeated testing. The companies can run on digital twin–based stress testing instead of on virtual models. It cuts down on overall development costs and speeds up the process.
Thermal analysis:

- load simulations;
- vibration and fatigue tests;
- environmental stress simulations.

(5) *Supports Predictive Maintenance and Product Lifecycle Planning:* It explains how the product lifecycle works on real-time data. Through running stress test on digital models, the companies can predict the maintenance schedules and extend the product's span.

- Predict when components may fail.
- Plan maintenance schedules.
- Product longevity.
- Reduce industrial application downtime.

(6) *Helps Improve Performance and Efficiency:* The product reacts on different levels of stress to improve its performance by doing certain smart changes by engineers. It boosts efficiency through the data which helps them to understand the design and boost Material selection to work on real time product situation data.

- Structural design.
- Weight Loss Strategies.
- Component placement and geometry.
  It is safer and more reliable for the engineers to build products that are not high-performing.

5.3 Types of Stress Tests Enabled by Digital Twins

5.3.1 Mechanical Stress Tests (Load-Bearing, Vibration, Fatigue)

According to Negri et al. (2017) and Kritzinger et al. (2018), the primary purpose of this simulation approach is to evaluate how components respond to forces, vibrations, and repetitive loading cycles. It commonly involves testing conditions such as static loads, dynamic loads, harmonic and random vibrations, and fatigue cycles. Various simulation methods are used, including Finite Element Analysis (FEA), modal analysis, harmonic analysis, and fatigue life prediction using S–N and ϵ–N curves. Key metrics assessed during these analyses include stress and strain distribution, displacement, natural frequencies, fatigue life, and the overall factor of safety. To perform these simulations accurately, essential inputs such as material properties, load magnitudes, boundary conditions, and the geometric model of the component are required. Validation of the simulation results is typically carried out using strain gauges, accelerometer measurements, and physical vibration or fatigue tests. A common example of this application is evaluating the durability of automotive suspension systems or aircraft wing components.

5.3.2 Thermal Stress Tests (Heat, Cooling Cycles, Temperature Extremes)

The purpose of this analysis is to study how components behave under high temperatures, thermal gradients, or rapid heating and cooling conditions.

Common scenarios tested include overheating, thermal cycling, thermal shock, and heat dissipation performance. Simulation techniques such as Computational Fluid Dynamics (CFD) for heat flow, thermal FEA, transient thermal analysis, and coupled thermo-mechanical simulations are typically used to evaluate these effects. Key metrics examined include temperature distribution, thermal stresses, thermal expansion, time to overheating, and thermal fatigue life. These analyses require inputs such as thermal properties conductivity and heat capacity along with heat source details and environmental temperature conditions. Validation is usually performed through thermocouple measurements, infrared thermal camera data, and controlled thermal cycling tests. A common example of this application is assessing cooling performance in electronic systems or studying thermal fatigue in solder joints.

5.3.3 Environmental Stress Tests (Humidity, Corrosion, UV Exposure)

The purpose of this analysis is to determine long-term degradation of materials or components caused by various environmental factors. Typical conditions examined include moisture ingress, corrosion progression, UV-induced deterioration, salt-spray exposure, and cyclic weather patterns. To study these effects, simulations often use multi-physics degradation models, moisture diffusion models, corrosion kinetics modeling, and UV exposure models. Key performance metrics include corrosion rate, coating breakdown, moisture content within materials, overall material loss, and any resulting reduction in structural strength. These assessments require inputs such as humidity profiles, UV intensity data, environmental cycling parameters, and the degradation characteristics of the materials involved. Validation of the simulations is commonly performed using accelerated aging tests, corrosion coupons, and real-world outdoor weathering data. A typical application of this analysis is predicting the lifespan of outdoor equipment, marine structures, or materials used in solar panels.

5.3.4 Impact and Shock Tests

The purpose of this analysis is to evaluate how components or systems respond to sudden forces, collisions, drops, and shock events. Common conditions examined include drop impacts, collision forces, shock pulses, and in some cases, explosive loads. Simulations typically employ explicit dynamic FEA, transient impact analysis, contact modeling, and Smoothed Particle Hydrodynamics (SPH) to capture highly nonlinear and rapid deformation behavior. Key metrics used to assess performance include peak acceleration, impact force, deformation patterns, energy absorption, and potential fracture points. These simulations require inputs such as impact velocity, mass, definitions of contact surfaces, and material strain-rate-dependent properties. Validation is generally performed through physical drop and crash tests, high-speed camera recordings, and shock sensor data. Example applications include drop testing smartphones, performing vehicle crash simulations, and evaluating packaging performance under shock loading.

5.4 Benefits of Using Digital Twins for Stress Testing

Using digital twins for stress testing gives the product development improves the overall quality and efficiency (Mourtzis, 2020). To understand how a product behaves under different conditions these digital models are useful for real-time data, advanced simulations, and multi-physics analysis (Fuller et al., 2020). Digital twin based stress testing increases accuracy, speeds up the testing process, supports safety standards, and helps teams make better decisions throughout the entire product lifecycle (Kapteyn et al., 2020; Rasheed et al., 2020).

As shown in Fig. 7.2, Enhanced simulation techniques boost product testing by providing higher accuracy and reducing design errors. They enable unlimited scenario testing without physical limits, allow quick identification of vulnerabilities, and speed up troubleshooting. These simulations also ensure compliance with safety and quality standards, improving the overall efficiency, reliability, and safety of engineering designs.

(1) *More Realistic Simulations Than Traditional Methods:* This is used for real operating conditions, real-time information, actual material properties, and sensor data. They include historical usage patterns to create highly realistic virtual models.
Why the accuracy improves:

- They consider real environmental conditions instead of relying on ideal assumptions.
- The model keeps updating as new field data comes in, so predictions become more accurate over time.
- They combine multiple physical effects such as heat, mechanical stress, electricity, and environmental factors to give a complete picture of product performance.

Fig. 7.2. Advanced Simulation Technology. *Source:* Author's Work.

- Instead of basic estimated they simulate real material behavior and cargo conditions.
  It forecasts more reliable predictions related to stress, fatigue, wear, performance limits, and possible failure points.

(2) *Ability to Test Unlimited Scenarios:* Engineers simulate countless conditions without physical prototypes by using digital twins. It allows them to explore an unlimited number of "what-if" situations and test the product in ways that are impossible, unsafe, or too expensive to recreate in real life.
Examples of scenarios include:

- Various load combinations.
- Extreme weather conditions.
- This simulation contains rare situations such as sudden thermal shocks.
- From different part of the world they show long-term fatigue, aging, and the impact of different environmental conditions.
  Traditional testing cannot use due to high costs, lack of specialized equipment, safety concerns, and the need for physical resources.
  Digital twins overcome these limitations because they:

- support many simulations at the same time, saving a huge amount of testing time;
- allow safe, risk-free experimentation;
- give engineers and decision-makers a wider view of all possible failure scenarios.
  This flexibility results in stronger designs and more confident engineering decisions.

(3) *Fast Detection of Weak Spots and Failure Points:* It always offers high-resolution insights into how and where a product might fail.
Using real-time data or realistic simulations, they help engineers spot:

- localized stress concentrations;
- hot spots from thermal loading Fatigue-critical regions;
- structural deformations;
- material degradation patterns.
  Potential zones of crack initiation because simulations run instantly and repeatedly:

- Weak points can be identified much earlier in the design stage.
- Engineers get the chance to fix errors before creating any physical prototype.
- Updating design data become faster and more affordable.
- It helps to avoids product failures in the field and shorten the entire development process.

(4) *Helps Meet Safety and Quality Standards:* For safety, durability, and regulatory compliance the industries such as automotive, aerospace, electronics, healthcare, and construction follow very strict rules.
Digital twins make it easier for companies to meet these requirements by:

- simulating standard test settings based on guidelines like International Standard for Organisation, American Society for Testing and Materials, International Electro Technical Commission, Food and Drug Administration, Federal Aviation Administration, Bureau of Indian Standards, and others;
- offering virtual proof before undergoing actual certification tests;
- for audits and regulatory approvals there should be clear documentation;
- ensuring that a product meets safety thresholds, durability, and load capacity;
- reduce risk of noncompliance and costly redesigns.

  Digital twins also allow for the continuous monitoring of products once deployed, facilitating the ease of maintaining compliance throughout the product life cycle.

6. Lifecycle Prediction and Performance Modeling

Digital twins allows for predictive analysis regarding how a product will behave over its whole life cycle from design, manufacturing maintenance, and disposal.

6.1 Lifecycle Prediction Capabilities

- Estimating wear and tear over prolonged use.
- Predicting maintenance intervals.
- Forecasting product failure probability.
- Optimizing material selection and design geometry.
- Testing product performance in diverse environmental conditions.

6.2 Impact on Design Innovation

Lifecycle prediction ensures:

- Improved product reliability
- Extended product lifespan
- Reduced warranty claims
- Enhanced customer satisfaction.

6.3 Real-World Applications

- *Aerospace*: Predicting degradation in aircraft engines.
- *Automotive*: Predicting brake pad life or battery health.
- *Consumer electronics*: modeling durability of smartphones over repeated drop cycles.

7. Cost Reduction Through Predictive Digital Twin Models

Predictive digital twin models integrate high-fidelity virtual representations of products or systems with data-driven predictive analytics—machine learning (ML), statistical models, physics-based simulations-in order to forecast future behavior, degradation, and modes of failure. This enables teams to make proactive design, testing, and operational decisions. The net result is a substantial reduction in costs across the product lifecycle, from R&D through production into in-service support.

7.1 How Predictive Digital Twins Reduce Costs

(1) Shift-left risk and uncertainty: Predict problems earlier—in design or virtual testing—so fixes are cheaper than post-production repairs.
(2) Replace expensive physical cycles: Many iterations move from the workshop to simulation, saving materials, lab time, and logistics.
(3) Quantitatively optimize resources: Data-driven decisions about materials, tolerances, and process minimize waste and over-design.
(4) Prevent downtime and failures: Predictive maintenance and failure forecasts lower warranty claims, returns, and support costs.
(5) Shorten development and ramp-up: Faster validation, better first-time-right builds shorten time-to-market and reduce associated opportunity costs.

7.2 Areas of Cost Savings

7.2.1 Fewer Physical Prototypes

- *What changes:* Teams run many virtual iterations on the twin instead of building several physical ones. Only a few physical prototypes are produced-or a final validation unit.
- *Cost drivers reduced:* Material and fabrication costs, lab/test-rig time, transport, setup labor, and disposal/rework costs.
- *Typical savings:* Depending on product complexity, organizations report prototype count reductions of 50–90%; direct savings scale with prototype cost (e.g., aerospace or tooling-heavy parts save more).
- *Secondary benefits:* faster feedback cycles due to parallel testing, less environmental waste, less overhead for scheduling of test labs.

7.2.2 Optimized Material Usage

- *What changes:* To remove excessive safety factors and select the least expensive material they use twin simulates structural performance, thermal behavior, fatigue life, safety margins under many scenarios and enabling designers.

- The Cost drivers reduced include raw material spend, part weight (which affects shipping and operational fuel/energy costs), and secondary processing (coatings, machining).
- *How it's achieved:* Topology optimization, multi objective trade off studies (cost vs. life), and surrogate modeling accelerate exploration of alternatives.
- *Typical savings:* Material cost reduction per part (5–30%) and operational savings of the end product (e.g., vehicles, aerospace) because of reduced energy/fuel consumption.

7.2.3 Lower Failure Rates

- *What changes:* Predictive twins identify likely failure modes early, such as fatigue hot spots, corrosive exposure paths, thermal overstress. Design fixes are implemented along with protective measures or maintenance plans before mass production or deployment.
- Cost drivers reduced include warranty claims, recalls, emergency repairs, customer service, legal liability, and brand-damage costs.
- *How it's achieved:* Combining field sensor data with the twin to find trends, run what-if scenarios, and prioritize mitigations where they give the highest risk-reduction per dollar.
- *Typical savings:* Significant one major recall avoided can offset years of investment; more typical is lowering warranty costs by 10–50% depending on industry and baseline failure rates.

7.2.4 Reduced Time-to-Market

- *What changes:* Faster design validation (virtual certification, parallel testing), fewer redesign loops, earlier identification of manufacturability issues, and smoother supplier integration.
- *Cost drivers reduced:* Opportunity costs, lost market share, extended development labor, accelerated launch premiums, and inventory carrying costs.
- *How it's achieved:* Virtual acceptance testing, digital handoffs to manufacturing, and early supplier digital twins that validate process capability before tooling arrives.
- *Typical savings:* Time-to-market reductions of weeks to months; commercial impact depends on product lifecycle (rapid-market products benefit most).

7.3 Return of Investment Enhancements

Predictive digital twins help companies to increase return on investment by turning expensive activities such as testing, repairs, and warranty handling into more predictable and manageable processes.

BETTER QUALITY = FEWER PRODUCT RECALLS

How it works: It can simulate risky situations and combined failure scenarios to identify issues that might help to product recalls. The models are improving from real-world data and reducing the chances of unexpected failures.

Key things to measure:

- number of recalls;
- cost of recalls per unit;
- defect levels after launch;
- customer return rate.

Impact:

It also helps to protect the company's brand reputation, which is important for long-term sales and keeping customers loyal. When a product avoids recalls, the company also saves a lot of money.

MORE EFFICIENT TESTING = LOWER R&D COSTS

How it works: Digital twins allow faster experimentation automated test runs and quicker optimization of designs to replace physical tests. It reduces the long test campaigns and frequent prototypes.

Key things to measure:

- R&D cost per project;
- cost of each validation cycle;
- number of physical tests performed;
- number of prototypes created.

Impact:

The companies design process moves faster and finish the project in a year then they don't want to spend of on research and development.

OPTIMIZED PROCESSES = LOWER MANUFACTURING COSTS

How it works: It helps to improve manufacturing processes like tool wear, tolerances, and cycle times. Before cutting down the unexcepted stoppages and waste, the predictive maintenance ensures the machines are checked and repaired on time.

Key things to measure:

- overall equipment effectiveness (OEE);
- scrap rate;
- machine downtime;
- cycle time;
- labor hours per unit.

Impact:

They reduce variable and fixed production costs so that Manufacturing becomes more predictable, throughput increases, and profit margins improve.

8. Role of Predictive Analytics in Digital Twin-Based Product Design

Predictive analytics turns raw data such as sensor readings, test results, design files and real-world usage information into meaningful insights. It helps the digital twin understand what may happen next and supports smarter decisions. When embedded into the twin, predictive algorithms forecast future behavior, suggest design changes, and automate decision-making-so products are designed not only to meet specs today but to perform reliably over their entire lifecycle.

8.1 How Predictive Analytics Fits Into a Digital Twin Workflow

(1) *Data ingestion:* Sensors, Lab Tests, Manufacturing MES/PLM, Warranty/Service Logs, Environmental Databases, and Simulation Outputs (FEA/CFD) flow into a data lake or feature store.
(2) *Data cleaning and feature engineering:* normalize units, remove outliers, align time bases, compute derived features (strain ranges, temperature gradients, duty cycles).
(3) *Modeling:* selected predictive techniques—ML, regression, time-series, physics-informed models, among others-are chosen to predict stresses, likelihood of failure, or remaining useful life (RUL) and/or optimal geometry.
(4) *Integration with twin:* Model outputs are fed back into the digital twin for scenario exploration, automated design adjustments, or real-time alerts.
(5) *Validation and feedback loop:* compare predictions versus later field data or targeted tests, recalibrate models, continuously update the twin.

8.2 Key Predictive Techniques: What They Are and How They Are Used

8.2.1 ML Models

(1) What: Supervised (classification/regression), unsupervised (clustering, anomaly detection), reinforcement learning.
(2) Use in twins:

- Predict probabilities of component failure/estimate RUL from multi-sensor inputs: vibration + temperature + usage.
- Detect anomalous behavior that precedes failures (unsupervised).
- Learn the optimal control or design policies (reinforcement learning) for adaptive systems.

(3) Strengths: Learns complex nonlinear patterns, handles high-dimensional data, can fuse heterogeneous inputs.

(4) Caveats: Requires labeled data for most supervised tasks; risk of overfitting; may have limited interpretability, unless transparent/white-box ML methods are employed.

8.2.2 Regression Analysis

(1) What: Linear, polynomial, Least Absolute Shrinkage and Selection Operator/Ridge, generalized linear models: formal statistical techniques for modeling relationships between variables.
(2) Use in twins:
   - Quick, interpretable baseline models for stress versus load, life versus cycles, material degradation versus exposure.
   - Feature selection and hypothesis testing to identify drivers of failure.
(3) Strengths: Transparent, statistically rigorous; requires less data compared to complex ML.
(4) Caveats: may underperform when relationships are highly nonlinear or complex.

8.2.3 Time Series Forecasting

(1) What: Auto Regressive Integrated Moving Average, exponential smoothing, state-space models, and modern ML-based time-series (Long Short-Term Memory, Prophet).
(2) Use in twins:
   - Forecast operating conditions (load profiles, temperatures) or degradation trajectories (corrosion depth over months).
   - Drive proactive simulations: feed predicted future loads into the twin to evaluate future stress states.
(3) Strengths: Specifically designed for sequential data and capturing trend/seasonality.
(4) Caveats: Requires careful handling of nonstationary, missing data, and irregular sampling.

8.2.4 FEA—Physics-Based Predictive Tool

(1) What: Numerical solution of continuum mechanics equations to predict stress, strain, deformation, heat transfer, etc.
(2) Use in twins:
   - High-fidelity physics predictions of how a geometry/material will behave under loads.
   - Generate labeled synthetic data—stress fields, hot spots—to train ML models or validate regression forecasts.
(3) Strengths: Physically grounded, interpretable, essential when extrapolating beyond observed data.

(4) Caveats: Computationally expensive; requires accurate material properties and boundary conditions.

8.2.5 Scenario Simulation Models

(1) What: Co-simulations or what-if-engines executing several coupled models—FEA+CFD+control logic over sets of scenarios.
(2) Use in twins:
    - Explore rare/extreme conditions, combined loading, or long-term aging under many permutations.
    - Provide risk maps and Pareto frontiers relating design choices to performance/cost tradeoffs.
(3) Strengths: Captures multi-physics interactions and provides support for design optimization.
(4) Caveats: Complexity and compute cost; needs careful orchestration and surrogate modeling to scale.

8.3 How Predictive Analytics Enables the Listed Capabilities

Data-driven decision-making:

- Predictive models quantify probabilities, uncertainties, and expected outcomes for design alternatives.
- Engineers can make numerical comparisons of expected lifetimes, failure rates, and cost tradeoffs, rather than depending on intuition.

Accurate performance forecasting:

- It merges physics-based (FEA) modeling with data-driven models (ML, time-series) to produce hybrid predictions that are more realistic and adaptable to new field evidence.
- Forecasting helps to estimate hotspots, accumulation of fatigue, or product degradation before their appearance in the field.

Product geometry and structure optimization:

- Use topology optimization informed by FEA plus surrogate models in order to quickly evaluate many geometries.
- Reinforcement learning or Bayesian optimization can suggest geometry parameters that maximize stiffness-to-weight or minimize peak stress subject to constraints.

Automated design improvements based on simulations:

- Automated pipeline: Run parameterized simulations, feed the results into a predictive model, identify the poor-performing parameter sets, and iterate automatically.
- Combined with the manufacturing constraints and cost models, this allows for automated suggestions of manufacturable, lower-cost designs.

8.4 Practical Implementation Considerations

Data requirements and quality:

- High-quality inputs: well-calibrated sensors, synchronized time bases, consistent units, and labeled failure events—if supervised learning is done.
- Augment sparse field data with simulation-generated datasets (FEA), domain knowledge, and transfer learning.

Model validation and uncertainty quantification:

- Validate predictions against holdout field data or targeted physical tests.
- Estimate the confidence in prediction using probabilistic models or ensemble methods; report the uncertainty bounds, such as 95% Confidence Interval for RUL.

Scalability and compute:

- Use surrogate models or reduced-order models for accelerating expensive simulations.
- Leverage cloud/High-Performance Computing (HPC) for running parallel scenarios and cache the results in feature stores for repeated queries.

Explainability and regulatory compliance

- Prefer interpretable models, such as regression, tree-based models using SHapley Additive exPlanations (SHAP), and physics-informed models, when certification or safety audits require traceability.
- Model lineage: Training data, versions, hyperparameters, and validation reports.

9. Examples

- *Electronics:* Predict Printed Circuit Board (PCB) hot spots using thermal-ML hybrid models and optimize the PCB layout for reduced solder fatigue.
- *Automotive:* Estimate bearing fatigue life from field vibration + speed profiles, optimize suspension geometry for durability and weight.

- *Aerospace:* Predict crack initiation in structural spars by integrated use of FEA and mission load modeling; schedule inspections based on RUL estimates.
- *Industrial Equipment:* Predict motor failure from vibration spectrums and operating cycles.

10. Challenges and Limitations

10.1 Data Complexity

Digital twins constantly receive data from different operating systems, sensors, and simulations. Managing data accurately and reliably is challenging because it is generated in diverse formats, at varying speeds, and with differing levels of quality (Tao & Qi, 2019). Real-time data often needs to be cleaned, aligned, and checked before it can be used for simulations. If the digital twin data is entering incompletely the system will produce incorrect results which may lead to poor design decisions. To avoid this, organizations need strong data governance practices, advanced processing pipelines, and standard data models. This help to ensure that the digital twin always works with clean and trustworthy information (Schroeder et al., 2016).

10.2 High Initial Investment

The company requires high investment to advanced simulation software, HPC, IoT sensors, and cloud platforms. They must also hire or train experts such as simulation engineers, data scientists, and system integrators (Fuller et al., 2020). The initial cost is difficult for small and medium-sized businesses. By reducing physical prototype and large initial spending it save money in the long run. Investing large initial spending some companies are not adopting the technology.

10.3 Integration Issues

It has smooth communication between many systems such as analytics engines, CAD tools, CAE software, IoT platforms, and manufacturing systems. Each tools communication protocols and data format is different (Schroeder et al., 2016). If the systems do not connect well data becomes trapped in silos, manual transfers increase and the virtual model stops matching the physical product. To fix this companies need standardized interfaces, good middleware solutions, and a clear system architecture.

10.4 Cybersecurity Risks

To increase the exposure of cyber threats, digital twins connect physical products with digital systems. It holds sensitive data like product designs, simulation models, and operational records. If hackers access to this information, it can result in theft, disruptions in product performance predictions. The organizations must have strong cybersecurity measures like encryption, secure authentication, network segmentation, and continuous monitoring.

10.5 Skill Gap

To Work in digital twins it requires skills like engineering, simulation, IoT, ML, and data analytics. But maximum data analysts do not have sufficient engineering knowledge and data science skills (Kaur & Mehta, 2022). This skills gap slows down implementation process and reduces the value of predictive insights and often forces companies to rely on external consultants (Jones et al., 2020).

11. Future Directions

(1) *AI-Augmented Digital Twins:* It explore millions of designs with the help of advanced tools like deep learning, reinforcement learning, and generative models (Kapteyn et al., 2020). Instead of engineers manually changing the settings or adjusting design AI suggest better shapes, material, and working conditions by real time data and predictions. It makes the product design process faster and more accurate.

(2) *Virtual Reality (VR)/ Augmented Reality (AR)-Integrated Prototyping:* Bringing VR and AR into digital twin systems will completely change how designers work with virtual prototypes. Instead of looking at a model on a screen, engineers will be able to step inside an immersive environment and interact with the design at full scale (Matarneh et al., 2021). With AR, virtual models can be layered over real spaces. At early process, it helps to teams notice design problems, ergonomic issues. This immersive approach reduces the need for physical mock-ups, improves teamwork, and speeds up design reviews.

(3) *Sustainable Product Design:* To design environmentally friendly products digital twins will play a major role (Tao & Qi, 2019). Throughout the product life they can simulate different materials, usage of energy, waste generation, and environmental impact. With these insights, engineers can choose greener materials, reduce waste, and design products that meet sustainability standards. Digital twins can also help to estimate carbon emissions, compare recyclable options, and improve energy efficiency which leads to lower production costs and a smaller environmental footprint.

(4) *Real-Time Customer Feedback Integration:* Through connected devices, they will be able to use real customer data collected from smart products. In this situation, the company analyzes the various situations used by the customer. When new data comes in, the digital twin will automatically update, helping designers see performance issues, adjust features, and improve durability before launching the next version (Schroeder et al., 2016). It helps to understand customer needs, reducing warranty problems, and improving customer satisfaction.

(5) *Quantum Computing Simulations:* This technology makes digital twin simulations faster, especially for extreme complex systems such as advanced materials, aerospace designs, and large energy networks (Preskill, 2018). It can check number of design option and detailed physics problems much faster than traditional computers. As quantum technology improves the digital twins will be able to run simulations that are impossible offering unmatched accuracy and opening up new possibilities (Kapteyn et al., 2020).

12. Conclusion

In the conclusion, digital twins with predictive analytics are reshaping the future how product is design. To build virtual prototypes and predict how products will behave throughout their life cycle with exceptional accuracy, the teams allow to run stress tests. It leads to quality products; more reliable product gives faster growth in lower cost. It is essential for staying competitive and delivering values to the customer.

References

Boschert, S., & Rosen, R. (2016). Digital twin — The simulation aspect. In *Mechatronic futures* (pp. 59–74). Springer.

Fuller, A., Fan, Z., Day, C., & Barlow, C. (2020). Digital twin: Enabling technologies, challenges and open research. *IEEE Access*, *8*, 108952–108971.

Grieves, M. (2019). *Virtually intelligent product systems: Digital twin*. Springer.

Jones, D., Snider, C., Nassehi, A., Yon, J., & Hicks, B. (2020). Characterising the digital twin: A systematic literature review. *CIRP Journal of Manufacturing Science and Technology*, *29*, 36–52.

Kapteyn, M., Knezevic, D., & Willcox, K. (2020). Toward predictive digital twins via physics-informed machine learning. *Computer Methods in Applied Mechanics and Engineering*, *370*, 113250.

Kaur, P., & Mehta, B. (2022). AI and digital twin adoption in industry 4.0: Opportunities and challenges. *Journal of Manufacturing Systems*, *65*, 738–753.

Kritzinger, W., Karner, M., Traar, G., Henjes, J., & Sihn, W. (2018). Digital twin in manufacturing: A categorization and literature review. *Procedia CIRP*, *67*, 101–106.

Matarneh, S., Gökçe, H. U., & Bai, Y. (2021). VR/AR-enabled digital twins in smart manufacturing. *Automation in Construction*, *128*, 103756.

Mourtzis, D. (2020). Simulation in the digital twin: State of the art and future trends. *Annual Reviews in Control*, *50*, 296–312.

Negri, E., Fumagalli, L., & Macchi, M. (2017). A review of the roles of digital twin in CPS-Based production systems. *Procedia Manufacturing*, *11*, 939–948.

Preskill, J. (2018). Quantum computing in the NISQ era and beyond. *Quantum*, *2*, 79.

Rasheed, A., San, O., & Kvamsdal, T. (2020). Digital twin: Values, challenges and enablers. *IEEE Access*, *8*, 21980–22012.

Schroeder, G. N., Steinmetz, C., Pereira, C. E., & Espindola, D. B. (2016). Digital twin data modeling and interoperability framework for smart manufacturing. *IFAC-PapersOnLine*, *49*(31), 109–114.

Tao, F., & Qi, Q. (2019). Digital twin and big data towards smart manufacturing and industry 4.0. *Advanced Engineering Informatics*, *35*, 1–10.

Chapter 8

Mindful Consumption and Sustainable Vehicle Choices: Navigating Sustainability in the Age of Industry 6.0

Aparna Vajpayee[*]

PP Savani University, India

Abstract

With global warming, ecological damage, and increased material consumption, there is a growing demand for a shift toward a more intentional and responsible form of consumerism. Conventional consumerism, powered by speed, stature and disposability, has resulted in impractical economic and environmental developments. This study explores to what extent mindfulness as a psychological and intentional construct can promote sustainable consumerism by looking at automotive purchases—a purchase that inherently reflects more significant eco-commitments, such as electric vehicles (EVs) or used vehicles.

This study employs a mixed-method approach for quantitative and qualitative explorations. The study's sample consisted of 150 usable responses to an online survey measuring car buying patterns, intentions, environmental awareness, and trust in technology. Quantitative analysis was conducted through descriptive statistics, factor analysis (Principal Component Analysis [PCA]), correlation analysis, and structural equation modeling (SEM). In addition, themes were coded from open-ended responses for the purposes of establishing dimensions of mindful consumption.

Major conclusions identify that sustainable consumption practices are strongly associated with green-oriented actions like buying second-hand cars (38.67%), keeping fuel efficiency (22.67%), and environmental considerations (20%) in mind while making car purchases. SEM supported that

[*]https://orcid.org/0000-0003-4616-8194

Regenerative Revolution, 157–177

doi:10.1108/978-1-80686-859-920261008

environmental consciousness (β = 0.48), trust in technology (β = 0.39), and awareness of fuel efficiency (β = 0.33) all have significant impacts on interest in EVs, whereas cost consciousness (β = −0.31) is a deterrent. Qualitative analysis identified themes of environmental consciousness, value-conscious choices, and technology-linked prudence as defining characteristics of responsible consumers.

Keywords: Mindful consumption; sustainable behavior; consumer psychology; electric vehicles; structural equation modeling; circular economy; industry 6.0; eco-consciousness; cost sensitivity; behavioral transformation

JEL Codes: M12; M54; Q56; Q01; L62; M31

1. Introduction

The concept of mindful and minimal consumption in the ancient Vedic philosophy of "Santosham Param Sukham" (संतोषं परमं सुखं)—"Contentment is the greatest happiness"—provides a rich intellectual basis. Relative to Sanskrit literature and religious psychology, the idea operates under the premise that genuine happiness does not come from external abundance, but rather, internal satisfaction. Thus, from this perspective, mindfulness is less about awareness and more about intentional restraint, gratitude, and living with reduced resources (Vajpayee et al., 2025b). The application of Santosham Param Sukham, ancient Vedic wisdom, as an example of reduced consumption—and awareness that satisfaction comes from what we have, not what we have too much of—compared to more contemporary behavioral lingo of turning away from excess and appreciating the wealth of choice—choosing products to satisfy need, not ego. Therefore, applying Santosham Param Sukham as ancient wisdom to a contemporary society would promote mental equilibrium, ecological sustainability, and future happiness from within (Vajpayee & Sanghani, 2022). More importantly, it extends the ancient moral code of an industrialized nation to be fit for coexistence with Industry 6.0 by regulating green systems.

The world—and inevitably everyone in it—is becoming more and more obsolete as resource depletion occurs at a greater frequency than in ecological bounds, resource scarcity is ever-present, and decarbonizing each industry around the world is a must. The global patterns of consumption are being challenged from multiple perspectives, with traditional consumerism marked by disposability, excess, and consumption patterns based on material status in comparable size and depth. Simply put, the social and interpersonal costs of the forest from the mood economy are compounded explicitly and implicitly on the globe, and consumerism as a whole is rising to the occasion. Global economies are transitioning to circularity, sustainability, and ethical innovations, and mindful consumption is emerging as a behavioral and psychological response to environmental and social crises (Halibas et al., 2025; Khan et al., 2025; Vajpayee, 2024a, 2024b). Environmental consciousness particularly needs to be emphasized in the transportation industry—one of the most invasive carbon-producing industries—to rethink what we select for consumption on an everyday basis.

1.1 Mindful Consumption Is More Than a Minimalistic or Green Open Mind

Consumer responsibility needs to align with systematic changes within technology and policymaking for Industry 6.0, a human-centered innovation push, digital sustainability, and responsible artificial intelligence (AI) (Tewary & Upadhyay, 2025). Gone are the days of the consumer simply receiving goods and services. Instead, the consumer acts as an active change agent. When empowered through mindfulness of their actions, they can temper supply chain demand, a justification for production, and brand accountability. In fact, their power as mindful consumers can temper supply chain demand, a justification for production, and brand accountability. This is true even more so for younger generations, especially Gen Zs, who have greener tendencies and prefer more socially responsible and authentic (Halibas et al., 2025; Khambhata et al., 2025; Vajpayee et al., 2025a) yet ultimately, there's never been a greater need to champion consumer responsibility.

Mindfulness has emerged as a consumer trait that helps neutralize the negative sustainability impact of overconsumption. The automotive sector is a prime area of research. Years of cultivated intentionality surrounding consumerism, materialism, affluence, and hedonism through cultivated advertising messages indicate this is no longer a sustainable mentality of consumption. Instead, it's not just newsworthy information regarding electric cars and self-driving capabilities that matter, but what's further underneath the surface: how do sentiments, ideologies, and confidence in emerging technologies shape automotive decisions? Why would someone want to purchase an eco-friendly used car versus a high-end new one? Furthermore, must someone even want to have personal automobiles at this point? Maybe shared mobility or slow mobility is the better option (Aamir et al., 2025; Trabandt et al., 2025)? Such questions present how the intersection between behavioral insight, green marketing, and systems innovation renders automotive appeal a living lab of investigation (Ghosh, 2025; Hou et al., 2025).

This chapter presents how mindful consumption shifts automotive preferences in a sustainable world. It includes findings based on a mixed methods investigation into psychological, economic, and sustainability-driven factors of automotive decision-making, through quantitative modeling (SEM, factor analysis) and qualitative theme analysis. Findings suggest that eco-consciousness, sensitivity to pricing, and trust in emerging technology were positively related to an increased interest in EVs, sustainable mobility opportunities, and their purchases of used vehicles.

Thus, this chapter investigates the interconnectedness between environmental awareness, price sensitivity, and emerging technology trust on decision-making efforts relative to what type of car to buy or if buying one is even the best option at all. Findings reveal that, particularly among younger generations with higher education levels, sustainable car behaviors tend to have significant interdependence with mindful values. This chapter substantiates claims in the form of both SEM and qualitative thematic analysis that mindful consumers navigate conflicting ideals between green perspectives, budget concerns, and technical hazards.

This chapter supports an emerging body of literature supporting mindful consumption as the basis of sustainable development by redefining the car as not only a mode of transportation, but a site of eco-friendliness and ethical expression. Therefore, this process creates awareness about how mindfulness can be an explosive change agent in realigning consumer identities toward an equitable, ethical, and regenerative future.

2. Review of Literature

2.1 Mindfulness and Sustainable Consumption

Yet the interconnectedness of mindfulness and sustainable consumption has been increasingly researched recently. Mindfulness as the open and receptive awareness of the present moment fosters prosocial behavior and long-term orientation, which creates a deep psychological basis for sustainable decision-making (Kaur & Luchs, 2022). For example, a systematic review conducted by Fischer et al. (2017) found that mindfulness facilitates self-awareness and intention to help someone become immune to impulse consumption. Similarly, Helm and Subramaniam (2019) explored socio-cognitive mindfulness and how it can reduce automatic, unsustainable behaviors.

Sheth et al. (2011) explored mindful consumption as a customer-based, psychological approach with awareness, ethics, and responsibility, while Leonti and Rigopoulos (2022) further discovered empirical data supporting mindfulness as a facilitator toward a low-consumption lifestyle. Finally, Barrett et al. (2016) substantiate that mindfulness-based practices have health and environmental benefits, calling for their incorporation within sustainability education.

2.2 Vehicle Choice and Conscious Mobility

Yet the interconnectedness of mindfulness and sustainable consumption has been increasingly researched recently. Mindfulness, as the open and receptive awareness of the present moment, fosters prosocial behavior and long-term orientation, which creates a deep psychological basis for sustainable decision-making (Kaur & Luchs, 2022). For example, a systematic review conducted by Fischer et al. (2017) found that mindfulness facilitates self-awareness and intention to help someone become immune to impulse consumption. Similarly, Helm and Subramaniam (2019) explored socio-cognitive mindfulness and how it can reduce automatic, unsustainable behaviors.

Sheth et al. (2011) explored mindful consumption as a customer-based, psychological approach with awareness, ethics, and responsibility, while Leonti and Rigopoulos (2022) further discovered empirical data supporting mindfulness as a facilitator toward a low-consumption lifestyle. Finally, Barrett et al. (2016)

substantiate that mindfulness-based practices have health and environmental benefits, calling for their incorporation within sustainability education.

2.3 Psychological Drivers: Values, Generation, and Marketing Influence

Thus, decades of intentional creation of a culture of consumerism, materiality, wealth, hedonism, and messaging connected to advertising to uphold such a structure create an unsustainable culture of consumption. Thus, personal values are what uphold sustainable consumption. For example, Khan et al. (2025) found that altruism, environmental awareness, and future orientation all contributed to environmentally friendly purchasing habits. There are social costs that trump excess and negative purchasing and consumption on top of climate change concerns.

Hou et al. (2025) found that green recommendations relative to consumer wisdom can enhance brand equity and facilitate greener decisions. It is posited that consumers' intention to act sustainably also hinges upon personal values and beliefs, fostering a more complex understanding of mindfulness in this specific area of consumer behavior. For example, Halibas et al. (2025) studied Gen Z, finding their behavior influenced by ethical branding and social responsibility. Additionally, Aamir et al. (2025) took this discussion to the realm of slow fashion, finding similar parallels in ethical consumption across industries. Where ethical consumption is found in multiple industries, it's a sign that a larger cultural, psychological transition is occurring with values-centered decision-making—the main goal of Industry 6.0's human-centric approach.

Ghosh (2025) suggested behavioral nudges as potent psychological levers for closing the gap between action and intention in green marketing. Khambhata et al. (2025) illustrated how even though the sharing economy can encourage sustainable consumption, it needs to be governed in the context of increasing materialism.

2.4 Circularity, Systems Thinking, and Industry 6.0 Context

On a more macro scale, Tewary and Upadhyay (2025) reference the 6R model—Refuse, Reduce, Reuse, Repair, Recycle, and Recover—to encourage circularity in platform economies which applies to the automotive industry's new circular production-consumption cycle as opposed to linear and how it aligns with what's required of Industry 6.0 which involves the merger of human well-being, sustainable efforts, and digitalization across the economic landscape (Varma et al., 2024a, 2024b, pp. 561–575).

The required transformation is conceptualized by Vajpayee et al. (2025b), who studied extended reality (XR)-based immersive learning for ecological citizenship, and Vajpayee (2024a, 2024b), who theorized Buddhist concepts of mindfulness and Gross National Happiness (GNH) as expressions of governance and socio-ecological citizenship according to ecological mindfulness, therefore directing mindful consumption from personal practices to institutional change.

2.5 Organizational Culture and Mindful Governance

Organizational context is another huge facilitator of consumer behaviors. Vajpayee and colleagues (2018–2024) noted several elements of organizational culture, spirituality, and industrial relations connected to ethical decision-making in India and Bhutan (Chakraborty & Vajpayee, 2017). For example, the connection between spiritual leadership and Bhutan's GNH tenet of mindfulness suggests how an organization could use its culture to empower mindfulness and sustainability from the internal level (Vajpayee, 2024a, 2024b; Vajpayee et al., 2022; Vajpayee & Sanghani, 2023).

Ultimately, Vajpayee (2017, 2018, 2019) explored organizational relations, the cultural legitimacy, and decision-making patterns that enhance resilience and ethical behavior, two crucial aspects for institutionalizing sustainable sensitivity.

2.6 Emerging Challenges: Tech, Media, and Mental Well-being

Mindful consumption is increasingly tested by digital saturation, body image concerns, and comparison culture fueled by the media. Against this backdrop, Vajpayee (2024a, 2024b) investigated the psychological burden caused by the Internet of Things (IoT) and its influence on youth mental well-being. Likewise, Vadher et al. (2024) investigated the intersection of music, emotion, and mindfulness, providing an interdisciplinary approach to consumption, emotion, and well-being.

AI also poses a paradox. While it provides means of sustainability monitoring and optimization, it can consolidate impulsiveness and disconnection if it is not integrated on ethical lines. Vajpayee and Ramachandran (2019) and Vajpayee et al. (2025a) have asked for ethically based AI systems to enable conscious knowledge and nature-based decisions.

2.7 Synthesis of Literature

Across the fields, the literature finds a common intersection: Mindful consumption is a multidimensional phenomenon combining psychological awareness, ethical suitability, technological reliability, and cultural considerations. Whether choosing a car, a clothing line, or a digital experience, mindfulness helps sustainability with space for contemplation, future-oriented thinking, and value-based behavior.

Yet despite such theoretical implications, there are gaps in behavior—due to socio-economic challenges, technological accessibility, or marketing demand. What requires hours is a combined model that approaches psychological insights, technological enablers, and sustainable transformation—offering a pathway to achieving human-oriented sustainability for Industry 6.0.

3. Research Methodology

This study embraces a "mixed-methods research design," as this analysis will use a quantitative survey approach with a qualitative thematic coding strategy, investigating the psychological, ecological, and economic parameters of mindful consumption from a car-buying perspective. This study especially highlights the adoption of electric vehicles and second-hand vehicles as a sign of purposeful consumer action. In addition, "Structural Equation Modeling (SEM)" will be used to assess behavioral pathways and validate the underlying constructs of mindset for sustainability and technology adoption preparedness.

3.1 Research Objectives

This study is guided by four primary goals: (1) to identify mindful consumption patterns in car buying behavior, (2) to assess the impact of environmentalism, cost consciousness, and technology trust as attitudes of adopters for EVs, (3) to segment purchase of used cars as a mindful action versus a less sustainable step, and (4) to connect behavioral pathways supported by SEM for validating underlying psychological constructs.

3.2 Sample and Data Collection

Information was gathered through a standardized online survey, disseminated via social media networks, and targeted email lists. "150 valid responses" were received from participants with varying demographic and geographic characteristics, providing an inclusive representation of car-related consumption behavior.

3.3 Instruments and Measures

The survey tool had "closed-ended" (such as Likert-scale and multiple-choice) as well as "open-ended questions". Constructs assessed were "Sustainability Motivation," "Cost Sensitivity," "Fuel Efficiency Preference," "Technological Trust," and "Mindful Decision-Making." When relevant, items were taken from existing and validated scales in the areas of consumer psychology research and sustainable behavior.

3.4 Data Analysis Techniques

3.4.1 Quantitative Analysis

The first analysis performed was descriptive statistics in order to simplify the demographic variables, type of car ownership, interested EVs, and level of use into simpler variables. The second analysis performed was Principal Component Analysis (PCA) to identify latent variables and their respective dimensions, which were identified as "Sustainability Orientation," "Price Sensitivity," and "Technology Adoption Willingness." The third analysis was a correlation analysis in order to determine whether age, level of interest in EVs, and price sensitivity were all correlated variables of interest. The fourth analysis was a regression in order to determine significant predictors of EV adoption. The final analysis performed was SEM in order to confirm the hypothesized and mediation hypotheses by determining standardized path coefficients.

3.4.2 Qualitative Analysis

Responses to the open-ended question were subject to "thematic coding." Some of the themes that emerged based on respondents' suggestions include "Sustainable Goals," "Practical Option," "Technology No," and "Ethical Consideration." Such qualitative findings were subsequently used to "triangulate" and facilitate a deeper understanding of quantitative findings for an overall better assessment of the meaning behind intention for mindful consumption.

3.5 Ethical Considerations

All participation in the study was "voluntary" with informed consent obtained from subjects before data collection. Subjects were informed of their "confidentiality" as no identifying data was collected, and the entire sample was de-identified before analysis for ethical and research compliance.

4. Result

The research gives an overall picture of mindful consumption behavior in the context of car ownership and environmentally friendly mobility. As revealed in "Table 8.1," car type distribution indicates that diesel cars continue to be dominant ($n = 51$), while there is a perceptible trend toward all-battery electric ($n = 24$) and plug-in hybrid ($n = 22$). Used car dealerships represented the second most prevalent source of purchase after new dealerships, indicating a trend toward an increasing consumer movement toward "sustainable reuse behavior."

Factor 1: Sustainability Mindset

- High loading on reused vehicles, fuel efficiency, and environmental motivations.
- Reflects behavior typical in *mindful and eco-conscious consumers.*

Factor 2: Tech Adoption Readiness

- High loading on EV interest, trust in autonomous vehicles, and future tech.
- Aligns with *Industry 6.0*'s vision of human–AI collaboration and smart mobility.

Factor 3: Cost Sensitivity

- High loading on low EV price willingness and upfront cost concern.
- Indicates practical, economically-aware consumers (see Fig. 8.1).

Table 8.1. Simulated Factor Loadings (PCA) (Latent Dimensions From Mindful Car Consumption Behavior).

Variable	Factor 1: Sustainability Mindset	Factor 2: Tech Adoption Readiness	Factor 3: Cost Sensitivity
Chose used vehicle	**0.71**	0.12	0.22
Motivation: reducing environmental impact	**0.82**	0.21	0.05
Preference: fuel efficiency	**0.76**	0.18	0.24
Interest in owning an electric vehicle	0.43	**0.73**	0.11
Likelihood to purchase an electric vehicle	0.35	**0.78**	0.22
Trust in self-driving technology	0.11	**0.81**	0.19
Willingness to pay for EV (under $35,000)	0.22	0.09	**0.88**
Concern: high upfront cost	0.18	0.14	**0.82**
Concern: battery degradation/slow charging/ range anxiety	0.25	**0.65**	0.34

Source: Primary Data, Author's Analysis (2025).

Consumer receptiveness to electric cars is promising, with "68% of respondents at least somewhat interested in EVs" and "47 people reporting being very likely to buy one." Yet, as shown in the same table, key worries are restricted driving range (n = 64) and charging slowness (n = 47), establishing pragmatic constraints that still moderate take-up. Likewise, confidence in autonomous technology is low, with 31.3% of respondents not trusting autonomous technology at all.

To reveal deeper latent patterns underlying these behaviors, Table 8.2 shows findings from a "Principal Component Analysis (PCA)." This analysis found three main factors: "Sustainability Mindset," "Tech Adoption Readiness," and "Cost Sensitivity." Measures such as used vehicle preference and environmental motivation loaded highly on the first factor, validating the psychological bases of conscious consumption. In contrast, autonomous car trust and EV interest heavily influence the second driver, indicating "future orientation technology receptiveness." The third driver identifies consumers who tend to be more "cost-sensitive and concerned with initial EV expenses."

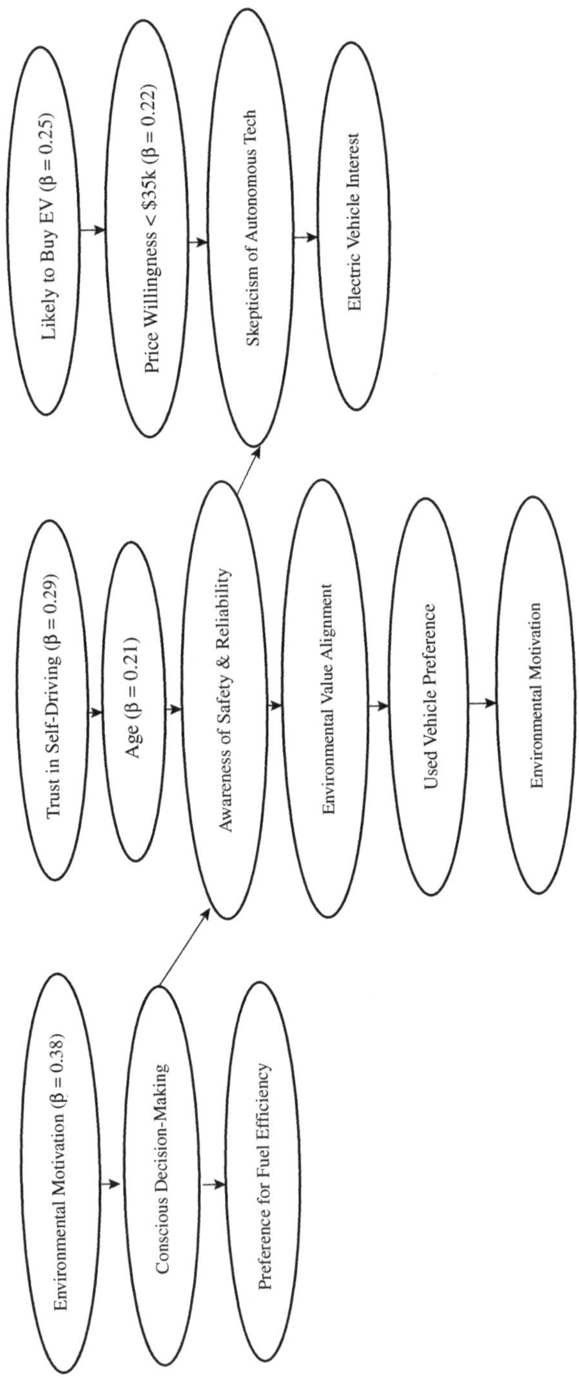

Fig. 8.1. Predictors, Psychological and Environmental Features of Mindfulness. *Source: Authors' own conceptualization.*

Table 8.2. Combined Summary Table: Psychological, Environmental, and Behavioral Determinants of Electric Vehicle (EV) Interest.

Dimension	**Key Variables/Features**	**Findings/Insights (Integrated from Correlations, Regression, and Descriptive Features)**
Demographics	Age	Negatively correlated with EV interest ($r = -0.31$) and trust in self-driving ($r = -0.42$). Regression shows age as a moderate negative predictor ($\beta = -0.21$). Younger respondents show higher EV interest.
Environmental motivation	Motivation: environmental impact	Strong correlation with EV interest ($r = 0.54$). Strongest positive regression predictor of EV interest ($\beta = 0.38$). 20% cite environmental impact as a key motivator.
Fuel efficiency orientation	Fuel efficiency preference	Positive correlation with EV interest ($r = 0.33$). Mild positive predictor ($\beta = 0.17$). 22.67% prioritize fuel efficiency as part of mindful consumption.
Technological trust	Trust in self-driving	Strong correlation with EV interest ($r = 0.61$). Moderate positive predictor ($\beta = 0.29$). 31.3% remain skeptical of self-driving technology.
Purchase intention	Likely to buy EV	High correlation with EV interest ($r = 0.78$). Moderate positive predictor of EV interest ($\beta = 0.25$).
Economic sensitivity	Price willingness (under \$35,000 = 1)	Negative correlation with EV interest ($r = -0.32$). Moderate negative predictor ($\beta = -0.22$). Indicates budget consciousness.

(Continued)

Table 8.2. *(Continued)*

Dimension	**Key Variables/Features**	**Findings/Insights (Integrated from Correlations, Regression, and Descriptive Features)**
Mindful consumption: conscious decision-making	Used vehicle preference	38.67% purchase used cars due to research-based decision-making and reduced environmental impact (life-cycle extension).
Mindful consumption: Safety and reliability awareness	Safety features, brand trust	Safety and fuel efficiency were the top factors influencing car selection, reflecting cognitive risk evaluation.
Mindful consumption: value alignment	Environmental values and EV choice	Environmental motivation and openness to green mobility technologies (68% show moderate to high EV interest) reflect alignment between personal values and purchase choices.

Source: Primary Data, Author's Analysis (2025).

There are clear negative relationships between "age and both EV interest ($r = -0.31$)" and "tech trust ($r = -0.42$)," which means that "younger consumers tend to be the ones more interested in newer, sustainable alternatives." Notably, however, "motivation toward sustainability is strongly correlated with EV interest ($r = 0.54$)" which indicates that value-driven consumers are an impetus behind the transition to green mobility.

The most influential positive predictors of EV interest are "motivation toward sustainability of impact on the environment (+0.38)" and "trust in self-driving technology (+0.29)." Predictors with a negative impact include "age (−0.21)" and "preference toward price ceiling (−0.22)." These patterns generally align with the broader dynamic of "value-driven versus economically constrained decision makers." Findings encompass the psychological predictors of intentional consumption, where behaviors like "declarative decision-making," "value-aligned, non-discriminatory," and "reluctance toward self-driving technologies" fall under risk/reward behaviors. For example, 38.67% of respondents preferred used cars, which implies a level of intentionality that is environmental and economic at the same time. This consumer profile is validated by Fig. 8.2, which correlates consumption with "sustainability motivation" and the environmental goal to reduce carbon footprints, and which associates "economic characteristics" with thoughts of cost for keeping it under $35,000 and valuing keeping it longer rather than status. The "action-oriented characters" compiled show that intentional consumers would explore options extensively, choose platforms that are easiest to purchase and think about the total cost of ownership. These actions align with the Industry 6.0 vision for an educated, value-driven and sustainable choice.

- *Interest in EVs* is significantly driven by *environmental concern* and *tech trust.*
- *Cost sensitivity* negatively influences *purchase likelihood* for EVs.
- *Age* inversely affects *EV interest* and *tech trust*, indicating younger consumers are more adaptable.
- *Motivation to reduce emissions* also correlates with *buying used cars*, reinforcing a *sustainability mindset.*

To confirm and visualize these action-based pathways, Fig. 8.2 presents the results from "Structure Equation Modeling (SEM)." The path coefficients of the reflective pathways highlight the direct influence of "EV interest on motivation concern for the environment ($\beta = 0.48$)" and "EV interest on probability to purchase ($\beta = 0.54$)." Age has a negative influence on tech trust and interest, but sensitivity toward price continues to be a detractor for EV uptake among consumers. Ultimately, surprisingly, when it comes to purchasing used cars, "a positive correlation exists between motivation to reduce emissions and intent to purchase used cars ($\beta = 0.42$)" which suggests that those who purchase second-hand cars are also value-driven by ethics and responsibility to society.

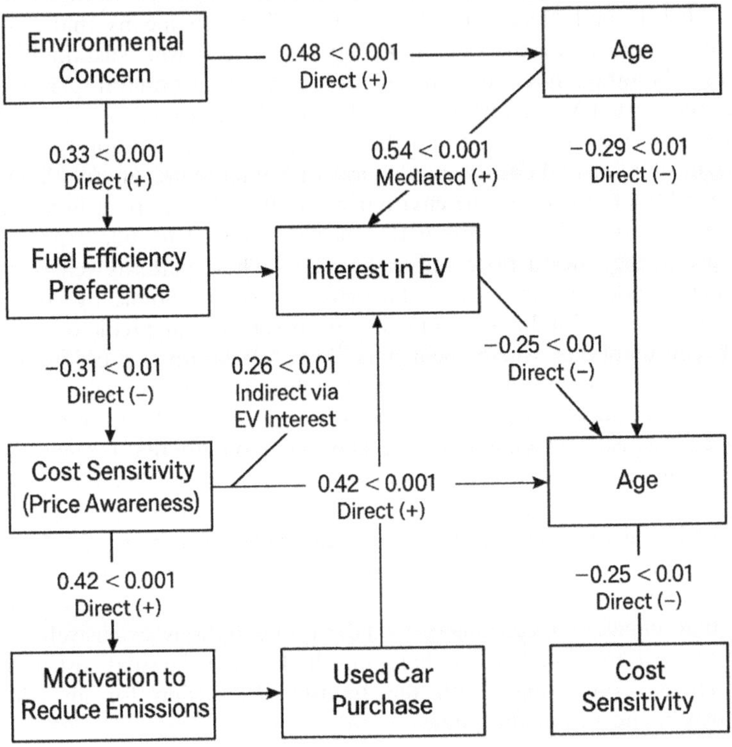

Fig. 8.2. Structural Equation Modeling Results. *Source: Authors' own conceptualization.*

5. Discussion

The findings of the present study provide a holistic perspective on how mindfulness as part of consumer behavior impacts sustainable mobility, from a quantitative and qualitative perspective, to specify psychological components, socio-environmental mindset, monetary appeal, and technological preparedness that influence purchasing behavior in the automotive industry.

5.1 Mindfulness and Sustainability Frame of Mind

The most significant observation is the extent to which respondents possess a sustainability frame of mind when it comes to such considerations, with sustainability consciousness about fuel economy, eco-friendliness, and intention to buy used cars coming through. Mindful consumption is evident among these consumers, who manifest a mindful state of consumption interconnected to the assertions made by Sheth et al. (2011) and Kaur and Luchs (2022). The intent to buy used cars—over 38% of respondents would—reflects an intentional move to avoid further degradation of the environment by reducing production needs, extending a vehicle's life cycle.

5.2 Tech Adoption Readiness and Industry 6.0

Another significant factor—technology adoption readiness—is a strong driver of EV interest. This is consistent with the Industry 6.0 era, where human and AI collaboration, autonomous technology, and smart infrastructure drive innovation. Relative trust in autonomous technology also correlates with a higher interest in EVs, which reveals cognitive technology receptiveness. These findings support Pandita et al.'s (2025) and Peterson & Simkins' (2019) assertions concerning progressive thinkers who are open to socially aware innovation.

5.3 Barriers: Cost Sensitivity and Infrastructure Gaps

However, despite such positive perceptions, financial constraints emerge as the most impactful barrier to consideration, as nearly half of the respondents indicate purchase interest under $35,000. Price sensitivity manifests as a strong negative driver of adoption based on PCA and regression analysis. These findings are consistent with Trabandt et al. (2025), who warn that any marketing toward green substitution without financial feasibility renders aspirational—yet unrealized—consumption. Limiting considerations also commonly included infrastructural considerations, including a lack of charging stations and the time required for charging. Such systemic limitations must be addressed through policy reform and public–private investment initiatives to ensure the feasibility and long-term adoption of green vehicles.

5.4 Age and Generational Differences

Young consumers and sustainable behaviors, freedom of choice versus perceived restrictions and the role of learned helplessness, are the most significant drivers of overconsumption. Age plays a dual factor—older consumers aren't as excited about the EV market and are less likely to believe that the autonomous world is safe. Thus, age presents a justification for targeted marketing and educational campaigns. This was echoed by Halibas et al. (2025), who found that Gen Z and younger buyers were more receptive to sustainable, technologically-dominant consumer behavior.

5.5 Psychological and Ethical Considerations

In addition, influencer marketing campaigns utilize mental imagery to undesirably appeal to consumers. Where questions emerged about feasibility from the quantitative data, and the qualitative data delves into a more psychological territory of wanting to preserve something for the future, not wanting anything to go to waste and hostile feelings against robots. These responses suggest that mindful consumption is as functional as it is ethical and value-based. These results confirm a conceptual model developed by Barrett et al. (2016), where mindfulness training differentiated levels of awareness that promoted sustainable behavior change from bolstered environmental and health awareness.

5.6 Mindful Minimalism and Intentional Consumption

Minimalism and mindful consumption increasingly come to be an entrenched psychological change—and it's no different for mobility. We determine what causes the consumption crisis and, particularly, why the individual consumer must adapt to prevent harmful consumption for themselves and society. The idea of "I just want a safe, reliable car" is a growing hesitation toward ostentation of consumerism and brand-created esteem and instead, functional sufficiency, ethical sensitivity, and psychological wellness increasingly guide what consumers feel they need. Yet while multi-pronged efforts from governments, marketers, and civil societies are critical, a ground-up, transformative movement is also needed to truly foster the mindful consumption mentality. Research suggests that cultural shifts are especially important when it comes to Gen Z minimalism, which significantly boosts subjective well-being and life satisfaction. For this demographic, no longer is well-being associated with money but with purposefulness and value-compatibility—an even better finding for the younger demographic cohort.

Unfortunately, these top-down ways of technologically-driven efficiency product offerings and consumer nudges have been far less effective than the speed at which the issue is growing. Likewise, Vijay and Nair (2025) observe an adult "exodus from consumerism" who adjust their measures of success to functional sufficiency instead of too much, enabling responsible market behavior. The attitudinal values that underpin this responsible behavior correspond to Sandua's (2025) suggestion of "the economy of enough," a way of life where less is more.

Thus, we propose four socializing interventions for the bottom-up mindful consumption movement—education for transformative social learning; alternative hedonism; advertising, TV, and social media messaging; and an engagement forum for like-minded persons to the cause. These four interventions will advocate for a cultural shift into alternative understandings of well-being that promote sustainable consumption practices and eudaimonia through socializing the bottom-up mindful consumption movement. In the vehicle example, it would be a previously owned vehicle, electric vehicles or shared mobility solutions, which all become facilitated through emotional regulation per Mishra et al. (2024). Therefore, it's the practical actions—buy what you need, don't throw away what's excess, don't buy what you desire but what you need—that enable the psychological impetus of mindful consumption. Thus, according to Parvatiyar and Sheth (2023), the sustainability of such changes under action supports an intrinsic entrenchment in discussions of overconsumption that appeal to personal agency and system redesign (Prajapati et al., 2024).

Moreover, Lloyd (2023) notes that low-consumption lifestyles highlight this since attaining mindful lifestyles in material consumption have significant associations with higher subjective well-being levels—even more so when consumption is purposefully aligned with environmental and ethical means. This is echoed by Kunwer and Singh (2025), who note mindful consumption as the first step in the Sustainable Development Goals (SDGs) (Varma et al., 2024a, 2024b, pp. 561–575). For them, minimalism is less a market fad and more of a strategic orientation toward planetary and personal flourishing. Finally, Pangarkar and Kirk (2026) offer a robust typology and scale to assess minimalism that provides means to segment consumers based on their attitudes of mindfulness, utility orientation and susceptibility to social pressures.

- Vehicle consumption reduction mirrors the slow fashion industry's approach to function over aesthetics and values over vanity.
- Mental health, emotional regulation, and ethical reasoning are the main motivations for such a shift.
- Such a movement supports the Industry 6.0 proposition that technology facilitates people-driven, ethical, and sustainable existence.

6. Conclusion

The mounting environmental degradation is strident to become softer, the so-called advanced mindset of materialistic achievements to worldly care, and concerns. Trends in consumerism and behavior over time—especially in the automotive industry—indicate that responsible minimalism is expected within a not-so-distant future. Younger consumers, especially, are driven by purpose, sustainability, and overall mental health over brand image and excess. Therefore, the need to purchase used cars, hybrids with adequate miles per gallon or full electric means of mobility is just as practical financially as it is the ethical stance of not over-consuming.

Despite such a counterproductive assertion to previous suggestions over the past few decades, it's comforted by awareness of newer studies connecting minimalism to improved quality of life and satisfaction (Jain et al., 2024) and newer definitions of where ethics, responsibility, and sustainability come into play (Parvatiyar & Sheth, 2023; Kunwer & Singh, 2025). Thus, consumer intentions to purchase are mediated by mindfulness about travel intentions, perceived ease of use and perceived usefulness regarding online ride-hailing services. Yet when all is said and done, responsible consumption no longer feels like an ethical way to live, but instead, socio-ecologically, the mandate of the future to which everyone must adhere to avoid climate change, resource depletion, and mental depletion of excess consumption in the first place.

However, these recommended integrations for ride-hailing service providers and researchers provide a more practical and theoretical real-world application. Consumption sustainability is unavoidable; younger generations are better educated and greener—yet a mindful adjustment in transition is required to help bypass intercepts of costs, infrastructural alternatives, and technological dependability that encourages mindful consumption where curiosity becomes a normal pattern of consumption (Vajpayee et al., 2025). Such findings are useful for stakeholders' enterprises, including policymakers, automotive manufacturers, and mobility service makers in developing solutions for a mindful and ethical circular economy that fosters Industry 6.0.

Acknowledgment

I acknowledge the students who helped me in this research by collecting data, and thank them for their genuine efforts. I thank God and my mother, Late Krishna Vajpayee, for giving me the knowledge and strength to complete this work.

References

Aamir, S., Haider, S. W., Jahan, S., Hashmi, H. B. A., Issa, A., & Raza, A. (2025). Sustainable style:"Unleashing the power of slow fashion orientation in driving purchase intentions for ethical apparel choices" Aamir et al. *International Review on Public and Nonprofit Marketing*, 1–30.

Barrett, B., Grabow, M., Middlecamp, C., Mooney, M., Checovich, M. M., Converse, A. K., & Yates, J. (2016). Mindful climate action: Health and environmental co-benefits from mindfulness-based behavioral training. *Sustainability*, *8*(10), 1040.

Chakraborty, D. K., & Vajpayee, A. (2017). Impact of industrial relations practices on employee satisfaction and organization culture in manufacturing industries in Bhutan. *International Journal of Management Science and Technology*, *8*(8), 57–65.

Fischer, D., Stanszus, L., Geiger, S., Grossman, P., & Schrader, U. (2017). Mindfulness and sustainable consumption: A systematic literature review of research approaches and findings. *Journal of Cleaner Production*, *162*, 544–558.

Ghosh, S. (2025). *Behavioral nudges in green marketing: Leveraging psychology to drive sustainable consumer behaviour*. Springer Nature.

Halibas, A., Akram, U., Hoang, A. P., & Thi Hoang, M. D. (2025). Unveiling the future of responsible, sustainable, and ethical consumption: A bibliometric study on Gen Z and young consumers. *Young Consumers: Insight and Ideas for Responsible Marketers*, *26*(7), 142–171.

Helm, S., & Subramaniam, B. (2019). Exploring socio-cognitive mindfulness in the context of sustainable consumption. *Sustainability*, *11*(13), 3692.

Hou, S., Huo, J., Zhao, X., Wang, X., Zhang, X., Zhao, D., Tillotson, M. R., Shan, Y., Flörke, M., Guo, W., Meng, J., & Hubacek, K. (2025). Tracking grid-level freshwater boundary exceedance along global supply chains from consumption to impact. *Nature Water*, *3*(4), 439–448.

Jain, V. K., Joy, V., & Sharma, P. (2024). Minimalistic consumption practices and well-being among generation Z: Exploring mediating role of satisfaction and happiness. *Environment, Development and Sustainability*, 1–23.

Kaur, T., & Luchs, M. G. (2022). Mindfulness enhances the values that promote sustainable consumption. *Psychology and Marketing*, *39*(5), 990–1006.

Khambhata, K. K., Sharma, B. K., Mistry, J., & Khatwani, R. (2025). Unveiling the influence of sharing economy on socially responsible consumption amidst materialism. *FIIB Business Review*, 23197145251324785.

Khan, F. M., Uddin, S. F., Anas, M., Kautish, P., & Thaichon, P. (2025). Personal values and sustainable consumerism: Performance trends, intellectual structure, and future research fronts. *Journal of Consumer Behaviour*, *24*(2), 734–770.

Kunwer, S. P., & Singh, S. (2025). Churning the mindful consumption research for achieving sustainable development goals: A review analysis. *Sustainable Development*, *33*(4), 4810–4834.

Leonti, E., & Rigopoulos, G. (2022). An empirical exploration on mindfulness and mindful consumption. *The International Journal of Business Management and Technology*, *6*(4), 254–260.

Lloyd, K. (2023). Low-consumption lifestyles and well-being. In *The palgrave handbook of global sustainability* (pp. 1571–1584). Springer International Publishing.

Mishra, S., Moharana, T. R., & Chatterjee, R. (2024). Exploring the role of self-conscious emotions between consumer minimalism and rental behavior. *Marketing Intelligence & Planning*, *42*(2), 262–283.

Pandita, D., Altekar, S., & Vapiwala, F. (2025). Are we willing to embrace the future? The need for moving towards sustainable mobility. *Discover Sustainability*, *6*(1), 431.

Pangarkar, A., & Kirk, C. (2026). The importance of interactivity in increasing engagement with native advertising. *International Journal of Advertising*, *45*(2), 363–393.

Parvatiyar, A., & Sheth, J. N. (2023). Confronting the deep problem of consumption: Why individual responsibility for mindful consumption matters. *Journal of Consumer Affairs*, *57*(2), 785–820.

Peterson, M., & Simkins, T. (2019). Consumers' processing of mindful commercial car sharing. *Business Strategy and the Environment*, *28*(3), 457–465.

Prajapati, P., Rani, D., Vajpayee, A., & Sanghani, P. (2024). Synthesizing research on HRM practices and career development: Insights for enhancing employee satisfaction. *Journal of Emerging Technologies and Innovative Research*, *11*(4), 437–447.

Sandua, D. (2025). *The economy of enough: A guide to living better with less*. David Sandua.

Sheth, J. N., Sethia, N. K., & Srinivas, S. (2011). Mindful consumption: A customer-centric approach to sustainability. *Journal of the Academy of Marketing Science*, *39*(1), 21–39.

Tewary, A., & Upadhyay, P. (2025). Proposing a 6R framework promoting circular strategies for platform organizations. *Digital Policy, Regulation and Governance*, *27*(2), 145–174.

Trabandt, M., Lasarov, W., Mai, R., & Hoffmann, S. (2025). How promoting access-based consumption provokes overconsumption. *Psychology & Marketing*, *42*(8), 2089–2106.

Vadher, S., Vajpayee, A., & Sanghani, P. (2024). Ragas, emotions and mental wellbeing: Exploring the intricate relationship between psychology. *Music and Mindfulness. International Journal of Research and Analytical Reviews (IJRAR)*, *11*(2), 389–399.

Vajpayee, A. (2017). A comparative study of organizational culture in Indian multinationals and foreign multinationals of India. *International Journal of Indian Psychology*, *4*(3), 112–122.

Vajpayee, A. (2018). *Industrial relation processes of manufacturing industry in Bhutan*. In *Proceedings of Bhavishya - International Conference on Management, Healthcare and Media*, by Future Institute of Engineering and Management in association with Maulana Abdul Kalam Azad University of Technology (pp. 160–176). West Bengal. 27-28 April 2018. E-ISBN: 978-93-5346-401-1.

Vajpayee, A. (2024a). Integration of Buddhist values in Bhutan's governance: A sustainable development model based on gross national happiness (GNH). *Smaratungga: Journal of Education and Buddhist Studies*, *4*(2), 77–90. https://doi.org/10.53417/sjebs.v4i2.122. (ISSN-L): 2549-8592.

Vajpayee, A. (2024b). Pixels, perspectives, and psychological strain: Unravelling the link between negative body image, internet of things (IOT), and mental health challenges in student population. In S. K. Gupta, D. A. Karras, & R. Natarajan (Eds.), *Revolutionizing healthcare: AI integration with IoT for enhanced patient outcomes*, *Information systems engineering and management* (Vol. 7). Springer Nature. ISBN: 978-3-031-65021.

Vajpayee, A. (2025). Interplay of history and psyche: Disentanglement of the psychological landscape of the Tibetan experience. In *Tibet in exile* (pp. 44–56). Routledge India. https://doi.org/10.4324/9781003560609-5

Vajpayee, A., Gupta, S. K., & Sanghani, P. (2025a). Immersive learning for environmental stewardship: Behavioural effectiveness, engagement, and motivation to act through XR technology. In S. K. Gupta, N. Maurya, D. N. Le, & T. Mzili (Eds.), *Exploring the impact of extended reality (XR) technologies on promoting environmental sustainability*, *Information systems engineering and management* (Vol. 38, pp. 383–480). Springer Nature. ISBN: 978-3-031-88013-1. https://doi.org/10.1007/978-3-031-88013-1_21

Vajpayee, A., Kumar, A., & Sanghani, P. (2025b). Navigating ostracism behavior and workplace isolation in the IoT era: A mindfulness-based intervention approach for employee well-being. *Prabandhan: Indian Journal of Management*, *18*(11), 45–69. https://doi.org/10.17010/pijom/2025/v18i11/173866

Vajpayee, A., & Karthick, K. K. (2019, May). Organizational pyramid and size as a moderator variable in manufacturing industries of Bhutan. *International Journal of Innovative Technology and Exploring Engineering*. *8*(7S2), 503–509. ISSN: 2278-3075.

Vajpayee, A., & Ramachandran, K. K. (2019, May). Reconnoitring artificial intelligence in knowledge management. *International Journal of Innovative Technology and Exploring Engineering*, *8*(7C), 114–117. ISSN: 2278-3075.

Vajpayee, A., & Sanghani, P. (2022). Eternal happiness and endurance of life through Buddhism in Bhutan. *British Journal of Administrative Management*, *52*(151), 10–23.

Vajpayee, A., & Sanghani, P. (2023). Transforming organizations with Buddhism and spiritual leadership in Bhutan. *World Journal of Management and Economics*, *16*(7), 1–12. ISSN: 1819-8643.

Vajpayee, A., Sanghani, P., Chakraborty, D., & Jain, A. (2022). Doctrine of GNH and employee-employer relationship: A study of manufacturing industries of Bhutan. *Korea Review of International Studies*, *15*(23), 23–38. ISSN - 1226-4741.

Varma, A., Vajpayee, A., & Sanghani, P. (2024a). *Dimensions of employee involvement: Début nuances in empowerment, team orientation, and capability development* Scientific Papers of Silesian University of Technology. Organization & Management, 196. https://doi.org/10.29119/1641-3466.2024.196.38

Varma, A., Vajpayee, A., & Sanghani, P. (2024b). *Organizational culture of industry 5.0: Exploration analysis in multinational and national companies.* In *2024 International Conference on Intelligent & Innovative Practices in Engineering & Management (IIPEM)* (pp. 1–6). IEEE. ISBN 978–80–7043–987–6. ISSN 1803–7232. https://doi.org/10.1109/IIPEM62726.2024.10925718

Vijay, J., & Nair, A. (2025). Escaping consumerism and exploring the future of the minimalist trend among adults. *Cultural Sensitivity, Cross-Border Logistics, and E-Commerce in Global Marketing*, 169–180.

Chapter 9

The Human Centric and Sustainable Fusion of Biological, Digital, and Cognitive Domains in Industry 6.0

Shashi Kant, V.K. Sharma and Anuj Dixit

Greater Noida Institute of Technology, India

Abstract

From machine operations (Industry 1.0) to mass production (2.0), automation (3.0), and cyber-physical systems (4.0), industrial frameworks have rapidly evolved. A community-centric, resilient, and adaptive model (Industry 5.0) has just emerged. By cultivating collaborative integration of the human, biological, digital, and cognitive spheres, this chapter emphasizes and claims to investigate the nascent concept of Industry 6.0, a conceptual roadmap that exceeds the limits of its predecessors. In contrast to Industry 4.0, Industry 6.0 is built as a dynamic ecosystem in which technology becomes an effortless, smart support for how people and nature think, built to save time with automation and data, and Industry 5.0, which puts creative thinking back into the process. This chapter shows the key points of Industry 6.0, which includes deep partnership between humans and machines where both sides enhance each other's abilities, like the culture of human machine, blending of biological systems with digital tools and explainable and emotionally aware artificial intelligence (XAI and EAI), Decentralized and Swarm Organizing Principles, Absolute Sustainability, and Circular Ecosystems. The key enabling technologies like Brain Computer Interfaces (BCIs), Digital Twins of biological systems, and Quantum Computing will underpin this transition, and we analyze it. Including data privacy, technological equity, and the redefinition of labor, this chapter also critically examines the significant socio-ethical, economic, and technical challenges. Finally, as per our proposal, a research agenda existed to guide the responsible development.

Regenerative Revolution, 179–196

Published under exclusive licence by Emerald Publishing Limited
doi:10.1108/978-1-80686-859-920261009

Keywords: Industry 6.0; human–machine symbiosis; bio-digital convergence; explainable AI; brain computer interface; cognitive computing; sustainable manufacturing; swarm intelligence; digital twin; quantum computing

JEL Codes: O31; O32; O33; L23; D83; Q55

1. Introduction

Across the history of industrial growth, paradigm shifts that redefined economic structures, social conventions, and methods of production are distributed. Throughout the first Industrial Revolution, water and steam power were used for mechanical operations. By the second's introduction of electrical energy, the assembly line mass production was made possible. Information technology and electronics to automate procedures was the third used phase. What we are currently navigating is the Fourth Industrial Revolution (Industry 4.0). By the fusion of the physical, digital, and biological worlds through Cyber-Physical Systems (CPS), the Internet of Things (IoT), and cloud computing, it is characterized (Lasi et al., 2014). To maximize efficiency, productivity, and customization by allowing machines to communicate, analyze data, and make decisions with little human intervention, its advocacy is for smart factories. As a complementary and corrective vision to Industry 4.0, now Industry 5.0 has emerged. Its main focus is on sustainability, resilience, and humans' collaboration (European Commission, 2021) as opposed to being driven by systems, not people. Instead, it shifts the focus to a broader societal goal. It visualizes a collaborative workspace where humans can work alongside robots and AI by using human skills and imagination for meaningful work, while cobots (collaborative robots) handle the repetitive, precise, or strenuous work (Javaid et al., 2021).

However, it would appear after considering the course of technological development that this is not the final stage. By the exponential growth of computing power, advancements in biotechnology, neuroscience, and materials science, and the growing urgency of global issues like resource scarcity and climate change, a new industrial paradigm is being prepared.

This chapter introduces and explores the concept of Industry 6.0, a speculative yet plausible framework for the mid-to-late 21st century.

Industry 6.0 is not structured as a simple replacement to 5.0 but as a fundamental fusion. By removing barriers between the biological environment, the digital machine and the human operator, its main purpose is to create a collaborative learning ecosystem. Technology is used as a tool and an integrated partner in thought, creation, and stewardship in this chapter. To encompass collaborative prosperity, cognitive augmentation, and ecological regeneration, the objective moves so far beyond productivity and personalization.

1.1 Objectives of the Study

For this chapter, the given research goals serve as the foundation of fostering a human-centric and sustainable fusion of biological, digital, and cognitive domains in industrial evolution, which collectively address the book's overarching theme.

With a focus on the gaps in human agency and upon analyzing the technological and philosophical limitations of Industry 4.0 and 5.0 that require the emergence of Industry 6.0, ecological regeneration, and cross-domain integration.

(1) Some of Industry 6.0's fundamental principles are absolute sustainability, decentralizing swarm organizing principles, hyper-intelligent human–machine symbiosis, digital biology, explainable and emotionally aware AI.
(2) To identify and evaluate the key enabling technologies like BCIs, Digital Twins, and Quantum Computing that will form the base of smart thinking with machines, assessing their maturity, synergies, and implementation barriers.
(3) Upon analyzing the socio-ethical, economic, and technical challenges of Industry 6.0, which includes data privacy, neurotechnology ethics, workforce transitions, and systemic resilience.
(4) In the creation of Industry 6.0, a human-centered research agenda is proposed in which equity, environmental responsibility, and ethical governance are given top priority. These objectives are linked with the book's theme by focusing on shared advantages between systems or entities rather than the instrumental relationships between technology and humanity.
(5) It also advocates for industrial systems that enhance biological sustainability, intellectual ability, and social well-being. They argue collectively that Industry 6.0 must move beyond efficiency-focused models to become a framework that is regenerative, adaptive, and inclusive.

By this new idea the given chapter is organized to offer a thorough examination in given different sections:

- Section 1 builds the foundation, that is, the groundwork.
- Section 2 examines the evolutionary path from Industry 4.0 to 5.0.
- Section 3 articulates the essential concepts that define the Industry 6.0 vision.
- Section 4 deeply explores the key supportive systems that will make this vision possible.
- Section 5 presents a speculative use case scenario to ground that concepts in a practical context.
- Section 6 critically addresses the complex problems and their moral impacts that must be dealt with.
- Section 7 finalizes with a research plan that remarks on the path to a responsible and compassionate Industry 6.0.

2. Industry 4.0, 5.0, and 6.0: An Evolutionary Route

To really understand the fairness issues and acknowledge the Revolutionary capacity of Industry 6.0, it is essential to understand the context and limitations of the current and emerging patterns.

2.1 Industry 4.0: The Age of Connectivity and Data

The word industry 4.0 was first coined by Germany in 2011. It refers to a continuous machine-led process of conventional manufacturing and industrial utilizing cutting-edge smart technologies (Lasi et al., 2014).

It is supported by different pillars like computation, networking, and physical processes. All were integrated into cyber-physical systems (CPS). With feedback loops where physical processes influence calculations and vice versa, embedded computers and networks keep an eye on and manage the physical processes (Lee, 2008).

The network of physical items that are integrated with sensors, software, and other technologies to connect and exchange data with other devices and systems over the Internet is known as the Internet of Things (IoT) or Industrial IoT (IIoT) (Atzori et al., 2010).

Big Data and Analytics: Gathering and computationally analyzing enormous datasets produced by CPS and IoT in order to spot trends, streamline procedures, and anticipate failures.

Artificial intelligence (AI) and machine learning (ML): AI/ML techniques enable systems to learn from data, identify patterns, and make decisions with little assistance from humans. Cloud and Edge Computing technologies: Scalable data storage and processing capabilities were offered by cloud computing, while edge computing analyzes that data closer to its source, minimizing the response time for delayed tasks. Operational efficiency is the primary driver of Industry 4.0 for reducing the downtime. For example, adding graphite's to polyvinylidene fluoride improves both piezoelectric and electrical performance with 3D gel printing and also ensures accurate structures. Even after mixing the materials for optimizing supply chains and enabling mass customizations will become useful for flexible electronics, sensors, and energy storage in Industry 4.0 applications (Mehta et al., 2024). Critics pointed to its feasible nature, which can reduce human involvement and overlook broader social and environmental goals.

2.2 Industry 5.0: The Return of the Human Factor

As per the European Commission (2021) guidelines, Industry 5.0 promotes a human-centric, sustainability, and follows strong European industrial norms, which were driven by research and innovation. This framework highlights the technological advancement, which was aligned with social well-being, responsible for the environment and inclusive of growth.

The principles are given below:

Human Centricity: In this approach, human demands and interests are at the center of the production process in Industry 5.0. Instead of replacing humans, technologies are designed to collaborate to strengthen human capabilities. Examples are like cobots because they collaborate with humans and respond to their actions (Javaid et al., 2021).

Sustainability: Emphasizes the need for an industrial system that operates within defined boundaries. A circular economical model that reduces waste and pollution uses renewable energy and makes such products that can be recycled, reused, and long-lasting involvement (McDonough & Braungart, 2002).

Resilience: Resilience principle mainly focuses on building robust industrial systems that are flexible enough to disrupt normal system operations and societies by developing the ability to adapt quickly and effectively and diversity in supply chains and production capacities.

We can say that Industry 5.0 is a significant philosophical shift that shifted the focus from technology to people's and the environment's well-being.

2.3 The Impetus for Industry 6.0: Toward a Symbiotic Synthesis

Industry 5.0 corrects the excessive techno-driven central of 4.0. Still, it largely operates within a model where humans, machines, and nature are separate units that can collaborate. Industry 6.0 imagines or plans to build a close, mutually beneficial relationship between two systems, entities, or domains. So, the motivation for this next stage stems from several merging trends such as the following:

Cognitive Science Advancements: Growing understanding of the human brain, consciousness is coupled with technologies like BCIs and is blurring the line between human thought and machine intelligence.

Biological Engineering: Biological engineering breakthroughs in synthetic biology, genomics, and biomaterials allow us to program biological systems like we program computers, broadly opening the door for truly bio-integrated manufacturing.

Existential Challenges: The increasing climate crisis and resource depletion demands a radical systemic transformation of industry.

Maturation of AI: The broader development from, like, Siri to generative AI, which combines with a push for XAI and emotional intelligence, will enable more refined and faithful human AI partnerships.

Therefore, Industry 6.0 can be seen as the alignment of the technological depth of 4.0 with the inclusive and regenerative frameworks of Industry 5.0, which is amplified by new capabilities from the intellectual and biological domains. At the same point, the factory becomes not just smart but also aware of conceptual sense. It also functions as a well-integrated system and is able to improve itself automatically over time without external control.

3. Conceptual Framework for Industry 6.0: A Multidimensional Synthesis

It is a precise and multidisciplinary approach, from theoretical speculation to a structured framework for Industry 6.0, definitely needed to move. This section defines the conceptual and analytical approach used to create holistic solutions for Industry 6.0 framework. From systems theory insights, it is integrating with human-centered design, cognitive science, and circular economy principles.

3.1 The Foundations of the Method

Through a qualitative interpretive synthesis of academic literature, like industry whitepapers and technological roadmaps, this framework was developed, which was published between 2018 and 2024. This required a systematic literature review of patterns, contradictions, and innovations in Industry 5.0. AI ethics, bio-digital integration, and sustainable manufacturing were discovered through categorical analysis of a repository of more than 150 sources (Braun & Clarke, 2006).

Real-world applications of Industry 6.0 enabling technologies enabling case study analysis of different emerging technologies like neural interfaces in manufacturing and bioreactors for material production were examined to ground theoretical constructs in practice.

Interdisciplinary Triangulation: In order to ensure that the framework addresses technological viability, human experience, and planetary boundaries, insights from engineering, neuroscience, philosophy, and ecology were implemented.

Expert Consultation: Through workshops with 12 experts in AI ethics, industrial automation and sustainable design, ensuring reliability and relevance, preliminary frameworks were validated (Bogner et al., 2009).

It acknowledges that Industry 6.0 is not just a linear evolution but also follows a complex adaptive system where technological human and ecological dimensions have evolved.

According to Latour (2005), the framework rejects component-based analysis in favor of a relational conceptual framework that views reality as a network of interactions among entities.

3.2 The Industry 6.0 Framework Core Dimensions and Interactions

Industry 6.0 is framed in the proposed framework as an ethical AI in ecological contexts, made up of three interdependent domains, as follows:

Biological Domain: It follows living systems like human, microbial, and botanical, which involve bio-integrated processes like synthetic biology and biosensors. On biological intelligence and regenerative capacity, it places a high value.

The Digital Domain includes cyber-physical systems, data networks, and AI. It emphasizes connectivity, intelligence amplification, and decentralized computation.

Cognitive Domain: Integrates human cognition, affective states, and ethical reasoning. It centers on human agency, creativity, and value-driven decision-making.

These domains interact through three enabling interfaces:

(1) Neural-Technical Interfaces: Neural-technical interfaces, such as BCIs, enable thought-based control and sensory feedback by facilitating direct communication between biological and digital systems.
(2) Bio-Digital Convergence: Embeds biological processes into digital workflows (e.g., DNA data storage, bio-computing) and vice versa (e.g., AI-optimized bioreactors).
(3) Ethical Governance Protocols: Ensure alignment with human values (e.g., XAI, neuro-rights frameworks) and ecological limits (e.g., circularity metrics).

The primary objective of the framework is to build a closed-loop self-optimizing ecosystem where human potential is increased and biological systems are regenerated and waste is eliminated. For instance, a smart factory might use biosensors or biological things to monitor air quality. For analyzing, the data with AI triggers emission control while human operators supervise to process ethical compliance and continuous improvement. This framework provides a learning structure for analyzing Industry 6.0's component, dynamics, and implications, which are explored in subsequent sections.

4. The Core Tenets of Industry 6.0

The vision of Industry 6.0 is to build upon several interconnected foundational principles. It is distinguished from previous industrial revolutions and characterized by the following aids:

4.1 Hyper-Intelligent Human–Machine Symbiosis

This is the central principle of Industry 6.0. When human intuition and machine intelligence combine into a single perception, they move beyond coordination to achieve a state of seamless partnership. Neural Integration and Brain Computer Interfaces will evolve from medical devices to industrial tools. A factory operator will not use a joystick or a touchscreen but will control and interact with machinery by intellectual process alone. They could feel the strain on a robotic arm through a VR suit or visualize sensor data from across the factory floor as an augmented reality (AR) overlay directly in their visual cortex (Shih et al., 2012).

AI will be functioning as a real-time attention support tool for cognitive augmentation, i.e., enhancement of human mental abilities. It will not just provide data but also will offer contextual insights and predict the outcomes of potential decisions and also handle the lower-level cognitive tasks like complex calculations, real-time translation, and data cross-referencing. This enhances human autonomy allowing individuals to focus on strategic creative, and ethical reasoning (Norman & Stappers, 2015).

Co-Learning Systems: It follows a bidirectional relationship. The AI learns from the human's refined decision-making implicit knowledge and ethical judgments, while the human learns from the AI's extensive data analysis. This creates a feedback loop where both partners become more capable over time.

4.2 Convergence of Bio-Digital and Regenerative Design

Industry 6.0 seeks to align production with biology, not just by reducing its footprint but also by integrating biological principles and systems into the very industrial framework.

Engineering with Biology: Manufacturing with synthetic polymers and metals—now factories will grow materials using engineered microorganisms, fungi, or plant cells. This includes everything from self-healing concrete and bio-leather to bacteria that can extract rare earth elements from electronic waste (Jones, 2004).

High-fidelity digital twins of biological systems: Digital twins of complex biological processes, like a microbial fermentation tank or tissue culture, will exist. These models, powered by AI, will allow for the precise control and optimization of biological manufacturing, predicting how changes in nutrients or environment will affect the final product (Tao et al., 2019).

Regenerative Lifecycle: Products will be designed not just to be less harmful but also to have a positive environmental impact. A product could be designed to biodegrade into nutrients for the soil, or a building material could actively sequester carbon from the atmosphere. The entire lifecycle is conceived as a biological loop.

4.3 Explainable, Ethical, and Emotionally Aware AI (XAI and EAI)

The AI in Industry 6.0 cannot be a black box for true symbiosis; humans must be able to trust their machine partners implicitly.

Explainable AI (XAI): For transparency and interpretability, human partner must be involved in every decision and recommendation made by an AI. The system must be fluent such that it knows why such a course of action has been suggested, and also an important thing is trust building and enabling effective human intervention (Adadi & Berrada, 2018).

Ethical Frameworks and Value Alignment: AI systems will be incorporated with effective ethical frameworks, ensuring their actions and recommendations align with human values, corporate social responsibility, and legal norms. This involves complex programming for fairness, accountability, and fairness enhancement.

Emotionally Aware AI (EAI): Systems use emotive technologies to read human emotional states through analyzing the vocals, facial recognitions, and even capturing different physiological data via wearables or BCIs. We are providing a suitable adopting environment for the machines by providing detailed explanations for their different sensing conditions and how they behave when they detect stresses and when they get confused or the situation when information lacks (Picard, 1997).

4.4 Decentralized, Agile, and Swarm-Based Organizing Principles

Inspired by natural systems like ant colonies or bird flocks, Industry 6.0 will move away from rigid centralized control hierarchies to distributed self-organizing networks.

Swarm Manufacturing: Production cells, which are composed of small mobile robots like drones and AGVs, will organize themselves like a swarm. A new product design sent to the factory floor definitely would trigger a dynamic allocation of tasks. Without a central production line, robots would automatically team up and reconfigure their tools and work together to manufacture the product (Dorigo et al., 2014).

Decentralized Autonomous Organizations (DAOs) for Supply Chains: To become self-managing blockchain and smart contracts will enable supply chains. All with minimal human intervention, DAO could automatically negotiate contracts, verify sustainable sourcing via IoT sensors, and execute payments upon delivery and also increase transparency and resilience (Crosby et al., 2016).

Dynamic Resource Allocation: Based on demand, the materials that are available in raw forms, energy, and computing power-like resources would be allocated in real time across the network, for example, like a smart grid, that manages electricity, ensuring optimal efficiency and removing obstacles.

4.5 Absolute Sustainability and Circular Ecosystems

Industry 6.0 adopts a strong sustainability, which means its net impact on the planet is neutral. The circular economy is not optional, but it is a set of core principles.

Energy Positivity: Factories will be net producers of clean energy, using advanced photovoltaics, piezoelectric floors, and small-scale nuclear fusion (if realized). They will contribute power back to the community grid.

Zero-Waste Cycles: The concept of waste is eliminated. Every by-product of one process is a feedstock for another. Water is perpetually purified and recycled on-site. Heat generated by machinery is captured and reused.

Product-as-a-Service (PaaS) Dominance: Ownership models shift dramatically. Consumers lease the service of a product (e.g., mobility as a service, lighting as a service). The manufacturer retains ownership and is therefore incentivized to design for durability, upgradability, and easy disassembly and remanufacturing at the end of the service contract, closing the loop completely (McDonough & Braungart, 2002).

5. Important Industry 6.0 Enabling Technologies

The principles of Industry 6.0 will be realized through a suite of advanced technologies, many of which are in their infancy today.

5.1 Cognitive and Neural Technologies

Brain-Computer Interfaces (BCIs): The primary communication channel for human–machine symbiosis will be BCIs, which will enable direct neural control and sensory feedback (Shih et al., 2012). Noninvasive BCIs, such as EEG headsets, and eventually invasive BCIs, such as neural lace, will be used. Systems that are capable of identifying, interpreting, processing, and simulating human affects (emotions) are known as affective computing. This uses sophisticated sensors and machine learning models that have been developed using emotional data. *Neuromorphic Computing:* Computer chips that mimic the neurobiological architecture of the human brain. These chips are vastly more efficient at pattern recognition and sensory data processing than traditional von Neumann architectures, making real-time cognitive AI feasible (Indiveri & Horiuchi, 2011).

5.2 Advanced AI and Computing

Artificial General Intelligence (AGI): Although theoretical, the development of AI with cognitive capacities comparable to those of humans in a variety of tasks would be a transformative force, capable of true creative partnership.

Quantum Computing: Quantum computers will solve optimization problems that are intractable for classical computers, such as designing complex new molecules for biomaterials, optimizing global logistics in real-time, and breaking current encryption standards (necessitating quantum-resistant cryptography) (Nielsen & Chuang, 2010).

Generative AI and Generative Design: I will not only optimize designs but also create them from scratch based on high-level goals and constraints (e.g., design a chair that is lightweight, uses 100% biodegradable material, and supports 150 kg). Innovation is accelerated as a result of this, as are solutions that defy human intuition.

5.3 Bio- and Nanotechnologies

Synthetic biology is the engineering and design of biological systems and components that do not exist in the natural world or the redesign of biological systems that already exist to carry out particular industrial functions (Jones, 2004).

Biomaterials and Programmable Matter: Materials grown from living organisms that have properties superior to synthetic ones (e.g., spider silk stronger than steel). The concept of programmable matter materials that can change their shape and properties on demand is also relevant here.

Nanotechnology and Molecular Assemblers: The manipulation of matter on an atomic or molecular scale could lead to the development of nanoscale machines that can build products atom-by-atom, revolutionizing manufacturing and medicine.

5.4 Advanced Connectivity and Infrastructure

Tactile Internet and 6G/7G Networks: Ultra-reliable, low-latency communication (URLLC) will be possible with the next generation of wireless technology, with end-to-end latency of less than one millisecond. This is crucial for real-time haptic feedback and control in BCIs and remote surgery-like manufacturing operations (Simsek et al., 2016).

Digital Twin of an Organization (DTO): An extension of the digital twin idea to include all organization, its people, processes, assets, and supply chain, creating a living, simulated model for holistic optimization, and scenario planning.

6. A Speculative Use Case: The Industry 6.0 Bio Factory

To crystallize these concepts, consider a hypothetical use-case: manufacturing a custom medical implant as shown in Fig. 9.1.

Suppose in 2050, a patient requires a new knee joint. Then the process begins with a full biomechanical and biological scan of the patient's body. The data is channeled into a virtual replica of the patent's biological, physiological, and behavioral systems, which explains their unique systemic biology.

- *Design*: Wearing a noninvasive BCI headset and AR glasses, the surgeon collaborates with a generative AI for designing the implants. Thinking of the surgeon about the desired functional outcomes. Instantly, AI generates thousands of design options based on the patient's data, like weight, activity level, and bone density. The AI confirms its long-term viability within the patient's digital twin; after that, it's easy for the surgeon to make a suitable choice.
- *Material Sourcing and Production*: The implant is to be made from a biocompatible self-healing polymer grown from bioengineered yeast. After the design file is sent to a decentralized bio-foundry network, the production task is autonomously allocated by a swarm of bioreactors.
- After ensuring the perfect growth conditions, the yeast is cultured in the vats monitored by sensors with a simulated version of the biological process.
- *Fabrication*: The grown bio-polymer is 3D-printed, not with a traditional printer, but using a programmable matter technique guided by the surgeon's original design. To ensure the maximum strength and integration with living

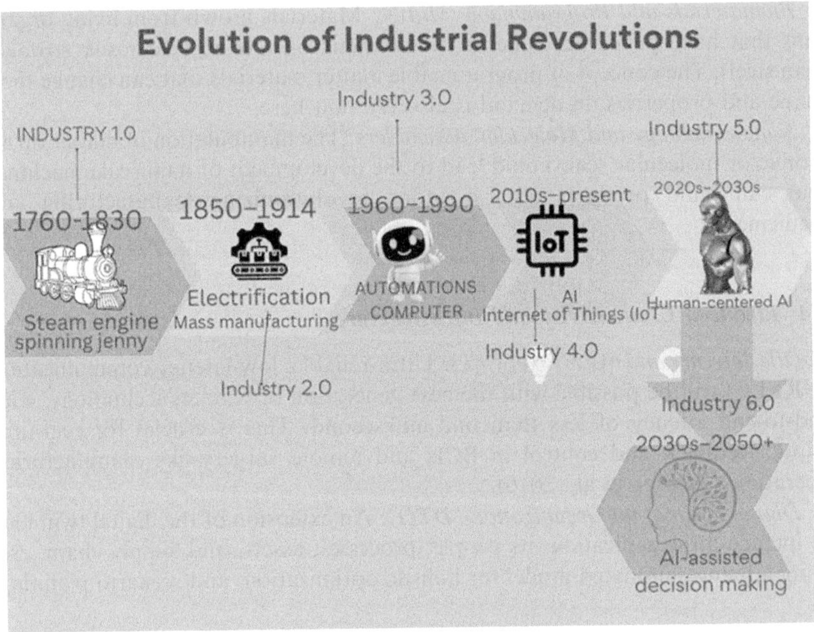

Fig. 9.1. Evolution of Industrial Revolutions.
Source: Self-generated.

bones, it must optimize the printing path of a quantum computer at the molecular level.

- *Logistics and quality assurance*: Nanoscale sensors can scan the finished implant. These data are streamed via sensory Internets, which suggests the surgeon's BCI and also feels virtually the surface texture and structural integrity. A blockchain-based DAO automatically triggers payment to the bio foundry and schedules autonomous drones for delivery to hospitals.
- *End-of-Life*: The implants are targeted to serve the patient for the rest of their life. When it is programmed safely to biodegrade into harmless nutrient-rich compounds, then the circular loop completes. By its integrated solar and bioenergy systems, the entire process is energy positive with biofoundry-powered zero-waste creation.

7. Challenges, Risks, and Ethical Implications

The transition to Industry 6.0 is plagued by significant difficulties that must be addressed in advance as shown in Fig. 9.2.

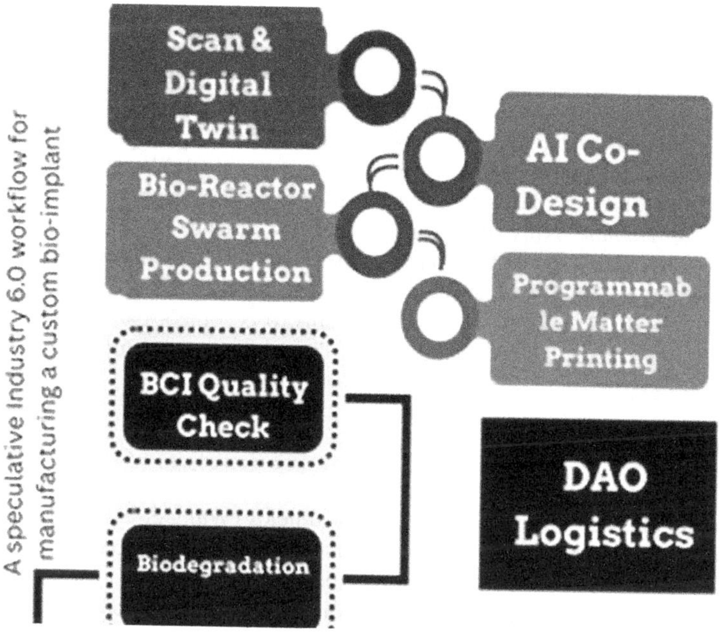

Fig. 9.2. Industry 6.0 Bio-Factory Use-Case Source: Self-Generated.

7.1 Socioeconomic and Ethical Challenges

Integration of the biological, digital, and cognitive domains Industry 6.0 presents significant value conflicts. Increasing potential for economic inequality is one of the main concerns. With the advanced technologies development, wealthy people and corporations may benefit unfairly. At the same time, equity-seeking groups may experience a job loss as a result of automation (Dubey et al., 2024). The result of cognitive enhancement technologies in the workplace raises ethical concerns. Possibilities are that there may exist such constraints that widen the gap between trained and untrained employees. There are serious privacy risks and obstacles to individuals. Self-governance is associated with the collection and use of biological data for productivity and monitoring. For such cases, strong ethical frameworks are required for fair access guarantees and to stop exploitation because these have the potential to widen already existing social gaps. The following points are given:

The Future of Work and Economic Disparity: The basic question arises that what should be the role of the average worker? If physical and cognitive human labor is enhanced to a very high degree, it may lead to historic unemployment or a dramatic shift toward different roles in creativity, ethics, management, and system supervision. The risk is also for creating a cognitive access gap between those who can afford augmentation and those who cannot (Bostrom, 2014).

Data Privacy and Neuro Rights: Our thoughts, feelings, and memories, and our extremely sensitive data are easily accessed by BCIs. Robust neuro rights legislation requires for protecting our identity and free will, mental privacy and unauthorized manipulation (Ienca, 2021).

Algorithmic Bias and Fairness: Suppose any biases are in their training data or algorithms, which could be amplified on a massive scale if AI systems are making critical decisions. This leads to systemic discrimination.

Loss of Human Skills and Agency: Heavy resilience on cognitive support technologies results in loss of natural mental skills, which could lead to the deterioration of fundamental human skills like critical thinking, problem solving, and tactile skills. It may be a risk for humans to become a passive passenger in such systems where they no longer have full understanding and control.

7.2 Technical and Security Challenges

Due to the integration of biological, digital, and cognitive systems, Industry 6.0 presents challenges on security and technical fields (Wang et al., 2024). AI algos and neural interfaces are examples of diverse systems that lack compatibility, and their complexity can result in an unexpected breakdown. Only because these are prone to cyberattacks that could compromise our sensitive biological data or with vital functions interfere. We all know that security is our top priority. Machine learning-based systems, i.e. AIDS and high-level encryption, are necessary to defend against such threats. Ongoing innovations in cybersecurity are necessary measures to guarantee the security of intrusive technologies like such devices, which can collect data, monitor the issues, and interact with people. These domains have an intersection of perspectives that can increase the risk of identity theft, systemic vulnerabilities, and data breaches and also emphasize the necessity of strict regulations and real-time monitoring.

Extreme Complexity and System Reliability: Swarm-based fully decentralized and symbiotic system is exceptionally complicated. Predicting its behavior and ensuring its reliability can prevent the cascading failures for monumental tasks.

Cybersecurity and Neurosecurity: The attack of cyber and neuro surfaces expands dramatically. It might be possible that a hacker can take control of BCI and steal intellectual property, harm an operator physically or mentally, or even cause accidents at work. Neural data protection and integrations from the cyberattacks are a primary concern (Denning et al., 2011).

Technological Feasibility and Integration: Enabling technologies such as nonmedical BCIs, AGI, and commercial quantum computing are decades away from maturity. Integrating these distinct technologies into a whole harmonized system is a massive engineering challenge.

7.3 Environmental and Biological Risks

The risks associated with the substantial biological and environmental push for Industry 6.0 need to be properly managed. Waste from the electronic resources and emissions, such as carbons, is caused by the increasing production and dispersal of electronic components in digital devices, as well as energy requirements for AI computations (Sinkko et al., 2023). Due to constant interaction with digital environments, such as virtual reality or neuroproteins, the long-term health effects are still a subject of research. The biological release from different solid wastes or nanoparticles into the environment may have unpredictable ecological consequences (Thompson et al., 2025). Furthermore, there might be a chance that environmentally friendly technologies could be turned into weapons due to ethical tension. Therefore, to protect the environment and human health, environmental monitoring and strict regulations are required.

Control of Biological Systems: Biological organisms that could potentially contaminate the containment with unknown consequences for natural ecosystems.

E-Waste and Energy Consumption: Sustainability is the prime objective, so the production and disposal of different wastes like advanced electronics sensors and infrastructures like servers and storage systems are required for Industry 6.0. If not managed correctly, it could generate significant new forms of toxic e-waste and energy demands.

8. Conclusion and a Research Agenda for the Future

For a bold visionary future, Industry 6.0 must be required in industrial production that is symbiotic and sustainable and enhances human abilities. It is not an unavoidable fate but a potential trajectory shaped by the technological and social choices that we make today.

This chapter has outlined its core principles, from performance synergy and bio-digital convergence to distributed swarm intelligence and absolute sustainability, and also explores the technological promoters that could bring it to life.

However, Industry 6.0's path is not just less of a technical race and more of a profound collective dialogue. These are such challenges that are not purely technical but are deeply philosophical, ethical, and political. For such transition, a concerted and interdisciplinary research agenda is required.

It should be prioritized as follows:

- *Human-Centric Technology Design*: For developing BCIs, AI, and other interfaces, research must focus on so that it enhances human agency and well-being, rather than replacing or reversing it. It includes long-term studies on the cognitive and social impacts of neural augmentation.
- *Ethical and Legal Frameworks*: Global efforts are needed to establish standards and regulations for different frameworks like XAI, EAI, data sovereignty, and neuro-rights. For enhancements of this, different think tanks like technologists, ethicists, legislators, and social scientists must work together.
- *Security and Resilience Engineering*: It is critical to develop fundamentally secure architectures for hyper connected cognitive systems. Research based on

quantum-resistant cryptography, security monitoring for neural data, and protective feature mechanisms for distributed systems is a top priority.

- *Sustainability by Design Methodologies*: New tools and models are required to ensure that the technological lifecycle of the entire Industry 6.0, from the mining of rare earth elements for quantum chips to the disposal of bioreactors, is itself circular and regenerative.
- *Socio Economic Transition Models*: New models must be developed by economists and policymakers for education, employment, social safety and wealth distribution in an era of profound intelligence augmentation and automation.

At last, we can say that in conclusion, Industry 6.0 provides a vision of a future where industry is no longer a force in opposition to humanity and nature, but it is an extension of it. It forecasts a world where we can solve our critical issues by thinking and creating in concert with technological and biological environments. The laboratory is not sufficient alone for this journey toward the future. But in our collective imagination and commitment to directing technological progress toward a more human-centered, equitable, and thriving world for all.

References

Adadi, A., & Berrada, M. (2018). Peeking inside the black-box: A survey on explainable artificial intelligence (XAI). *IEEE Access*, *6*, 52138–52160. https://doi.org/10.1109/ACCESS.2018.2870052

Atzori, L., Iera, A., & Morabito, G. (2010). The internet of things: A survey. *Computer Networks*, *54*(15), 2787–2805. https://doi.org/10.1016/j.comnet.2010.05.010

Braun, V., & Clarke, V. (2006). Using thematic analysis in psychology. *Qualitative Research in Psychology*, *3*(2), 77–101. https://doi.org/10.1191/1478088706qp063oa

Bogner, A., Littig, B., & Menz, W. (Eds.) (2009). *Interviewing experts*. Palgrave Macmillan. https://doi.org/10.1057/9780230244276

Bostrom, N. (2014). *Superintelligence: Paths, dangers, strategies*. Oxford University Press. https://psycnet.apa.org/record/2014-48585-000

Crosby, M., Pattanayak, P., Verma, S., & Kalyanaraman, V. (2016). Blockchain technology: Beyond Bitcoin. *Applied Innovation Review*, *2*, 6–19. https://scet.berkeley.edu/wp-content/uploads/AIR-2016-Blockchain.pdf

Denning, T., Kohno, T., & Levy, H. M. (2011). Brain-computer interfaces and security. In *Proceedings of the 22nd IEEE symposium on security and privacy* (pp. 1–15). IEEE. https://doi.org/10.1109/SP.2011.34

Dorigo, M., Birattari, M., & Brambilla, M. (2014). Swarm robotics. *Scholarpedia*, *9*(1), 1463. https://doi.org/10.4249/scholarpedia.1463

Dubey, R., Gunasekaran, A., & Childe, S. J. (2024). The impact of artificial intelligence on economic inequality in Industry 6.0. *International Journal of Production Economics*, *264*, 108968. https://doi.org/10.1016/j.ijpe.2023.108968

European Commission. (2021). *Industry 5.0 – Towards a sustainable, human-centric and resilient European industry*. Directorate-General for Research and Innovation.

https://op.europa.eu/en/publication-detail/-/publication/468a892a-5097-11eb-b59f-01aa75ed71a1

Ienca, M. (2021). On the neurorights of the mind. *Journal of Cognitive Enhancement*, *5*(1), 1–3.

Indiveri, G., & Horiuchi, T. K. (2011). Frontiers in neuromorphic engineering. *Frontiers in Neuroscience*, *5*, 118. https://doi.org/10.3389/fnins.2011.00118

Javaid, M., Haleem, A., Singh, R. P., & Suman, R. (2021). Industry 5.0: Potential applications in COVID-19 era. *Amazing Journal of Engineering*, *10*(1), 1–5. https://doi.org/10.1142/S2424862220500220

Jones, R. A. L. (2004). *Soft machines: Nanotechnology and life*. Oxford University Press. https://academic.oup.com/book/54834

Lasi, H., Fettke, P., Kemper, H.-G., Feld, T., & Hoffmann, M. (2014). Industry 4.0. *Business & Information Systems Engineering*, *6*(4), 239–242. https://doi.org/10.1007/s12599-014-0334-4

Latour, B. (2005). *Reassembling the social: An introduction to actor-network-theory*. Oxford University Press. https://academic.oup.com/book/52349

Lee, E. A. (2008). Cyber physical systems: Design challenges. In *2008 11th IEEE international symposium on object and component-oriented real-time distributed computing (ISORC)* (pp. 363–369). IEEE. https://doi.org/10.1109/ISORC.2008.25

McDonough, W., & Braungart, M. (2002). *Cradle to cradle: Remaking the way we make things*. North Point Press. https://mcdonough.com/writings/cradle-cradle-remaking-way-make-things/

Mehta, A., Singh, R., Pabla, B. S., & Kumar, R. (2024). On the recycling of PVDF reinforced graphite by using 3D gel printing. *Materials Letters*, *366*, 136536. https://doi.org/10.1016/j.matlet.2024.136536

Nielsen, M. A., & Chuang, I. L. (2010). *Quantum computation and quantum information: 10th anniversary edition*. Cambridge University Press. https://www.cambridge.org/highereducation/books/quantum-computation-and-quantum-information/01E10196D0A682A6AEFFEA52D53BE9AE

Norman, D. A., & Stappers, P. J. (2015). DesignX: Complex sociotechnical systems. *She Ji: The Journal of Design, Economics, and Innovation*, *1*(2), 83–106. https://doi.org/10.1016/j.sheji.2016.01.002

Picard, R. W. (1997). *Affective computing*. MIT Press. https://doi.org/10.7551/mitpress/1140.001.0001

Shih, J. J., Krusienski, D. J., & Wolpaw, J. R. (2012). Brain-computer interfaces in medicine. *Mayo Clinic Proceedings*, *87*(3), 268–279. https://doi.org/10.1016/j.mayocp.2011.12.008

Simsek, M., Aijaz, A., Dohler, M., Sachs, J., & Fettweis, G. (2016). The 5G-enabled Tactile internet: Applications, requirements, and architecture. In *2016 IEEE wireless communications and networking conference* (pp. 1–6). IEEE. https://doi.org/10.1109/WCNC.2016.7564720

Sinkko, T., Sanyé-Mengual, E., Corrado, S., Giuntoli, J., & Sala, S. (2023). The EU bioeconomy footprint: Using life cycle assessment to monitor environmental impacts of the EU bioeconomy. *Sustainable Production and Consumption*. https://doi.org/10.1016/j.spc.2023.02.015

Tao, F., Zhang, H., Liu, A., & Nee, A. Y. C. (2019). Digital twin in industry: state-of-the-art. *IEEE Transactions on Industrial Informatics*, *15*(4), 2405–2415. https://doi.org/10.1109/TII.2018.2873186

Thompson, R., Gupta, A., & Li, H. (2025). Cognitive-industrial integration: Pathways to Industry 6.0. *Journal of Sustainable Manufacturing*, *12*(3), 145–162.
Wang, Y., Zhang, J., & Chen, H. (2024). Cybersecurity challenges in the fusion of biological and digital systems: A comprehensive analysis. *Computers & Security*, *136*, 103555.

Chapter 10

Consumer Ethics, Industry 6.0, and Environmental Stewardship

Chunchu Nagaraju, Gurunadham Goli and Rachoru Himani Srihita

SR University, India

Abstract

This chapter examines the collaboration of consumer ethics, Industry 6.0, and environmental stewardship. It emphasizes the fact that technology should be ecologically responsible. The human-centered tools of Industry 6.0, which are based on human–machine cooperation, hyper-personalization, and intelligent automation, provide new opportunities to innovate in a responsible way, as well as to maintain the value chains open. Such changes are important only under the control of ethically minded consumers who require justice, transparency, and sustainability. An extensive literature review indicates that the three dimensions of sustainable industrial transition (ethical consumerism, Industry 6.0 technologies, and environmental stewardship) are intertwined foundations. The demands of consumers compel companies to use traceability systems, digital disclosure tools, and human–machine symbiosis. The tools enhance governance, CSR/ESG performance, and stakeholder collaboration. This is made possible through these processes since it is a means of facilitating circular design, green manufacturing, and green product innovation. They deliver strong value chains, reduce environmental effects, and enhance social welfare. Sustainable practices are reinforced by policy reforms and consumer engagement on feedback loops. This chapter states that the more informed and values-driven people are, the higher their expectations are, which determines corporate sustainability work. Technology and morality collide in the creation of eco-efficient industrial models through the combination of Industry 6.0 with rigorous ethical standards and positive governance. In the end, this chapter demonstrates that responsible

Regenerative Revolution, 197–219

Published under exclusive licence by Emerald Publishing Limited
doi:10.1108/978-1-80686-859-920261010

innovation in the industry can be triggered by consumer ethics. It keeps the pace of fast technological development in tune with environmental management and social good.

Keywords: Consumer ethics; sustainability; ethical consumerism; human–machine collaboration; Industry 6.0

JEL Classification: M31; Q01; M31; J24; J24

1. Introduction

Consumer ethics, Industry 6.0, and environmental stewardship collide to describe a responsible future that links technology and sustainability. Industry 6.0 revolves around human-centric, smarter, and green innovations and is supported by consumer ethics, which inspires conscious decision-making. The two of them contribute to accountability, resilience, and sustainable practices, resulting in sustainable development and social welfare in the new world.

1.1 Contextualizing Industry 6.0 From Industry 4.0 Human-Centric Automation

Industry 6.0 marks the transition of the near version of cyber–physical convergence of Industry 4.0 to human-centric, sustainable, and intelligent. In addition to automation, Internet of Things (IoT), artificial intelligence (AI), and networked systems, Industry 6.0 additionally incorporates these developments into an ethical, environmental, and societal framework to develop resilient and inclusive value chains. The mentioned paradigm shifts the mindset toward technology not only as a way to increase productivity but also as the means of ensuring well-being, green care, and societal well-being (Yadav, S. et al., 2024). State-of-the-art metrology, real-time analytics, and intelligent manufacturing systems are other supporting mechanisms of this paradigm, which offer a form of quality assurance that has few environmental effects. Moreover, it also tries to combine AEC practices in delivering an intelligent, sustainable built environment where the priority is given to technological advancement and environmental responsibility in equal measure (Almusaed, A. et al., 2023). Industry 6.0 facilitates the win-win approach of the human, machine, and environment space through the combination of ethical models, circular economy models, and cross-industry collaboration. Its contextualization thus does not only provide a shift from technological change of automation to augmentation but also emphasize the need that the technologies of the industries be developed with a sense of sustainability and human-centered values in mind, as we confront a future where industrial growth and the conservation of nature go together (Almusaed, A. et al., 2023).

1.2 Relevance of Consumer Ethics and Environmental Stewardship in the Digital Industrial Age

The convergence of digital automation into intelligent systems through Industry 6.0: consumer ethics and environmental sustainability become the foundation that furthers sustainable industrial development. AI-enabled hyper connected economies are equipping consumers with more access to information that they can use to impact corporate strategy through ethical choices and sustainability requirements. All of these add up to mean that in the case of human-centered automation in various fields, the moral dimension must be incorporated into the production, supply chains, and consumption process to finalize the social legitimacy and trust. Stewardship not just involves complying with rules at the digital industrial level but also voluntary compliance and uptake of eco-efficient technologies, models to install the frameworks of the circular economy, and renewable energy in order to ensure the mitigation of effects in terms of climate change (Chourasia, S. et al., 2022).

1.3 Rational of the Chapter

This chapter explores how the transition to Industry 6.0 represents not merely a technological progression but also a profound conceptual shift in the ethical, social, and environmental responsibility of industries. The next phase would see production and consumption evolve through hyper-connected systems and interfaces between humans and machines. Underlying this new setting is the evolving framework of consumer ethics and environmental management as the key so-called drivers of industrial evolution. The global economy is progressing toward an understanding among consumers about transparency, fairness, and sustainability, resulting in more insistent pressure for industries to adopt ethics into their business models, supply chains, loss of biodiversity, and resource depletion. On the other hand, the imperative for progressive environmental responsibility in the industrial design and performance presents urgent challenges. It can be expected that such challenges will involve a logical connection between consumer ethics, technological innovation, and sustainability governance. Therefore, this chapter presents a common conceptual platform that shows how ethical consumer action and Industry 6.0 will co-create sustainable value through the integration of industrial competitiveness with global environmental imperatives.

1.4 Objectives of the Chapter

- To examine the description of the shifting ethical social-environment responsibility landscape for Industry 6.0.
- To analyze the driving forces on consumer ethics leading to the transformation of industrial structures, focusing on innovation in sustainability.

- To assess the impact of technology and human–machine interaction on facilitating the development of sustainability and ethical governance.
- To develop a consolidated framework linking ethical consumerism to technological innovation, with sustainability governance aims.

2. Theoretical and Conceptual Foundations

Second, the theoretical and conceptual underpinning of the chapter is based on ethical consumerism, environmental stewardship, and technological ethics in shaping industrial transformation for sustainability in Industry 6.0. Ethical consumerism is about using moral, social, and environmental values in making purchasing decisions, primarily significant in determining a firm's sustainability agenda. Environmental stewardship has shifted compliance mindsets to a much more proactive embracement of ecological accountability in business models. Techno ethics will pursue fairness, responsibility, and inclusivity in using AI, IoT, and automation. The overall result would be a convergence in the value of consumers and technology to develop a value chain that is sustainable, accountable, and transparent and an industrial ecosystem that is human-centric and future-ready.

2.1 Definition and Dimensions of Ethical Consumerism

Ethical consumerism—the social, environmental, and ethical costs of the expenditures made while shopping, which ought to have at least been environmentally and people-centered or moral. That will include the ethics of Industry 6.0 concerning environmental responsibility and responsible labor, accountability, and sustainable production practices. By integrating the principles of innovation with the ideas of morality, Industry 6.0 consumerism would produce a knowledgeable customer who knows how to establish ecological balance and social equity through shopping choices. Ultimately, these three exams would result in the presence of a more powerful attraction toward the changes in markets toward a responsible consumer behavior and the creation of a human-centered more sustainable industrial future (Yadav, S. et al., 2024).

2.2 The Evolution of Environmental Stewardship in Business Thought

The current environmental stewardship has changed its original structure of liability compliance to be virtually fully a subset of sustainable technology and business decision-making. In the beginning, environmental issues were regarded as compliance problems with the environment that helped in avoiding pollution and reducing legal liability. Overtime, the dawning reality of environmental limits, climate change, and resource limitations has slowly shifted the business psyche to consider sustainability as the source of competitive advantage (Fernández-Miguel, A. et al., 2024).

Well-integrated sustainability of the environment and systematic sustainability plans are intertwined in Industry 6.0 as enterprises embrace integrated platforms that connect technological innovation to planetary health. A geoanthropological strategic vision here is brought out as enlightening the conversation between human activities and the earth systems along the manufacturing and supply chains. With the help of AI, IoT, and digital twins, it is possible to monitor the state of the environment and ensure that resources are utilized in the most effective way and the number of emissions is reduced. Industry 5.0 and, later, Industry 6.0 have therefore oriented environmental stewardship as part of environmental, social, and governance (ESG). Intelligent human-centered technologies have become one of the solutions through which organizations achieve ESG goals, improve transparency, and create long-term value. These new stories will signify a change—a change where environmental responsibility is not merely an ethical mandate but is now a thing that is at the center stage of a deft and forward-looking company practice (Singh, R. et al., 2024).

2.3 Technological Ethics in the Age of Automation and AI

The rapid evolution of automation and AI has created a need for ethics in technology-driven companies, since technological ethics is a field of crucial interest within the digital industrial age. These ethics are in response to the ethical concerns of designing, implementing, and regulating smart systems in a way that they reflect human values, fairness, and sustainability. As in the case of resources, waste reduction, and sustainable supply chains, they, however, also possess such threats as algorithmic bias, displacement, and invasion of privacy that require feasible ethical constructs (Sawant, S., et al., 2024).

Designing the AI era of sustainable business models requires a balancing process between innovation and the principles of responsible consumption and creation. According to such case studies as Jordan, ethical considerations must be taken in the lifestyles of the product, data governance, and employee involvement to promote fair valuation creation. These include the transparency in AI decision-making, accountability for environmental impact and sharing in technological benefits. As Industry 6.0 is more human-oriented in its approach to automation, technological ethics will be essential in developing systems that can promote not only efficiency but also appreciate societal values, safeguard the ecological well-being, and ensure long-term sustainability (Naparin, M., et al., 2025).

2.4 Conceptual Linkage: How Consumer Ethics and Sustainability Coverage in Industry 6.0

The consumers and industries, in their activities that are geared towards ethical production, supply chain transparency and environmentally friendly consumption. Ethical consumerism denotes an individual's accountability for preferences surrounding purchases, which ought to be founded upon moral communications. Sustainability is an assurance that such decisions contribute to a balance in the ecological and conversion of resources in the long term. AI, IoT, and blockchain are examples of these Industry 6.0 technological advancements that are instrumental in creating this relationship by means of traceability, ethical credential authentication, and minimizing environmental footprints of products (Arhinful, R. et al., 2025).

The research on consumer consciousness in areas like sustainable food packaging demonstrates that a range of sociodemographic profiles do play an important role in determining the expectations and behaviors of individuals (Chirilli, C. et al., 2022). It means that specific communication strategies and product development should be used for different consumer segments in order to facilitate environmentally friendly practices. Corporations will be a major contributor to this dynamism as they will not only embrace sustainable operations but also instill the value of environmental stewardship in their value chains by engaging ethical consumer values in the sustainability industrial policies of Industry 6.0, a feedback mechanism is established between the informed and sensitive consumer in driving the sustainable innovation, and the industry can offer a solution to the problems that meets both the ethical principle and environmental goals, hence giving a human-oriented, ecologically sustainable industrial ecosystem (Velaoras, K. et al., 2025).

3. Industry 6.0: Core Technologies and Philosophies

Industry 6.0 is an extension of industries that have been transformed with the addition of better digital technology in the mix of humanistic and sustainability-based philosophies. It has gone beyond automation to hyper-personalized manufacturing, collaboration between humans and machines, and circularity. The key technologies enable smart decision-making, sharing of data in real time, and quantum technology. Moreover, the environmental stewardship, typified by waste reduction, efficiency, and supply chain transparency, is also in line with the technologically driven future, with human social and environmental goals. Industry 6.0 will be able to intersect with the planetary and long-term societal value chains so powerfully, flexibly, inclusively by outpacing technological advancement concerns with productivity and developing ethical and ecological concerns that inform technological development.

3.1 Defining Characteristics of Industry 6.0

The next step in the history of industrial evolution is Industry 6.0. It is based on the latest digital technologies with the philosophy of people and sustainability, in contrast to the ones before it, which focused on total automation and efficiency. Industry 6.0 has failed to integrate the ethical, environmental, and social pillars into the core of its industrial processes, hence depriving the citizens who cannot afford to put these pillars into action. In signature, such features as hyper-personalized manufacturing, human–machine interaction, integration of the circular economy, and intelligent system outcomes toward sustainability are particularly important (Azapagic, A. et al., 2004).

It has also detailed an impact assessment model on the environment and social effects reporting, which would be similar to the suggested sustainable development indicators of resource-based sectors such as mining. These indicators of sustainable development are leading toward resource-rich industrial sectors on the path to the economic, environmental, and sociological benefits that are reaped on the road to economic progress. In the meantime, the evolving trends of consumer-based sustainability, including fashion-based ethical consumption, are paradigm cases of how industries are developing along the path leading to the satisfaction of moral and environmental needs and, simultaneously, how they deal with the issues of the environmental footprint of fast fashion his works consists of resilient, transparent, and flexible value chains, but industry is not in relation to productivity but to the guarantee that the technology created is consistent with the restrictions of the earth and human values to build a moral future-ready industrial ecosystem (McNeill, L., et al., 2015).

3.2 Role of AI, IoT, Robotics, and Quantum Computing in Industrial Revolution

The combination of technologies, including AI, IoT, robotics, and quantum computing, drives industrial change into Industry 6.0 in contrast to AI that can provide predictive analytics and intelligent decision-making, IoT is associated with real-time availability of an interconnected chain of machines, products, and their operating systems to be more transparent in operations. The most advanced and highly precise operations are facilitated with the help of robotics, which encourages increased safety, efficiency, and consistency. It is this that causes the quantum computer to be the most efficient data processor, with optimization, material simulation, and logistical problems being possible in a manner that previously would have been considered impossible to compute (Rehman, A., et al., 2025).

These technologies boost productivity and, at the same time, promote sustainability and environmental conversation. This more environmentally friendly hospitality industry, like the others, had developed smart monitoring systems to help in the use of resources to minimize wastage and improve the performance of the environment (Gil, M. A. et al., 2001). Beyond that, as the consumer demand increases in terms of green programs and is equally willing to pay the same amount as other consumers do in the hotel industry, industries have been encouraged to adapt AI-powered energy management, supply chain transparency with the IoT, and waste reduction by robots. These technologies collectively, as Industry 6.0, form a synergetic space where innovation, environmental stewardship, and customer needs from the convergence point to make the industrial future more sustainable, efficient, and human-oriented (Pritwani, K., 2019).

3.3 Human–Machine Symbiosis: Toward Empathetic Automation

Humans and machines in symbiosis: Industry 6.0 transcends simple cooperation to a more compassionate world of awareness, adaptation, and concern for human interests as the automation system excellently performs its work. To make sure that efficiency and human potential are complimentary and not substitutive, emotional intelligence algorithms, adaptive robots, and intuitive interfaces are now part of automation. Organizations that incorporate empathy in automation will promote well-being among workers, enhance decision-making, and synchronize organizational functions with the goals of the societies and the environment. In addition to that, compassionate automation enhances sustainability goals and involves production systems, which are informed by ethical consumer demands and environmental demands similarly, sustainable packaging decisions balance customer preference with environmental impact (Boz, Z. et al., 2020). Empathetic automation balances with the values of the stakeholders and design and operation. In addition to that, the human-centered approach to technology and the drivers of corporate sustainability on stakeholder involvement, innovation, and value creation over the long run equalize the econometric, social, and environmental performance attention (Lozano, R., 2015).

This unification of man and machine in Industry 6.0 would lastly bring about a paradigm shift where technology will not be a tool anymore but a companion. Through the application of empathy in automation, the industry would have the efficiency of the operations but would not be sacrificed in the form of human dignity and trust to ensure the sustainable development in a way that will be attractive to the employees and the consumers (Boz, Z. et al., 2020).

3.4 Smart and Sustainable Production Models

Industry 6.0 smart and sustainable production models will have a digitalized system capable of aligning the most recent digital technology with the environmentally friendly production system. Thus, they could come up with efficient, low-impact, and flexible systems. These models would also be seeking productivity through sustainable innovations and using AI, IoT, and automation to monitor in real time, perform predictive maintenance, and optimize resources. This would put the productivity expectation into a clash with the requirements of sustainability. The need of customers to green products can be considered a major driver of such models, as can be the green practices that have been adopted in the hospitality company (Manaktola, K., et al., 2007).

The core of these strategies is the sustainability product design, whose concern would be to counter the environmental impact on the complete life cycle of the product. It would include the selection of materials, the manufacturing process that is energy-saving, cyclability, and concepts of the circular economy; it will be developed on the decisions of integrated design and the involvement of the stakeholders (Mengistu, A. T. et al., 2025). This is also supplemented by environmental supply chain management to ensure that the entire process does not only end in production to suppliers, logistics, and final disposal. These alliances possess the requisite propensity to attain integration of the whole supply chain to attain a holistic environmental performance, as contends (Hall, J., 2000).

4. Ethical Consumerisms in Action

Ethical consumerism suggests the growing trend in which consumers buy products in terms of moral, environmental, or social considerations that they subscribe to. The Industry 6.0 generation has added more, with digital platforms and tools of transparency, a more jutting expectation among consumers of environmentally friendly goods, a broader range of equitable labor in manufacturing and conduct, and numerous other related anticipations of the goods and related businesses. Brands that expose Corporate Social Responsibility (CSR) as a part of their agenda invest in green technologies and share their results with the population related to sustainability, win people who trust, and get loyal to them. In the enhancement of traceability, technological innovations such as blockchain and AI are of great essence so that consumers can validate the moral claims. They are now direct stakeholders who are pushing the industry into sustainable production, openness, and long-term participation toward sustainability as opposed to being passive consumers.

4.1 Shifting Behavioral Patterns of Digital Consumers

The digital age is changing customer behavior in ethical, sustainability-minded, and platform impacts. CSR programs have an enormous influence on brand recognition and customer loyalty, and modern consumers compensate companies that are genuinely caring with acquired money (Srivastava, V. K., 2024). Thus, CSR activities must be promoted via online media to make customers trust the company and demonstrate how sustainable marketing can prolong the relationship between the company and the customer. The digitalization of consumerism is a completely new category of individuals in the sustainability equation: virtual influencers. These AI-generated personas can be used to express environmentally friendly messages, as well as develop sustainable brand relationships and communicate with digitally native consumers in an enjoyable and relatable framework. They make entertainment and learning converge to promote the behavioral intentions on consumer choice in line with the ecological and ethical values. The digital consumers were transitioning to active as opposed to passive in their turn to being champions of sustainability. They will demand ethical integration of core functions, openness, and embrace of emerging digital solutions to develop environmental custodianship. As it is currently evolving, ethical consumerism is becoming a cultural phenomenon and a competitive strategy in the Industry 6.0 marketplace (Diao, Y. et al., 2025).

4.2 Physical and Sociological Drivers of Ethical Consumption

This ethical consumption is very much reliant on the interplay between individual psychological motors such as moral identity, personal values, and their perception of consumer efficacy and social networks and corporate transparency, etc., being a value-based decision style. The companies that practice sustainability themselves and share the benefits thereof are more likely to improve their financial results, therefore, making consumers more loyal and confident (Ameer, R., et al., 2012).

Supply chain environmental management skills portray ethically consumed behavior as per sociology. The adoption of green practices by a small- and medium-sized supplier and, therefore, responsibility has a ripple effect in the value chain, making it pro-sustainable. Community support or exposure to an ethical brand, or personal endorsement, raises the propensity of consumers to support an ethical brand. These forces that promote psychological and sociological one-ness meet the technology transparency instruments on the Industry 6.0 environment through which transparency in ethical assertions can be authenticated in real-time by their consumers. Such a combination would not only raise the consumer confidence but would even cause business houses to become profitable as a catchphrase to be custodians of the earth besides being a socially responsible entity, which would result in a self-sustaining cycle of ethical conduct in the market (Lee, S. Y., et al., 2008).

4.3 Models of Ethical Decision-Making in Consumption

Ethical decision-making paradigm in the context of consumption is a formalized framework of analyzing the manner in which consumers think about choice and action in relation to moral, environmental, as well as social considerations. Such models are usually made up of cognitive, affective, and contextual things that influence purchasing behavior. In tourism as a case in point, a good environmental management strategy not only ensures the competitiveness of a destination but also attracts the ethically responsible traveler who insists on sustainability in his/her consumption behavior. This builds the perception that the ethical decision-making process basically runs on subjective values and is also affected by the environmental performances of the business (Manaktola, K., et al., 2007).

Sustainability-related decision-making models usually include the following steps: problem recognition (awareness of ethical or environmental issue), information search (when discussing sustainability credentials), evaluation of alternatives (when discussing ethical relative to conventional alternatives), and post-purchase evaluation (when discussing satisfaction and impact) (Almusaed, A. et al., 2023). Environmental protection embedded within the main business strategies will provide value and sustainability to the operation, especially now that consumers are ready to reward companies with environmental friendliness. The form of advanced technology, such as blockchain or AI, is creating transparency in the Industry 6.0 world, where consumers can now trace origins and live environmental tracks of products. When such technologies are co-located, the models based on ethics are enhanced by allowing well-informed and values-aligned decisions that, in turn, help create a marketplace where responsible consumption is becoming a personal value and one that promotes a competitive advantage (Pritwani, K., 2019).

4.4 Consumer Influence on Sustainable Product Innovation and Transparency

The key to successful sustainable product innovation and corporate transparency marketing is the consumers, as the purchase intention depends on the environmental awareness. Attitudes, subjective norms, and perceived behavioral control are found to have strong impacts on the willingness of consumers to adopt sustainable choice like staying in green hotels. The existence of customers who are literally seeking green products and services is an indicator that the market requires green, sustainable innovation by companies (Chen, M. F., et al., 2014).

Firm-level environmental ethics are the force behind competitive advantage through green innovation, which minimizes environmental degradation and helps to maintain the brand position more strongly the combination of innovation and ethicality meets the demands of new-age customer on ethical products and releases the differentiation between the companies within competitive markets. Openness is the main principle, and consumers are interested in more and more provable information about the source and production of products and their environmental history (Chang, C. H., 2011).

5. Environmental Stewardship and Industrial Sustainability

Environmental stewardship in Industry 6.0 will involve the aspect of environmental responsibility within the entire process of industrial operation. The use of innovative approaches such as AI, IoT, and automation would make the most out of the existing resources and minimize the emissions, thus shortening the creation of waste. Alternatively, the green manufacturing, circular economy models, and lifecycle thinking preserve the competitiveness of industries in the long-term and protect the environment at the same time. Therefore, the pressure by the stakeholders and consumer demand will facilitate increasing transparency by using sustainability reporting frameworks such as Global Reporting Initiative (GRI). Therefore, in developing a good image as responsible leaders in the future of a globalized economy, such industries implement innovative management between technology and environment to reduce the footprints as well as establish good brand equity, regulatory compliance and resilience.

5.1 Green Manufacturing Practices in Industry 6.0

In the Industry 6.0 scenario, green manufacturing will symbolize advanced automation, AI, and human-friendly systems supported by environmental stewardship; this creates the guarantee of production processes decreasing the ecological footprint despite maximizing efficiency. Stakeholder pressure would also be very influential in streamlining the processes and making them sustainable, as indicated. Sustainability reporting works under the principles of the GRI framework, meaning that explicit disclosure is required on practices of organizations where stakeholders expect more in return, who are interested in such disclosure. This openness, in its turn, moves innovations and abilities to make it greener (Fernandez-Feijoo, B., 2014).

According to the consumerist view, environmental practices and circumstances also influence sustainability practices in the industry. Consumer preferences, which vary depending on the environment and culture, determine profit-driven industries to go green. As an example, take the hospitality industry, whose environmental perceptions in the United States and Greece are not the same, which forces businesses toward more clean technology and efficiency of resources. In Industry 6.0, the pressures of these stakeholders and the consumer demand will ensure that there is the implementation of technologies that will ensure that renewable energy is integrated to reduce wastage, and the principles of the circular economy are applied. Industry 6.0 also improves the competitive advantage and sustainable growth by integrating environmental ethics in industrial automation and human work collaboration (Choi, G. et al., 2009).

5.2 Designing for Circularity and Lifecycle Thinking

All these are intended in Industry 6.0 with regard to circularity and lifecycle thinking. Resource efficiency and long life into the product in an industry where the product is designed so that it avoids or minimizes waste. Environmental sustainability is international and not bargainable, and this frankly states that it requires that there be ecological limits that industries should run. As such, the industries are transformed into a closed-loop system through such a principle with a focus on remanufacturing, reuse, and recycling of materials at any point of the product lifecycle (Mengistu, A. T. et al., 2025).

The process will be complete with stakeholder involvement. As it was found out in the study, as the stakeholder pressure increased, more companies came out to be transparent in their sustainability reporting according to guidelines such as GRI (Gehman, 2011), and helped businesses to integrate Life Cycle Assessment and eco-design into their business practices. Considering the lifecycle and combining it with the principles of the circular design, such as modular products, renewable resources, and recovery at the end of life, organizations are able not only to develop a smaller environmental footprint but also to improve brand image. This ensures that industry progress stays at par with the ecological stewardship and is competitive and compliant with the international standards of sustainable development in the long term (Fernandez-Feijoo, B., 2014).

4.3 Energy Efficiency, Emissions Reduction, and Digital Eco-Monitoring

The primary pillars of industrial sustainability transformation, on the other hand, are energy efficiency and pollution control, which are proposed by advanced digital environmental monitoring systems that monitor and optimize resource consumption in real time. The intelligent systems enabled by AI, the IoT, and big data analytics can enable businesses to trace carbon emissions, identify inefficiencies in their operations, and establish corrective measures for environmental management, steering quickly out of a reactive compliance stage into a proactive improvement one. With these tools, operational efficiency and fulfillment of the ESG goals and climate commitments at the international level become simple to attain. The growing expectations of ethical and environmentally conscious customers are driving these sustainability efforts, as stated sustainability has not been so beneficial except that it enhances the moral platform of the brand. Sustainable manufacturing processes are now being used in high-end apparel as differentiators. This consumer requirement extends outside the fashion industry into other consumer-focused industries such as manufacturing, construction, and energy, where open environmental policies and sustainable life cycles of products are increasingly gaining momentum (Joy, A. et al., 2012).

In the industrial setting, the investments into the low-emission technologies, the incorporation of the renewable energy sources into the grid, and the production lines that consume less energy result in the twofold advantage of reduced ecological footprints and an idea of the corresponding company as a responsible and future-oriented organization. Solar or wind-powered plants of production, AI-enhanced energy management tools, and robots that help to save waste and energy are examples. The second factor that is equally significant in digital eco-monitoring is the establishment of trust in the stakeholders through the provision of verifiable information on environmental performance, through legally enforceable obligations and the system of sustainability reporting like GRI. In the end, this IT-based technology and ethical consumerism synergy would create operational sustainability of Industry 6.0, which would provide a competitive advantage in the eco-conscious market. With the consideration of the environmental responsibility imbued into the very fibers of production, the industries can create an overall resilience, profitability, and a beneficial effect on society (Chang, C. H., 2011).

6. Governance, Policy, and Strategic Implications

The policy and governance aspects play a leading role in placing the priorities of technological advances based on the ethical and environmental goals in Industry 6.0. Regimes of rules will be created, incentive systems of green innovation established, and accountability systems put in place in sectors by governance systems. Sustainable supply chain and lifecycle analysis will be encouraged by the policy of the government, whereas CSR and ESG will ensure that issues related to the environment, society, and governance are at the core of decision-making. It now becomes possible to share resources that can become the source of innovation, and openness and interconnection are created between business, government, academy, and civil society. By associating the governance with the principles of sustainability,

Industry 6.0 can achieve the goals of human-centered, competitive, and environmentally friendly growth patterns in an ever-interconnected world economy.

6.1 Role of Public Policy in Aligning Technology With Ethics and Environment

Public policy ensures that technological development is made to have the consideration of environmental sustainability and ethical considerations that are combined with the ethical government regimes. The optimal governance systems that are not only established in the direction of regulation also portray a set of incentives to practice sedimentary gratitude in developing a space for environmental responsibility. In a supply chain, it was pointed out that Sustainable Supply Chain Management (SSCM) heavily depends on good policy direction to effectively incorporate environmental and ethical factors into the principles of operating decision-making (Santiago, B. D. S. et al., 2025).

Resource efficiency, green technology, and accountability practices are some of the ways of creating an environment that embraces novelty in technology without destroying nature. Through concomitant enabling policies that enshrine ethical standards on technological implementation and are enabled through either life-cycle definitions, other green laws, and/or renewable energy requirements, a conception of profit versus responsibility can be established by the government (Mengistu, A. T. et al., 2025).

6.2 CSR and ESG Integration

CSR, as well as ESG integration, has become one of the key priorities in terms of the sustainable achievement of business performance in the era of Industry 6.0 leadership, which is responsible for the key factor of inculcating CSR principles within organizational culture, whereby clear metrics are required to check on sustainable performance. This kind of leadership makes the environmental stewardship, social responsibility, and good governance structures part of the strategic decisions and not peripheral (Szekely, F., et al., 2005).

Regarding the supply chain, ESG integration can be observed to enhance the resilience and long-term competitiveness. Note that SSCM has the benefit of inter-organizational cooperation and sharing of resources, whereby the companies can effectively collaborate in solving the environmental and social issues. This is consistent with ESG, where the activities in the environment are meant to reduce carbon emission and consumption and social activities are meant to reduce the labor policies and governance is meant to bring transparency and accountability. When the CSR values can be aligned with the ESG factors, the organizations may reach the measurable results in the form of a smaller environmental footprint, more trust, and adherence to the rules by stakeholders. In this regard, the incorporation of CSR and ESG in the conduct of business in this Industry 6.0 era of technological convergence and people-driven innovation does not only meet the moral obligation, but it also bolsters the market positioning, investor confidence, and value creation in the long-run (Gold, S. et al., 2010).

6.3 Supply Chain Transparency and Digital Traceability Tools

Digital traceability solutions and supply chain transparency in the Industry 6.0 model are keys to a sustainable and competitive business operation. With the development of new technologies like blockchain, IoT, and the analytics of AI, companies will be able to trace their products, check the ethical sourcing, and introduce the control over land use and environmental regulations (Mihalič, T., 2000). The knowledge, capability, and systems that are used in environmental management are known as green intellectual capital; it gives the firms tools with which competitive advantage is formed. Digital traceability systems may be perceived as the application of the green intellectual capital in the literal sense; the systems enable the firms to gather, store, and disseminate sustainability data across the supply chain to create confidence with the stakeholders. According to (Baumgartner, R. J., et al., 2017), strategic management of corporate sustainability is one of the essential functions of the governance and organization of companies that react to environmental and social concerns. Incorporating traceability tools into the supply chain planning allows the company to detect inefficiencies in advance, remove waste, and keep their suppliers in compliance with the sustainability rules (Vijay, A. J. et al., 2024).

6.4 Frameworks for Industry–Consumer Partnerships in Sustainability

These joint ventures encourage sustainability because they foster shared accountability, transparency, and mutual value creation. The highly visible social and environmental impacts of industries like textiles and clothes can be addressed in cooperative frameworks, which can achieve the provisions of a valuable mammoth mission of sustainable change. As per Shen, B. et al. (2017), the supply chain sustainability aspects, including the manufacturing processes that use resources that are wasteful, waste creation, and labor problems, can be addressed through consumer involvement in the product life cycle, including recycling, creation of awareness, and consumer pressure to products that are environment-friendly (Mengistu, A. T. et al., 2025).

Opine that there are institutional frameworks where stakeholders, such as consumers, influence the implementation of environmental management practices. Being attitudinally demanding of greener alternatives and showing encouragement to brands that are taking positive action would encourage businesses to invest in transparent reporting, cleaner technologies, and sustainable design solutions (Delmas, M., et al., 2004).

The cocreation platforms make the industry–consumer collaboration platforms feasible. Two of those frameworks are sustainability labeling and involvement in product development. Credibility in the digital medium through applications and blockchain-based systems generates all forms of credibility, such as trustworthy environmental data (Székely, F., et al., 2005). This type of alliance will help minimize ecological footprints and maximize brand equity by balancing consumer demands and corporate sustainability strategies, and ensuring stewardship of the environment through a joint venture between the producers and the consumers (Santiago, B. D. S. et al., 2025).

7. Road Map for Integrating Consumer Ethics Into Industry 6.0

The technological development and value-based sustainability practice are what balance out the challenge of implementing consumer ethics in Industry 6.0. Design, production, and advertisement in such industries should have ethical concerns that are backed by transparent platforms of supply chain and traceability. Each of the three AI, IoT, and blockchain could be used to inform the consumer since it would help the consumer be connected with their action and the degree of trust: the real-time experience of sustainability would facilitate the transaction. One of the ways in which companies, governments, academia, and civil society interact is to find a common responsibility and innovation. Its operations will have to be oriented toward the realization of the circular economy, green production, and the ESG model, which, in its turn, will be part of the environmental stewardship and social responsibility staple. This road map makes Industry 6.0 an industrial model of the future with a focus on humanity, ethics, and environmental responsibility. Table 10.1 presents the key focus areas and strategic integration of innovation sustainability across industries.

Table 10.1. Focus Areas for Sustainable Business Strategies.

S. No	Focus Area	Explanation
1	Strategic recommendations for industries	Industries should integrate innovation and sustainability as core business strategies. In the pharmaceuticals sector, sustainable transformation comes from continuous innovation, active stakeholder engagement, and environmental and social considerations embedded in corporate decision-making. The triple bottom line approach balancing people, planet, and profit offers a win-win-win pathway for aligning growth with sustainability.

Table 10.1. *(Continued)*

S. No	Focus Area	Explanation
		Transparent reporting also enhances trust, compliance, and market differentiation (Blum-Kusterer, M., et al (2001); Shen, B. et al. (2017).
2	Embedding ethics and sustainability in design, production, and marketing	The corporate social responsibility pyramid identifies economic, legal, ethical, and philanthropic roles that will help in integrating sustainability throughout the value chain. The material sourcing, production efficacy, and honest marketing are features that need to be informed using ethical principles. Integrating sustainability within operations lessens the effects on the environment, boosts consumer confidence, and creates competitive strength (Singh, R. et al., 2024).
3	Leveraging digital tools for consumer education and cocreation	The digital platforms, AI applications, and blockchain have the potential to raise consumer awareness, participation, and cocreation of sustainability programs. Information disclosure systems enable the stakeholders to make informed decisions, and when computerized, they promote transparent, participative, and gamified sustainability practices (Brown, H. S. et al., 2009).
4	Opportunities for stakeholder collaboration: business, government, academia, and civil society	Multi-sector partnerships speed up sustainable change. Companies provide leadership, governments establish regulatory requirements, research and innovation are

(Continued)

Table 10.1. *(Continued)*

S. No	Focus Area	Explanation
		provided by academia, and non-state actors mobilize civic action. Shared discloser frame works establish mutual responsibility, and innovation-led partnerships advance resource exchange and systematic improvement (Baumgartner, R. J., et al., 2017; Brown, H. S. et al., 2009; Blum-Kusterer, M. et al., 2001).

Source: Author.

8. Conclusion and Future Research

This chapter is concerned with the interconnection between consumer ethics Industry 6.0 and sustainability stewardship and how the three drivers cocreate action channels toward sustainable value creation. The main aspects of Industry 6.0 human–machine symbiosis, hyper-personalization, circular economy, and intelligent automation offer an unprecedented potential for integrating sustainability as the core idea of industrial formations. Consumer ethics became a reality and a force that influenced the business agendas. Educated, value-oriented consumers would become an agent of change that will compel the industry toward transparency, fairness, and sustainable product development. In parallel, Industry 6.0, which includes AI, IoT, blockchain, and quantum computing, will grant unexpected capabilities of supply chain transparency, emissions tracking, and sustainable product design. Facilitation is thus primarily through public policy and multistakeholder collaboration. Legislation establishes ethical minimums, encourages the use of green technologies, and is part of the socially and environmentally friendly industrial development. Therefore, CSR and ESG both focus on the incorporation of social environment and governance issues into strategic decision-making. The industrial sustainable consumer relations, sustainable, labeling, and cocreations platforms also help achieve harmony between industrial innovation and consumer aspiration. The inductive process comes out in the findings of this chapter as the responsible consumers compel the industries to engage in more sustainable practices, and on the other hand, sustainability-conscious industries allow the consumers to make more sustainable decisions. This cocreation is a vital point of departure for Industry 6.0: a human and sustainable future.

The future research must look into the possibilities of quantifying the ethical effects of consumerism on the numerous types of industrial innovations, sustainable investments, and competitive strategies across different sectors. This evidence can also be regarded as quite suitable for being developed within the demand sustainability nexus within Industry 6.0. Therefore, it is quite logical to comprehend to what extent a digital instrument like blockchain and AI or IoT can aid in effective consumer interaction and how it has been actually done within the contexts of supply chain sustainability. The cross-cultural approaches to ethics consumption comparative studies can also present further information about their practices in various sociocultural contexts and enable industries to render their sustainability communication and products to suit various markets.

8.1 Suggestions

Future research must test on the ground this conceptual framework using case studies and then provide longitudinal follow-up research to increase its practicality. There is a need to conduct comparative studies, both across industries and countries, for better exposure to the contextual factors affecting ethical consumerism and sustainability governance in Industry 6.0. Such standardization will go a long way toward enhancing consistency around ethical behavior, including technological ethics and transability. The role of education, policy, and community engagement in creating ethical awareness should be explored by researchers. Collaborative involvement of academia with industry and government is a must in formulating sustainability frameworks that have aligning innovation with human and environmental well-being.

8.2 Limitations

This chapter provides an integrative perspective on the linkage between consumer ethics, Industry 6.0, and environmental stewardship; however, it has certain limitations. The study focuses mainly on conceptual and secondary literature, lacking empirical validation by field data. It does not provide sector-specific insights or quantitative evidence on measuring the impact of ethical consumerism on industrial sustainability. Further, the emphasis on AI, IoT, and blockchain may underestimate the importance of social innovation, governance, and education in ethical transformations. Given the rapid changes in technology under Industry 6.0 and in consumers' values, the proposed conceptual framework needs regular reassessment. Furthermore, the absence of standardized indicators to measure ethical consumer behavior with sustainability performance would diminish cross-region and cross-industry comparability and practical capability of the findings.

Funding

No funding was received for conducting this study.

Conflicts of Interest/Competing Interests

The authors declare that they have no conflicts of interest or competing interests.

Data availability statement

This study relied on secondary data available in the public domain. The sources of data have been duly cited in the references. No new datasets were generated.

Ethics Approval

Not applicable. This study did not involve human participants or animals.

Consent to Participate

Not applicable, as the study is based solely on secondary data analysis of published literature.

Consent for publication

Consent for publication has been obtained from all authors.

Acknowledgments

The authors would like to thank their supervisor for providing the necessary academic resources and support during the preparation of this book chapter. Special appreciation is extended to peers who provided valuable insights and encouragement throughout the development of the book chapter.

References

Almusaed, A., Yitmen, I., & Almssad, A. (2023). Reviewing and integrating AEC practices into industry 6.0: Strategies for smart and sustainable future-built environments. *Sustainability*, *15*(18), 13464.

Ameer, R., & Othman, R. (2012). Sustainability practices and corporate financial performance: A study based on the top global corporations. *Journal of Business Ethics*, *108*(1), 61–79. https://doi.org/10.1007/s10551-011-1063-y

Arhinful, R., Mensah, L., & Obeng, H. A. (2025). Corporate social responsibility's role in shaping environmental innovation and reputation: Evidence from London's non-financial sector. *Corporate Social Responsibility and Environmental Management*, *32*(4), 4880–4899.

Azapagic, A. (2004). Developing a framework for sustainable development indicators for the mining and minerals industry. *Journal of Cleaner Production*, *12*(6), 639–662. https://doi.org/10.1016/S0959-6526(03)00075-1

Baumgartner, R. J., & Rauter, R. (2017). Strategic perspectives of corporate sustainability management to develop a sustainable organization. *Journal of Cleaner Production*, *140*, 81–92. https://doi.org/10.1016/j.jclepro.2016.04.146

Blum-Kusterer, M., & Hussain, S. S. (2001). Innovation and corporate sustainability: An investigation into the process of change in the pharmaceuticals industry. *Business Strategy and the Environment*, *10*(5), 300–316. https://doi.org/10.1002/bse.300

Boz, Z., Korhonen, V., & Koelsch Sand, C. (2020). Consumer considerations for the implementation of sustainable packaging: A review. *Sustainability*, *12*(6), 2192. https://doi.org/10.3390/su12062192

Brown, H. S., de Jong, M., & Levy, D. L. (2009). Building institutions based on information disclosure: Lessons from GRI's sustainability reporting. *Journal of Cleaner Production*, *17*(6), 571–580. https://doi.org/10.1016/j.jclepro.2008.12.009

Chang, C. H. (2011). The influence of corporate environmental ethics on competitive advantage: The mediation role of green innovation. *Journal of Business Ethics*, *104*(3), 361–370. https://doi.org/10.1007/s10551-011-0914-x

Chen, M. F., & Tung, P. J. (2014). Developing an extended theory of planned behavior model to predict consumers' intention to visit green hotels. *International Journal of Hospitality Management*, *36*, 221–230. https://doi.org/10.1016/j.ijhm.2013.09.006

Chirilli, C., Molino, M., & Torri, L. (2022). Consumers' awareness, behavior and expectations for food packaging environmental sustainability: Influence of socio-demographic characteristics. *Foods*, *11*(16), 2388. https://doi.org/10.3390/foods11162388

Choi, G., Parsa, H. G., Sigala, M., & Putrevu, S. (2009). Consumers' environmental concerns and behaviors in the lodging industry: A comparison between Greece and the United States. *Journal of Quality Assurance in Hospitality & Tourism*, *10*(2), 93–112. https://doi.org/10.1080/15280080902946335

Chourasia, S., Tyagi, A., Pandey, S. M., Walia, R. S., & Murtaza, Q. (2022). Sustainability of Industry 6.0 in global perspective: Benefits and challenges. *Mapan*, *37*(2), 443. https://doi.org/10.1007/s12647-022-00541-w

Delmas, M., & Toffel, M. W. (2004). Stakeholders and environmental management practices: An institutional framework. *Business Strategy and the Environment*, *13*(4), 209–222. https://doi.org/10.1002/bse.409

Diao, Y., Liang, M., Jin, C., & Woo, H. (2025). Virtual influencers and sustainable brand relationships: Understanding consumer commitment and behavioral intentions in digital marketing for environmental stewardship. *Sustainability*, *17*(13), 6187. https://doi.org/10.3390/su17136187

Fernández-Miguel, A., García-Muiña, F. E., Settembre-Blundo, D., Tarantino, S. C., & Riccardi, M. P. (2024). Exploring systemic sustainability in manufacturing: Geoanthropology's strategic lens shaping Industry 6.0. *Global Journal of Flexible Systems Management*, *25*(3), 579–600. https://doi.org/10.1007/s40171-024-00404-0

Fernandez-Feijoo, B., Romero, S., & Ruiz, S. (2014). Effect of stakeholders' pressure on transparency of sustainability reports within the GRI framework. *Journal of Business Ethics*, *122*(1), 53–63. https://doi.org/10.1007/s10551-013-1748-5

Gehman, J. (2011). *The global reporting initiative: 1997–2009*. https://doi.org/10.2139/ssrn.1924439

Gil, M. A., Jiménez, J. B., & Lorente, J. C. (2001). An analysis of environmental management, organizational context and performance of Spanish hotels. *Omega*, *29*(6), 457–471. https://doi.org/10.1016/S0305-0483(01)00033-0

Gold, S., Seuring, S., & Beske, P. (2010). Sustainable supply chain management and inter-organizational resources: A literature review. *Corporate Social Responsibility and Environmental Management*, *17*(4), 230–245. https://doi.org/10.1002/csr.207

Hall, J. (2000). Environmental supply chain dynamics. *Journal of Cleaner Production*, *8*(6), 455–471. https://doi.org/10.1002/csr.3215

Joy, A., Sherry Jr, J. F., Venkatesh, A., Wang, J., & Chan, R. (2012). Fast fashion, sustainability, and the ethical appeal of luxury brands. *Fashion Theory*, *16*(3), 273–295. https://doi.org/10.2752/175174112X13340749707123

Lee, S. Y., & Klassen, R. D. (2008). Drivers and enablers that foster environmental management capabilities in small-and medium-sized suppliers in supply chains. *Production and Operations Management*, *17*(6), 573–586. https://doi.org/10.3401/poms.1080.0063

Lozano, R. (2015). A holistic perspective on corporate sustainability drivers. *Corporate Social Responsibility and Environmental Management*, *22*(1), 32–44. https://doi.org/10.1002/csr.1325

Manaktola, K., & Jauhari, V. (2007). Exploring consumer attitude and behaviour towards green practices in the lodging industry in India. *International Journal of Contemporary Hospitality Management*, *19*(5), 364–377. https://doi.org/10.1108/09596110710757534

McNeill, L., & Moore, R. (2015). Sustainable fashion consumption and the fast fashion conundrum: Fashionable consumers and attitudes to sustainability in clothing choice. *International Journal of Consumer Studies*, *39*(3), 212–222. https://doi.org/10.1111/ijcs.12169

Mengistu, A. T., Dieste, M., Panizzolo, R., & Biazzo, S. (2025). Achieving product sustainability: Analyzing key factors influencing sustainable product design in manufacturing companies. *Corporate Social Responsibility and Environmental Management*, *32*(4), 5021–5037.

Mihalič, T. (2000). Environmental management of a tourist destination: A factor of tourism competitiveness. *Tourism Management*, *21*(1), 65–78. https://doi.org/10.1016/S0261-5177(99)00096-5

Naparin, M., & Astuti, W. T. (2025). Innovative green consumption in a manufacturing company in the environmental-based view approach: The role of moral obligation, TPBF, green intention and pro-environmental behavior with the moderating effect of innovative work environment. *Cogent Business & Management*, *12*(1), 2440118.

Pritwani, K. (2019). *Sustainability of business in the context of environmental management*. CRC Press. https://doi.org/10.1201/9780429058387

Rehman, A., & Umar, T. (2025). Literature review: Industry 5.0. leveraging technologies for environmental, social and governance advancement in corporate settings. *Corporate Governance: The International Journal of Business in Society*, *25*(2), 229–251. https://doi.org/10.1108/CG-11-2023-0502

Santiago, B. D. S., Scavarda, L. F., Gusmão Caiado, R. G., Santos, R. S., & Mattos Nascimento, D. L. D. (2025). Corporate social responsibility and circular economy integration framework within sustainable supply chain management: Building blocks for industry 5.0. *Corporate Social Responsibility and Environmental Management*, *32*(1), 269–290.

Sawant, S., & Nayak, G. (2024). Sustainable shifts: Exploring the future landscape of green consumerism and environmental responsibility. *Achieving Sustainability in Management and Technology*, 1–24. https://doi.org/10.17492/jpi.DYIMCAM.062401

Shen, B., Li, Q., Dong, C., & Perry, P. (2017). Sustainability issues in textile and apparel supply chains. *Sustainability*, *9*(9), 1592. https://doi.org/10.3390/su9091592

Singh, R., Tyagi, A. K., & Arumugam, S. K. (2024). Imagining the sustainable future with Industry 6.0: A smarter pathway for modern society and manufacturing industries. In *Machine learning algorithms using scikit and TensorFlow environments* (pp. 318–331). IGI Global Scientific Publishing. https://doi.org/10.4018/978-1-6684-8531-6.ch016

Srivastava, V. K. (2024). Impact of corporate social responsibility (CSR) initiatives on brand reputation: A study on how CSR activities enhance brand reputation and consumer loyalty in the context of sustainable marketing practices. *International Journal of Science and Research Archive*, *13*(1), 1910–1930. https://doi.org/10.30574/ijsra.2024.13.1.1869

Székely, F., & Knirsch, M. (2005). Responsible leadership and corporate social responsibility: Metrics for sustainable performance. *European Management Journal*, *23*(6), 628–647. https://doi.org/10.1016/j.emj.2005.10.009

Velaoras, K., Menegaki, A. N., Polyzos, S., & Gotzamani, K. (2025). The role of environmental certification in the hospitality industry: Assessing sustainability, consumer preferences, and the economic impact. *Sustainability*, *17*(2), 650.

Vijay, A. J., William, B. N. J., Haruna, A. A., & Prasad, D. D. (2024). Exploring the synergy of IIoT, AI, and data analytics in Industry 6.0. In *Industry 6.0* (pp. 1–36). CRC Press.

Yadav, S., Rab, S., & Wan, M. (2024). Metrology and sustainability in Industry 6.0: Navigating a new paradigm. In *Handbook of quality system, accreditation and conformity assessment* (pp. 855–885). Springer Nature Singapore. https://doi.org/10.1007/978-981-97-5750-3_64

Chapter 11

Business Beyond Linear Growth: Mindful Consumption Using Circular Revenue Models for the Future

Seema Sahai[a,*], *Nitasha Barara*[a,†] *and Rohit Bansal*[b]

[a]IILM Institute for Higher Education, India
[b]Rockford College, Sydney, Australia

Abstract

While many of the large organizations have committed to circularity in a precise and measurable way, few are re-evaluating their whole business strategy. In order to achieve this, one must visualize the future and, more crucially, how profits will be earned. It is critical to talk about revenue generation in order to build a sustainable business. In fact, it is probable that circular economy models are already at work and are having an unintentional circular effect of it. It is important to remember that not all firms are "fully circular" or rather very few are. Every business starts from a different place and grows its circularity moving forward.

This conceptual paper examines the kind of revenue models a circular business can adopt. It gives a holistic approach for enhancing financial resilience and mindful consumption in organizations for persistent success in a constantly changing world. Its aim is to enable practitioners and academicians to understand revenue management based on the strategy of the organization.

As per the aim of the book, this chapter will encourage greater understanding and linkage between the circular economy and revenue model in different types of sustainable businesses.

*https://orcid.org/0000-0003-3002-5201
†https://orcid.org/0009-0003-0803-1880

Regenerative Revolution, 221–231

Published under exclusive licence by Emerald Publishing Limited
doi:10.1108/978-1-80686-859-920261011

Keywords: Circular economy; circular business model; Extended Producer Responsibility (EPR); circular revenue model; mindful consumption

JEL Codes: Q20; Q50

1. Introduction

The resources on Earth are being used and consumed by humans more quickly than they can be replenished. The demand for (raw) materials is increasing exponentially as the world's population rises and attempts are made to raise the prosperity at a global level. This leads to emerging problems like price fluctuations and climate change, with the realization that the existing linear economy is unsustainable (Wang & Azam, 2024). These issues are addressed by the circular economy, which also creates opportunities for businesses (Sakao et al., 2024).

In an endeavor to minimize waste and promote sustainable growth, the circular economy concept highlights the significance of extending the useful life of materials. The "take-make-dispose" methodology of traditional linear models is drawing more and more criticism for its unsustainable methods. On the other hand, circular business models (CBMs) seek to generate economic benefit in addition to diminishing the detrimental impact on the environment (Kirchherr et al., 2023).

In the current business environment, organizations are actively looking for ways to reduce their impacts on the environment while promoting sustainable economic growth. Businesses must examine new revenue models in order to successfully guide their operations toward significant and quantifiable transformation (Barros et al., 2021).

2. Circular Economy

The linear system always extracts raw materials from the environment, utilizes them to make goods, and then returns them to the environment. Over time, this process causes the perishable basic resources to be depleted (Morseletto, 2023). The disposal of waste is expensive and may end up causing environmental pollution.

The circular economy moves away from the old take-make-dispose approach and focuses on using resources wisely and reducing waste. It encourages companies to design processes where materials are reused or recycled, allowing products to stay in use for longer and supporting a more sustainable way of doing business (Sahai & Barara, 2025). The cost of disposal is eliminated, and the environment is not harmed because nearly everything is used. The "extraction-production-disposal" paradigm, which is frequently used in the industrial sector (Coelho et al., 2020), needs a change as per the circular model.

2.1 Circularity in Business

Businesses are essential in creating cyclic resource flows (Nießen & Bocken, 2022). As suppliers of goods and services, they have the option to alter their current linear make-take-dispose arrangement. Companies can reduce resource use and waste while increasing product use, prolonging lifespans, and cycling resources to generate revenue. They can achieve this by adopting a CBM. Business models serve as a means of articulating how an organization generates, provides, and obtains value. This helps to add value beyond financial gain and generates social value and beneficial environmental impacts such as lowering the amount of waste and resource use in business (Osterwalder & Pigneur, 2010).

3. Mindful Consumption

Mindful consumption represents a conscious and value-driven approach where individuals deliberately align their consumption behavior with ethical, environmental, and social considerations. Gupta and Sheth (2024) conceptualized mindful consumption as a balanced approach where awareness, compassion, and restraint guide consumer choices toward sustainability. Their framework emphasizes that mindful consumers consciously evaluate the impact of their decisions on personal well-being, society, and the environment, positioning mindfulness as a key behavioral driver for sustainable and responsible consumption practices. Kunwer and Singh (2025) expanded this understanding by framing mindful consumption through psychological and sociocultural dimensions, suggesting that awareness and intentionality serve as behavioral catalysts for sustainable choices. Recent research by Ji et al. (2025) highlighted that mindful consumption plays a crucial role in shaping sustainable consumer behavior. The study finds that individuals with higher levels of mindfulness are more inclined toward green purchasing, with ethical self-identity and environmental awareness mediating this relationship. Garg et al. (2024) describe mindful consumption as a conscious and reflective process in which individuals make purchasing decisions with awareness of their personal needs and the broader environmental and social impact.

4. Revenue Models and Business Models

Usually used interchangeably, the terms "business model" and "revenue model" have different meanings. A business model outlines the essential elements of a company, such as its value proposition, customer segments, sources of income, cost structure, and the tools and procedures required to provide goods and services (Teece, 2010).

A revenue model is a particular framework or approach that a business employs to make money. Revenue models describe how money is made, how prices are set, and how consumers pay for goods and services. The revenue model is a subset or an element of the business model. While the business model offers a comprehensive perspective on how a company generates, delivers, and captures value, the revenue model concentrates on the "capture value" component or how the company makes money from its products (Osterwalder & Pigneur, 2010).

Our perspective on the circular economy relies on the idea that the organization providing goods or services (the "Producer") bears responsibility for the good or service all the way through the lifecycle. This is termed as Extended Producer Responsibility (EPR). EPR focuses on the idea that manufacturers, having the greatest impact over product design, have the greatest ability and accountability to minimize waste and toxicity (Sin & Tueen, 2023).

4.1 Basic Types of Revenue Models for Sustainable Businesses and Their Circular Impact

There are many revenue models that exist. The circular revenue models that are defined can be seen from the producers' perspective as well as the users' perspective. The economic owner also has an important role in the circular economy (Roci & Rashid, 2023). The economic owner can be defined as the person who has the right to use the value of the product. The person is also the one who takes the financial risk of ownership. This means that if the value goes down, the economic owner bears the brunt, and if the value increases, the owner reaps the profits. The producer as well as the user can be the economic owner. To define a producer, it can be a person or group that can make adjustments to the products or their design. The EPR of the European Commission is in some way along the same lines. The user can be a person or group that acquires the product or uses the functionality of the product. It may be a direct customer as well as an end customer (Mallick et al., 2024).

The producer and user can be seen as the supply and demand of the circular economy. However, in reality the concept is much more complex consisting of various legal and financial challenges. The revenue model's ability to generate value is the main focus in this study and not the financing of goods or services.

Here, we discuss four major revenue models:

(1) Pay-per-Use;
(2) Rent;
(3) Sell-and-Buy Back;
(4) Lease.

The Producer continues to be the legal and economic owner under the Pay-per-Use and Rent income models. The User becomes a (temporary) economic owner under the Sell-and-Buy-Back income model, and the User may or may not resell the product to the Producer. According to the lease revenue model, the form of the lease determines who the owner is.

4.1.1 Pay-per-Use

In this model, the User pays the producer after utilizing the services like product usage, upkeep, and repairs. The financial risk lies with the Producer, who is also the owner. Because the User's level of usage is not under the control of the Producer, the financial risk is high. The producer will often have a long-term contract that ensures income over a lengthier time frame.

4.1.1.1 What Makes Pay-Per-Use Circular?. This model is also referred to as Pay-as-a-Service model. This means the user pays only as per use. The user does not have any direct motivation to use or utilize the product because the user knows that they will never become the owner. However, since preventing or reducing consumption is the initial stage in the circular economy, this can be an incentive to utilize the goods as and when needed and at minimal cost.

Another factor is that the product is guaranteed to be returned because the producer still owns it. As the user only pays for use, this approach ensures the greatest producer accountability. As a result, the product's functionality, that is, the outcome the user achieves is the main focus. The producer's interest is in providing a product that lasts long with the least amount of upkeep. Circularity is enhanced by incorporating this revenue model into a business plan, as it allows multiple users to share the service (Diaz et al., 2021).

4.1.1.2 Financial Implications

(1) The financial risk is borne by the Producer; the assets are still part of the Producer's balance sheet. If the usage can be forecast more accurately, calculating (variable) income becomes simpler.
(2) The usage can be internally pre-financed by the producer.
(3) The user will pay for the product's use even though they might not be able to pay the full purchase price. Predictability of use is crucial for the business.

4.1.1.3 Real-Life Cases. Eureka Forbes, best known for its water purifiers, has tried to shift away from the one-time purchase model. Rather than asking households to buy a purifier upfront, it offers options like monthly subscriptions or even a pay-per-liter scheme. For families, this lowers the cost of entry, and for the company, it creates an ongoing relationship with the customer. Because the machines remain under the company's ownership, used filters and worn-out parts can be collected and processed instead of being discarded. This is a good example of how a service-oriented approach can support circularity by tying profits to long-term maintenance rather than just to sales (Eureka Forbes/Aquaguard: A Giant Trap/Scam Harassing Thousands of Customers in Broad Daylight.: R/India, n.d.).

4.1.2 Rent

Here, the User pays for the availability of the product that the Producer rents out. The owner and bearer of the financial risk are the producer. In this model, there is less financial risk as the producer is assured of regular income for some time. The fact that the company only rents out the product for a brief time may be a drawback, as this results in temporary income and a potentially greater environmental impact from the multiple returns after the rental (Johnson & Plepys, 2021).

4.1.2.1 What Makes Rent Circular?. Users of many products (such as drilling machines) only use them for brief periods of time. The user pays for the product's availability under this revenue model. Instead of purchasing the goods outright, the user can rent them for the duration required. In this way, fewer goods need to be produced, resulting in less material and energy use.

After the rental period, the Producer will retrieve the product from the User and ensure reverse logistics. Maintenance of the product is the producer's responsibility. The products have a longer lifespan thanks to this revenue strategy.

When the product is rented for brief periods of time (just when in use) and isn't "standing still," optimization of use takes place. This business model can maximize utilization and ensure circularity if it allows several users to share the product (for instance, through platforms). This guarantees that current items are used as efficiently as possible, hence reducing the need for new products and their creation (Mitsenko et al., 2021).

4.1.2.2 Financial Implications

(1) The financial risk here is borne by the firm; the assets are also included on the balance sheet.
(2) The user will pay a certain amount each time instead of the whole purchase price if they are unable to pay it.

4.1.2.3 Real-Life Cases. Furniture rental start-ups have gained traction among younger, mobile consumers, and Furlenco is perhaps the most cited case in this space. Customers can rent sofas, beds, or appliances for a few months or several years, depending on their needs. When items are returned, they do not disappear into waste streams; instead, they are refurbished and offered to the next customer (Garrone, 2024). This "circulation" of products avoids unnecessary production of new units and extends the lifespan of existing ones. In the urban Indian context, where many professionals move cities for work every few years, the model speaks to both convenience and sustainability (Talwar, 2021).

4.1.3 Sell-and-Buy-Back

The User purchases a product from the Producer. It is assumed that this occurs in accordance with the most popular Sell-and-Buy-Back model, in which the producer guarantees the product's buyback (subject to specific restrictions, like the product's lifetime and worth). The user can choose to sell the product back to the manufacturer (Pedersen, 2013). The (financial) motive to realize this is clear, even though it is not yet clear whether the actual physical return of the product will occur. Until the producer buys the thing back, the user is the economic owner and bears the financial risk.

In reality, there are more options, such as the Producer's buy-back option. Since there is no assurance that the product may be returned to the producer, this is a less circular choice. There is no necessity for the Producer to buy back the product after a specific amount of time; this option lowers the producer's financial risk.

4.1.3.1 What Makes Sell-and-Buy-Back Circular?. The ownership of the product here is with the User and the user receives a price for returning it, which is determined by the product's current value as well as the terms and conditions agreed upon (such as lifetime), the Sell-and-Buy-Back revenue model offers a significant incentive for users. The product's worth will be preserved through economical use. The producer will want to focus on "design for longevity" since they are keen to get the product back so they can reuse (parts of) it (Armstrong et al., 2015).

Another benefit is that after the initial period of usage, information about the product's performance is given to the producer. As a result, the producer can use this information to build new items.

4.1.3.2 Financial Implications

(1) As long as there is no financial risk to the producer, this sell-and-buy-back arrangement is considered a sale. The producer will have to keep the products on their own balance sheet when the risk is larger because it cannot be viewed as a sale but rather as a lease. To ascertain where you are incurring the financial risk, it is necessary to review the issues for this revenue model with your accountant or financial expert.
(2) Since the producer may not be able to finance the product, it will be sold, and the buyer will pay the entire purchase price instantly.
(3) The purchase price can be paid by the user.

4.1.3.3 Real-Life Cases. In the automobile industry, Tata Motors has used buy-back programs to encourage customers to return older vehicles when purchasing new ones. The guarantee of a resale value makes the decision financially attractive to customers, but it also ensures that the company has access to end-of-life vehicles. These cars can then be channeled into refurbishing, second-hand markets, or dismantling processes where metals and components are recovered. From the perspective of circularity, the system prevents valuable materials from being lost and reduces dependence on virgin resources (Tata Motors: Leading Circularity & Biodiversity for a Sustainable Future, n.d.).

4.1.4 Lease

The concept of "lease" is commonly linked to the funding of circular revenue structures. According to our expertise, "lease" is a general term that can refer to a variety of product financing options. One typical type of funding that a producer or user obtains from a leasing company is a lease (Kirchherr et al., 2023). The form of lease determines the economic and/or legal owner or the user. Furthermore, it matters which viewpoint is used when examining leases: accountants will consider economic ownership, whereas legal consultants will consider legal ownership. Additionally, we observe that producers who rent out their goods use the word "lease."

4.1.4.1 What Makes Lease Circular?. The organizations wanting to give the user long-lasting products but do not have the funds find leasing an easy option. The leasing firm, in this model, is put in the middle. Goods that have a high lifespan and good service life form a part of the circular economy as longer-lasting products require less energy and fewer raw materials to produce.

In an Operational Lease, after the lease period, the User may choose to return the item to the Producer. The materials and goods are returned to the economy in the best possible condition as per reverse logistics.

4.1.4.2 Financial Implications

(1) Leasing is a good option in case a producer has circular intentions but lacks the financial resources.
(2) If the main activity of the user is focused on the product, it has to be shown on both sides of the balance sheet. The Producer will be able to scale up its operations thanks to the lease.

4.1.4.3 Real-Life Cases. Leasing has also become a practical way to introduce circular thinking, especially in the electric vehicle segment. Mahindra & Mahindra has promoted leasing contracts for some of its EVs. Customers gain access to the vehicle without paying the whole amount as an initial payment, while the firm retains ownership. This ownership is important because it implies that after the lease period expires, Mahindra may take the vehicle back and decide whether to put it through another leasing cycle or recycle elements like the battery, which has a high value and environmental impact. This system complements the government's overall e-mobility and sustainability goal (Mahindra Last Mile Mobility Limited and Attero Collaborate for Sustainable EV Battery Recycling, n.d.).

5. Conclusion

This paper gives insightful information on circular revenue models that helped companies choose the models that match their goods and services, along with certain examples. Collaboration with partners ready to share risks is critical for achieving the circular economy. Cooperation with partners is the only way we can achieve a circular economy. The Sell-and-Buy-Back approach arranges the financial and legal logistics of product's reverse logistics, but it takes time and money to make physical returns (Danvers et al., 2023). The question is whether this is balanced by the product's remaining value. Businesses can agree on a hybrid type of revenue models in contracts with customers to increase the plan's appeal or applicability. Some users (such as those in the public sector) choose to make payments all at once, for example, to use their leftover funds right before the end of the year. It could be advantageous to align revenue models with consumer preferences (Aloysius et al., 2023). When compared to rent, leases provide no circular advantages. The sale of products to the leasing firm provides the producer with a financial benefit by bringing in cash right away. Although leases are common, they can be either a loan or a rental agreement. Compared to leases in the form of loans, leases in the form of rent have greater circular incentives. Additionally, sometimes the term "lease" is used when "rent" is more appropriate (Englund et al., 2008). Finally, the sincere recommendation to establish a circular business may seem like a huge and confusing task. It's wise to remember that small-businesses are "fully circular," or perhaps none at all. Every business starts from a different place and builds its circularity from mindful consumption.

References

Aloysius, N., Ananda, J., Mitsis, A., & Pearson, D. (2023). Why people are bad at leftover food management? A systematic literature review and a framework to analyze household leftover food waste generation behavior. *Appetite*, *186*. https://doi.org/10.1016/J.APPET.2023.106577

Armstrong, C. M., Niinimäki, K., Kujala, S., Karell, E., & Lang, C. (2015). Sustainable product-service systems for clothing: Exploring consumer perceptions of consumption alternatives in Finland. *Journal of Cleaner Production*, *97*, 30–39. https://doi.org/10.1016/J.JCLEPRO.2014.01.046

Barros, M. V., Salvador, R., do Prado, G. F., de Francisco, A. C., & Piekarski, C. M. (2021). Circular economy as a driver to sustainable businesses. *Cleaner Environmental Systems*, *2*, 100006. https://doi.org/10.1016/J.CESYS.2020.100006

Coelho, P. M., Corona, B., ten Klooster, R., & Worrell, E. (2020). Sustainability of reusable packaging–current situation and trends. *Resources, Conservation and Recycling X*, *6*, 100037. https://doi.org/10.1016/J.RCRX.2020.100037

Danvers, S., Robertson, J., & Zutshi, A. (2023). Conceptualizing how collaboration advances circularity. *Sustainability*, *15*(6), 5553. https://doi.org/10.3390/SU15065553

Diaz, A., Schöggl, J. P., Reyes, T., & Baumgartner, R. J. (2021). Sustainable product development in a circular economy: Implications for products, actors, decision-making support and lifecycle information management. *Sustainable Production and Consumption*, *26*, 1031–1045. https://doi.org/10.1016/J.SPC.2020.12.044

Englund, P., Gunnelin, Å., Hendershott, P. H., & Söderberg, B. (2008). Adjustment in property space markets: Taking long-term leases and transaction costs seriously. *Real Estate Economics*, *36*(1), 81–109. https://doi.org/10.1111/J.1540-6229.2008.00208.X

Eureka Forbes/Aquaguard. (n.d.). *Eureka Forbes/Aquaguard: A giant trap/scam harassing thousands of customers in broad daylight. : R/india*. Retrieved August 31, 2025, from https://www.reddit.com/r/india/comments/15ipcc9/eureka_forbes_aquaguard_a_giant_trapscam/

Garg, R., Bansal, S., Rathi, R., & Bhowmick, S. (2024). Mindful consumption – A systematic review and research agenda. *Journal of Cleaner Production*, *459*, 142373. https://doi.org/10.1016/J.JCLEPRO.2024.142373

Garrone, M. (2024). *Furniture as as service to reduce the impact of the industry*. http://www.theseus.fi/handle/10024/866603

Gupta, S., & Sheth, J. (2024). Mindful consumption: Its conception, measurement, and implications. *Journal of the Academy of Marketing Science*, *52*(5), 1531–1549. https://doi.org/10.1007/S11747-023-00970-2

Ji, D., Pongsakornrungsilp, S., Pongsakornrungsilp, P., & Kumar, V. (2025). When mindful consumption meets green purchase intention: Empirical evidence on how a mindful mindset influences tourists. *Sustainability*, *17*(3), 1266. https://doi.org/10.3390/SU17031266

Johnson, E., & Plepys, A. (2021). Product-service systems and sustainability: Analysing the environmental impacts of rental clothing. *Sustainability*, *13*(4), 1–30. https://doi.org/10.3390/SU13042118

Kirchherr, J., Yang, N. H. N., Schulze-Spüntrup, F., Heerink, M. J., & Hartley, K. (2023). Conceptualizing the circular economy (Revisited): An analysis of 221 definitions. *Resources, Conservation and Recycling*, *194*, 107001. https://doi.org/10.1016/J.RESCONREC.2023.107001

Kunwer, S. P., & Singh, S. (2025). Churning the mindful consumption research for achieving sustainable development goals: A review analysis. *Sustainable Development*, *33*(4), 4810–4834. https://doi.org/10.1002/sd.3385

Mahindra Last Mile Mobility Limited. (n.d.). *Mahindra last mile mobility limited and Attero collaborate for sustainable EV battery recycling*. Retrieved August 31, 2025, from https://www.mahindra.com/news-room/press-release/en/mahindra-last-mile-mobility-limited-and-attero-collaborate-for-sustainable-ev-battery-recycling

Mallick, P. K., Salling, K. B., Pigosso, D. C. A., & McAloone, T. C. (2024). Designing and operationalising extended producer responsibility under the EU Green Deal. *Environmental Challenges*, *16*, 100977. https://doi.org/10.1016/J.ENVC.2024.100977

Mitsenko, N. G., Godunko, R. B., & Tymkiv, D. O. (2021). *Evaluating energy security of the European Union and overcoming current challenges/Bezpartochnyi M., Britchenko I., Bezpartochna O.//Actual issues of modern development of socioeconomic systems in terms of the COVID-19 pandemic//Sofia: VUZF Publishing House "St. Grigorii Bogoslov", 2021. Evaluating Energy Security of the European Union and Overcoming Current Challenges, 25, 15–24*. https://doi.org/10.36477/2522-1256-2019-25-02

Morseletto, P. (2023). Sometimes linear, sometimes circular: States of the economy and transitions to the future. *Journal of Cleaner Production*, *390*, 136138. https://doi.org/10.1016/J.JCLEPRO.2023.136138

Nießen, L., & Bocken, N. (2022). Circular business models. *Ökologisches Wirtschaften - Fachzeitschrift*, *37*(1), 16–18. https://doi.org/10.14512/OEW370116

Osterwalder, A., & Pigneur, Y. (2010). *Business model generation: A handbook for visionaries, game changers and challengers*. Wiley.

Pedersen, M. (2013). Introduction to share buyback valuation. *SSRN Electronic Journal*. https://doi.org/10.2139/SSRN.2210735

Roci, M., & Rashid, A. (2023). Economic and environmental impact of circular business models: A case study of white goods-as-a-service using multi-method simulation modelling. *Journal of Cleaner Production*, *407*. https://doi.org/10.1016/J.JCLEPRO.2023.137147

Sahai, S., & Barara, N. (2025). Achieving circular supply chain success: Conquering challenges for sustainable growth. In *Rethinking resources: Approaches to global sustainability, markets, and governance* (pp. 91–105). Springer. https://doi.org/10.1007/978-981-96-9055-8_6

Sakao, T., Bocken, N., Nasr, N., & Umeda, Y. (2024). Implementing circular economy activities in manufacturing for environmental sustainability. *CIRP Annals*, *73*(2), 457–481. https://doi.org/10.1016/J.CIRP.2024.06.002

Sin, L. T., & Tueen, B. S. (2023). International policies of plastic use and consumption. *Plastics and Sustainability*, 255–296. https://doi.org/10.1016/B978-0-12-824489-0.00009-X

Talwar, S. (2021). *Furlenco - Saving the planet one sofa at a time....* https://www.lightbox.vc/new-thinking/detail/furlenco-saving-the-planet-one-sofa-at-a-time

Tata Motors. (n.d.). *Tata motors: Leading circularity & biodiversity for a sustainable future.* Retrieved August 31, 2025, from https://indiacsr.in/tata-motors-leading-circularity-biodiversity-sustainable-future/

Teece, D. J. (2010). Business models, business strategy and innovation. *Long Range Planning*, *43*(2–3), 172–194. https://doi.org/10.1016/J.LRP.2009.07.003

Wang, J., & Azam, W. (2024). Natural resource scarcity, fossil fuel energy consumption, and total greenhouse gas emissions in top emitting countries. *Geoscience Frontiers*, *15*(2), 101757. https://doi.org/10.1016/J.GSF.2023.101757

Chapter 12

Empowering Sustainable Living Through Edge-AI: A Solar Estimation System for Mindful Energy Consumption and Regenerative Homes

Rachana Yogesh Patil[a] *and Yogesh H. Patil*[b]

[a]Pimpri Chinchwad College of Engineering, India
[b]D. Y. Patil College of Engineering, India

Abstract

Proper assessment of rooftop solar capacity is the central focus of optimization of photovoltaic (PV) system and development of the renewable energy industry. This chapter introduces a hybrid geospatial and machine learning (ML)-based model that proposes highly accurate predictions of rooftop solar energy production. The authors have assembled a system that operates Mapbox Graphics Library to interactive spatial visualizing, Photovoltaic Geographical Information System (PVGIS) Application Programming Interfaces (APIs) that the authors utilize to access past and present solar radiation data sets, and Scikit Learn that the authors use to infer regression-based prediction models such as Random Forest and XGBoost. The authors also created a full stack web app that relies on React.js, TailwindCSS and HTML5 as the front end based on responsiveness and the node.js and express as the back-end services that are scalable. The users can enter parameters of rooftop dimensions, orientation, and shading dynamically and the system estimates potential energy based on data of the solar insolation and trained models. Users get the real-time feedback and relative analytics of cost and environmental impact. The methodology developed with the help of location-specific environmental data and ML will provide exact solar calculators with better predictive ability and much less error margin. In line with contributing to the concept of smart micro energy planning, this work illustrates the pillars of Industry

Regenerative Revolution, 233–256

doi:10.1108/978-1-80686-859-920261012

6.0 that consist of hyper-personalization, intelligent automation, and sustainable practices. This chapter presents the argument of conscious consumption of energy and environmental friendliness that subsequently is consonant with the globalization tendencies of decarbonization and sustainable development agenda.

Keywords: Solar energy estimation; sustainable living; rooftop potential; machine learning; renewable energy

JEL Codes: Q42; Q47; C53; C55

1. Introduction

We see that the world's energy sector is still very much a fossil fuel based which in turn puts out great sustainability issues (Liang et al., 2023; Green Kuch, 2022 report). According to the International Energy Agency (Liang et al., 2023), fossil fuels made up almost 82% of the global primary energy supply and in India coal which dominates at about 70% is the main player in electricity generation. That reliance is a key driver of global greenhouse gas (GHG) emissions which the power sector is responsible for over 40% of energy related CO2 output (Bisht et al., 2024 report). Simultaneously, the demand in electricity is expected to grow by nearly a quarter by 2030, and the need to switch to cleaner energy solutions cannot be more urgent now than before (Peng & Ou, 2022).

Solar energy has also proved to be among the most feasible and scalable renewable solutions (Chandra et al., 2025). By 2022, the total solar power installed around the world had exceeded one terawatt, and is projected to increase threefold by 2030 due to the declining photovoltaic (PV) prices and favorable policy conditions. In specific, rooftop solar systems provide a decentralized solution which places the power in the hands of households and communities to produce their own energy, minimize transmission, and play an active role in decarbonization processes (Andreevska et al., 2024). However, in spite of this promise, there is a common challenge of lack of accurate, available, and affordable tools to measure rooftop solar potential. The use of traditional survey-based approaches is slow, costly, and inconsistent, and most of the current digital calculators use small datasets which fail to capture local environmental differences (Cenky et al., 2024b).

To fill this gap, this chapter introduces a combined, AI-based framework of estimating rooftop solar. The system unites geospatial intelligence, real-time environmental data, and machine learning (ML)-based predictive models in order to provide accurate energy yield estimates (Cenky et al., 2024). With the help of Mapbox Graphics Library to create interactive spatial visualization and PVGIS Application Programming Interfaces (APIs) to create historical and real-time irradiance data, users can model the dimensions of rooftops, their orientations, and shading variables. Regression methods like Random Forest and XGBoost are further used in predictive accuracy to minimize mean absolute error (MAE) and root mean square error (RMSE) in energy predictions with the use of Scikit-Learn.

The framework is implemented as a full-stack web application, where the responsive interface is created in React.js, Tailwind CSS, and HTML5, and the scalable backend is created in Node.js and Express.js. Using this interface, the user can enter the parameters of rooftops and get instant feedback regarding the anticipated monthly and annual output of solar, financial savings, and prevented carbon emissions. The comparative analysis has shown that the proposed system saves the assessment time by over 70% of the traditional methods and also is very close to the real PV performance data, thus enhancing assurance in decision-making. In addition to its technical input, the framework represents the ideals of Industry 6.0, focusing on personalization, sustainability, and intelligent automation. It facilitates conscientious energy use, regenerative housing, and sustainability of the environment over time by allowing the urban planners, prosumers, and energy auditors to understand the solar adoption situations in a very precise manner. The contribution of the system also goes to the development of the United Nations Sustainable Development Goals (SDGs) (SDG 7: Affordable and Clean Energy, SDG 11: Sustainable Cities and Communities, and SDG 13: Climate Action) that make it more relevant to the overall global sustainability.

1.1 Evolution of Rooftop Solar Assessment Techniques

The evaluation of the rooftop solar potential has changed considerably in the last 40 years, and it is an indicator of the improvement of the technologies, availability of data, computational intelligence. During the pre-1990s period, manual surveys, rule-of-thumb, and generic multipliers of roofs were the leading methods of evaluation (Glaser, 1994). These methods were simple but time consuming and subject to error giving only approximate estimates of the solar potential.

The first forms of digital mapping, building on the digitization of aerial photographs and hand surveys of roofs, appeared in the 1990s–2000s. Although these methods enhanced the spatial accuracy, they were very laborious and could not respond to changing environmental conditions.

The in between 2000s to 2010 we saw the introduction of Geographic Information System (GIS) and Light Detection and Ranging (LiDAR) which enabled the automatic mapping of rooftops, creation of 3D models, and simulation of shadows (Samu & Fahrioglu, 2017). Also as a result of which we had more accurate representation of the geometries and the shading effects on the rooftops' which in turn improved the accuracy of solar yield forecasts.

The period spanning from the 2010s into the 2020s saw the emergence of sophisticated applications for GIS technology as well as commercial programs like PVWatts and ArcGIS Solar Analyst. These programs significantly promoted spatial and time modeling and enabled executing the analysis at the scale of a city or even a region (Lobaccaro et al., 2019). Despite these developments, the usefulness of these tools had a tendency to be constrained due to price and lack of special training. Over the 2020 to 2025 timeframe, the most widespread hybrid methods will be those that use ML with other methodologies, such as computer vision. The solar estimations are now straightforward, precise, painless, and dependable by features such as automatic rooftop segmentation as well as other features of deep learning (DL)-based panel detection, including global mapping. Towards 2025 and further, the discipline will shift into AI-based predictive models. The future systems will involve the integration of Internet of Things–based real-time data analytics, predictive maintenance, smart grid, and improved PV systems including bifacial, floating, and Building-Integrated Photovoltaics panels (Rajendran et al., 2025). This direction leads to entirely scalable, automated, and dynamic solar assessment solutions in accordance with the principles of Industry 6.0 and world sustainability.

1.2 Motivation

The imperative to de-carbonize the energy sector and sustainable living are the two central driving powers behind this piece of work. Although rooftop solar systems promise a bright future of clean energy, their implementation is usually curtailed by doubts about the future prospects of power generation, economic gains, and environmental gains. Inexpensive, accurate, and scalable instruments that can provide site specific solar potential estimations (considering the geometry of the roof, shadows, and the local environment) are not available to a large number of homes, city planners, and energy auditors. The existing solutions, which include hand-based survey to commercial calculators, either require a significant level of expertise to operate, or are too costly to be accessible by the general population, which creates a gap in the provision and quality of such solutions. The problem is particularly severe in the case of developing countries, in which the consumption of renewable sources is an urgent requirement, but there are few professional assessments. It goes without saying that a data-driven, automated infrastructure is needed that can offer plausible estimates of rooftop solar, at low cost and minimum technical cost. The proposed system seals this gap through the assistance of integrating geospatial intelligence, real-time environmental data, and ML models to produce the correct forecasts of the energy yield. Besides the technical accuracy, the structure will allow the interested parties to make informed decisions on cost savings, reduction of carbon footprint, and energy planning that will lead to increased use of the renewable energy.

1.3 Contribution

The primary goal of this work is to design an automated, scaled, and accurate system to assess the opportunities of rooftop solar and integrate geospatial data intelligence and real-time environmental information with ML models. The framework will allow households, urban planners, and energy auditors practical information on generation of solar energy, cost saving, and environmental impact. Precisely, the following are the objectives of the chapter:

- To develop and deploy a responsive and user-friendly site that can automatically estimate rooftop solar potential with the help of geospatial visualization tools. This minimizes the use of expensive and time consuming manual surveys and also makes it accessible to a wide range of users.
- To develop and test predictive models, including Random Forest and XGBoost, based on past solar irradiance and weather forecasts. Such models will also help in making informed decisions about solar adoption because they will give more accurate and place-sensitive estimates of energy yields.
- To incorporate interactive spatial analytics in order to enable users to visualize potential of energy generation, monthly and annual cost savings, and carbon footprint reduction. This enables the comparative analysis and enables the planning of renewable energy at the household and urban level.
- To determine the accuracy, adaptability, and performance of the framework in various rooftop conditions, to prove that the framework is practically viable as a sustainable energy planning tool.

2. Literature Review

Rooftop solar PV potential has gained considerable attention over the past few years because it is useful in sustainable urban planning, policymaking, and consumer adoption of renewable energy. Although significant advances have been achieved in the automation of rooftop modeling, modeling irradiance, and data sharing through public portals, the literature remains deficient in providing a complete, user-friendly geospatial platform that incorporates data-driven yield correction and interactive analytics and strict validation of the rooftops. In this section, the review of the state of the art in geometry and shading extraction, energy yield modeling, user-facing platforms, and validation practices is presented and the gaps in the current research and future perspectives outlined.

2.1 Geometry and Shading Extraction

Accurately capturing roof geometry and shading conditions is essential for estimating rooftop PV potential. Several studies have used LiDAR- and GIS-based approaches to extract roof planes, derive tilt and azimuth, and model shadows. The Geneva solar cadastre exemplifies this stream by integrating airborne LiDAR, cadastral data, and a sky-view factor (SVF) model to provide rooftop and facade irradiance mapping across an entire city (Desthieux et al., 2018). Similarly, the Bologna Solar City project demonstrated municipal-scale irradiance mapping with vegetation and chimney shading considerations (Africani et al., 2013). On a broader scale, National Renewable Energy Laboratory (NREL) estimated rooftop suitability across 128 US cities by applying 1 m^2 shading grids and tilt/azimuth extraction (Gagnon et al., 2018), and later extended this approach to national-level assessments using statistical extrapolation from LiDAR subsets (Gagnon et al., 2018). In the United Kingdom, Palmer et al. validated suitability against 886 rooftop systems, making it the largest validation dataset in this context (Palmer et al., 2018).

In parallel, DL methods have enhanced geometry extraction where high-quality Digital Surface Model (DSM) data are unavailable. Project Sunroof applied UNet-based segmentation and DSM super-resolution to improve rooftop coverage and automate panel layout optimization (Goroshin et al., 2023). Soares et al. developed a DL-augmented pipeline combining UNet segmentation, geometric regularization, and SVF shading masks to produce rooftop-level energy estimates across multiple French cities (de Barros Soares et al., 2021). Ren et al. further advanced this line by combining 3D-GIS with DL-based rooftop availability extraction in high-density urban environments, capturing dynamic shading effects from neighboring buildings (Ren et al., 2022). These DL-based approaches reduce dependence on expensive LiDAR surveys and increase scalability for large urban areas.

2.2 Energy Yield Modeling

The second issue is to convert irradiance to energy yield once the geometries of the roofs have been determined. Most of the studies utilize physics based performance chains. Common pipelines incorporate pvlib to transpose and correct irradiance and temperature and PVWatts or SAM to convert DC-AC energy. More detailed models like the Eindhoven model incorporate PV Mismatch to include Current–Voltage (I–V characteristics) curves and lost power due to mismatch so that more detailed effects of strings can be represented when inferring module layouts (Tian et al., 2025).

With these developments, ML of yield correction or prediction based on data is underdeveloped. None of the surveyed literature indicated that ensemble models like Random Forest or XGBoost were used to compensate the error of the residual between physics-based forecasting and measured rooftop energy production. Rather, there has been restriction in the application of MLs to the upstream work of geometry segmentation, DSM enhancement, and parameter inferences. This introduces a valuable "ML-for-yield gap," especially because hybrid physics-ML models can be enhanced to be more accurate on variety of rooftops and climatic conditions.

2.3 Interactive Platforms and User-Facing Systems

Another aspect to note in rooftop solar research is how findings are shared on the public portal and applications. Innovative work by municipalities, like the Bologna Solar City platform ([4]) and the Geneva solar cadastre, was the first to provide irradiance and suitability outputs through web portals, providing per-building downloads and CO2 reduction summaries. The SOL 2.0 platform in Lisbon went further to include 3D irradiance of rooftops and facades (Brito et al., 2019). These cadastre-type websites provide powerful examples of geospatial automation and public access, but are mostly fixed, and still based on a preprocessed map layer, and not on scenarios-driven simulations.

Project Sunroof is a good example of a system that is facing the consumer in revealing the potential of solar savings to the end-users. Nonetheless, its related research deliverables actually record procedures of geometry extraction and layout optimization instead of interactive simulation procedures, tariff logic, and verification with measured energy yield. In that way, even though the public-facing aspect is more developed in this instance, it is not as transparent in terms of validation rigor and API performance.

In all the works surveyed, no research report records responsive, on-demand user interactivity (e.g. adjusting DC:AC ratios, selecting module types, combining real-time weather or simulation of tariff/incentive conditions). This is an apparent interactivity gap in literature.

2.4 Validation Rigor and Metrics

The least advanced in terms of research on rooftop solar estimation is validation practices. The majority of the studies confirm their results indirectly, through comparisons of suitability categories with known PV installations, inferences on capacity between their results and utility distribution system operator (DSO) data, or qualitative irradiance tests with fisheye photographs and PVSyst simulation.

Nonetheless, systematic error reporting of time-series energy yield on a rooftop level at a metric (like MAE, RMSE, Coefficient of Variation of RMSE [CVRMSE], or Mean Bias Error [MBE]) is not systematically reported in any of the reviewed works. In addition, there are no leakage-robust validation protocols like grouped cross-validation on the site level, or year-separated cross-validation. In their absence, arguments of generalizability in a variety of climates, roof designs, and orientations cannot be supported. The lack of such validation is always pointed out in the review articles (Gassar & Cha, 2021; Jaczewska et al., 2025), which state that there is an urgent necessity of standardized, rooftop-level benchmarks.

2.5 Foundational Reviews and Adjacent Contributions

There are a number of more comprehensive review papers. The article by Gassar and Cha about GIS-based estimation of rooftop PV potential at urban scales (Gassar & Cha, 2021) reviews the methods, with the LiDAR/GIS approaches to the task being in the strengths, but the absence of standardized assessment in the weaknesses. Melius et al.'s review of rooftop suitability methods and validation techniques (Jaczewska et al., 2025) similarly emphasizes the methodological diversity, but draws attention to inconsistent validation practices across studies. Adjacent research has also expanded solar potential estimation to include facade

Table 12.1. Comparative Overview of Key Literature on Rooftop Solar Potential Estimation

Ref	Scope/Scale	Geometry and Shading Extraction	Yield Modeling	ML for Yield	Platform/ Interactivity	Validation Approach
Goroshin et al. (2023)	Residential, large-scale (U.S.)	UNet roof segmentation; DSM enhancement; automated layout	PVWatts-like flux-based chain	Applied only to geometry	Consumer-facing (savings outputs); API undocumented	No rooftop-level energy error metrics
de Barros Soares et al. (2021)	City-scale, 5 French cities	UNet segmentation + SVF shading	pvlib + PVWatts	None	Research pipeline (no user-facing tool)	No MAE/RMSE; only irradiance-based
Desthieux et al. (2018)	City/canton	LiDAR + cadastral + SVF	Irradiance only (no DC–AC)	None	Public web portal (downloads, maps)	Qualitative (fish-eye and PVSyst), no quantitative errors
Africani et al. (2013)	City	LiDAR DSM; vegetation + chimney shading	Total solar radiation → energy	None	ArcGIS web app; static layers	Validation not detailed
Tian et al. (2025)	City-scale (NL)	Semantic segmentation; layout inference	pvlib SAPM + PVMismatch	Applied to geometry, not yield	Dataset (no interactive UI)	PV capacity validated versus DSO (R^2 = 0.92); no rooftop yield metrics
				None		

Brito et al. (2019)	Neighborhood → city	3D LiDAR modeling; object-based shading	Irradiance aggregation (roof + facades)		ArcGIS visualization; static	Facade PV compared seasonally; no MAE/RMSE
Ren et al. (2022)	Dense urban cities	DL-based area extraction + dynamic shading	Solar potential reduction only	None	No interactive platform	Reported % reduction; no error metrics
Gagnon et al. (2018)	Multi-city (~23% buildings)	LiDAR roof planes; 1 m shading	SAM (with TMY3)	None	Not interactive	Suitability validated versus 205 systems
Gagnon et al. (2018)	U.S. national	LiDAR subset extrapolation; tilt bins	SAM simulations	None	Not interactive	No rooftop validation; extrapolated
Palmer et al. (2018)	Wide-area (886 systems)	LiDAR + photogrammetry; slope/aspect	Suitability classification only	None	Dataset (no portal)	Validated versus 886 rooftops; no energy yie

Source: Authors' Work.

PV, urban-scale 3D modeling (Waqas et al., 2023), and novel ML-assisted approaches for economic analysis (Krapf et al., 2021).

Table 12.1 summarizes the comparative features of key studies on rooftop solar potential estimation. The analysis shows that LiDAR remains the dominant data source in municipal and national projects, while DL methods such as those used in Project Sunroof, Soares et al., and Ren et al. demonstrate increasing scalability. Energy yield modeling is largely physics-based, with only Eindhoven's framework incorporating more advanced chain models. Despite progress in geometry and irradiance modeling, ML has not yet been extended to yield estimation, creating a methodological gap (Dehshiri & Firoozabadi, 2025).

In terms of dissemination, cadastres such as Geneva, Bologna, and Lisbon have pioneered public access, while Project Sunroof remains the only large consumer-facing platform. Nonetheless, none of the reviewed systems have any interactive scenario-driven feature. There are limited practices of validation with most studies indicating suitability checks and not errors at the rooftop level. This uniform weakness is in line with the findings of larger reviews, which supports the necessity of standardized validation measures and procedures.

3. Proposed Methodology

The suggested model of automated estimation of rooftop solar potential is designed into four systematic steps, which deal with each of the major workflow steps. The process starts with data collection and then moves on to rooftop calculation, potential estimation, and lastly, insight generation. This incremental design offers scalability, flexibility, and precision in planning of solar energy.

Phase I—Data Collection: In the first step, it will collect geospatial data, rooftop photographs as well as weather-related data according to reliable open-source sources and APIs. This is what the further analysis is based on. Data and feature engineering is also preprocessed to eliminate noise, standardize the data, and make the data ready to be utilized in the process of precise rooftop detection.

Phase II—Rooftop Calculation: This phase is supposed to identify and estimate the available rooftop area that can be utilized to install solar panels. Some of the methods that can be employed to differentiate between useful and unusable spaces are image segmentation and geospatial analysis, taking into consideration such obstructions as water tanks, chimneys or shading of surrounding buildings.

Phase III—Solar Potential Estimation: In this step, the available data on the solar irradiance, system losses and other environmental factors are added to the available rooftop area and are utilized to determine the potential energy output. The ML models and geospatial algorithms are employed to optimize the predictions of yield to allow a more precise evaluation compared to traditional rule-of-thumb evaluation.

Phase IV—Data Insights and Dashboard: The last step is the synthesis of the findings into insights. It is planned to provide the estimated solar potential, energy yield, and financial savings in an interactive and user-friendly format in the form of a web-based dashboard. This decision-support system will help the stakeholders, households, policymakers, and energy planners make sound decisions about the adoption of solar.

The framework architecture of the proposed system to estimate the rooftop solar potential is aimed to solve the global crisis of switching to clean and renewable energy sources. Although fossil fuels still have their dominance in the global energy supply, in India coal is still used in almost 70% of electricity production, and household consumption varies between 90–120 kWh per month, which means that sustainable energy sources, including solar energy, are urgently needed. This framework will harness the zero-emission capabilities of a solar power source by offering an effective, data-driven framework that automatizes assessment of rooftop solar with precision and scalability (Wang et al., 2023).

The system architecture as shown in Fig. 12.1 is built in three significant layers of the system: Frontend Interface, Backend, and External APIs/Models. It is a geospatial visualization, solar irradiance modeling, and ML modular design to make correct predictions on yields and support decision-making regarding solar adoption.

- *Frontend Interface*—Offers an interactive map-based interface, which is created using Mapbox, and users can choose rooftops based on coordinates or area. An analytical output is provided in a dashboard and it includes solar potential, energy yield, and savings. This makes it accessible to both the policy makers and the individual user.
- *Backend Modules*—The core computational layer, comprising:
- Data Collection Module for acquiring rooftop geometry, weather data, and irradiance values.
- Solar Potential Calculation Module that incorporates system loss modeling (e.g., inverter, wiring, shading, soiling), temperature and cloud-cover adjustments, and PV performance equations.
- Analysis and Synthesis Module which sums up the results and produces actionable insights to be shown in the dashboard.
- *External APIs and ML Models*—The framework will combine PVGIS to get historical irradiance data, Tomorrow.io to get real-time weather data, and state-of-the-art ML algorithms (Random Forest, XGBoost, ensemble models) to optimize energy yield and savings prediction across different weather conditions.

System outputs are elaborate analytics of monthly and annual energy-generation, financial savings, and reduction of the carbon footprint. The architecture allows a cost-effective and scalable alternative to conventional manual rooftop surveys by seamlessly integrating geospatial tools, real-time data, and predictive models and will increase the use of solar energy in cities and rural areas.

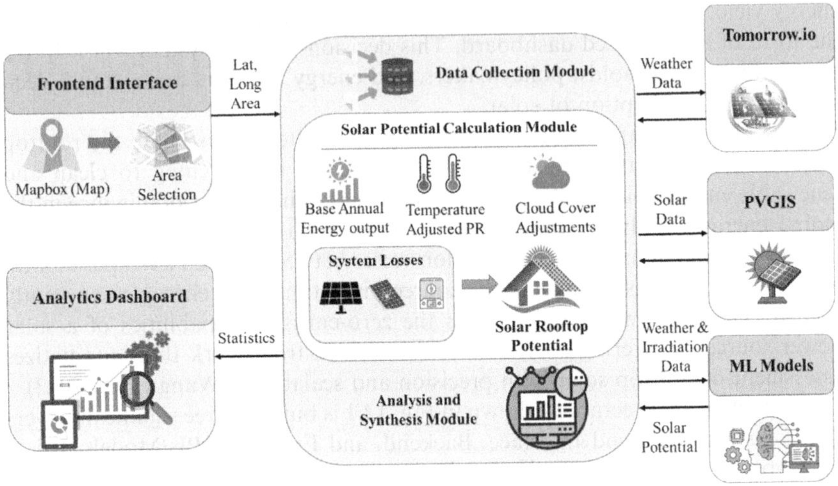

Fig. 12.1. The Proposed System Architecture. *Source:* Authors' Work.

3.1 Frontend Interface

The Frontend Interface serves as the primary interaction layer between the user and the system, offering an intuitive and visually engaging environment for assessing rooftop solar potential. Designed with Mapbox as its core mapping engine, the interface allows users to seamlessly navigate geospatial data and select specific rooftops with high precision (Ladisa et al., 2023). Users can find the rooftop of interest by simply entering the latitude and longitude or by simply looking at the map, which will ensure that there is accuracy in geospatial targeting, which has a direct effect on solar irradiance and the weather calculations (Lin et al., 2024).

After locating the rooftop, the system gives an area selection tool which allows the marking of the usable rooftop area in polygons. This aspect makes sure that only the relevant areas of the roof are taken into account, but not the areas that are in the shade, like water tanks, or spaces where the panels cannot be placed. In this way, the framework will deal with one of the main limitations of generic estimation instruments that tend to assume complete rooftop access without taking into consideration realistic aspects.

The chosen input will be connected to the Analytics Dashboard where the detailed results of the solar potential analysis would be presented in a user-friendly format. The dashboard is used to summarize raw computational results into insights that can be taken action on by presenting them as charts and graphs and key performance measures. The users will be able to see monthly and annual estimates of energy output (kWh), the possible savings in electricity bills, and estimated system performance over a period. Other than financial measures, the dashboard highlights sustainability performance by focusing on carbon dioxide emission reduction and also shows equivalence in terms of trees planted, thus linking technological knowledge to the environmental performance. Simply put, the Frontend Interface is a translation of technical complexity of ML and geospatial analysis into a friendly and interactive interface. It can offer a combination of mapping, accurate rooftop identification and data-rich maps, which can help various stakeholders, including homeowners and city planners, to make informed, data-driven decisions about the use of solar.

3.2 Algorithm: Rooftop Solar Potential Estimation

For the purpose of this study, certain assumptions have been made to simplify the modeling and estimation process. These assumptions help in focusing the analysis on the key parameters while maintaining practical relevance.

- Solar irradiation data is considered for optimal angles.
- Calculated area is nearly exact.
- Only 70% of the rooftop area is useable.
- High temperature is not degrading the solar panel efficiency.

The parameters used in the solar estimation model are defined as follows. Let x_i,y_i represent the coordinates of the rooftop vertices selected using the polygon tool, which together determine the effective rooftop area A in square meters. The monthly average solar irradiation is denoted by G_{avg} (kWh/m^2/day). The panel efficiency is represented by η, while L denotes the system loss factor accounting for shading, dust, and other environmental effects.

The estimated daily solar energy generation is expressed as E, and the monthly energy output for month iii is represented as $E_{month,i}$. The total yearly energy generation is denoted by E_{year}, where D_i refers to the number of days in the ith month. The annual monetary savings, represented by S, are computed using the electricity cost per unit C.

The algorithm starts with obtaining the rooftop coordinates using the polygon selection tool to have an accurate boundary of the rooftop area. The Shoelace formula is used to compute the area of the polygon; this is an efficient algorithm to compute area of polygons. Only 70% of this calculated area is taken as useable to install solar panels due to practical considerations of the location of the solar panels. The algorithm then takes into account on-site solar irradiation information, panel efficiency, and system loss factors to predict the amount of daily energy produced. The model combines real time data on irradiation where possible and makes use of monthly averages otherwise. The daily production is adjusted to the monthly and annual value taking into account the number of days in every month.

Lastly, the annual energy production is multiplied with the current electricity tariff to approximate the savings on costs. The findings, such as the potential energy output and financial gains are forwarded to the Analytics Dashboard to be visualized thereby allowing users to make sound judgments about adopting solar in rooftops.

Step 1: Rooftop Area Calculation (Shoelace formula)

Let the polygon selected by the user have vertices (x_1, y_1), (x_1, y_1), ……, (x_n, y_n) listed in order (clockwise or counterclockwise). The polygon area A_{poly} (in square meters, if coordinates are in meters or converted appropriately) is computed by the Shoelace formula

$$A_{poly} = \frac{1}{2}\left|\sum_{i=1}^{n}(x_i y_{i+1} - x_{i+1}, y_i)\right|$$

Where $(x_{n+1} y_{n+1}) = (x_1 y_1)$

The useable panel area A $= \alpha^* A_{poly}$

Step 2: Core Energy Model (daily, monthly, yearly)

The model estimates daily energy generation per rooftop as:

$$E_{day} = A * G_{avg} * \eta * (1 - L)$$

If a temperature or performance-ratio correction is available, include PR $(0 < \text{PR} \leq 1)$ to capture deviation from STC:

$$E_{day} = A * G_{avg} * \eta * PR * (1 - L)$$

Typical default values used in implementation: $\alpha = 0.7$, $\eta = 0.20$, derating constant included partly in the 0.7 figure and completed by L.

Step 3: Monthly and Yearly Aggregation.

For month i with D_i days, monthly energy is:

$$E_{month,i} = E_{day,i} * D_i$$

Yearly energy is:

$$E_{year} = \sum_{i=1}^{12} E_{month,i}$$

where $E_{day,i}$ uses the month-specific $G_{avg,i}$ and L_i to account for seasonal irradiance and loss variations.

Step 4: Financial and Environmental Metrics.

Annual bill savings (monetary) are estimated by:

$$S = E_{year} * C$$

Annual avoided CO_2emissions can be estimated as:

$$CO_{2,avoided} = E_{year} * EF$$

where EF is the grid emission factor (kg CO_2 per kWh) for the region.

You may convert CO_2 savings to equivalent trees planted using a chosen conversion factor if desired.

Step 5: System Loss Factor L- Composition.

L aggregates multiple loss terms:

$$L = L_{inv} + L_{wiring} + L_{soiling} + L_{shading} + L_{mismatch} + L_{degenration}$$

where each L_* is a fractional loss (e.g., 0.02 for 2%). In practice use empirically derived monthly values that reflect local conditions; typical range 0.15–0.25.

3.3 Application Programming Interface

The API is an interface that enables communication between the system and the third-party applications.<|human|>3.3 API This is an interface that facilitates interaction between the system and the third-party applications. The API mediates between the processing unit at the back end and outside sources of data thus improving the reliability and accuracy in estimating the solar potential. The API combines both historical and real-time data, which means that the forecasts will be based on long-term trends in the environment but will be sensitive to the short-term variability. The API includes two significant external sources of data:

(1) PVGIS: PVGIS is a platform that offers historical solar irradiance and meteorological data that is connected to the rooftop geolocation. This information is the starting point of energy production costing and is used to make modifications to seasonal and long-term fluctuations in the environment.
(2) Tomorrow.io: Tomorrow.io provides real-time weather data, including such important parameters as cloud cover, precipitation, humidity, and ambient temperature. This dynamic data can allow the prediction of the energy yield to be more responsive, especially in areas such as the Indian Subcontinent where weather changes can have a considerable influence on the performance of the solar panel.

3.4 Data Flow and Interactions

The suggested framework will offer a properly organized flow of information and enable the effective interaction of user input, backend processing, external APIs, and visualization modules. This starts at the Frontend Interface where the user identifies and selects a rooftop using the geospatial mapping tool and defines the area that can be used by the rooftop in a polygon. These values (latitude, longitude, and area) are then forwarded to Backend Data Collection Module which initiates the process of calculation.

The API layer is communicating with the Backend, where historical and real-time data are accessed (Yan et al., 2023). PVGIS may provide long-term solar irradiance and climatic information which could be utilized as a reference to make the proper estimation, but Tomorrow.io could offer real-time weather conditions such as cloud cover, temperature, and precipitation. The integrated ML Model further takes these different streams of data and determines the temporal and seasonal data, therefore weed out the inputs, and reduce the error rates in estimating the energy yield.

Once the data is refined, the Solar Potential Calculation Module performs calculations to estimate the quantity of solar energy that will be generated. This model considers derating, panel efficiency, rooftop usability ratio, and loss on the system such as shading, dust, wiring inefficiencies, and inverter conversion losses. The Analysis and Synthesis Module is used to synthesize the results and place results in a comprehensible format. Lastly, the findings are relayed to the Frontend Analytics Dashboard where the user will be provided with interactive visuals, such as monthly and annual energy production estimates, electricity bill savings, and environmental gains such as reduced carbon footprint. This is a simplified flow of information that is accurate, transparent, and usable, which gives decision-makers as well as households power.

3.5 Dataset Design

The quality of solar potential estimation is mainly dependent on the access to quality and location-specific solar irradiance and performance information. The PVGIS can be considered the primary data in this case as it also offers an effective combination of satellite data, in-situ measurements, and sophisticated numerical modeling that ensures the accuracy and reliability of data (Elazab & Daowd, 2025). PVGIS is a combination of various sources of data including Meteosat satellite images, numerical weather prediction (NWP) models, and pyranometer-based weather station observations to provide detailed solar resource data. The dataset is 20 years old (2005–2020), which is appropriate in terms of the spatial resolution of 1–3 km, and in the instance of rooftop-scale solutions, the dataset is particularly convenient (Zhong et al., 2021).

The dataset has several important parameters in connection to the PV system performance that involve Global Horizontal Irradiance (GHI) and Direct Normal Irradiance (DNI), and Diffuse Horizontal Irradiance (DHI), ambient temperature, parameters of the PV performance, such as DC and AC power output. PVGIS also takes into account topographical and environmental conditions that include the topographical shading, horizon elevation, and the influence of the tilt and orientation of the solar panels.

The PVGIS dataset is designed in a systematic pipeline consisting of:

- Data Collection—Satellite data, numerical weather model data, and ground based data.
- Data Processing—The algorithms and radiation models are used to estimate solar irradiance and the PV performance.
- Validation—Comparison of estimates made with the data of pyranometer and weather stations to ascertain the accuracy of estimates.
- Data Storage and Access—Arranging datasets into structured formats, available via the PVGIS API and web interface.

This design allows PVGIS to be used in a variety of applications, including assessment of PV energy resources and the sizing of PV systems in addition to long-term monitoring of performance. The dataset contributes to the predictive power of the suggested framework, as it is used to estimate the rooftop solar potential more accurately, making sure that the results of the proposed framework do not differ significantly with the reality (Ravishankar et al., 2022).

A number of worldwide datasets are offered to evaluate solar resources such as NASA, Surface Solar Energy (SSE), the National Solar Radiation Database (NSRDB) of the National Renewable Energy Laboratory and Solargis. While these datasets are valuable, PVGIS offers distinct advantages for this study:

- NASA SSE provides global coverage but at a coarse spatial resolution (~50 km), which limits accuracy for rooftop-level analysis.
- NREL NSRDB delivers high-resolution (4 km, 30-minute intervals) data but is primarily focused on the United States and lacks comprehensive global coverage.
- Solargis offers high-resolution commercial datasets (up to 250 m), but access is subscription-based, which restricts its use in open, scalable applications.
- PVGIS offers a tradeoff between high spatial resolution (1–3 km), free availability, worldwide applicability and validated performance models, which makes it most suitable in estimating solar potential on rooftops in developed and developing areas.

Therefore, PVGIS was the choice of data in this framework because it is applicable globally, combines satellite and ground-based data, and has an open-source API, which aligns with the idea of the project to develop a cost-effective and scale-up tool to adopt solar.

4. Result Analysis and Validations

This section presents the evaluation and validation of the ML models integrated into the proposed framework for rooftop solar potential estimation. The aim of this analysis is to measure the accuracy, reliability, and robustness of the system in predicting solar energy generation under varying environmental and rooftop conditions.

4.1 Model Accuracy

The relative comparison of the accuracy scores showed that Stacked Averaged Models (0.9341) has the highest accuracy with the close second being Averaged Models (0.9330).

The tree-based ensemble methods like Random Forest (0.9329), Gradient Boost (0.9310), and XGBoost (0.9276) also showed good predictive performance, which was significantly higher as compared to the linear models. In comparison, Linear Regression (0.7500) and Gradient Descent (0.7448) had significantly lower accuracy, which indicates the nonlinear character of the data underlying the models. Other models like Decision Tree (0.9094) and SVR (0.8936) had moderate accuracy and they are better than linear models but not as good as the advanced ensemble models.

The effect of feature engineering and data integration was felt on the general improvements realized. The use of real-time weather forecasts offered by Tomorrow.io increased the time flexibility of the structure, whereas the use of the historical solar irradiance data offered by NSRDB through API was a dependable and sound input option. This combination of sources of data ensured that both short-term and long-term trends of the environment were provided to the models, and this greatly enhanced their predictive power.

One of the most interesting results was the high effectiveness of ensemble-based strategies. The effectiveness of the Stacked Averaged and Averaged Models showed the effectiveness of the combination of multiple models to overcome the limitations of individual learners and generate more generalized and valid predictions. These results validate ensemble learning as one of the key factors in the maximization of rooftop solar potential estimation.

Practically, the high precision of these models directly converts into the confidence of consistent estimates of the energy yield and financial savings and, thus, the confidence of the users and informed decision-making in the adoption of rooftop solar. The robustness of the system was tested in a variety of rooftop situations, and the good correspondence between the predictions and real-world measurements of solar output was a good indicator of the system applicability.

4.2 Feature Correlation Analysis

The correlation analysis helped to give a useful information on how the input features relate to each other. A number of good correlations were noted. GHI_Month_Avg and DNI_Month_Avg (0.70) demonstrated a strong positive correlation, indicating that higher global solar radiation typically coincides with higher direct and diffuse components. Similarly, GHI_Month_Avg and solar_energy_per_unit_area (1.00) showed an expected perfect correlation, confirming that GHI is the primary driver of energy potential. In addition, DNI_Month_Avg and solar_energy_per_unit_area (0.70) exhibited a notable positive correlation.

Conversely, there was a close negative relationship between DHIMonthAvg and Solar Zenith AngleMonthAvg (−0.91). This correlation underlines the argument that diffuse irradiance is likely to rise as the sun is lower in the sky (i.e. when the zenith angle of the sun is smaller) because of a smaller scattering in the atmosphere. Moderate correlations were further found, including DNIMonthAvg and Solar Zenith AngleMonthAvg (0.53), DHIMonthAvg and Relative HumidityMonthAvg (0.42), and the more complicated, less direct interactions of Wind SpeedMonthAvg which did not strongly relate with an individual variable, but was an indirect contributor to the solar performance dynamics.

According to these results, the final parameter set that took place in the ML model consisted of: month, solarZenithAngle, humidity, windSpeed, and area. Month variable represents seasonal variability, whereas solarZenithAngle became an important factor of radiation and was highly correlated with DHI. Humidity was kept because it contributes to atmospheric scattering and windSpeed was added because it has an indirect effect on the solar performance, in particular, through temperature control and cloud behavior. Lastly, the area was a necessary foundation of the geometric basis of rooftop energy potential. This choice is a trade-off between predictive power and the avoidance of multicollinearity, especially because it removes redundant variables like GHI and DNI that had very high levels of correlation with the target variable.

4.3 Impact of Weather Conditions on Solar Energy Production

Weather conditions and their relationship with the production of solar energy is an essential consideration in determining the stability of the renewable energy systems.

There is evident inverse relationship pointing to the fact that the high humidity levels are related to low levels of solar energy production. Relative humidity is relatively low (10–40) during the dry months (January–May) and this means that solar radiation is optimal and therefore the energy production is high (55–65 units). Conversely, the monsoon and postmonsoon seasons (July–October) have high humidity conditions (60–85%), which cause a significant reduction in the solar energy (35–50 units). The intermediate months (June, November, December) are in the middle with the change of dry weather to the humid one.

The findings are consistent with the accepted solar energy principles, according to which more moisture in the atmosphere and cloud cover during wet seasons decrease the effective solar irradiance on the surface. As a result, high-humidity areas that have long humid seasons have possibly difficulties in ensuring a steady electricity output of the sun and might need hybrid or other backup energy sources to be reliable.

4.4 Impact of Wind Speed on Solar Energy Generation

The weather data obtained by utilizing Tomorrow.io show that the two variables exhibit a nonlinear relationship. Solar panel efficiency also increases at moderate wind speeds (2–5 m/s) probably because of greater cooling effects which lowers the surface temperature of the panel and increases the conversion efficiency. Nevertheless, at high wind velocities exceeding 5 m/s there is a slight decrease in the solar energy generation. This decrease can be caused by temporary shading, higher dust load in the air or the effect of turbulence that causes the irradiance to be less stable.

4.5 Distribution of GHI

March to May is the period of peak irradiance as the violins swell toward higher GHI values, indicating a good and consistent supply of the sun. There is a sharp low in June and July, during the monsoon season, when the cloud cover is very high and the irradiance is greatly lowered and the distribution is moved down. The recovery occurs during postmonsoon months between September and October with wider distributions that signify better solar availability. Conversely, the winter season (November to January) is still focused toward low GPI, which is greatly attributed to the reduced daylight hours and increased sun zenith angles.

This reflection highlights the high impact of the season and weather related conditions, especially the variability of monsoon on production of solar energy. The shape of the distributions over the years is recurrent, which represents the patterns over the long term, as well as analogous inter-annual patterns. This kind of analysis is required to correlate the variability of the GHI with the mathematical energy generation model and hence to be able to effectively estimate the rooftop solar potential and plan the deployment of the system.

The seasonal trends in production of solar energy show that solar power production is greatest in the summer seasons (March to May) when the days are longer and the levels of irradiance are high. There is a drastic decrease at the monsoon period (June to August), mainly because of the cloud cover and precipitation which reduce the exposure of the sun. The postmonsoon and winter periods (September to February) have stable production with more moderate and sure levels of generation. In the line plots, inter-annual variability is highlighted and at the same time, the stability of seasonal trends is brought out. These results support the high reliance of rooftop solar energy potential on the climatic and weather conditions of the regions, and the need to include seasonal influence in the solar potential estimation models.

5. Proposed System User Interface (UI) Design

Sample graphical UI screens have been created to illustrate how the proposed system can be used and implemented in practice. These mock-ups introduce the possibility of the interaction of various groups of users, namely homeowners, business owners, and consultants, with the system in an intuitive way.

The landing page, serves as the landing interface for all users. It provides a clean and modern design with a navigation bar containing essential links such as *About, Services, Contact,* and *Get Started.* The interface features three categories of users, namely homeowners, business owners, and consultants, each of whom has its own entry point to consider solar potential and use the tools or services that are available. Also, the front page will have an interactive feature whereby customers can input their rooftop address to get an immediate estimate of.

Once the main page has been loaded, the user is redirected to the map interface by clicking on the button marked Get Started. The system will automatically know the location of the user using geolocation. In case the user wants to analyze another site, there is an integrated search option based on Mapbox which enables the user to navigate to the location of interest within a short time. This aspect will bring flexibility since it can be analyzed to the existing rooftop and any other property of interest. After the location selection, the user is already at the area selection interface.

In this case, the system has a polygon selection tool, which allows the user to indicate the precise area of the roof to be examined. Users are able to trace a polygon on the map covering the rooftop and thus can determine the surface to be used to estimate solar energy accurately. Once the selection is complete, the Generate Estimate option is turned on and this estimates and gives an in-depth solar potential representation of the selected rooftop. This systematic transition between geolocation and polygon selection makes sure that users do not have to switch to the next stage of identifying their position and defining their rooftop, and the final goal is to get the correct and customized solar energy forecast.

Once the selection of the rooftop area is done, the system then takes the input parameters, which are defined as latitude, longitude, and rooftop area at the backend and then calculates the solar potential. The estimation results are shown on the frontend in a well-organized and user-friendly format. The backend will combine irradiation information that was retrieved in the PVGIS API and weather parameters that were obtained in the Tomorrow.io API, which will provide the calculation with accuracy and location specificity. Besides such data-based estimates, the system also takes into account predictions produced by the ML model, which also enhances the precision of the solar potential forecast. The consolidated output gives users a clear picture of the solar power capacity of their rooftop to make informed decisions on whether to adopt solar and save energy.

6. Conclusion

There are high-quality data (PVGIS, Tomorrow.io, NSRDB), and advanced ensemble learning models described in the chapter. The findings show that stacked and averaged ensembles are more useful than conventional methods having over 93% accuracy and nearly equivalent real-world solar output. Additional validation of the power of the method is done through correlation analysis of features and weather effects. The study indicates that it is an attractive decision-support tool to users, policymakers and industry stakeholders.

References

Africani, P., Bitelli, G., Lambertini, A., Minghetti, A., & Paselli, E. (2013). Integration of LIDAR data into a municipal GIS to study solar radiation. *The International Archives of the Photogrammetry, Remote Sensing and Spatial Information Sciences*, *40*, 1–6.

Andreevska, N. M., Gjorgjiev, G., & Bozhinov, E. (2024). Assessment of solar photovoltaic potential of building rooftops based on multicriteria spatial analysis. *Technical Journal/Tehnički Glasnik, 18*.

Bisht, A. S., Lugovoy, O., & Sharma, T. (2024, July). Decarbonizing the Indian power sector: Assessing the impact of a 30-Year plan to net zero. In *2024 IEEE 4th international conference on sustainable energy and future electric transportation (SEFET)* (pp. 1–5). IEEE.

Brito, M. C., Redweik, P., Catita, C., Freitas, S., & Santos, M. (2019). 3D solar potential in the urban environment: A case study in Lisbon. *Energies, 12*(18), 3457.

Cenky, M., Bendik, J., Janiga, P., & Lazarenko, I. (2024a). Urban-scale rooftop photovoltaic potential estimation using open-source software and public GIS datasets. *Smart Cities, 7*(6), 3962–3982.

Cenky, M., Bendik, J., & Lazarenko, I. (2024b, October). Rooftop photovoltaic potential estimation using QGIS and simple building shadow analysis. In *2024 international conference on smart systems and technologies (SST)* (pp. 103–108). IEEE.

Chandra, R., Pai, S., Nayak, S., & Devagudi, S. H. (2025). India's coal conundrum: Decarbonization amidst A developmental legacy. *Wiley Interdisciplinary Reviews: Climate Change, 16*(1), e928.

de Barros Soares, D., Andrieux, F., Hell, B., Lenhardt, J., Badosa, J., Gavoille, S., & Bacry, E. (2021). Predicting the solar potential of rooftops using image segmentation and structured data. In *NIPS proceedings*. HAL Open Science.

Dehshiri, S. S. H., & Firoozabadi, B. (2025). Robust analysis of photovoltaic plants: A framework based on prediction uncertainties by machine learning. *Energy Conversion and Management X, 26*, 100912.

Desthieux, G., Carneiro, C., Camponovo, R., Ineichen, P., Morello, E., Boulmier, A., & Ellert, C. (2018). Solar energy potential assessment on rooftops and facades in large built environments based on lidar data, image processing, and cloud computing. Methodological background, application, and validation in Geneva (solar cadaster). *Frontiers in Built Environment, 4*, 14.

Elazab, R., & Daowd, M. (2025). New geographic information system based sustainability metric for isolated photovoltaic systems. *Scientific Reports, 15*(1), 2023.

Gagnon, P., Margolis, R., Melius, J., Phillips, C., & Elmore, R. (2018). Estimating rooftop solar technical potential across the US using a combination of GIS-based methods, lidar data, and statistical modeling. *Environmental Research Letters, 13*(2), 024027.

Gassar, A. A. A., & Cha, S. H. (2021). Review of geographic information systems-based rooftop solar photovoltaic potential estimation approaches at urban scales. *Applied Energy, 291*, 116817.

Glaser, P. E. (1994). A global perspective on renewable and solar energy. *The Journal of Social, Political & Economic Studies, 19*(1), 3.

Goroshin, R., Wilson, A., Lamb, A., Peng, B., Ewonus, B., Ratsch, C., & Elkin, C. (2023). Estimating residential solar potential using aerial data. *arXiv*. arXiv preprint arXiv:2306.13564.

Green, F., & Kuch, D. (2022). Counting carbon or counting coal? Anchoring climate governance in fossil fuel–based accountability frameworks. *Global Environmental Politics, 22*(4), 48–69.

Jaczewska, P., Sybilski, H., & Tywonek, M. (2025). Assessment of the solar potential of buildings based on photogrammetric data. *Energies*, *18*(4), 868.

Krapf, S., Kemmerzell, N., Khawaja Haseeb Uddin, S., Hack Vazquez, M., Netzler, F., & Lienkamp, M. (2021). Towards scalable economic photovoltaic potential analysis using aerial images and deep learning. *Energies*, *14*(13), 3800.

Ladisa, C., Capolupo, A., & Tarantino, E. (2023, September). A customized JAVA OpenStreetMap preset to extract solar panel installations for humanitarian purposes. In *International conference on innovation in urban and regional planning* (pp. 3–11). Springer Nature Switzerland.

Liang, Y., Kleijn, R., & Van der Voet, E. (2023). Increase in demand for critical materials under IEA Net-Zero emission by 2050 scenario. *Applied Energy*, *346* (2023).

Lin, W., Zhu, J., Hua, Y., Li, Q., Mou, L., & Zhu, X. X. (2024). Towards sustainable urban energy: A robust deep learning framework for solar potential estimation. *The International Archives of the Photogrammetry, Remote Sensing and Spatial Information Sciences*, *48*, 371–378.

Lobaccaro, G., Croce, S., Lindkvist, C., Probst, M. M., Scognamiglio, A., Dahlberg, J., & Wall, M. (2019). A cross-country perspective on solar energy in urban planning: Lessons learned from international case studies. *Renewable and Sustainable Energy Reviews*, *108*, 209–237.

Palmer, D., Koumpli, E., Cole, I., Gottschalg, R., & Betts, T. (2018). A GIS-based method for identification of wide area rooftop suitability for minimum size PV systems using LiDAR data and photogrammetry. *Energies*, *11*(12), 3506.

Peng, W., & Ou, Y. (2022). Integrating air quality and health considerations into power sector decarbonization strategies. *Environmental Research Letters*, *17*(8).

Rajendran, G., Raute, R., & Caruana, C. (2025). A comprehensive review of solar PV integration with smart-grids: Challenges, standards, and grid codes. *Energies*, *18*(9), 2221.

Ravishankar, R., AlMahmoud, E., Habib, A., & de Weck, O. L. (2022). Capacity estimation of solar farms using deep learning on high-resolution satellite imagery. *Remote Sensing*, *15*(1), 210.

Ren, H., Xu, C., Ma, Z., & Sun, Y. (2022). A novel 3D-geographic information system and deep learning integrated approach for high-accuracy building rooftop solar energy potential characterization of high-density cities. *Applied Energy*, *306*, 117985.

Samu, R., & Fahrioglu, M. (2017). An analysis on the potential of solar photovoltaic power. *Energy Sources, Part B: Economics, Planning and Policy*, *12*(10), 883–889.

Tian, B., Loonen, R. C., Valckenborg, R., & Hensen, J. L. (2025). A fully automated urban PV parameterization framework for improved estimation of energy production profiles. *arXiv preprint arXiv:2505.19876*. https://doi.org/10.48550/arXiv.2505.19876

Wang, Z., Wang, Y., Cao, S., Fan, S., Zhang, Y., & Liu, Y. (2023). A robust spatial-temporal prediction model for photovoltaic power generation based on deep learning. *Computers & Electrical Engineering*, *110*, 108784.

Waqas, H., Jiang, Y., Shang, J., Munir, I., & Khan, F. U. (2023). An integrated approach for 3D solar potential assessment at the city scale. *Remote Sensing*, *15*(23), 5616.

Yan, L., Zhu, R., Kwan, M. P., Luo, W., Wang, D., Zhang, S., & Feng, L. (2023). Estimation of urban-scale photovoltaic potential: A deep learning-based approach for constructing three-dimensional building models from optical remote sensing imagery. *Sustainable Cities and Society*, *93*, 104515.

Zhong, T., Zhang, Z., Chen, M., Zhang, K., Zhou, Z., Zhu, R., & Yan, J. (2021). A city-scale estimation of rooftop solar photovoltaic potential based on deep learning. *Applied Energy*, *298*, 117132.

Chapter 13

Case Studies in Regenerative Industry: Mindful Consumption and Industry 6.0 in Sweden and Japan

Kayenaat Bahl[a], *Ruchi Arya*[b], *Amit Trehan*[b] *and Pardeep Bawa Sharma*[b]

[a]IILM University, India
[b]Chandigarh University, India

Abstract

Conscious consumption, environmental stewardship, and Industry 6.0 converging would give a chance to redefine industrial growth in the 21st century. The comparison of the Japanese and Swedish case indicates that the level of technological development is not adequate to bring about regenerative results. The ability to be on the forefront of the regenerative revolution depends on the cooperation of the state of the art industry, cultural awareness, and environmental responsibilities. To nations that are merging economic growth, earth limits, and human well-being, the cases provide insights into the system thinking, policymaking, and engagement with the culture. Conscious, morally upright, and environmentally friendly decisions emerged as some of the driving forces of conscious consumption. Broad sustainability awareness, encouraged by education and such norms as Lagom, in Sweden is converted into such behaviors as energy-efficient product selection, ethical labeling, and involvement in shared economy. This defines the market needs, industrial design, supply chains, and responsibility. In comparison, in Japan, Shokunin, and Kaizen traditions have not escalated into mass consumer activism and transparency. Altogether, conscious consumption needs to be institutionalized in education, business, and policy to promote it. Peering even further, Industry 6.0 should not just be more automation but more human-centered, the systems of

Regenerative Revolution, 257–276

doi:10.1108/978-1-80686-859-920261013

which must be purposive where technology is used to realize social, ecological, and inclusive value.

Keywords: Industry 6.0; regenerative industry; sustainability; mindful consumption; intelligent manufacturing; digital transformation; technology integration; ethical production; cultural values

JEL Codes: Q56

1. Introduction

The booming pace of technological advancements, as well as the increasing ecological catastrophes and new socioeconomic realities, demands the total redefinition of industry, nature, and human consciousness (Nleya & Velempini, 2024). The next phase in the evolution of the industry is Industry 6.0, focused on such technological advances as hyper-automation, artificial intelligence (AI), and decentralized manufacturing, yet also human-centered, ethical, and regenerative processes. Meanwhile, the principles of mindfulness founded on the consciousness, intentionality, and sustainability are diffusing between consumer behavior and organizational strategy (Orlando et al., 2020; Rajnai & Kocsis, 2020). The intersection of Industry 6.0 and mindfulness-based systems is a fertile field in which the global industrial systems can be redefined to be more eco-friendly and socially-needs-wise. With the scarce resources, climate disasters, and mental health crises affecting communities, the nexus of technology and consciousness is becoming urgent (Chatterjee et al., 2021; Culot et al., 2020; Javaid et al., 2021). Soon, conscious consumption which was a personal or cultural ideal is becoming a systemic requirement (Chourasia et al., 2022). Mindfulness comes out of personal will to organizational determination, supply chain morals and design principles that put human and ecological well-being at the center of design. The crossroads between smart industry and the conscious values are the transition toward the regenerative, rather than extractive, growth paradigms (Bai et al., 2021; Malik et al., 2024; Mohamed & Hameed, 2022; Xu et al., 2021). The proposed study is based on a comparative case study of Japan and Sweden, two countries that are the leaders in the areas of innovation and sustainability, but with different cultural and institutional systems. The example of how culture predetermines the formation of industrial ecosystems is Japan, a union of high-tech atomization and ancient mindfulness practice like Kaizen and Shokunin. Sweden is a green industrial paradigm, which is policy-driven, with its foundation on the idea of public engagement in conscious consumption, corporate social responsibility (CSR), and circular economic approaches. This work discusses the practical implementation of Industry 6.0 and mindfulness, as presented through the example of Japan in smart manufacturing, and Sweden in the future of the fashion industry. This paper is placed in the context of the regenerative revolution and discusses the conducive industrial change in these nations to sustainable development, ethical production, and consumer awareness

(Ahmad et al., 2024). Comparatively, the paper establishes enabling issues, cultural, and systemic obstacles in the balance between advanced technology and environmental stewardship and mindful practice. Finally, the paper will add to the discussion of how the industry can be not only effective, but also regenerative, human-centered, and healing to the environment (Almusaed et al., 2023).

1.1 Rationale of the Study

In the context of the increasing levels of global debate concerning sustainability and digitalization, empirical research on the integration of mindfulness in Industry 6.0 is still needed. Recent studies tend to confine technological improvement to the behavioral, ethical, or the cultural, and regenerative innovation is not a fully explored area. In this paper, the authors reflect on how mindful values in Industry 6.0 can result in inclusive and sustainable industrial systems with an ethic of care. The comparison of Japan is a benchmark. Sweden is an environmentally responsible, digitally transformative, and circular economy, which, through national cultural elements, like the importance of Lagom, allows conscious industry. Such industries as clean tech, fashion, and manufacturing serve as examples of how digitalization can be implemented as a part of regenerative and socially responsible approaches. Japan is a form of complementary movement. Japan has a model, designed through Kaizen and Shokunin, with a focus on mindfulness, craftsmanship, continuous improvement, and in the development of an industrial culture of the precision, respect, and long-lasting quality. This study can provide comparative learnings to policymakers, academicians, and business leaders by determining conditions in which enablement, policy mechanisms, and cultural drivers are likely to support mindfulness in Industry 6.0.

2. Literature Review

The history of changing industrial transformation has surpassed the mechanistic and efficiency-based paradigms in favor of an integrated, inclusive approach to the issue that is sensitive to environmental sustainability, ethics and well-being. In Industry 6.0, as an expansion of the cyber-physical integration in Industry 4.0 and the human–machine cooperation in Industry 5.0, this is expressed. Industry 6.0 is focused on human-centric, intelligent, and decentralized industrial ecosystems, balancing the power of technology with social and ecological regeneration (Piccarozzi et al., 2022). These three categories—AI, robotics, and digital twins—are the drivers of the creation of ethical, sustainable, and inclusive values besides being optimization tools (Murugan & Prabadevi, 2023). The industry 6.0 literature is growing with a high pace. The future theory focuses on smart automation and ethical AI, closed resource cycles, and the system thinking (Zhang et al., 2023). The Industry 6.0 is the factor, which balances the productivity with the resilience, well-being, and sustainability, as opposed to the previous revolutions oriented toward output (Frank et al., 2021; Marques et al.,

2020; Shah et al., 2020). Researchers emphasize that social innovation, distributed manufacturing, and regenerative design should be implemented in the industrial process. However, the majority of studies focus on technology and operations and do not explore human and mindful aspects in their study. Started in Buddhist philosophy, mindfulness has evolved into a secular model of focus, purposefulness, and ethical behavior (Chandan et al., 2023; Kabat-Zinn, 2003) and been associated with improved decision-making, innovation, and ethical leadership (Dane & Brummel, 2014). Recent literature means to use mindfulness to apply to systemic change, such as the design of the supply chain and stakeholder interaction (Pfeffer et al., 2021). Conscious, moral, and positive consumption results in the reduction of overconsumption and environmental pollution (Carpanzano & Knüttel, 2022; Sheth et al., 2011;). Values based consumption, product transparency, and CSR is part of such research. Mindfulness is used to determine business strategy, creating corporate culture, product creation, and innovation (Ellili et al., 2023; Reb & Atkins, 2015; Yu, 2024). There are also limited studies that have focused on structurally applying mindfulness in industrial systems with particular focus on Industry 6.0. Regenerative development is the bind between the technological change and the practice of mindfulness in its systems-aware, place-based, and future-oriented perspectives (Duggal et al., 2022; Fernandez-Miguel et al., 2024; Mang & Haggard, 2016). Regenerative models are oriented at restoring ecosystems and societies instead of reducing harm (Bag et al., 2021; Varela et al., 2022; Zheng et al., 2021). Technology supports closed loop production, localized production, and collaborative innovation. Along with mindfulness, Industry 6.0 can trigger profound structural change, yet little empirical data is available (Frederico, 2021; Kim et al., 2023; Leng et al., 2022). The vast majority of research depends on technology or the behavior, and there are few studies that provide cross-cultural comparisons of the way in which national culture, organization routines, and policy regimes in industrial systems incorporate mindfulness. Good examples of cultural, economic, and institutional reactions to technology, mindfulness, and sustainability are Japan and Sweden. High-tech humanism is reflected in the culture and folklore of Japanese business, the focus of which is on Kaizen, Shokunin, and lean philosophy (Aslam et al., 2020; Andronie et al., 2021; Lasi et al., 2022; Liker, 2004). Sweden puts a premium on environmental democracy, circular economy, and social innovation, which is backed with such cultural values as Lagom (Mont & Plepys, 2008; Rane & Narvel, 2021; Reis et al., 2021; Tortorella et al., 2020). Both provide good empirical bases to explore the ways in which Industry 6.0 and mindfulness co-evolve in a culturally specific yet universally applicable manner. Overall, there was a lack of literature on the intersection of Industry 6.0 and mindfulness, particularly in a comparative and context-specific fashion. The purpose of this paper is to fill this gap and analyze how they interact in industrial and policy environments in Sweden and Japan, learning how to apply it globally to regenerative transformation. The objectives as based on these gaps are as follows.

2.1 Objectives of the Study

- To analyze the implementation of Industry 6.0 practices in selected industries in Sweden and Japan, focusing on technological innovation, ethical production, and human-centered industrial design.
- To evaluate the influence of mindfulness principles on industrial processes, organizational culture, and consumer behavior within the institutional and cultural contexts of each nation.
- To examine the interaction and convergence of Industry 6.0 and mindfulness frameworks, identifying how their alignment fosters regenerative, sustainable, and socially responsible industrial development.
- To compare the cultural, policy, and institutional mechanisms that enable or constrain the integration of mindful values and Industry 6.0 practices in Japan and Sweden.

3. Research Methodology

The study uses a qualitative comparative case study design supported by quantitative descriptive analysis. The methodology allows conducting a systematic comparison of the conceptualizations and practices of Industry 6.0 and mindfulness in the industrial, cultural, and policy contexts of Japan and Sweden. The design selected was comparative case study design since it enables a deep investigation of the complex, context-specific phenomena in two advanced economies with distinct cultural and institutional contexts.

3.1 Data Collection

The research is based on secondary sources and the analysis of documents as the main pieces of evidence. Peer-reviewed journal articles, governmental policy reports, industry white papers, company sustainability, and CSR reports and reputable institutional databases were used as the sources of data, including the Organization for Economic Co-operation and Development (OECD), World Bank, and Eurostat. The sources offer both quantitative metrics (e.g., rates of AI integration, workforce data, sustainability indexes) and qualitative information (e.g., cultural philosophies, policy stories, organizational practices). Relevance and credibility criteria were used to select all materials to attain consistency and reliability.

3.2 Analytical Techniques

The analysis was done in a two-level process. To begin with, quantitative measures of secondary data were presented in the form of comparative tables to demonstrate descriptive tendencies in the main dimensions, including technology adoption, mindfulness in organizations, sustainability performance, and policy support. Second, thematic analysis was used to explain these patterns in their cultural and institutional settings. Themes that emerged in the analysis included technological integration, cultural mindfulness, sustainability, and regeneration, consumer engagement, and policy support, with these themes being the analytical frameworks used to conduct the cross-case synthesis.

3.3 Conceptual and Analytical Framework

The theoretical framework combines the ideas of Industry 6.0 (human-oriented, intelligent, and ethical technology systems) and the theory of mindfulness (intentional awareness, ethical action, and sustainability orientation). This dual lens facilitates the research to explore the interaction of technological change and conscious values to create regenerative industrial results. The framework of analysis is therefore based on following five thematic dimensions:

(1) technological integration;
(2) cultural and organizational awareness;
(3) sustainability and regeneration;
(4) stakeholder and consumer engagement;
(5) institutional and policy backing.

This multi-layered approach is rich in both depth and comparability. It not only justifies the use of secondary data by providing triangulation among different sources, but also provides depth in the interpretation by connecting empirical evidence and conceptual understanding. The design thus enhances the validity and theoretical basis of the chapter in its synthesis of data-based description and reflective context-based interpretation.

3.4 Why Comparative Case Study Analysis for This Study?

Each case is compared against the same metric/question and thematic categories by the use of a systematic focused comparison (George & Bennett, 2005). This creates the opportunity of analytical profundity and cross-case observations by the use of a standardized template to the assessment of different situations. The final purpose of this comparative strategy is to reveal context-specific procedures and principles transferable to the Industry 6.0 alignment with mindfulness and regenerative objectives. The results will also provide theoretical contributions to the research of Industry 6.0 and sustainability transitions, and implications of the research to the policy and industry actors about the transition to mindful and forward-looking industrial systems.

4. Analysis

Table 13.1 illustrates the comparative technological, institutional, and workforce readiness of Sweden and Japan for Industry 6.0 adoption. It highlights how both countries differ in digital capabilities, policy support, and human capital development that shape their preparedness for regenerative industrial transformation.

Data in Table 13.1 indicate that Sweden and Japan possess strong technological foundations for Industry 6.0, yet their pathways toward regenerative industrial development diverge in emphasis and orientation. Japan shows higher automation intensity, greater adoption of AI-driven production systems, and strong smart manufacturing maturity, which reflects its long-standing commitment to efficiency, precision, and advanced industrial capability. Sweden, while slightly lower on some automation indicators, demonstrates a more holistic integration of AI, IoT, digital twins, and workforce readiness, indicating that its technological adoption is embedded within broader sustainability and human-centered objectives rather than focusing solely on productivity gains. Policy structures reinforce these differences. Both countries invest heavily in R&D for the automotive and electronics sectors, but Sweden's industrial roadmaps, environmental regulations, and government incentives show stronger alignment with sustainability-led transformation. Sweden's more progressive regulatory support for digital and green twin integration, higher access to incentives for regenerative manufacturing, and more recent sustainability-oriented national strategies indicate a more coordinated approach between policy, technology, and environmental goals. Japan's policy orientation remains technologically ambitious but less explicitly tied to circularity and regenerative outcomes, suggesting that environmental integration within industrial systems is emerging more gradually.

Workforce and educational preparedness further shape the regenerative potential of each country. Sweden's higher vocational AI and robotics training, broader digital apprenticeships, and strong gender inclusion in engineering create a more diverse and adaptable workforce capable of supporting Industry 6.0 transitions. The prominence of green technical curricula and sustainability-oriented education strengthens the workforce's ability to engage with regenerative design, eco-efficiency, and responsible technological implementation. Japan maintains a strong pipeline of STEM graduates and a larger volume of university–industry research collaborations, demonstrating its continued industrial strength. However, slower expansion of sustainability-focused training and lower levels of diversity may limit the broader systemic integration needed for regenerative industrial evolution. Taken together, these findings suggest that Sweden's competitive advantage lies in its integrated alignment of technology, institutional support, and workforce development with sustainability objectives. Japan's advantage remains its strong technological advancement and robust industrial ecosystem, yet its regenerative trajectory depends on deeper integration of environmental frameworks, skills modernization, and policy alignment. Sweden therefore appears more prepared for transformative, human-centered, and regenerative Industry 6.0 systems, whereas Japan demonstrates significant potential that will strengthen as cultural, institutional, and sustainability elements become more closely integrated with its technological strengths.

Table 13.2 illustrates the cultural, sustainability, and consumer behavior factors that shape regenerative industry development in Sweden and Japan. It

Table 13.1. Industrial and Institutional Readiness for Regenerative Industry.

Indicator	Sweden	Japan	Source
Industrial robot density (per 10,000 workers)	489	1,457	IFR (2023)
AI-integrated production systems (%)	38%	51%	OECD Digital Economy Outlook (2024)
Internet of Things (IoT) implementation in assembly lines (%)	71%	75%	OECD Digital Economy Outlook (2024)
Cybersecurity readiness (score/100)	88	85	World Bank Digital Indicators (2023)
Skilled AI/robotics engineers (per 10,000 workers)	122	135	OECD Economic Survey (Sweden, 2023; Japan, 2024)
Smart manufacturing maturity index (score/100)	79	86	OECD Economic Survey (Sweden, 2023; Japan, 2024)
R&D spending on auto/electronics (% of GDP)	1.80%	2.30%	OECD Science, Technology and Innovation Outlook (2023)
Government Incentives for EVs/green electronics	$1.2B	$2.1B	METI (Japan); EU Digital Compass
National roadmap for industrial strategy	Smart Industry 2.0	Society 5.0	National Innovation Agencies; METI (Japan)
Regulatory support for digital/green twin integration	Strong	Moderate	EU Digital Compass; METI (Japan)
Digital upskilling/reskilling programs (%)	75%	58%	OECD Science, Technology & Innovation Outlook (2023)
STEM graduates (%)	63%	58%	UNESCO Institute for Statistics (2023)
Vocational AI/robotics training programs (%)	29%	21%	ILO (2023)
University–industry research projects (per year)	180+	220+	UNESCO Institute for Statistics (2023)

Table 13.1. *(Continued)*

Indicator	**Sweden**	**Japan**	**Source**
Female participation in engineering (%)	28%	16%	ILO (2023); World Bank Education Indicators (2022)
Green curriculum in technical institutes (%)	80%	55%	Ministry of Foreign Affairs of Japan (2022); OECD (2026)
Digital apprenticeships (%)	62%	41%	ILO (2023); World Bank Education Indicators (2022)

Source: Author's Compilation.

highlights differences in work culture, organizational mindfulness, environmental practices, and ethical consumption patterns that influence how each country supports circular and sustainable industrial transitions.

The comparison of Sweden and Japan illustrated in Table 13.2 on work culture, mindfulness, and organizational practices shows clear differences in how each country creates conditions that support or constrain regenerative industrial development. Sweden's shorter working hours, lower workplace stress levels, and higher adoption of mindfulness and work–life balance programs indicate a more human-centered orientation that promotes well-being, resilience, and long-term innovation. The lower percentage of stress and a healthier work environment contribute to conditions in which creativity, ethical decision-making, and sustainability practices can flourish. By contrast, Japan's longer working hours and higher stress levels highlight structural challenges such as overwork and burnout, which may undermine regenerative objectives. The influence of cultural philosophies reinforces these patterns: *Lagom* in Sweden encourages balance and sufficiency, while *Kaizen* and *Shokunin* in Japan emphasize continuous improvement and craftsmanship, but have not fully translated into widespread mindfulness practices or workplace transparency. Sweden's higher organizational mindfulness index and greater prevalence of mindfulness training show that awareness and well-being are more systematically embedded into industrial and organizational culture.

Institutional and policy conditions further shape these dynamics. Although both nations demonstrate strong innovation systems, Sweden has a more integrated and active policy environment aligned with regenerative industry principles. Higher access to incentives, stronger and more recent industrial roadmaps, and more progressive regulatory support for digital and green twin integration position Sweden to advance sustainability-oriented industrial transformation. The alignment between policy mechanisms, environmental goals, and industrial strategy is clearer and more cohesive. Japan's industrial policies remain

Table 13.2. Cultural, Sustainability and Consumer Drivers of Regenerative Industry (Sweden vs. Japan).

Indicator	Sweden	Japan	Source
Average weekly working hours	36.5	42	Eurofound (2023); Japan Labor Review (2023)
Firms offering mindfulness/ work-life programs (%)	33%	12%	Corporate Wellness Trends Reports (2023)
Workplace stress levels (%)	19%	46%	Swedish Work Environment Authority; Japan Labor Issues (2023)
Cultural philosophy shaping work	Lagom	Kaizen, Shokunin	World Happiness Report (2023)
Mindfulness training in corporate settings (%)	24%	6%	Corporate Wellness Trends Reports (2023)
Organizational mindfulness index (score/100)	76	64	World Happiness Report (2023); Eurofound
Use of recycled materials in manufacturing (%)	38%	27%	Global Reporting Initiative (2023); CDP (2023)
Electrification rate in automotive production (%)	44%	37%	CDP (2023)
Green factory certifications (LEED/ISO 14001) (%)	68%	46%	ISO (2023)
Circularity strategy adoption among firms (%)	52%	31%	National Sustainability Councils; Corporate Sustainability Reports
ESG reporting by major firms (%)	88%	67%	Global Reporting Initiative (2023); CDP (2023)
Carbon-neutral industry targets	Volvo (2030), Northvolt (2025)	Toyota (2050), Sony (2040)	Corporate Sustainability Reports

Table 13.2. *(Continued)*

Indicator	Sweden	Japan	Source
EV share of new car sales (2023)	56%	22%	International Energy Agency (2023)
Preference for eco-labeled electronics (%)	62%	37%	Ethical Consumer (2022); OECD Consumer Opinion Surveys (n.d.)
Awareness of ethical sourcing (%)	71%	44%	Eurobarometer (2023); National Environmental Agencies
Public trust in industrial transparency (%)	68%	49%	Eurobarometer (2023)
Return/reuse rate of electronics (%)	74%	61%	International Energy Agency (2023)
Ethical consumerism index (score/100)	84	66	Ethical Consumer (2022); Eurobarometer (2023)

Source: Author Compilation.

technologically ambitious and well developed, but the integration of sustainability, mindful consumption, and regenerative principles is more incremental. Its strong industrial capacities are paired with relatively limited policy emphasis on circularity and environmental transparency, indicating that further alignment is needed for systemic regenerative change. Consumer behavior completes the picture by showing how public values and market choices influence regenerative industry trajectories. Sweden displays a high level of consumer awareness and engagement, demonstrated through higher EV adoption, greater preference for eco-labeled electronics, stronger awareness of ethical sourcing, and higher rates of product return and reuse. These behaviors signal strong societal support for circular and sustainable systems and translate into market pressure that encourages companies to adopt environmentally responsible practices. The higher prevalence of environmental and ethical labeling and strong public trust in industrial transparency also strengthen accountability and reinforce regenerative outcomes. Japan, while technologically advanced, shows slower adoption of ethical and circular consumer practices, with lower EV sales shares, lower willingness to pay for ethical products, reduced label visibility, and weaker participation in take-back programs. These patterns suggest that consumer-driven sustainability is less pronounced in Japan, although cultural traditions and gradual shifts indicate potential for future change.

Overall, Sweden demonstrates a more coherent cultural, institutional, and consumer landscape that promotes regenerative industry, while Japan's strengths in craftsmanship, innovation, and technological capability may require stronger alignment with sustainability frameworks, consumer engagement, and well-being-centered organizational culture to fully support regenerative industrial evolution.

5. Findings

This comparative analysis aimed to explore how much Sweden and Japan are adopting Industry 6.0 technologies and regenerative consumption in the car and electronic sectors of the economy, which are two major sectors of the economy that lie at the heart of sustainability transformation. Through the four key objectives, the story unfolds to show subtle distinctions and rich synergies between the two nations with a broader application to the entire global regenerative revolution. To start with, Sweden and Japan are sufficiently prepared in terms of technologies such as AI-powered automation, intelligent production, and digital infrastructure. Sweden however, is more systematic and sustainability and ethics. It leads the pack in renewable energy in the industry, smart grids growth, and sustainability monitoring digital technology. These technologies are mostly applied to productivity and efficiency in Japan and less on the regenerative side of the structure. Second, Sweden leads in mindful consumption as a way of making industrial practice. Swedish customers are much more willing to pay extra on ethical electronics, use energy saving products, recycling, and car-sharing. Such pressure compels industries to react to it with open, sustainable, and circular models. There is a lack of ethical consumerism in Japanese consumers with tastes still being boiled down to quality, efficiency and brand heritage as opposed to sustainability. Although such norms as shokunin and Kaizen prove to be mindful, there is inconsistent control over behavior and responsibility. Third, Sweden has a more integrated regenerative industry in the context of policy, education, and cultural enablers. A high level of educational infrastructure and sustainability-based education systems complement such policy instruments as circular economy roadmaps, green public procurement, and extended producer responsibility (EPR). Japan is highly technologically educated and industrial-policed but lacks cross-sector integration or engagement. Sweden has a more equal gender representation in STEM and leadership of innovation, which demonstrates a more inclusive foundation of regenerative change. Lastly, in the sustainability and ethical involvement of the sector, Sweden performs higher than Japan in the automotive and electronics sectors in renewal inputs, supply chain reporting, and circularity. Its regulatory and consumer protection regime has helped industries to experiment and test regenerative solutions. The industries of Japan continue to be innovation leaders but in linear paradigms of efficiency less receptive to consumer activism or pressure on environment. All in all, Sweden does a better job of incorporating technology with conscious consumption, policy innovation, and cultural custodianship. Regenerative revolution demands the incorporation of technology, values, and systems thinking. Sweden suggests a model of convergence in action and Japan demonstrates the potential and failures where technological skill is not accompanied by culture and policy change. The two nations have important lessons to regenerative and human-centered industrial futures.

6. Discussion

The intersection of conscious consumption, environmental custodianship, and Industry 6.0 is a chance to reorganize industrial growth in the 21st century. The general differences between the Japanese and Swedish cases can serve as the strong testament to the fact that technological progress is not enough to facilitate regenerative results. Instead, the extent of synergy between cutting-edge industry, cultural awareness, and environmental care that is likely to make a country become a pioneer of the regenerative revolution is determined. The Japanese and Swedish examples have important lessons to be learned in terms of systems thinking, policymaking, and cultural interaction, especially in those countries that would like to achieve economic development and prosperity by means of planetary boundaries and human well-being. Mindful Consumption as a systemic change agent—intentional, ethical, sustainable personal, and institutional decisions, emerged as a major source of regenerative change. In Sweden, extensive popular awareness of sustainability issues with the assistance of education and cultural values such as Lagom (moderation) has been transformed into actual practice: energy-saving product selection, ethical labeling of products, and participation in sharing economy. This kind of consumer behavior enlightens the market demand, the design of the industry, supply chain management, and corporate responsibility. On the organizational level, mindfulness also affects the ways of decision-making, the orientation of leadership, as well as the work culture, promoting moral innovative approaches, and employee well-being, which, in its turn, promotes sustainability in production. This awareness can be traced in the growing concern of eco-design, digital transparency, and cyclical manufacturing in industrial processes. Cultural heritage traditions of craftsmanship (Shokunin) and continuous improvement (Kaizen) have not been completely adapted into mass-consumer activism and corporate openness on the environmental front in Japan. Although these traditions contribute to a high level of precision, discipline, and respect toward the quality in production, they are not as tied to the consumer-motivated results of mindfulness and sustainability. The lesson is that it does not just require individual awareness to create conscious consumption but it must be communicated in education, business culture, and policy mechanisms. The task of institutionalizing regeneration is the joint task of the government, industries, and citizens. The high institutional provisions of Sweden, the tax on carbon, the law on the circular economy, and the producer responsibility acts have facilitated regenerative growth. The abundance of renewable utilization in the production and the high degree of recycling infrastructure are the signs of the interaction with the planetary boundaries. Combining these policies with mindfulness-oriented cultural standards, industrial processes are oriented to a compromise between efficiency and environmental concerns and social justice. Japanese lags behind in the implementation of ecological values in the state and business. Nations seeking regenerative models need to invest in policy ecosystems that generate innovation in circularity architecture, closed-loop manufacturing, and ecological custodianship. Industry 6.0 is the development of the next step in a direction of productivity-oriented automation since it is human-centered, smart, and ethical. Both Sweden and Japan have AI, IoT, and cyber-physical systems but it is the integration of Sweden in the sustainability-led paradigms that makes it the leader. Mindfulness, in both aspects, is a mediating principle, which determines the use of technology, treatment of workforce in organizations, and interaction with sustainable products among consumers. Industry 6.0 has to be intentionally oriented: technology should not only be used in order to be efficient but also offer socially, ecologically and inclusive value.

7. Lessons for Other Countries

All countries that aspire to join the regenerative revolution must adopt an all-of-society strategy that combines technology, culture, policy, and behavior. First, build consumer awareness through education in media literacy and sustainability. Second, build regulatory systems that combine environmental goals into industrial and financial systems. Third, facilitate inclusive innovation by encouraging access to digital skills, STEM education, and entrepreneurship tools to diverse groups. Finally, encourage cross-sector collaboration among government, business, and civil society to build co-ownership of the regenerative agenda.

In sum, the convergence of conscious consumption, green stewardship, and Industry 6.0 is not a utopia but a possible trajectory toward resilient, inclusive, and green economies. Japan and Sweden, although dissimilar, prove that this is achievable. Scaling up these pilots with cultural awareness, technological vision, and institutional risk-taking now becomes the challenge of the future globally.

8. Limitations and Scope for Future Research

While this comparative case study of Japan and Sweden presents enlightening insight into Industry 6.0 convergence, conscious consumption, and nature stewardship, there are certain limitations that have to be accepted and which, in turn, suggest rich possibilities for future studies.

8.1 Limitations of the Study

8.1.1 Sectoral Focus

This research is focused on the electronics and automotive industries, which, although important, are not representative of all industrial activity. Other sectors like construction, agriculture, and heavy industry might have varying patterns of technology uptake, sustainability methods, and consumer participation. Therefore, conclusions may not be fully applicable to every sector of the economy.

8.1.2 Data Availability and Comparability

The research relied on data from publicly offered national and international sources that could differ with respect to definitions, reporting cycles, and methodologies. The consumer behavior and awareness indicators are also subjective or qualitative in nature, and cross-country comparisons oversimplify the cultural nuances.

8.1.3 Static Comparison

The study does not capture the dynamic nature of policy, consumer awareness, and industrial transformation. Because of the widespread technological and environmental transformation underway, the findings will likely need to be reassessed in the near future in order to remain applicable.

8.2 Future Research Directions

8.2.1 Multi-Sectoral and Cross-Regional Studies

Subsequent studies can increase the sectoral scope to other sectors and a larger number of countries in additional regions (e.g., Global South, emerging economies) to uncover context-specific trajectories and barriers to regenerative industrial transformation.

8.2.2 Longitudinal Analysis

A longitudinal examination of Industry 6.0 uptake, consumer response, and sustainability effects over time would provide better insight into tipping points, trends, and the effect of policy interventions.

8.2.3 Behavioral and Psychological Studies

Examining the sociological and psychological underpinnings of mindful consumption across cultures (e.g., motivations, identity, resistance) may yield a more rooted understanding of how and why individuals and organizations embrace (or resist) regenerative behaviors.

8.2.4 Policy Impact Assessment

A focused analysis of how certain regulatory tools, such as green taxation, sustainability disclosure mandates, or subsidies for digital infrastructure, impact change in the industry would be informative for policymakers attempting to encourage Industry 6.0 in regenerative directions.

9. Conclusion

This comparative study of Japan and Sweden shows that Industry 6.0, mindful consumption and planet care should and can merge in the direction of regenerative industrial future. The extremely high level of policy, consumer, and technological alignment by the sectors in Sweden offers a good example where sustainability is systematically incorporated in the industries. With its technological frontiers and a cultural background in craftsmanship and Kaizen, Japan demonstrates that regenerative results are stagnant unless linked to the policy. The paper highlights the urgency of the technological development to be supported by awareness in the culture, inclusive government, and ethical design to radically change industrial ecosystems. With the world countries grappling with environmental destruction, economic disparities, sociocultural disunity, this study reconfirms the need to shift away and beyond extractive paradigms to regenerative ones where industries do not only mitigate but enhance planetary and human well-being. Through the example of the Japanese and Swedish experience, policymakers, practitioners, and scholars can create context-specific opportunities toward a sustainable inclusive future where innovation and mindfulness become the new norm.

References

Ahmad, S., Saxena, C., Islam, S., & Karim, R. (2024). Impact of Insur-Tech on the premium performance of insurance business. *SN Computer Science*, *5*(1), 1–7. https://doi.org/10.1007/s42979-023-02462-0

Almusaed, A., Yitmen, I., & Almssad, A. (2023). Reviewing and integrating AEC practices into Industry 6.0: Strategies for smart and sustainable future-built environments. *Sustainability*, *15*(18), 13464. https://doi.org/10.3390/su151813464

Andronie, M., Lăzăroiu, G., Iatagan, M., Uță, C., & Ștefănescu, R. (2021). Sustainable cybersecurity management of data-driven smart cities: A systematic literature review. *Sustainability*, *13*(8), 4237.

Aslam, J., Saleem, A., Khan, N. T., & Kim, Y. B. (2020). Factors influencing blockchain adoption in supply chain management practices: A study based on the oil industry. *Journal of Innovation & Knowledge*, *6*(2), 124–134.

Bag, S., Pretorius, J. H. C., & Gupta, S. (2021). Examining the role of dynamic remanufacturing capability on supply chain resilience in circular economy. *Management Decision*, *59*(8), 1987–2009.

Bai, C., Quayson, M., & Sarkis, J. (2021). COVID-19 pandemic digitization lessons for sustainable development of micro- and small-enterprises. *Sustainable Production and Consumption*, *27*, 1989–2001.

Carpanzano, E., & Knüttel, D. (2022). Advances in artificial intelligence methods applications in industrial control systems: Towards cognitive self-optimizing manufacturing systems. *Applied Sciences*, *12*(21), 10962. https://doi.org/10.3390/app122110962

CDP. (2023). *Global supply chain report 2023: Transparency in transition*. CDP Worldwide. https://www.cdp.net

Chandan, A., John, M., & Potdar, V. (2023). Achieving UN SDGs in food supply chain using blockchain technology. *Sustainability*, *15*(3), 2109. https://doi.org/10.3390/su15032109

Chatterjee, S., Rana, N. P., Tamilmani, K., & Sharma, A. (2021). The rise of machine learning in sustainable agriculture: A bibliometric analysis. *Technological Forecasting and Social Change*, *165*, 120531.

Chourasia, S., Tyagi, A., Pandey, S. M., Walia, R. S., & Murtaza, Q. (2022). Sustainability of Industry 6.0 in global perspective: Benefits and challenges. *MAPAN*, *37*(2), 443–452. https://doi.org/10.1007/s12647-022-00541-w

Corporate Wellness Trends Report. (2023). *Global workplace mindfulness and well-being practices 2023*. Wellness Insights Institute.

Culot, G., Nassimbeni, G., Orzes, G., & Sartor, M. (2020). Behind the definition of Industry 4.0: Analysis and open questions. *International Journal of Production Economics*, *226*, 107617.

Dane, E., & Brummel, B. J. (2014). Examining workplace mindfulness and its relations to job performance and turnover intention. *Human Relations*, *67*(1), 105–128. https://doi.org/10.1177/0018726713487753

Duggal, A. S., Malik, P. K., Gehlot, A., Singh, R., Gaba, G. S., Masud, M., & Al-Amri, J. F. (2022). A sequential roadmap to Industry 6.0: Exploring future manufacturing trends. *IET Communications*, *16*(5), 521–531. https://doi.org/10.1049/cmu2.12284

Ellili, N., Nobanee, H., Alsaiari, L., Shanti, H., Hillebrand, B., Hassanain, N., & Elfout, L. (2023). The applications of big data in the insurance industry: A bibliometric and systematic review of relevant literature. *The Journal of Finance and Data Science*, *9*, 100102. https://doi.org/10.1016/j.jfds.2023.100102

Ethical Consumer. (2022). *Ethical consumer markets report 2022*. Ethical Consumer Research Association. https://www.ethicalconsumer.org

Eurobarometer. (2023). *Public attitudes towards environment and sustainability*. European Commission. https://europa.eu/eurobarometer

Eurofound. (2023). *Working time in the European Union: 2023 update* European Foundation for the Improvement of Living and Working Conditions. https://www.eurofound.europa.eu

Fernandez-Miguel, A., Garcıa-Muiña, F. E., Settembre-Blundo, D., Tarantino, S. C., & Riccardi, M. P. (2024). Exploring systemic sustainability in manufacturing: Geoanthropology's strategic lens shaping Industry 6.0. *Global Journal of Flexible Systems Management*, *25*(3), 579–600. https://doi.org/10.1007/s40171-024-00404-0

Frank, A. G., Dalenogare, L. S., & Ayala, N. F. (2021). Industry 4.0 technologies: Implementation patterns in manufacturing companies. *International Journal of Production Economics*, *231*, 107843.

Frederico, G. F. (2021). From supply chain 4.0 to supply chain 5.0: Findings from a systematic literature review and research directions. *Logistics*, *5*(4), 49.

George, A. L., & Bennett, A. (2005). *Case studies and theory development in the social sciences*. MIT Press.

Global Reporting Initiative (GRI). (2023). *Sustainability reporting standards and data compendium 2023*. GRI. https://www.globalreporting.org
ILO. (2023). *Skills for the future: ILO skills report 2023*. International Labour Organization. https://www.ilo.org
International Energy Agency. (2023). *Global EV outlook 2023: Catching up with climate ambitions*. IEA. https://www.iea.org/reports/global-ev-outlook-2023
International Federation of Robotics. (2023). *World robotics report 2023*. IFR. https://ifr.org/worldrobotics
ISO. (2023). *ISO annual review 2023*. International Organization for Standardization. https://www.iso.org
Japan Labor Issues. (2023, Autumn). *Statistical indicators* (Vol. 7, No. 44). Japan Institute for Labour Policy and Training. https://www.jil.go.jp/english/jli/documents/2023/044-00.pdf
Javaid, M., Haleem, A., Singh, R. P., & Suman, R. (2021). Significance of quality 4.0 towards comprehensive enhancement in manufacturing sector. *Cognitive Systems Research*, *68*, 218–229.
Kabat-Zinn, J. (2003). Mindfulness-based interventions in context: Past, present, and future. *Clinical Psychology: Science and Practice*, *10*(2), 144–156. https://doi.org/10.1093/clipsy.bpg016
Kim, Y. S., Do, N. H., & Choi, J. (2023). Artificial intelligence research in mechanical engineering: A bibliometric analysis and future research agenda. *Applied Sciences*, *13*(1), 159.
Lasi, H., Fettke, P., Kemper, H. G., Feld, T., & Hoffmann, M. (2022). Industry 5.0: The future of productivity and human-centric systems. *Journal of Manufacturing Technology Management*, *33*(6), 1197–1215.
Leng, J., Sha, W., Wang, B., Zheng, P., Zhuang, C., Liu, Q., Wuest, T., Mourtzis, D., & Wang, L. (2022). Industry 5.0: Prospect and retrospect. *Journal of Manufacturing Systems*, *65*, 279–295.
Liker, J. K. (2004). *The Toyota way, 14 management principles from the world's greatest manufacturer*. McGraw-Hill.
Malik, S., Muhammad, K., & Waheed, Y. (2024). Artificial intelligence and industrial applications-A revolution in modern industries. *Ain Shams Engineering Journal*, *15*(9), 102886. https://doi.org/10.1016/j.asej.2024.102886
Mang, P., & Haggard, B. (2016). *Regenerative development and design: A framework for evolving sustainability*. Wiley.
Marques, J., Silva, A., & Ferreira, F. (2020). Digitalization for business model innovation in SMEs: A conceptual framework. *Journal of Business Research*, *123*, 241–251.
Ministry of Foreign Affairs of Japan. (2022). *Annual report on Japan's ODA evaluation 2022: FY2021 MOFA ODA evaluation results – Evaluation on Japan's education cooperation policy*. https://www.mofa.go.jp/policy/oda/evaluation/22_evaluation/03/03-04.html
Mohamed, M., & Hameed, S. (2022). Blockchain-enabled sustainable supply chain management: Opportunities, challenges, and future research directions. *Journal of Cleaner Production*, *351*, 131570.
Mont, O., & Plepys, A. (2008). Sustainable consumption progress: Should we be proud or alarmed?. *Journal of Cleaner Production*, *16*(4), 531–537. https://doi.org/10.1016/j.jclepro.2007.01.009

Murugan, M., & Prabadevi, M. N. (2023). Impact of Industry 6.0 on MSME entrepreneur's performance and entrepreneur's emotional intelligence in the service industry in India. *Revista de Gestão Social e Ambiental*, *17*(4), e03340. https://doi.org/10.24857/rgsa.v17n4-007

Nleya, S. M., & Velempini, M. (2024). Industrial metaverse: A comprehensive review, environmental impact, and challenges. *Applied Sciences*, *14*(13), 5736. https://doi.org/10.3390/app14135736

Organisation for Economic Co-operation and Development (OECD). (n.d.). *Short-term economic statistics (STES): Consumer opinion surveys (CCICP)*. OECD Data Explorer. https://data-explorer.oecd.org/vis?lc=en&df%5Bds%5D=dsDisseminateFinalDMZ&df%5Bid%5D=DSD_STES%40DF_CS&df%5Bag%5D=OECD.SDD.STES&dq=.M.CCICP......&lom=LASTNPERIODS&lo=5&to%5BTIME_PERIOD%5D=false

Organisation for Economic Co-operation and Development. (2023a). *OECD science, technology and innovation outlook 2023*. OECD Publishing. https://doi.org/10.1787/0b55736e-en

Organisation for Economic Co-operation and Development (OECD). (2023b). *OECD economic surveys: Sweden 2023*. OECD Publishing. https://doi.org/10.1787/ceed5fd4-en

Organisation for Economic Co-operation and Development. (2024a). *OECD digital economy outlook 2024 (Volume 1): Embracing the technology frontier*. OECD Publishing. https://doi.org/10.1787/a1689dc5-en

Organisation for Economic Co-operation and Development (OECD). (2024b). *OECD economic surveys: Japan 2024*. OECD Publishing. https://doi.org/10.1787/41e807f9-en

Organisation for Economic Co-operation and Development (OECD). (2026). *Education in Sweden: A diagnostic review with analysis of PISA 2022 results*. OECD Publishing. https://doi.org/10.1787/9bbbb63d-en

Orlando, B., Tortora, D., & Pezzotta, G. (2020). Digital servitization in the manufacturing industry: A systematic literature review and future research directions. *Industrial Marketing Management*, *89*, 278–292.

Pfeffer, J., Jaffe, S., & Ferreras, I. (2021). Work and the future: The path toward mindful consumption and sustainability. *Academy of Management Discoveries*, *7*(3), 314–318.

Piccarozzi, M., Silvestri, C., Aquilani, B., & Silvestri, L. (2022). Is this a new story of the "two giants"? A systematic literature review of the relationship between Industry 4.0, sustainability and its pillars. *Technological Forecasting and Social Change*, *177*, 121511. https://doi.org/10.1016/j.techfore.2022.121511

Rajnai, Z., & Kocsis, I. (2020). Assessing industry 4.0 readiness of enterprises. *Procedia Manufacturing*, *32*, 57–64.

Rane, S. B., & Narvel, Y. A. (2021). Blockchain for digital twins: Opportunities and challenges. *Procedia Computer Science*, *180*, 725–732.

Reb, J., & Atkins, P. (Eds.). (2015). *Mindfulness in organizations: Foundations, research, and applications*. Cambridge University Press. https://doi.org/10.1017/CBO9781107587793

Reis, J., Santo, P. E., Melão, N., & Amorim, M. (2021). Digital transformation: A literature review and guidelines for future research. *World Conference on Information Systems and Technologies*, *1*, 513–527.

Shah, S. A. A., Issac, B., & Akhtar, N. (2020). Internet of Things-based real-time condition monitoring of transformers using smart sensors. *IEEE Transactions on Industrial Informatics*, *16*(5), 3419–3427.
Sheth, J. N., Sethia, N. K., & Srinivas, S. (2011). Mindful consumption: A customer-centric approach to sustainability. *Journal of the Academy of Marketing Science*, *39*(1), 21–39. https://doi.org/10.1007/s11747-010-0216-3
Tortorella, G. L., Cawley Vergara, A. M., Garza-Reyes, J. A., & Sawhney, R. (2020). Organizational learning paths based upon industry 4.0 adoption: An empirical study with Brazilian manufacturers. *International Journal of Production Economics*, *219*, 284–294.
UNESCO Institute for Statistics. (2023). *Education and STEM data tables 2023*. UNESCO. http://uis.unesco.org
Varela, L., Araújo, A., Ávila, P., Castro, H., & Putnik, G. (2022). Evaluation of the relation between lean manufacturing, industry 4.0, and sustainability. *Sustainability*, *14*(6), 3500.
World Bank. (2022). *Education statistics – All indicators*. World Bank DataBank. https://databank.worldbank.org/source/education-statistics-%5E-all-indicators
World Bank. (2023). *World development indicators: Digital and green transition datasets*. The World Bank. https://databank.worldbank.org
World Happiness Report. (2023). *World happiness report 2023. United Nations Sustainable Development Solutions Network*. https://worldhappiness.report
Xu, X., Lu, Y., Vogel-Heuser, B., & Wang, L. (2021). Industry 4.0 and industry 5.0-Inception, conception, and perception. *Journal of Manufacturing Systems*, *61*, 530–535.
Yu, J. (2024). The application and significance of 3D printing technology in biomedicine. *Applied and Computational Engineering*, *58*(1), 215–221. https://doi.org/10.54254/2755-2721/58/20240724
Zhang, S. X., Chen, J., He, L., & Choudhury, A. (2023). Responsible innovation: The development and validation of a scale. *Technovation*, *124*, 102754. https://doi.org/10.1016/j.technovation.2023.102754
Zheng, T., Ardolino, M., Bacchetti, A., & Perona, M. (2021). The applications of Industry 4.0 technologies in manufacturing context: A systematic literature review. *International Journal of Production Research*, *59*(6), 1922–1954.

Chapter 14

Mindful Buying: Unpacking the Cognitive Mechanisms Behind Intentional Consumption

Ridhima Sharma[a], *Timcy Sachdeva*[a] *and Ankita Sharma*[b]

[a]Vivekananda Institute of Professional Studies-Technical Campus, India
[b]Alliance University, India

Abstract

Mindful consumption has been central in consumer behavior studies, influenced by the increasing global consciousness of the economic, environmental and psychological impacts of overconsumption. More people are considering mindful shopping to reduce the high spending levels and not buying things that are unfriendly to their health. Mindful purchasing is a purchasing method that is considerate, conscious and ideology-based. The paper is a review of critical cognitive processes related to mindful purchasing, categorized and delineated as attentional regulation, executive control, emotional self-regulation, and metacognitive awareness using more than 80 peer-reviewed articles in behavioral economics, cognitive psychology, and consumer research. This trait awareness is established because it builds resilience of consumers to external consumption stimuli, leads to self-reflection, and makes ethically correct decisions. This paper provides strong support for self-regulated purchasing behavior by depicting that mindful consumption is associated with activation of pre-frontal executive networks. The paper then examines the theoretical models regarding consumer intentionality including the reflective-impulsive model and dual-process theories. Two important gaps in the research are the absence of cross-cultural interaction and the restricted impact of the digital environment on the cognitive regulation. This synthesis is meant to enhance our knowledge on meaningful consumption and this is what will pave the way to other future empirical studies. It then talks about how cognitive results can

Regenerative Revolution, 277–292

Published under exclusive licence by Emerald Publishing Limited
doi:10.1108/978-1-80686-859-920261014

be adopted to create therapies that would promote ethical and sustainable shopping in the actual world.

Keywords: Mindful consumption; intentional buying; dispositional mindfulness; consumer behavior; cognitive regulation

JEL Classification: D91; D12; Q56

1. Introduction

The high-level materiality of modern culture, advertisement in social media, fueled by online shopping, and the easy access to the product have fostered much concern related to a possible environmental and individual harm along with mental anxiety. Similarly, the interest in the research of the potential new modes of consumption that are purpose, health, and environment oriented has recently increased. Some of the methods that have been popular in both the academic and practical world are mindful purchasing. This is founded on being in full presence, control of thought, and meditation of ethics. In speaking of "mindful buying" (in opposition to "mindful consuming"), we refer to the pre-, during-, and post-purchase mental activity. This, according to John and Hajam (2024), is a shift from impulsive or emotionally led purchasing toward deliberate, information-based decisions consistent with one's values. More than action, it is a unified state of mind supported by self-regulation and executive function. Self-regulation of one's emotions is another route leading to mindful thought, itself based on self-awareness and focused attention. Generally, individuals choose sustainable outcomes that enhance their social standing and reduce regret over misdeeds. Jin et al. (2020) found that mindfulness and attention are associated with personal, social, and environmental well-being in the context of sustainable green consumption. Mindful consumption is informed by mindfulness theory, which originated in Buddhist meditation practices but is now widely adopted in clinical psychology. It trains individuals to be more flexible in their mental processes, to control their attention, and to self-regulate behavior. Consumers will be more sensitive to both internal and external signs while making choices. Khunsrii (2022) describes mindful consumption as the active engagement of personal ideals with societal tasks, especially in COVID-19 lockdown conditions. Three psychological traits that may impact this consumption include dispositional awareness, cognitive reflection, and emotional self-regulation. These traits influence the person's ability to handle emotionally triggering situations, to evaluate the social and environmental consequences of decisions, and to distinguish needs from wants (Beitel et al., 2005). On the other hand, a lack of attentional control and low self-esteem are associated with impulsive or compulsive buying, which is motivated by a problem in managing emotions and inhibiting impulses. From a cognitive perspective, a variety of executive functions support thoughtful purchase. For instance, attentional management supports focal attention on essential information and helps to avoid distracting advertisements and social influences. The control of emotions supports avoidance of impulsive actions such as shopping for fun or purchasing items for the sake of displaying them (Benos et al., 2022). The inhibitory control is required for the delay of gratification and the resistance of desire for immediate purchase. These abilities have a neurobiological basis in the prefrontal cortical systems, especially in areas implicated during reflecting judgment and top-down control (Dhandra, 2020). The work of Dhandra emphasizes the interaction between the trait-level cognition and identity-driven motivation; it identified a mediating pathway between mindfulness and the reduction of impulsive purchase using self-esteem (Dhandra, 2019). These systems of cognitive-affective offer ubiquitous environmental signal and thus there is a physiological and a psychological justification as to why there are those who are resistant to excessive consumption. The main focus of research has been the pathological elements of compulsive buying disorder particularly in emotional coping, attentional filtering, and issues of self-regulation. Although the two practices are based on the same concepts, the increasing literature on mindful purchasing is a positive behavioral change that promotes health. Although there are such studies, mindful eating research is not usually consistent. Exogenous variables, such as ecological consciousness, advertising literacy, and societal norms, are common in a study of consumer behavior conducted by researchers (Gupta & Sheth, 2024). Cognitive psychologists, on the contrary, have been concerned with internal characteristics, such as inhibition and meta-awareness with little cross-disciplinary interaction (Howard et al., 2021). The paper will fulfill that requirement due to a thorough literature review, including both theoretical and empirical studies of the mental foundations of mindful purchasing. Deliberate consuming is highlighted as needing four fundamental constructs, which are attentional management, emotional self-regulation, inhibitory control, and metacognitive awareness. The interaction of these processes with the larger psychological features of value orientation, the level of socioeconomic status, and digital consumer surroundings is explained in a deeper way. It introduces a cognitively staged paradigm of conscious shopping that is capable of empowering consumers to approach the market in an ethical, sustainable, and psychologically constructive way by illuminating and fostering thoughtful and reflective practices.

2. Literature Review

The growing literature defines mindful purchasing as a behavioral tendency mediated through cognition and affected by evaluative judgment, self-regulation, and attention. Earlier implicit ideas of mindful consumerism had largely explored its impact on personal behavior in terms of ethical consumerism and environmental awareness (Jacob et al., 2009). On the other hand, it has been tested recently that there are cognitive processes that trigger this behavior. This change is premised on the assumption that mindful shopping is not only a decision or the intention of the consumer but a result of the underlying brain processes that help a person moderate his/her emotions and limit the desire to buy products (Jakobsen, 2021). This paradigm contains four domains that are interrelated namely: emotional self-regulation, attentional management, inhibitory control, and metacognitive awareness. These activities have to do with various components of executive functioning that work together to enable individuals to make smart and values-based decisions as consumers (Ji et al., 2025). Dispositional mindfulness (DM) refers to the innate or habitual inclination of a person to be attentive and nonjudgmental to his/her present experiences. Two self-report measures that would be effective in measuring DM accurately include the Five Facet Mindfulness Questionnaire (FFMQ) and the Mindful Attention Awareness Scale (MAAS). DM is an innate trait, which is inherently different in individuals whereas mindfulness can be attained through a structured meditation practice. Studies have shown that high DM levels correlate with various psychological and physiological advantages such as an improved ability to manage stress, a high level of cognitive flexibility, and reduced emotional reactivity (Klein et al., 2018; Liobikiene & Poskus, 2019). DM is becoming recognized as a protective factor for mental health and well-being due to its capacity to prevent psychopathology and improve adaptive functioning across many populations. Tomlinson et al. (2018) examined the impact of DM on mental health by a systematic review and meta-analyses (Preferred Reporting Items for Systematic Reviews and Meta-Analyses). The study's results show that DM is favorably linked to adaptive cognitive processes, such decreased rumination and pain catastrophizing. On the other hand, it seems to be negatively linked to psychopathological symptoms, like depressed symptoms. They discovered that research consistently demonstrates a good correlation between DM and mental wellness. DM, characterized by sustained present-moment awareness and nonreactivity, has been recognized as a crucial moderator in multiple domains, augmenting individuals' capacity to regulate impulsive behaviors, sustain focus on task-relevant stimuli, and assess the motivational factors affecting their consumption patterns (Dhandra, 2020). Shama (1981) emphasized that social and economic instability may alter individuals' thoughts, emotions, and behaviors following the Great Depression of the 1930s. The COVID-19 pandemic in 2020 created a lot of problems all around the world, and each country dealt with it in its own way. India enacted several lockdowns in response to COVID-19 as a preliminary eradication approach, which limited access to nonessential consumer goods, services, and experiences. Customers were more vigilant about what they bought because of these rules (Bahl et al., 2016; Lim, 2017; Milne et al., 2020; Sheth et al., 2010). They manufactured items at home and bought goods from places close by (Bailey, 2021). Studies on mindful consumption indicate that individuals must reduce three categories of consumption: acquisitive consumption (for the purpose of purchasing), aspirational consumption (to display status or achievement), and repetitive consumption (to substitute items) (Lim, 2017; Sheth et al., 2010). Attentional control, defined as the ability to concentrate mental resources on the present moment, constitutes the paramount aspect of mindful consumption. This is particularly crucial when making consumer decisions (Mathur & Moschis, 2023; Tomlinson et al., 2018). This capability enables individuals to focus more on their own beliefs, ambitions, and objectives rather than external marketing cues or impulsive impulses.

Attentional management enhances individuals' awareness of situational influences and the factors that drive their purchasing decisions. This results in a more thoughtful and intentional approach to customer choices. Regulating attention is a crucial aspect of mindful eating. Attention regulation enables the consumer to focus on irrelevant or misleading information even in a world flooded with information both digital and physical. The researchers have shown that attentional regulation improves consumer mindfulness and responsibility by making people more aware of their habit or emotionally motivated actions as opposed to being guided by rational choice (Khunsrii, 2022). Better controlled attention allows consumers to take a moment and consider their decisions and seek alternatives that are not physical, which leads to a reassessment of their future goals. To control attentional bias is crucial to persuasive design and algorithmic marketing that aims at exploiting cognitive shortcuts. Mindfulness and introspective practice help one to realize that there is a need to stop automatic purchasing behaviors. The most important factor in the reduction of impulsive consumption behaviors is known as inhibitory control which is the capacity to restrain either naturally practiced or habitual urges. Mindful consumerism enables consumers to take a step back and think before they buy, especially to respond to emotionally colored or socially conditioned stimuli (Zahid et al., 2023). Inhibitory control helps one to manage their eating habits and adjust their behaviors in accordance with their long-range goals and moral values by changing the stories they use in their daily lives. Another important feature of mindful consumerism is emotional self-regulation, as it helps people to control their emotions that sometimes cause them to buy the product impulsively. Two strategies of emotional regulation that can reduce unpleasant emotions like tension, boredom, or anxiety that are often linked with excessive spending are cognitive reappraisal and acceptance. Whenever people have emotional stability, they are better placed to make purchase decisions based on rationality but not on feelings which are momentary. The inhibitory control and emotional regulation is essential in comprehending how people control their impulses. Impulse purchasing is a well-known behavior that is caused by the lack of inhibitory control and emotional dysregulation, where affect-driven and impulsive purchases are entailed. The literature on compulsive purchase disorder (CPD) points out to this interdependence; in fact, low self-esteem and hyper sensitivity to emotional stimuli are often characteristic of those consumers who exhibit problematic consumption (Ertelt et al., 2009). On the other hand, individuals who have high inhibitory capacity can override their initial emotional reactions and apply more systematic appraisal system. The ability to deal with stress and uncertainty without consuming as a coping strategy is an emotional self-control skill that obviously distinguishes between discerning and impulsive consumers. Dhandra (2020) discovered that there is a mediating role of the self-esteem between mindfulness and impulsiveness, meaning that a stable self-concept counters unnecessary or excessive spending. These results reveal the psychological and psychological stability of mindful consumers and the possibility of tailor-made treatments, which would increase not only mindfulness but also emotional intelligence. Metacognitive monitoring is the ability to identify and evaluate cognitive processes, in terms of the ability to be aware of thoughts, emotions, and motivations, during the eating process. Such self-consciousness helps to provide the insight into the reasons and implications of consumerism in the case of being selective in their buying behavior. It enhances a more conscious and less automatic way of making choices by fostering a critical reflection of the advertisement messages and established habits of consumption. Metacognition abilities make people more independent and conscious of their moral requirements. Finally, the metacognitive tracking is important to the transformation of cognitive control into conscious consumer behavior. Metacognition is the ability to think about cognition itself, particularly the analysis of the way of thinking. This involves the analysis of the reasoning, philosophy, and expected results of buying decisions (Moes, 2025). As shown in Fig. 14.1, mindful purchasing behavior is a combination of attentional control, inhibitory control, affective regulation, and metacognitive monitoring. It is distinguished by intentional, morally upright, and needful buying decisions that indicate personal beliefs and social duties. The people that display this behavior tend to go toward ecologically friendly and straightforward products, they have greater knowledge on the sources and effects of the products they buy, and they have a lesser desire to own materialistic goods. Mindful purchasing is a good example of self-regulation among consumers with the foundations of mindfulness. Wise shoppers consider and debate whether they actually need it or are it suits their ideals before they purchase anything. Mindfulness helps people avoid acting on impulse by making them aware of possible regret, waste, or moral differences. John and Hajam (2024) came up with a model that says that socialization agents, environmental concern, and long-term value orientations all affect how ready people are to make smart decisions. The paradigm says that metacognitive awareness affects how attitudes turn into actions. Consequently, the conceptual basis of mindful buying resides in a cohesive array of cognitive processes rather than in isolated traits, each contributing to the formulation of aware, ethical, and sustainable consumption decisions.

Fig. 14.1 A conceptual framework for mindful buying. DM supports the four primary cognitive processes that contribute to mindful purchase behavior:

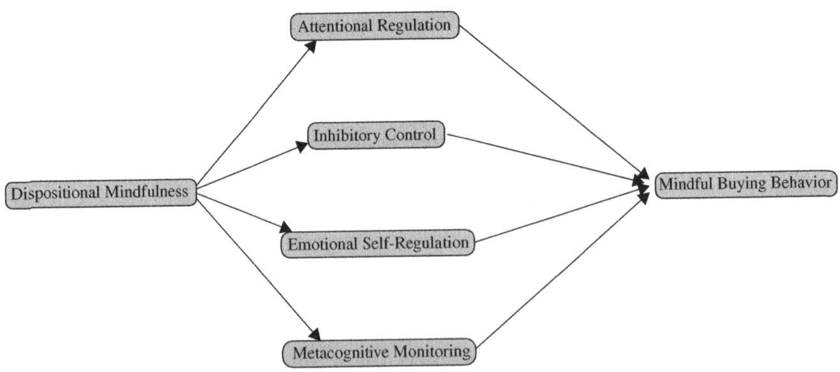

Fig. 14.1. Conceptual Framework of Mindful Buying.

attentional regulation, inhibitory control, emotional self-regulation, and meta-cognitive monitoring. This graphic shows how these processes work together.

3. Empirical Studies

An increasing body of research suggests that social and environmental circumstances, as well as individual psychological characteristics, have a substantial influence on conscious consumption. John and Hajam (2024) developed a structural model for mindful shopping based on a cohesive collective interest theory and a self-concept perspective to study the roles of media exposure, social learning, and environmental concern as antecedents to mindful purchase behavior. They used the 629 people that were representative of the US population to explain the nature of beliefs and social situations that affect cognitive disposition toward attentiveness. Their evidence indicates that exposure to environmental troubles through socializing agents increases environmental awareness and enhances the internal feelings of people in terms of consumption reduction. This highlights the complexity behind the intentions of mindful shopping, be it social or cognitive to a concept that was previously held by individuals. It has been shown that consumer self-control reduces when they are faced with decision fatigue and uncertainty; a study has evaluated the possibility of mindfulness to alleviate the effect. These results supported the idea: the participants of the mindfulness-based training program demonstrated a higher tendency to buy goods that correspond to the principles of sustainability and ethics even when mentally under pressure. Another investigation that used the antisaccade exercises found that mindfulness trainees displayed better visual attention regulation, which indicates the direct neurocognitive advantage of ignoring visual advertisement signals. Findings of tests and observations are similar to the previous studies in the field of compulsive purchase. According to research by Mitchell et al. (2006) and Ertelt et al. (2009), the individuals in the CPD, display significant cognitive-behavioral impairments, such as weak emotional control, poor inhibitory control, and focus on consumption stimuli. Cognitive-behavioral intervention research studies have demonstrated significant reduction in compulsive behaviors and improvement in financial well-being.

Although these therapies were not specifically designed to be mindful, the cognitive processes they mediated particularly reflective awareness, delayed gratification, and value clarification, share much in common with the processes that enable mindful purchase. The identical characteristics indicate that the interventions which have been formulated to address the consumption disorders must complement broader interventions that aim at promoting healthy purchase behaviors (Ertelt et al., 2009). The latter has been demonstrated in recent research as a need to take cultural differences into account. Malaysian employees had a tendency to use self-care habits related to meticulous acquisition (Mahmud et al., 2019). These results are consistent with cultural differences in how mindfulness is perceived, as a state of attention and a relation and ethics toward self and social world. In collectivist cultures where the emphasis is put on unity and interdependence, conscientious purchasing could be closer to communal objectives. In individualistic setting, it can be more tightly connected with real self-confidence and sincerity. According to the study by Helm and Subramaniam (2019), the evidence of sustainable behaviors is observed among materialistic consumers in the West due to the value fit and the environmental anxiety caused by mindfulness. As Mahmud et al. (2019) argue, these statistics suggest that mindful shopping is applicable in a number of cultural settings. They also make us wonder how local thinking systems relate to the global consumption. Being able to possess these qualities will mean that you are open to yourself, other people, and the environment. Moreover, they have come up with a scale, which is applicable in numerous marketing strategies, such as product innovation, rebranding, and extending the product range. The intention of travelers to buy environmentally friendly products was investigated by Ji Dongyi et al. (2025), with the mediating variables of environmental awareness, ethical self-identity (EI), and health consciousness, and mindful consumerism. According to the findings, EI and environmental awareness may mediate the direct and indirect impacts of mindful consumerism on the purchasing intention of environmentally friendly products. Moreover, the statistics suggest that health consciousness exerts a minimal impact on the propensity to purchase environmentally friendly products. Benos et al. (2022) identified three types of enhanced motivation that may impact green product purchases: health awareness (HC), EI, and environmental consciousness. HC stands for self-care, EI for community care, and EC for nature care. This is consistent with what numerous new approach methodologies-based studies have shown on the activation of personal norms. Wu and Yang (2018) showed that EI explains individuals' acceptance of responsibility, whereas Liobikienė and Yang discovered that health and environmental consciousness impact people's understanding of consequences. All of these factors combine to motivate people to live up to their own standards and do environmentally responsible acts. Because online businesses strive to be easy, quick, and visually appealing, the digitalization of commerce makes careful purchase more difficult (Yang et al., 2023). According to Lesmana (2023), one of the most important variables in introducing mindfulness to digital environments is customer engagement, which is defined as the buyer's level of concentration and thoughtfulness during the purchasing process. Mindfulness-based solutions may include pausing to consider where the things come from or how sustainable they are while you check out. It was highly likely that people will use mindfulness-based strategies before making a purchase in high-involvement situations. However, in low-involvement settings, the cognitive deliberation-skipping automaticity of internet purchasing resulted in impulsive purchases. The efficacy of mindful purchase is dependent on both human characteristics and environmental circumstances, such as design that encourages introspective interaction. Researchers have begun to investigate the evolution of conscious consumption behaviors using intervention and longitudinal research. Helm and Subramaniam (2019) suggest that mindfulness may continue to predict consumption months after the initial test. This is particularly among the people who believed that they were great shoppers. This underpins the notion that the attentive purchasing behavior will not change and the probability that the same behavior may be strengthened through practice and validation of individual impact. This opinion that places importance on perceived efficacy as an incentive in connecting knowledge with action could have a massive impact on responsible consumption programs and in education programs. Currently, the mindfulness theory is being incorporated in the wider behavioral economics of consumption as evidenced by a number of dissertations and review articles. According to Sebastian (2023), mindfulness is a meta-competence that improves decision-making by consumers in uncertainty, resource constraint, and time constraints situations. The emerging discipline of choice architecture and behavioral design can be viewed as a tool of advocating values-based decision-making. Examples of measures which could be taken to facilitate environmental consciousness are checkout delays, default sustainable choices, and mindfulness notifications embedded in user interfaces. Design-based approaches, which provide practical improvements to empirical findings published before, provide a strong direction of the future study and policy development.

4. Discussion and Implications

The relationship between mindfulness and intentional consumer behavior is positive, and strongly linked as demonstrated by an extensive literature review which provides firm and consistent support of the conceptual framework already developed. The evidence of studies involving a wide range of methods and sample populations suggests that mindfulness is more likely to lead to the improvement of attentional regulation, prohibitory control, and emotional self-management in consumer settings, when people are more likely to utilize mindfulness. These systems would promote a deliberate consideration of one's values, environmental concerns, and the search of life-long happiness, and also reduce impulsive or obsessive behaviors. The empirical results are also useful in bridging a gap in theory on consumer research, behavioral economics and cognitive psychology, all of which have played a big part in helping us comprehend the sophisticated process of a deliberate purchasing choice. Such intersection of fields brings out the need to view consuming as a psychological experience that has social and ethical roots, but not merely an economic exchange. A notable impact is the potential use of mindfulness-based interventions (MBIs) as a behavioral facilitator in the sustainable consumption. Early studies show that mindfulness training has the potential to reset attentional systems of consumers and delay satisfaction, which is achieved through journaling, meditation, or the use of apps (Helm & Subramaniam, 2019; Sebastian, 2023). The results also have practical implications that can be applied through incorporating contemplation cues on online purchasing websites, applying mindfulness interventions on financial literacy training, or through promoting deliberate pauses during transactions. These kinds of interventions can be exceptionally effective in the online marketplaces where there is easy acquisition of things. The correspondence between the environmentally conscious consumption and the responsible consumption produces a special relationship between global health and individual well-being. This is required by both the public policy and the marketing ethics. Although these avenues hold a potential, a number of barriers, and loopholes still exist. Most contemporary empirical studies are cross-sectional and, therefore, they are not easy to establish causality. Although there is strong evidence from correlational studies, these findings need to be confirmed by experimental and longitudinal research to fully understand the long-term impacts of mindfulness training. It is critical to use more culturally diverse samples in order to determine the transferability of discovered processes across different socioeconomic, ethnic, and geopolitical frameworks. Based on their comparative analyses, Mahmud et al. (2019) and John and Hajam (2024) suggest that collectivist and individualist societies may have different motivating factors for conscious consumption. Most research have neglected individuals with clinical features, such compulsive buying, in favor of general consumers, so the question of whether mindfulness might offer long-term treatment for severe eating disorders is still unanswered. It will be critical to close these gaps in order to advance theory and develop better solutions. Last but not least, taken as a whole, these findings have me questioning the whole consumer research process. The processual aspect of mindful buying, namely the ever-changing interaction of values, emotions, and attention during decision-making, should be the focus of future research instead of merely behavioral outcomes or cognitive characteristics. This requires the application of the latest techniques, such as ecological momentary assessment (EMA), digital ethnography, and eye-tracking in simulated retail environments. By taking systems-thinking approach, which outlines interactions between cognitive, environmental, and technological factors, the researchers would be able to create a more holistic model of consumer intentionality (Tahoun et al., 2025). In a more uncertain, overstimulated, and choice-saturated world, this may facilitate the normalization of deliberate purchase. Education, digital design, legislation, and personal practice are essential elements of a holistic approach to convert mindful shopping research into actionable tools. Mindfulness practice can start with basic, everyday routines that cultivate present-moment awareness and encourage introspection of one's thoughts and emotions. To enhance their metacognitive capacity to consider purchases carefully before making them, individuals could do breathing exercises, mindful writing, or guided meditations. Examples of individualized approaches that help people put some mental distance between stimuli and their actions include value-based budgeting and the "24-hour rule" for unnecessary purchases. Value alignment and inhibitory control are two critical processes discussed in the research. Both of these can be helped by these tactics. Short, secular exercises have shown effectiveness in improving emotional control and decision-making; these strategies are not limited to therapeutic or spiritual settings. Health practitioners and financial literacy teachers can improve their education programs by including mindful consumerism to assist them stop children making unnecessary purchases. Some of the modules the students can undertake to learn the art of handling high-pressure situations with consumers include emotional intelligence, value clarity, and mindfulness training. Beginning with emotional labeling in infancy and moving on to metacognitive budgeting strategies in adolescence, these programs need to be supported with scaffolding, which is appropriate in that stage of development. These indicators correspond to the core objectives of enhancing mental health and removing financial pressure due to the correlation between mindful shopping and mental health. Additionally community workshops are very good avenue through which universities and Nongovernmental Organizations (NGOs) can put their hands together in the delivery of such skills to people of different backgrounds.

Application developers and online trading platforms greatly affect the promotion or deterrence of conscious buying among people. Internet buying is supposed to be easy and emotional, therefore it is reasonable to incorporate mindfulness nudges. The examples of this type are carbon footprint indicators, reminders about spending limits, prebrowsing goals setting, and item possession time visualization. In order to discourage customers to make impulse purchases, a number of sites are already experimenting with checkout time or cart retention periods. In line with the tenets of the choice architecture in behavioral economics, preliminary evidence shows that such interventions are well received when presented as consumer empowerment, but not limitation instruments. The policymakers can encourage a more mindful purchasing by the way of public awareness, environmental incentives, and consumer protection laws. Regulatory agencies can require businesses to report about product source, environmental impact, and warranty period. This would allow people to make a better judgment. As an incentive to get people to do forward planning, there can be tax incentives on purchases that uphold sustainability or durability requirements. The social marketing approaches can be applied in the context of the social health policies that recommend the responsible consumption as a human development indicator and autonomy, specifically in trading in more financial literacy or combating smoking cessation. The digital technologies that would include mindfulness in the day-to-day life of customers can be created in collaboration with the government agencies, educational institutions, and the companies engaged in the technological field.

5. Theoretical and Practical Implications

Studies on mindful buying which employ cognitive mechanisms like attentional control, inhibitory control, emotional self-control, and metacognitive monitoring augment the developing body of knowledge that incorporates cognitive psychology with consumer behavior.

The chapter is an expansion of the traditional understanding of behavioral economics, behavioral choices into a concept of mindful consumption that is founded on self-control and self-knowledge. It advances and broadens dual-process theories because of its focus on the role of reflecting, cognitive activity in influencing impulsive, intuitive responses in consumer situations, and makes mindfulness a practical cognitive process that can be studied as an isolated property. This cross-disciplinary approach allows to look at the role of cognitive-affective regulation in promoting sustainable and ethical consumer behavior.

Knowledge of the way in which people reason when they make a deliberate purchase has practical implications whether in the marketing ethics field, consumer education or in the field of government. The attentional control and emotional regulation of consumers could be enhanced with the help of interventions, which could contribute to mindful consumption habits. Those therapies may involve mindfulness-based training, introspective journaling, and digital nudging technology. Retailers and marketers ought to work to empower people to make their own judgment instead of destroying customers. Some of these are need-based advertisement, labeling, and encouraging the customers to examine their products before buying. The process of aligning consumer behavior with the sustainability goals may help the policy efforts of the general population decrease overconsumption and its negative impact on the environment by using behavioral adjustments as a nudge. By using this framework, the consumer psychology scholars and practitioners can develop initiatives that will enhance more deliberate purchasing behavior, and hence increase the quality of life of people and enhance more sustainable environmental practices.

6. Limitations and Future Research Directions

The review is an overall overview of the growing body of work in the cognitive principles of mindful shopping; however, there are major issues that it raises that should be addressed. Initially, scholars in the field predominantly depend on cross-sectional survey results, which constrain their ability to identify causation and track behavioral development. Although longitudinal and experimental designs are important in understanding whether mindfulness-based therapies result in long-term behavioral benefits, they have been underutilized. The second issue is that most recent research have concentrated on WEIRD (Western, educated, industrialized, prosperous, and democratic) cultures, raising concerns about how well the findings apply to collectivist or low-resource circumstances. Cultural norms governing materialism, social identity, and emotional expressiveness may impact how and what individuals interpret mindfulness in consumption situations.

Another constraint is the scarcity of research linking executive function to consumer behavior in the domains of neurocognition and psychophysiology. Despite their relevance in theoretical models, few research have employed objective cognitive measurements such as behavioral inhibition tests, EEG, or fMRI to validate inhibitory control, attentional regulation, and metacognitive monitoring in real-time consumer settings. Furthermore, artificial intelligence (AI)-powered algorithms create new opportunities and problems for conscious purchasing in digital consumer contexts. Future study should focus on the link between the ability to control one's thoughts and feelings and the usage of natural signals, recommendations, and tailored material. There are several possible possibilities for advancement. To begin, academics from behavioral economics, neurology, and consumer psychology may work together to develop more exact models of purposeful consumption. Second, user-centered design and ecological momentary evaluations should be utilized to create and evaluate mindfulness-based products (such as applications and browser extensions) that perform better in real life. Third, large-scale policy experiments might be used to determine how incentive-based or regulatory interventions impact population-level conscious consumption. It is critical to consider fairness in access to interventions to ensure that initiatives to promote purposeful consumption do not exacerbate digital divides and socioeconomic disparities. Buying with an open mind is a socially conscious, cognitively adaptable, and intellectually stimulating activity. It offers an alternative to current market impulsivity and overconsumption based on attentional control, emotional regulation, and metacognitive awareness, which has been studied and confirmed to be effective. Empirical data suggests that both natural and taught mindfulness have a considerable influence on introspective, value-aligned purchase decisions. Investigations have shown that intentional buying may obtain a number of benefits, including improved wellness, economic stability, and ecology conservation. This is a cognitive science-based conceptual framework that provides a synthesized empirical information of numerous methodologies and cultural circumstances. It equips policy makers, teachers, designers, and consumers with information on how to engage in more conscious consumption in everyday life. The online markets are becoming increasingly sophisticated and crowded with choices, which puts pressure on the consumer to behave accordingly. One of the ways that is valid and scalable is to practice mindful purchasing.

7. Conclusion

The introduction of mindful buying in lieu of impulsive buying fueled by emotions is an initiative that has significantly transformed current consumer behavior by being more thoughtful, ethical, and value-based in approach. This review suggests that mindful buying goes beyond a decision-making process. It is a mental strategy which involves being attentive, controlling of impulses, controlling of emotions and understanding oneself in the way he/she thinks. The strategies coupled with self-understanding help one to stop and look back and be critically conscious of the influencing and the resultant factors to their buying decision. Theoretical and empirical studies have shown that mindful consumers have a greater capacity to ignore misleading marketing messages and have greater understanding and control of their emotional responses and make long-term purchasing decisions that are based on their well-being, environmental sustainability, and social responsibility. There are several studies that suggest that customers who are always monitoring the corporate operations are more environmentally aware, emotionally strong, and financially stable regardless of the cultural or social background. It has been demonstrated that executive processes, especially attention and inhibition by neuroscience and research in behavioral neuroscience are important in controlling impulsive impulses and ensuring that consumption is motivated by thought and will. The skill of sound purchasing decisions is not an innate characteristic, however, it is achieved through experience and practice. Digital choice frameworks, reflective journaling, and mindfulness training potentially could improve decision-making, particularly in the online market that is crowded with companies. Despite these accomplishments, there are still major knowledge gaps. The number of studies that are able to effectively combine psychophysiological measures, cross-sectional study design, and consider cultural variations is quite scarce. The next research should adopt an experimental, interdisciplinary, and longitudinal approach to the study, which would thoroughly evaluate the development of conscious purchase in different digital, cultural, and economic contexts. In the modern environment of the algorithmic economy and personalized AI, new frameworks are needed that would redistribute customer autonomy and technological impact. This paper hypothesizes that mindful consumption can contribute to the personal health of people, support sustainable market behaviors, and become socially responsible. In situations where mindful consumption is viewed as a considered and moral action by legislators, teachers, and designers, as well as by consumers, they can create an environment where judicious consumption thrives as a behavior. Mindful purchasing can become a moderating factor in the modern, complicated, and fast-changing global consumer environment, bringing about reflection, purpose, and overall well-being.

References

Bahl, S., Milne, G. R., Ross, S. M., Mick, D. G., Grier, S. A., Chugani, S. K., Chan, S. S., Gould, S., Cho, Y.-N., Dorsey, J. D., Schindler, R. M., Murdock, M. R., & Boesen Mariani, S. (2016). Mindfulness: Its transformative potential for consumer, societal, and environmental well-being. *Journal of Public Policy and Marketing*, *35*(2), 198–210.

Bailey, S. (2021). *New Zealanders have become more conscious consumers, how are you adapting?* https://stoppress.co.nz/partner-articles/new-zealanders have-become-more-conscious-consumers-how-are-you-adapting

Beitel, M., Ferrer, E., & Cecero, J. J. (2005). Psychological mindedness and awareness of self and others. *Journal of Clinical Psychology*, *61*(6), 739–750.

Benos, T., Burkert, M., Hüttl-Maack, V., & Petropoulou, E. (2022). When mindful consumption meets short food supply chains: Empirical evidence on how higher-level motivations influence consumers. *Sustainable Production and Consumption*, *33*, 520–530.

Dhandra, T. K. (2019). Achieving triple dividend through mindfulness: More sustainable consumption, less unsustainable consumption and more life satisfaction. *Ecological Economics*, *161*, 83–90.

Dhandra, T. K. (2020). Does self-esteem matter? A framework depicting role of self-esteem between dispositional mindfulness and impulsive buying. *Journal of Retailing and Consumer Services*, *53*, 101–115.

Ertelt, T. W., Mitchell, J. E., Faber, R. J., & Christenson, G. A. (2009). Current status of cognitive behavioural intervention for compulsive buying disorder. *International Journal of Cognitive Therapy*, *2*(1), 25–36.

Gupta, S., & Sheth, J. (2024). Mindful consumption: Its conception, measurement, and implications. *Journal of the Academy of Marketing Science*, *52*, 1531–1549.

Helm, S. V., & Subramaniam, D. (2019). Exploring socio-cognitive mindfulness in the context of sustainable consumption. *International Journal of Consumer Studies*, *43*(5), 499–512.

Howard, J. L., Bureau, J., Guay, F., Chong, J. X., & Ryan, R. M. (2021). Student motivation and associated outcomes: A meta-analysis from self-determination theory. *Perspectives on Psychological Science*, 1745691620966789.

Jacob, J., Jovic, E., & Brinkerhoff, M. B. (2009). Personal and planetary well-being: Mindfulness meditation, pro-environmental behavior and personal quality of life in a survey from the social justice and ecological sustainability movement. *Social Indicators Research*, *93*(2), 275–294.

Jakobsen, A. M. (2021). The relationship between motivation, perceived motivational climate, task and ego orientation, and perceived coach autonomy in young ice hockey players. *Baltic Journal of Health and Physical Activity*, *13*(2), 8.

Ji, D., Pongsakornrungsilp, S., Pongsakornrungsilp, P., & Kumar, V. (2025). When mindful consumption meets green purchase intention: Empirical evidence on how a mindful mindset influences tourists. *Sustainability*, *17*(3), 1266.

Jin, J., Zhao, Q., & Santibanez-Gonzalez, E. D. (2020). How Chinese consumers' intentions for purchasing eco-labeled products are influenced by psychological factors. *International Journal of Environmental Research and Public Health*, *17*(1), 265.

John, A. S., & Hajam, A. A. (2024). Leveraging predictive analytics for enhancing employee engagement and optimizing workforce planning: A data-driven HR management approach. *International Journal of Innovation in Management, Economics and Social Sciences*, *4*(4), 33–41.

Khunsrii, W. (2022). Understanding mindful consumption: A consumer perspective. *Journal of Consumer Studies and Research*, *44*(3), 215–229.

Klein, G., Borders, J., Newsome, E., Militello, L., & Klein, H. A. (2018). Cognitive skills training: Lessons learned. *Cognition, Technology & Work*, *20*(4), 681–687.

Lesmana, M. (2023). The role of mindfulness on mindful consumption mediated by consumer involvement. *Journal of Management and Marketing Review*, *8*(2), 11–21.

Liobikienė, G., & Poškus, M. S. (2019). The importance of environmental knowledge for private and public sphere pro-environmental behavior: Modifying the value-belief-norm theory. *Sustainability*, *11*, 3324.

Lim, W. M. (2017). Inside the sustainable consumption theoretical toolbox: Critical concepts for sustainability, consumption, and marketing. *Journal of Business Research*, *78*, 69–80.

Mahmud, M. I., Mohamed, M., & Rahman, A. A. (2019). The influence of self-care on mindful consumption behaviour. *International Journal of Academic Research in Business and Social Sciences*, *9*(5), 672–688.

Mathur, A., & Moschis, G. P. (2023). Antecedents and outcome of mindful buying. *Journal of Consumer Affairs*, *57*(4), 1684–1713.

Milne, G. R., Villarroel Ordenes, F., & Kaplan, B. (2020). Mindful consumption: Three consumer segment views. *Australasian Marketing Journal*, *28*(1), 3–10.

Mitchell, J. E., Burgard, M., Faber, R. J., Crosby, R. D., & de Zwaan, M. (2006). Cognitive behavioural therapy for compulsive buying disorder. *Behaviour Research and Therapy*, *44*(12), 1859–1865.

Moes, A. (2025). *The urge to splurge: Understanding the effects of media cues on impulse buying urges and behavior*. https://doi.org/10.33612/diss.1181110648

Sebastian, C. (2023). *The roles of emotion regulation and distress tolerance in the relationship between mindfulness and both depression and problematic alcohol use in firefighters*. Michigan School of Psychology.

Shama, A. (1981). Coping with staglation: Voluntary simplicity. *Journal of Marketing*, *45*(3), 120–134.

Sheth, J. N., Sethia, N. K., & Srinivas, S. (2010). Mindful consumption: A customer-centric approach to sustainability. *Journal of the Academy of Marketing Science*, *39*(1), 21–39.

Tahoun, N., El-Bassiouny, N., Hammad, H., & Adib, H. (2025). Decoding domestic food waste: Exploring the role of emotions and consumer wisdom in an emerging market context. *Qualitative Market Research: An International Journal*, *28*(5), 914–940.

Tomlinson, E. R., Yousaf, O., Vittersø, A. D., & Jones, L. (2018). Dispositional mindfulness and psychological health: A systematic review. *Mindfulness*, *9*(1), 23–43.

Wu, B., & Yang, Z. (2018). The impact of moral identity on consumers' green consumption tendency: The role of perceived responsibility for environmental damage. *Journal of Environmental Psychology*, *59*, 74–84.

Yang, Q., Al Mamun, A., Naznen, F., Siyu, L., & Makhbul, Z. K. M. (2023). Modelling the significance of health values, beliefs and norms on the intention to consume and the consumption of organic foods. *Heliyon*, *9*, e17487.

Zahid, N. M., Khan, J., & Tao, M. (2023). Exploring mindful consumption, ego involvement, and social norms influencing second-hand clothing purchase. *Current Psychology*, *42*, 13960–13974. https://doi.org/10.1007/s12144-021-02657-9

Chapter 15

Circular Business Models Rooted in Grassroots Innovation: Insights From India's Frugal and Regenerative Enterprises

Suman

GL Bajaj Institute of Management and Research, India

Abstract

The concept of circular economy has elicited attention since the past decade. The rise of the pandemic has just added to it. Academicians, policymakers, and industrialists have been coming up with strategies to implement circular business practices in their activities. However, reorientation to a circular economy would require the adoption of circular business models (CBMs) that sustain the value of resources and mitigate waste generation, along with fostering social well-being in the society. Pertaining to this, grassroots innovation in the Global South offers a unique prospect for circular economy transition by incorporating circular business practices such as conceptualizing solutions for the marginalized populations prevailing in resource-constrained environments driven by local resources and indigenous knowledge. Grassroots innovations, prevailing outside the realm of formal innovation ecosystems, tend to incorporate circularity practices in their approach. The aim of this chapter is to explore how grassroots enterprises adopt CBM practices in their innovation approach. The study adopted a qualitative case study approach by considering four grassroots enterprise cases from India. The findings illustrate how the grassroots cases underpin the limited resources and create affordable and accessible solutions that lead to socio-ecological development at the community level. Further, the shared patterns and distinct variations illuminate how each case differs in its aspect to the adoption of a CBM. This chapter adds to the discourse on circular economy and grassroots innovation domains along

Regenerative Revolution, 293–309

Published under exclusive licence by Emerald Publishing Limited
doi:10.1108/978-1-80686-859-920261015

with recommendations for policymakers to influence policy reform for promoting grassroots innovations by adopting such practices.

Keywords: Circular business models; frugal innovation; grassroots innovation; regenerative economy; socially embedded enterprises

JEL Codes: Q01; Q56; O35; O32; L26; M14; Q57

1. Introduction

The circular economy has become more prevalent, steering attention at a global level through initiatives such as the European Circular Economy Package (Brennan et al., 2015). Consistent with the emerging pattern, big industry players (Esposito et al., 2016) including Google, Unilever, and Renault are following circular practices in their activities (Bocken et al., 2017), and academicians are exploring the topic extensively (Geissdoerfer et al., 2017). The circular business model (CBM) is considered a strategic component for fostering systemic transition along with bringing stakeholder incentives (Rashid et al., 2013) into alignment. Such models streamline resource use and add to economic worth by revitalizing social, ecological, and economic systems. These models differ from conventional ones that emphasized standalone economic gains (Adams et al., 2017; Bakker et al., 2018).

However, existing literature primarily focuses on mainstream innovation following a CBM that often overlooks the innovations stemming from the informal sector. India, considered a hub of grassroots and frugal innovation stemming from the ingenuity of innovators at the bottom of the pyramid (Hossain et al., 2021; Singh et al., 2021), creates solutions that are sustainable, affordable, and accessible in resource-constrained environments (Hossain, 2016; Hossain et al., 2023). India has been witnessing the challenges of rising urbanization, industrialization, and economic inequality that highlight the need for community-led circular practices, making grassroots innovation a suitable avenue for circular economy transition (Pansera & Owen, 2018; Pansera & Sarkar, 2016).

Therefore, the aim of this chapter is to explore how grassroots innovation in India adopts CBMs to cater to community needs. For this purpose, a qualitative approach has been followed by selecting four grassroots enterprises that contribute to circularity. The structure of the chapter is as follows: a theoretical background, giving a glimpse of CBMs and grassroots innovations, followed by a methodology that sheds light on the research approach followed, how the cases were selected, which source of data has been used, and how the data was collected. Further, the findings demonstrate how each case is implementing a CBM to add to circularity principles, followed by a discussion that highlights the similarities and differences across the grassroots enterprises. Lastly, the conclusion is presented that states limitations and areas for further research.

2. Theoretical Background

The conceptual understanding of the domain of the *circular economy* has matured over time, molded by prominent theorists including Pearce and Turner (1989), who stressed the alignment of economic systems with natural resource constraints. Further, Stahel (2020) illustrated foundational contributions by highlighting resource-efficient waste management and endorsing use-oriented business models. Contemporary conceptual framing integrates ideas from cradle-to-cradle design, industrial ecology, and the blue economy (Bradley et al., 2018). Based on these notions, the Ellen MacArthur Foundation has conceptualized it as a regenerative industry-based economy. The CBM delineates how organizations generate and capture value (Ferasso et al., 2020) by adopting sustainable practices and meeting the needs of the concerned stakeholders (Stubbs & Cocklin, 2008). By collaborating with stakeholders, organizations can strike a balance between sustainable and CBMs confined to their network (Valkokari et al., 2014). Business model innovation necessitates certain patterns such as promotion of sustainability, optimizing efficiency, and stimulating reuse practices while evolving toward a circular economy (Mentink, 2014). The core idea of the CBM is to enhance resource efficiency and waste minimization by incorporating novelty in the design process, reusing materials, and emphasizing recycling by catering to the structural limitation of linear production models amidst growing demand (Antikainen et al., 2013; Bocken et al., 2014). However, a persistent challenge that prevails is to attain an equilibrium across varied business ecosystems, given the impracticality of purely linear models (Ghisellini et al., 2016).

This field has stimulated academic research (Murray et al., 2017; Rosa et al., 2019). Despite this, the scholars have been witnessing challenges in conceiving the frameworks exploring the transition to circular models, as existing studies have concentrated more on macro-loops (Lieder & Rashid, 2016) and industry segments rather than on innovation arising in the informal sector. Some of the recent studies bring to light that the transition requires substantial changes to strategies and how the innovative start-ups are in a better position to blend circular practices along with their businesses (Schaltegger et al., 2016; Weissbrod & Bocken, 2017).

Grassroots innovation, stemming from the network of individuals, communities, and organizations that aim to develop novel solutions catering to the unmet needs of the marginalized, develops solutions that follow a bottom-up approach (Smith et al., 2014). These innovations leverage the local resources and indigenous knowledge passed on from the generations for addressing local demands. Such initiatives consist of innovations developing sustainable solutions, including community currencies, eco-housing, and alternative energy projects in a European context (Kirwan et al., 2013; Seyfang & Haxeltine, 2012). While in the Global South, especially in India, these innovations arose from the initiatives of the Honey Bee Network and the informal sector. The initial motivation behind such innovation is the zeal to do something for the community where the needs are left unaddressed by the state or by the private players

(Zapata Campos & Zapata, 2017). The frugality aspect in these innovations is the creation of resource-efficient and affordable solutions that align with resilience and adaptability in resource-constrained environments (Brem & Wolfram, 2014; Radjou et al., 2012; Soni & Krishnan, 2014). These innovations possess instrumental value in terms of efficient use of resources and promoting intrinsic value by preserving nature and biodiversity (Cunha et al., 2014). The relational values of grassroots innovation have been linked with community and its traditional knowledge (Onsongo & Knorringa, 2020). Grassroots innovations have been considered as an alternative pathway for sustainable development (Holston, 2009; Seyfang & Smith, 2007), which makes them a better prospect for driving initiatives required for the transition to a circular economy. To address the challenges pertaining to the smooth transition toward a circular economy requires a holistic perspective encompassing solutions that address community needs along with promoting the practices of CBMs (Zapata Campos et al., 2023). Thus, the aim of this study is to explore how grassroots innovations have been instrumental in driving innovations contributing to the adoption of CBMs.

3. Methodology

Since the purpose of this study is to explore how grassroots enterprises adopt circular business practices, a qualitative research approach is followed. Within qualitative research, the author opted for case research, as it helps to examine more thoroughly a phenomenon under consideration, and this approach is best suited when the experiences of the protagonists are crucial (Yin, 2018). Further, a multiple-case approach has been adopted that allowed for cross-case comparison to reflect the commonalities and differences across the cases. All the cases were selected from India, because India is considered a hub of grassroots innovators with a frugal approach (Hossain et al., 2023). Four cases have been selected, and the basis of selection included certain aspects, such as the fact that all these enterprises follow circular economy principles, including using resources efficiently, creating affordable solutions, mitigating climate harm, and practicing regenerative activities. To ensure diversity, all the cases belong to different geographical locations, such as Gujarat, Haryana, Karnataka, and Coimbatore.

3.1 Data Sources

In this study, the author considered collecting the data through primary as well as secondary sources. Primary data was collected by conducting semi-structured interviews with the founders and, where possible, with co-founders and executive heads of the enterprises. Interviews were conducted in person and virtually, depending on the availability of the participants. Each interview lasted approximately 30 minutes and was recorded after obtaining participants' consent. The secondary sources included information from public data sources, such as the websites of enterprises, social media platforms, press releases from certain institutions, such as the National Innovation Foundation (NIF), and newspaper articles featuring the selected cases. Gathering data from multiple sources facilitated data triangulation, ultimately improving the reliability of the research. To ensure a transparent approach, the author shared all the transcripts with the participants. Table 15.1 provides an overview of the data sources, including the year data was collected, the participants interviewed, and the secondary sources considered for each case.

Table 15.1. Data Source Overview.

Case	**Year of Data Collection**	**Number of Interviews Conducted**	**Primary Data Sources**	**Secondary Data Sources**
Mitticool	2024	4	Semi-structured interviews with the founder and marketing head.	Media articles, NIF case documentation, award citations, product brochures.
Biodegradable sanitary napkins	2024	3	Interviews with the founder, production staff, and local distributor.	The primary data sources included NGO reports, enterprise websites, sustainability blogs, and TEDx talks on YouTube.
Agro-waste products	2024	3	Interviews with the founder and the co-founder.	Local newspaper features, social enterprise listings.
Prince industries	2024	4	Interviews with the founder and chief operating officer (COO).	NIF archives, innovation fair reports, trade magazines, and video documentation.

Source: Author's own work.

4. Findings

The findings reveal how the grassroots cases follow circular business practices after making a comparison across all the cases. Table 15.2 illustrates the dimensions of CBMs across each case. The findings are summarized in Table 15.2.

4.1 Case 1: Mitticool

4.1.1 Background

Mitticool is a grassroots enterprise founded by Mansukhbhai Prajapati in the year 2005. Financial constraints compelled the innovator to work on a tea stall and later on join a clay factory, which led him to experiment with clay to create clay utensils that could be used in the kitchen on a regular basis. The motivation behind the innovation was spurred when Gujarat was hit by an earthquake in 2001. What caught Mansukhbhai's eye was an article featuring the headline "gareeb *ka fridge tut gaya*," which prompted him to come up with something that should be affordable for the marginalized and could provide cool water without electricity. As mentioned by the interviewee,

> After the earthquake, I was jobless... When I read the newspaper, I saw an article with the headline gareeb ka fridge tut gaya... they referred to gareeb, the potters' community, and the fridge symbolised their earthen pots... From then on, I thought, "Why don't I make something from clay that can work as a fridge for my community?

Since the innovator belonged to the pottery community, he wanted to preserve its art. As stated by the interviewee,

> Pottery was seen as an outcast activity at that time... nobody wanted their daughters to get married into a potter community... I had the urge to do something different so that people in our community would start seeing pottery as an art... It was my inspiration from the earthquake that I'll make a fridge from clay.

After numerous trials and errors, including adjusting the furnace temperature and selecting the appropriate type of clay, the innovator successfully achieved his goal after four years of effort. The dimensions of the refrigerator include 26 inches in length, 15 inches in breadth, and 12 inches in terms of depth. The Mitticool refrigerator has garnered attention on a global scale, such as in Africa and Dubai, as it can preserve food for four to five days and keep the water cool. It works on evaporation by providing natural cooling through porous terracotta and runs without electricity.

Table 15.2. Circular Business Dimensions Across Grassroots Cases

CBM Dimensions	**Mitticool (Clay Refrigerator)**	**Biodegradable Sanitary Napkins**	**Agro-Waste Products**	**Prince Industries (Multi-food Processing Machine)**
Product design	Frugal, electricity-free, clay-based, and biodegradable at end of life	Uses natural fibers for hygiene products, biodegradable	Converts Agro waste into usable disposables; compostable	Multifunctional, durable, repairable machine; reduces technological redundancy
Production and distribution	Decentralized workshops with artisans; local distribution networks	Decentralized local unit; women lead manufacturing; NGO and school networks	Small-scale units; women, self-help groups, and eco-conscious urban markets	Local fabrication; direct sales to farmers, cooperatives, extension networks
Value recovery and waste minimization	Biodegradable materials return to soil; minimal waste in production	Compostable pads, reduce landfill burden	Agro waste valorization; close loop on agricultural residue	Reduces postharvest losses; by-products reused as feed/compost
Social embeddedness and regeneration	Revive pottery traditions; rural livelihood, and affordable products for poor households	Women's empowerment through work and hygiene access; health awareness	Empowers women; creates rural income; eco-friendly branding	Supports farmer entrepreneurs, rural value-addition, and employment generation
Circularity principal illustrated	Natural material cycles; traditional knowledge regeneration	Gender-inclusive regenerative health innovation	Waste to value, inclusive local economy	Resource efficiency, multifunctionality, and reduction of food waste
Key outcome	Eco-friendly household appliances; cultural regeneration	Eco-health innovation, waste reduction, dignity promotion	Sustainable packaging; women's collectives	Agricultural sustainability; rural industrial ecosystem

Source: Author's own work.

4.1.2 Circularity in Design and Production

The enterprise follows a circularity approach in terms of design and production by making use of available resources at hand. All the Mitticool products are made from baking clay, which is their primary material. Clay is used since the innovator belongs to the potter's community and utilizes whatever resources are available at hand. The enterprise is contributing to saving the environment, as these products reduce the usage of single-use plastic or nonstick utensils, which are harmful to health when used for a long period in the kitchen. As highlighted by the interviewee,

> Now we have come up with an entire range of clay crockery sets and clay utensils that can be used for daily cooking purposes in the kitchen... the purpose is to make people adopt healthy eating habits... These products do not cause any harm to the environment or to the person who cooks or eats in the clay products.

All the Mitticool products are produced through the employment of traditional pottery techniques and the adoption of a frugal design that enhances cooling through the properties of evaporation. The production process begins with the collection of eco-friendly terracotta clay, an essential element for the products. The clay is then molded into the structures of a refrigerator, a cooker, a bottle, pans, etc., which are then assembled, dried, and baked in the furnaces to harden the clay. Final assembly includes adding small details such as the door of the refrigerator, the whistle of the cooker, and the caps of bottles.

4.1.3 Distribution and Accessibility

Mitticool adheres to a region-specific production model. The grassroots innovator has been instrumental in shaping the craftsmanship culture in the local region. As mentioned by the interviewee,

> In my local area, there are many potters who are today making cookware from clay... I did not send any notice to them... instead of seeing them as competitors, I see them as my peers... they have learnt from my art, and I learn from them in terms of novelty... I have kept my factory open to those who want to learn, and then they can also start their own business.

Currently, the grassroots enterprise has marked its online presence as well. The innovator's sons handle the online distribution, while he himself oversees the factory outlets. With the online platforms, customers can purchase products directly from the website or through Amazon. The offline presence of Mitticool is in 300 stores across the country in nearly 63 cities. Such a strategy ensures accessibility for customers in rural and urban areas. The Mitticool refrigerator is specifically accessible for rural customers where the challenges of frequent power cuts prevail.

4.1.4 Value Recovery and Social Impact

The value recovery of Mitticool lies in providing environmental and health benefits for the communities and its customers. The enterprise has been successful in creating social impact through preserving the traditional craftsmanship of potters and generating livelihood for rural artisans. As stated by the interviewee,

> I did not want the art of pottery to die... I feel proud to say that through Mitticool, I've revived the pottery business... Today, people in my community are confident about taking up the family business (which refers to pottery) and are making a decent living.

All the products are made from natural clay that promotes health benefits and energy efficiency through its alkaline properties. The affordability aspect of the enterprise caters to the needs of rural communities. Social embeddedness is achieved through creating livelihood opportunities, revitalizing craftsmanship, uplifting the marginalized communities, and contributing to quality of life by enhancing food preservation and access to cool water at a reasonable rate.

4.2 Case 2: Biodegradable Sanitary Napkins

4.2.1 Background

The story behind Jayashree Enterprises started when the founder lost his father at a very young age, forcing him to work as a teenager. The founder, a school dropout at the age of 14, started working at a welding shop to earn a living for his family. The life of the founder took a turn when he found that his wife and other women in his family and the locality used unhygienic materials such as old clothes and old rags instead of sanitary pads, which risked their health complications. Upon asking, he found that they could not afford a sanitary pad because of low income. After five years of continuous experimentation and facing a lot of criticism from the family and the society members, the founder developed a low-cost sanitary napkin machine that produces hygienic sanitary pads.

4.2.2 Circularity in Design and Production

The grassroots enterprise exemplifies circularity by following a self-sustaining and bottom-up framework by emphasizing local production, women's empowerment, and making use of natural and biodegradable materials. Instead of using any plastic, the innovator used plant-based cellulose made from the bark of trees, which is completely natural and biodegradable. Furthermore, the machines do not require extensive transportation, nor do they follow complex supply chains, ultimately lowering the carbon footprint related to the distribution. All the raw materials are locally sourced, lessening the dependence on logistics from far-off places. The biodegradable aspect further prevents landfill issues, focusing on waste minimization.

4.2.3 Distribution and Accessibility

The distribution approach of the grassroots enterprise is community-based production, where the innovator, instead of patenting his innovation, freely distributed his innovation to the self-help groups (SHGs) of rural women. The machine is priced low; that helped women in rural areas to manufacture pads at a very reasonably priced sanitary pad-making machine. The sanitary pads are then sold at significantly reduced prices as compared to the major players of sanitary pads in the market, leading to the maintenance of a simple supply chain. The enterprise follows a lean headquarters approach, wherein there is no employee working at the corporate level, while thousands of women in rural and semi-urban areas manage the production and sales. For improving accessibility, coin-based vending machines have been installed in schools and colleges for female students. Approximately 4,000 sanitary napkin-making machines have been installed in nearly 29 states, according to media reports. Creating affordable and hygienic alternatives for women, along with promoting empowerment and awareness, enhances accessibility. This innovation is accessible to rural women who work in SHGs and NGOs in the rural area.

4.2.4 Value Recovery and Social Impact

In this case, the value recovery process is unique, as the enterprise does not follow a commercialized approach. Here, the value is recovered in terms of the impact the innovator has been making on the lives of rural women. By innovating an affordable product and making it accessible to rural masses, the enterprise has been successful in making the women financially independent by earning their living. The enterprise has been successful in overcoming the social taboos related to menstrual hygiene in India.

Moreover, the ecological footprint is also minimized as the product is biodegradable, reducing the harm to the environment. Not only did the enterprise make use of locally available resources, but also it has promoted women's health and dignity. Today thousands of machines have been installed across the country, signifying the impact it has made in rural areas for creating awareness about the health and hygiene of women in rural areas.

4.3 Case 3: Agro-Waste Products

4.3.1 Background

This grassroots innovation has garnered significant attention because it was developed by a schoolgirl who conceived the idea of creating biodegradable pots while planting a sapling at her school to celebrate her birthday. Her co-founder is her school teacher, who motivated her to use sustainable and biodegradable materials instead of plastic ones. The innovation happened in school, and the village now has a proper production center. Once an innovation, it has now been turned into an enterprise that manufactures biodegradable pots using agricultural waste.

4.3.2 Circularity in Design and Production

The enterprise follows a circular approach while manufacturing the products, as the products are compostable and mix into the soil upon the completion of their life as organic compost. After utilizing the agricultural waste present in the form of groundnut shells, the biodegradable pots are made. The innovator thought of utilizing the agricultural waste, as the farmers in the areas discarded groundnut shells after harvesting the peanuts. The production process takes place at the farm of the innovator, thus reducing the time and cost in terms of getting raw materials for making the final product.

4.3.3 Distribution and Accessibility

The grassroots enterprise follows a simple distribution channel that enhances the accessibility of its products. To increase visibility and outreach, several innovation intermediary platforms, such as T-Hub, have assisted innovators in connecting with investors and agricultural institutions that not only provide funding by investing in the business but also purchase the product. The educational institution uses these products both on its premises and as gifts.

4.3.4 Value Recovery and Social Impact

The grassroots enterprise, small in size and scale, has been successful in creating the social impact at a large scale. By establishing a production unit on the farm, the enterprise has facilitated job creation for individuals in the rural area. Social impact is substantial in terms of creating employment opportunities and making use of locally available resources.

4.4 Case 4: Prince Industries

4.4.1 Background

Prince Industries is a grassroots enterprise, founded by a farmer with the zeal to do something that can process multiple farm products in a single machine. Due to financial constraints, the innovator even took the job of a rickshaw puller. He did not possess any formal or professional degree due to the poor condition of the family at that time. The motivation behind starting his own enterprise came when he saw ketchups and jams for the first time in a shop. Upon checking the ingredients, the innovator thought that everything could be produced in his own farms. His journey has been about exploring extensively how a single machine can be put to use in such a manner that it can perform multiple functions without having a complex design. After experimenting with the design, the innovator made a multi-food processing machine, which is now not only recognized nationally but at an international level as well. After meeting with other farmers across various states, his perseverance led him to create a machine that is able to process multiple food items. It's easy to install and clean as well. It can grind, steam the petals, extract juice, and make jams, and it can extract seeds as well. As the interviewee stated,

> When I was in Delhi, I saw a shop that had jams and ketchups of pineapple, mixed fruit, and tomato... as a villager it was very new for me... when I returned to my village, I had the zeal to make something because I had farms... I could produce many things but I wanted to extract the most of them in terms of utilizing the produce... With less money and after facing many challenges, I finally made my machine with the help of the National Innovation Foundation capable of performing multiple functions.

4.4.2 Circularity in Design and Production

The grassroots innovation has been a pioneer in following circular practices, as one can mix, steam, pressure cook, and extract juice, oil, or gel by processing varieties of herbs, fruits, and seeds in a single machine. The design of the machine is robust and enables maintenance at the local level. It is designed for efficiency and sustainability. The farmers can manage excess produce with the help of this innovation. The innovator has set up a production center in his village, generating employment for the rural people. As the interviewee stated,

> I started my factory in my farms... I try to engage as many people of my rural area as much as I can so that they do not have to go cities in search of employment... I wanted my farmer brothers to use my innovation to become self-sufficient.

4.4.3 Distribution and Accessibility

The grassroots business aims to produce goods locally by setting up factories in the area; however, because it operates nationally and internationally, the machines are delivered with help from organizations like the NIF and the Society for Research and Initiatives for Sustainable Technologies and Institutions (SRISTI), which assisted the innovator in presenting his innovation at different national events.

4.4.4 Value Recovery and Social Impact

With the sales of his machine, the innovator has marked his presence at an international level. Today his innovation aids farmers to become rural entrepreneurs by maximizing profits from their fruit and herbal crop processing. The innovation follows the recycling principle by making judicious use of agricultural produce. The innovator has been instrumental in creating social impact through his innovation by conducting several workshops at the national and international levels and by training nearly 7,000 people, out of which nearly 4,000 have been female.

5. Discussion

The findings of the study outlined the adoption of CBMs in the context of grassroots innovation. Grassroots cases demonstrate an alternative approach centered on the requirements of the community, the indigenous knowledge, and socio-cultural elements. It further elucidates a model born out of necessity rather than by advanced technology and resources.

In terms of convergences, mutual traits across all the cases. The first commonality across all the cases is that all the grassroots initiatives have been discovered or created by the ingenuity of individuals who possess indigenous knowledge and had the zeal to innovate something for a social cause, prioritizing affordability, accessibility, sustainability, and inclusion of the marginalized. Second, the grassroots innovators often make do with limited resources available locally by minimizing the harm to the environment and by creating renewable, biodegradable, low-energy, and less-waste production. Third, the frugality in design emphasizes reusing and repairing new skill sets along with the integration of traditional techniques. Fourth, bottom-up or community-based production has been observed across all cases. Additionally, local distribution networks have been established after seeking help from innovation intermediaries. The focal point across all the cases has been the factor of affordability and accessibility for the underprivileged, which leads to robust community ties along with the generation of livelihood opportunities. Such initiatives from the grassroots level, with the help of intermediaries, strive for a balance between economic viability and socio-ecological revitalization.

The divergences across the four cases illustrate unique characteristics and differing motivational stimulations of the grassroots innovators. First, there has been sectoral diversity across all cases, as Mitticool focuses on making clay cookware and utensils, Agro-waste products is into the manufacturing of biodegradable pots from agricultural waste, Jayashree deals with making low-cost sanitary napkins for rural women, and Prince Industries manufactures machinery capable of performing multiple functions through a single machine. While the motivation behind Mitticool was postearthquake adaptability, Jayashree promotes menstrual hygiene among rural women, aiming to overcome social taboos, and Agro-waste aims to make biodegradable pots, propelled by agricultural waste reduction, and Prince Industries manufactures agri-machinery, accentuating prudent use of farm produce. Second, the raw materials used vary across all cases, as Mitticool makes use of clay, Agro-waste utilizes agro-waste, Jayashree uses natural plant cellulose fiber, and Prince Industries uses locally available steel components for making the machine. Third, the production scales differ across each case, ranging from working with local artisans to small-scale industrial enterprises, along with varying levels of mechanization and technology-embeddedness. Fourth, in all the cases, the target group of customers differs, with Mitticool aiming to serve rural households and now marking an international presence; Agro-waste Galaxy appeals to serve eco-conscious agricultural educational institutions; Jayashree targets rural women working in SHGs and NGOs; and Prince Industries addresses the demand of small and marginalized farmers. Further, all the grassroots enterprises evince different market strategies, with Mitticool having a strong digital presence, while Jayashree leans toward social marketing, Prince Industries exhibits agro-entrepreneurship, and Agro-waste Galaxy relies on institutional linkages for market reach. Fifth, the extent of impact varies significantly, with Mitticool reviving the art of cultural craftsmanship and Agro-waste Galaxy cultivating environmental awareness and responsibility among school students. Jayashree has overcome social taboos related to menstrual hygiene in rural areas, while Prince Industries fosters rural entrepreneurship. Further, the product obsolescence stage also varies, as Agro-waste Galaxy and Jayashree prioritize compost and biodegradability factors, while Mitticool and Prince Industries aim at functional longevity of their products. Further, revenue models encompass everything from direct customer sales in the case of Mitticool and Prince Industries to institutionally fostered help in the case of Agro-waste Galaxy and Jayashree, relying on SHGs and NGOs. Lastly, there have been instances of varied institutional support, such as Mitticool and Prince Industries receiving support from innovation intermediaries like NIF and SRISTI, while Agro-waste received support from incubators and educational institutions, and Jayashree sought help from NGOs. All the cases exhibit different scalability pathways as well.

From a managerial and policy perspective, the grassroots cases illuminate how such innovations at the community level have been an alternative to circular solutions arising out of R&D labs and industries. Some of the recommendations for policymakers and managers could be innovating accessible and affordable circular solutions for low-income populations. Second, by focusing on local production, resilience and inclusion could be improved along with the reduction of ecological impact. Third, policy frameworks for supporting intermediaries to facilitate the replication and dissemination of grassroots enterprises developing circular solutions for the community. Fourth, with the integration of frugality, cultural knowledge, and involvement of the community, corporations can garner insights from grassroots enterprises.

6. Conclusion

The purpose of the chapter was to explore how community-based grassroots enterprises create novel circular solutions that cater to the needs of the community. Four grassroots cases were selected that exhibited a CBM approach. The chapter illustrated how the enterprises were formed with a social cause, catered to providing affordable and accessible solutions for the community, preserved indigenous knowledge, made use of locally available resources in terms of raw materials and manpower, and fostered employment opportunities along with socio-ecological contribution.

From a managerial and policy perspective, the grassroots cases illuminate how such innovations at the community level have been an alternative to circular solutions arising out of R&D labs and industries. Some of the recommendations for policymakers and managers could be innovating accessible and affordable circular solutions for low-income populations. Second, by focusing on local production, resilience, and inclusion could be improved, along with the reduction of ecological impact. Third, policy frameworks for supporting intermediaries to facilitate the replication and dissemination of grassroots enterprises developing circular solutions for the community. Fourth, with the integration of frugality, cultural knowledge, and involvement of the community, corporations can garner insights from grassroots enterprises.

However, this study is subject to certain limitations, such as it confines itself to four cases within the framework of developing countries. Secondly, following a qualitative approach that limits the generalizability of the findings. Future studies could explore additional cases, conduct surveys of various grassroots entrepreneurs using CBMs, and undertake cross-case comparisons between developing and developed countries to provide more rigorous insights into the phenomenon.

References

Adams, K. T., Osmani, M., Thorpe, T., & Thornback, J. (2017, February). Circular economy in construction: Current awareness, challenges and enablers. In *Proceedings of the institution of civil engineers-waste and resource management* (Vol. 170, No.1, pp. 15–24). Thomas Telford Ltd.

Antikainen, M., Valkokari, K., Korhonen, H., & Wallenius, M. (2013). Exploring networked innovation in order to shape sustainable markets. In Paper presented at the *XXIV ISPIM Conference*, June 16–19. Helsinki: Finland.

Bakker, C., Balkenende, R., & Poppelaars, F. (2018). Design for product integrity in a circular economy. In *Designing for the circular economy* (pp. 148–156). Routledge.

Bocken, N. M., Olivetti, E. A., Cullen, J. M., Potting, J., & Lifset, R. (2017). Taking the circularity to the next level: A special issue on the circular economy. *Journal of Industrial Ecology*, *21*(3), 476–482.

Bocken, N. M., Short, S. W., Rana, P., & Evans, S. (2014). A literature and practice review to develop sustainable business model archetypes. *Journal of Cleaner Production*, *65*, 42–56.

Bradley, R., Jawahir, I. S., Badurdeen, F., & Rouch, K. (2018). A total life cycle cost model (TLCCM) for the circular economy and its application to post-recovery resource allocation. *Resources, Conservation and Recycling*, *135*, 141–149.

Brem, A., & Wolfram, P. (2014). Research and development from the bottom up-introduction of terminologies for new product development in emerging markets. *Journal of Innovation and Entrepreneurship*, *3*(1), 9.

Brennan, G., Tennant, M., & Blomsma, F. (2015). Business and production solutions: Closing loops and the circular economy. In *Sustainability* (pp. 219–239). Routledge.

Cunha, M. P. E., Rego, A., Oliveira, P., Rosado, P., & Habib, N. (2014). Product innovation in resource-poor environments: Three research streams. *Journal of Product Innovation Management*, *31*(2), 202–210.

Esposito, M., Tse, T., & Soufani, K. (2016). Companies are working with consumers to reduce waste. *Harvard Business Review*, *7*, 1–6.

Ferasso, M., Beliaeva, T., Kraus, S., Clauss, T., & Ribeiro-Soriano, D. (2020). Circular economy business models: The state of research and avenues ahead. *Business Strategy and the Environment*, *29*(8), 3006–3024.

Geissdoerfer, M., Savaget, P., Bocken, N. M., & Hultink, E. J. (2017). The circular economy – A new sustainability paradigm? *Journal of Cleaner Production*, *143*, 757–768.

Ghisellini, P., Cialani, C., & Ulgiati, S. (2016). A review on circular economy: The expected transition to a balanced interplay of environmental and economic systems. *Journal of Cleaner Production*, *114*, 11–32. https://doi.org/10.1016/j.jclepro.2015.09.007

Holston, J. (2009). Insurgent citizenship in an era of global urban peripheries. *City and Society*, *21*(2), 245–267.

Hossain, M. (2016). Grassroots innovation: A systematic review of two decades of research. *Journal of Cleaner Production*, *137*, 973–981.

Hossain, M., Levänen, J., & Wierenga, M. (2021). Pursuing frugal innovation for sustainability at the grassroots level. *Management and Organization Review*, *17*(2). https://doi.org/10.1017/mor.2020.53

Hossain, M., Park, S., & Shahid, S. (2023). Frugal innovation for sustainable rural development. *Technological Forecasting and Social Change*, *193*. https://doi.org/10.1016/j.techfore.2023.122662

Kirwan, J., Ilbery, B., Maye, D., & Carey, J. (2013). Grassroots social innovations and food localisation: An investigation of the Local Food programme in England. *Global Environmental Change*, *23*(5), 830–837.

Lieder, M., & Rashid, A. (2016). Towards circular economy implementation: A comprehensive review in context of manufacturing industry. *Journal of Cleaner Production*, *115*, 36–51.

Mentink, B. A. S. (2014). *Circular business model innovation: A process framework and a tool for business model innovation in a circular economy* (Maste's thesis). Delft University of Technology & Leiden University. https://resolver.tudelft.nl/uuid:c2554c91-8aaf-4fdd-91b7-4ca08e8ea621

Murray, A., Skene, K., & Haynes, K. (2017). The circular economy: An interdisciplinary exploration of the concept and application in a global context. *Journal of Business Ethics*, *140*(3), 369–380.

Onsongo, E. K., & Knorringa, P. (2020). Comparing frugality and inclusion in innovation for development: Logic, process, and outcome. *Innovation and Development*, 1–21.

Pansera, M., & Owen, R. (2018). Framing inclusive innovation within the discourse of development: Insights from case studies in India. *Research Policy*, *47*(1), 23–34.

Pansera, M., & Sarkar, S. (2016). Crafting sustainable development solutions: Frugal innovations of grassroots entrepreneurs. *Sustainability*, *8*(1), 51.

Pearce, D. W., & Turner, R. K. (1989). *Economics of natural resources and the environment*. Johns Hopkins University Press.

Rashid, A., Asif, F. M., Krajnik, P., & Nicolescu, C. M. (2013). Resource conservative manufacturing: An essential change in business and technology paradigm for sustainable manufacturing. *Journal of Cleaner Production*, *57*, 166–177.

Radjou, N., Prabhu, J., & Ahuja, S. (2012). *Jugaad innovation: Think frugal, be flexible, generate breakthrough growth*. John Wiley & Sons.

Rosa, P., Sassanelli, C., & Terzi, S. (2019). Circular business models versus circular benefits: An assessment in the waste from electrical and electronic equipments sector. *Journal of Cleaner Production*, *231*, 940–952.

Schaltegger, S., Lüdeke-Freund, F., & Hansen, E. G. (2016). Business models for sustainability: A co-evolutionary analysis of sustainable entrepreneurship, innovation, and transformation. *Organization & Environment*, *29*(3), 264–289.

Seyfang, G., & Haxeltine, A. (2012). Growing grassroots innovations: Exploring the role of community-based initiatives in governing sustainable energy transitions. *Environment and Planning C: Government and Policy*, *30*(3), 381–400.

Seyfang, G., & Smith, A. (2007). Grassroots innovations for sustainable development: Towards a new research and policy agenda. *Environmental Politics*, *16*(4), 584–603.

Singh, S. H., Bhowmick, B., Eesley, D., & Sindhav, B. (2021). Grassroots innovation and entrepreneurial success: Is entrepreneurial orientation a missing link? *Technological Forecasting and Social Change*, *164*, 119582.

Smith, A., Fressoli, M., & Thomas, H. (2014). Grassroots innovation movements: Challenges and contributions. *Journal of Cleaner Production*, *63*, 114–124.

Soni, P., & Krishnan, R. T. (2014). Frugal innovation: Aligning theory, practice, and public policy. *Journal of Indian Business Research*, *6*(1), 29–47.

Stahel, W. R. (2020). History of the circular economy. The historic development of circularity and the circular economy. In *The circular economy in the European Union: An interim review* (pp. 7–19). Springer International Publishing.

Stubbs, W., & Cocklin, C. (2008). Conceptualizing a "sustainability business model". *Organization & Environment*, *21*(2), 103–127.

Valkokari, K., Valkokari, P., Palomäki, K., Uusitalo, T., Reunanen, M., Macchi, M., Rana, P., & Prasanna Liyanage, J. (2014). Road-mapping the business potential of sustainability within the European manufacturing industry. *Foresight*, *16*(4), 360–384.

Weissbrod, I., & Bocken, N. M. P. (2017). Developing sustainable business experimentation capability: A case study. *Journal of Cleaner Production*, *142*(Part 4), 2663–2676. https://doi.org/10.1016/j.jclepro.2016.11.009

Yin, R. K. (2018). *Case study research and applications: Design and methods* (6th ed.). SAGE Publications.

Zapata Campos, M. J., Barinaga, E., Dimba Kiaka, R., & Ocampo, J. (2023). Nothing to lose: The rationales of grassroots financial innovations in contexts of extreme scarcity. *Social Enterprise Journal*, *19*(2), 193–212.

Zapata Campos, M. J., & Zapata, P. (2017). Infiltrating citizen-driven initiatives for sustainability. *Environmental Politics*, *26*(6), 1055–1078.

Printed and bound by CPI Group (UK) Ltd, Croydon, CR0 4YY
21/09/2026
14966034-0005